BUILDING CYCLES
AND BRITAIN'S GROWTH

By the same Author

★

AN INTRODUCTION TO MATHEMATICS
FOR STUDENTS OF ECONOMICS

BUILDING CYCLES AND BRITAIN'S GROWTH

BY

J. PARRY LEWIS

incorporating material of the late
BERNARD WEBER

MACMILLAN
London · Melbourne · Toronto

ST MARTIN'S PRESS
New York
1965

MACMILLAN AND COMPANY LIMITED
Little Essex Street London WC 2
also Bombay Calcutta Madras Melbourne

THE MACMILLAN COMPANY OF CANADA LIMITED
70 Bond Street Toronto 2

ST MARTIN'S PRESS INC
175 Fifth Avenue New York 10010 NY

PRINTED IN GREAT BRITAIN

To my parents

CONTENTS

PREFACE

WHEN Professor Brinley Thomas was working on his *Migration and Economic Growth* he appointed me as his Research Assistant. In many ways this present book stems from his, for it was he who impressed upon me the importance of the building cycle, and gave me a chance to study it. He has taken a great and active interest in it since I first began to write it six years ago. My debt to him is enormous.

The interest and kindness of Professor H. G. Johnson gave me the chance to continue my studies in Manchester, and so not only to alter the balance of the book but also to meet the continuous stream of new people and ideas with which the Faculty of Economics abounds. One of the first of these was Dr Shirley Lerner, who had borrowed some of Bernard Weber's papers from Professor Cairncross. Weber had almost completed the first draft of a thesis on the British building cycle, when he suddenly became ill with poliomyelitis and died. Professor Cairncross willingly sent me the vast pile of papers that he had accumulated, and at once the task before me changed. At first it seemed that Weber's thesis could be published with a little editing, but a more careful study of his papers revealed two difficulties. One was that several weaknesses existed in the manuscript as it stood. The other was that the papers had a great deal of information which was not mentioned in the draft. Clearly there was still a great deal of work to be done.

Weber's original data covered thirty-odd towns in various parts of the country. His bulging files bore eloquent testimony not only to his own energy and persistence, but also to the labours and patience of Town Clerks, City Surveyors and Architects throughout the country. One way or the other Weber contrived to add very considerably to the output of data by local-authority employees. Hamish Richards had obtained data for South Wales by visiting a large number of towns, and he kindly placed it all at my disposal. When it came my turn to visit fifty local authorities in the Manchester area I was always slightly amazed to find that the various local government officials were prepared to go to such trouble as they did in order to assist me. Weber, Richards and I have produced our data only through their kindness.

The examination of the Manchester data, and my wider reading, slowly compelled me to abandon my idea of either editing Weber's draft or padding it out. In several places I quote his work at length. For the rest I can only say that when one has burrowed in a pile of paper several feet high, covered with every jotting of a dedicated scholar, one is bound to absorb more than one realises. I suspect that if Weber could see what I have written he would not only agree with it, but would see more of his own thought in it than I am now able to see for myself. He was a provoking, honest and inspired researcher whose early death was a very great loss.

Some other debts can be mentioned more briefly, even though they are equally important. Professor Cairncross has constantly encouraged and advised me. He also put me in touch with Professor Saul, who generously gave me much of his own data, and patiently advised and corrected me as I all too frequently floundered in a subject more his than mine. Other historians who helped me in various ways were Dr. Chaloner and Mr. Musson, although I must be at pains to emphasise that the usual statement that the people mentioned in the Preface are not to be held responsible for one's sins is especially true in the case of these two colleagues of mine. Dr. E. Cooney gave me a great deal of guidance and encouragement.

Within my own department I owe especial debts to Professor Johnston, not only for frequent advice but also for practical assistance, to Professors Carter and Williams, whose knowledge of the building industries enabled them to help me in many particular problems, as well as generally. All three have eased my task considerably, and it is no reflection on them that, like so many British dons, I have had to embark on a piece of major research work with hardly any research assistance until the very last moment. Through the kindness of Professor H. G. Johnson, and the co-operation of Professors Brinley Thomas and Victor Morgan, I was able to devote one year entirely to research as a Research Fellow in Economic Statistics at Manchester University. In the following year I had the part-time assistance of Mr. Leslie Simister at the time I was least certain of my ideas and least able to use him. For the next three years I had no assistance at all, other than computing assistance. This is the fault of nobody I know, nor of the University. It is a state of affairs that typifies the conditions under which research is so often conducted in British universities. I have no doubt that, like this book, a great deal of research would be more thorough, and leave fewer ends, if a little more money were available, and if postgraduate students were given larger grants rather sooner. The additional speed made since July 1963, when one of my recent students, Mr. Graham Capper, began to assist me before taking up his duties at Keele in October, when another recent student, Mr. John Eaton, became my part-time Research Assistant, emphasises how much more I could have done if help had been available. On the other hand, I was fortunate in having excellent computing aid, especially that of Mrs. H. Collins and Mrs. M. Watts. At the galley stage I had the assistance of Mr. K. Holden, who checked the diagrams for me.

My colleague, Mr. D. J. Coppock, whose interest in this subject is older than mine, has often given me invaluable criticism, and also placed at my disposal his private copy of H. Feinstein's important thesis. Another colleague, Mr. David Bugg, is responsible for almost all of the work done on the Mercury and Atlas computers. Professor R. G. Lipsey has patiently and diligently coaxed and bullied me into making more precise and rigorous statements of my views. At a critical time Mr. G. C. Archibald came to his assistance. Their generous expenditure of time on my behalf has been excelled only by that of Mr. R. C. O. Matthews, who has commented in detail at various stages, and spent several hours discussing certain points with me. Professor R. G. D. Allen has also left me much in his debt. Mr. W. Fletcher made a number of valuable comments at the galley stage.

My old friend and colleague at Cardiff, Mr. Lionel Williams, carefully read and commented upon the whole manuscript. This, however, was the least of his efforts, for it was his continuous and patient insistence, over a period of many years, that economic theorists have so much to learn from a critical study of history that probably, more than anything else, really defined the shape of this book — even though he himself would have written it very differently.

I feel sure that over this long period I have also been helped by many others, in ways I have temporarily forgotten. To them I tender my apologies as well as my sincere thanks. The manuscript was expertly typed by Miss Pauline O'Brien, who patiently interpreted my sometimes very confused manuscript.

The cover design, by Mr. Geoffrey Lambert, is based partly on a photograph of the redeveloping Manchester taken by Mr. Franklin Medhurst from the roof of one of the University buildings.

It is a particular pleasure to thank, once again, my publishers and printers for their splendid and patient co-operation.

J. Parry Lewis

January 1965

ABBREVIATIONS USED IN LEGENDS
TO FIGURES

(listed in order of first appearance)

Ashton   T. S. Ashton, *Economic Fluctuation in England, 1700–1800*, Oxford, 1959.

B.H.S.   B. R. Mitchell and Phyllis Deane, *Abstract of British Historical Statistics*, Cambridge, 1962.

Hoffmann   W. Hoffmann, *British Industry, 1700–1950* (English edition), Oxford, 1955.

C. and W.   A. K. Cairncross and B. Weber, 'Fluctuations in Building in Great Britain, 1785–1849', *Economic History Review*, s.s., vol. ix, 1956, pp. 283–97.

Shannon   H. A. Shannon, 'Bricks—A Trade Index, 1785–1849', *Economica*, N.S., no. 3, 1934, pp. 300–18.

Cooney (1)   E. W. Cooney, 'Long Waves in Building in the British Economy of the Nineteenth Century', *Economic History Review*, s.s., vol. xiii, 1960, pp. 257–69.

Kenwood   A. G. Kenwood, 'Residential Building Activity in North-Eastern England, 1853–1913,' *The Manchester School*, vol. xxxi, 1963.

G.R.S.   A. D. Gayer, W. W. Rostow and A. J. Schwartz, *The Growth and Fluctuations of the British Economy, 1790–1850*, Oxford, 1953.

Thomas (1)   Brinley Thomas, *Migration and Economic Growth*, Cambridge, 1954.

Farnie   D. A. Farnie, *The English Cotton Industry, 1850–1896*, 1953, M.A. Thesis in the Library of the University of Manchester.

Ellison   T. Ellison, *The Cotton Trade of Great Britain*, London, 1886.

Morris and Williams   J. H. Morris and L. J. Williams, *The South Wales Coal Industry, 1841–1875*, Cardiff, 1958.

Finlay Gibson   Finlay Gibson, *The Coalmining Industries of the United Kingdom*, Cardiff, 1921.

Thomas (2)   Brinley Thomas (ed.), *The Welsh Economy: Studies in Expansion*, Cardiff, 1962.

Cairncross   A. K. Cairncross, *Home and Foreign Investment, 1870–1913*, Cambridge, 1953.

Cooney (2)   E. W. Cooney, 'Capital Exports and Investment in Building in Britain and the U.S.A., *Economica*, N.S., vol. xvi, 1949, pp. 347–54.

Feinstein   C. H. Feinstein, *Home and Foreign Investment, 1870–1913*. (Dissertation for the Degree of Ph.D., University of Cambridge, 1959.)

Weber (1)   B. Weber, 'A New Index of Residential Construction, 1838–1950', *Scottish Journal of Political Economy*, vol. ii, 1955, pp. 104–32.

Singer   H. W. Singer, 'An Index of Urban Land Rents and House Rents in England and Wales, 1845–1913', *Econometrica*, vol. ix, 1941, pp. 221–30.

Bowley   A. L. Bowley, *Wages and Income since 1860*, Cambridge, 1937.

Saul   S. B. Saul, 'English Building Fluctuations in the 1890's', *Economic History Review*, vol. xv, 1962, pp. 119–37.

CHAPTER I

INTRODUCTION

Between the idea
And the reality
Between the motion
And the act
Falls the Shadow.
                    T. S. ELIOT, *The Hollow Men*

THE appearance of a book that impinges upon several fields of
skill requires some explanation. Originally this volume was
to have been an econometric study, yet it has become a
historical survey interrupted with economic theory, digressing into
town-planning, and paving the way for a large simulation model to
be published separately. Nobody can hope to acquire sufficient
expertise in all these fields to ensure that he perpetrates no error,
and this is especially true of history. More than once I have wondered
whether it would not be wiser for me to leave history to the historians,
and to content myself with writing nearer to my training, but always
I have been forced to conclude that the building cycle presents a
problem of method as well as of theory, and that if it is to be properly
studied either a mathematically minded economist must turn to
history, or an economic historian must invoke some mathematics.
Economic problems cannot always be solved by a single method,
any more than a house can be built with a single skill. Ideally the
solution is for men of different skills to combine, but since, in this
case, there seemed to be little likelihood of that happening, I have
had to try to acquire a new skill for myself. I have been aided by
master craftsmen standing behind me, tapping my shoulder and
guiding my hand, but each improvement they have wrought has
made me more aware of how much better somebody else would have
done that particular part of the whole. My only excuse for presenting
the final product to a world of economists of whom most could have
done some part better than I have done it is that, viewed as a whole,
it seems to have sufficient to say for me to hope that its many imperfections will not detract too much from what I believe to be its
basic merit.

Brinley Thomas has suggested that from the time of the Potato Famine right up to 1914 the British and American economies exhibited inverse 'long swings' of about 18-20 years' periodicity, typified by the building cycle, and with a migration cycle, originating partly in a birth cycle, providing the link between these two halves of the Atlantic Economy.[1] My original intention was to frame this theory in econometric terms, and then to test it. There is not, however, a great deal of point in simply building formulae around what statistics exist, and working out a mass of coefficients and significance values. Too often an econometric investigation that 'gives a good fit' provides no real explanation. Sometimes the numerical coefficients are of use in subsequent analytical approaches, but even this is so only if the right kind of relationship has been posited before the calculations are begun. The first task of the econometric historian is to check that he introduces no equation whose behavioural implications go contrary to history. If he fails to do this then 'a good fit' may be both fortuitous and misleading.

It was almost immediately apparent that this kind of checking was going to be difficult, for little had been written on the course of British building in the nineteenth century. One of the few things that had been written was Cairncross's analysis of building in Glasgow,[2] and this confirmed my opinion that an adequate explanation of building had to be sought at a local level. Already I had seen that fluctuations in building in South Wales differed appreciably from those in England,[3] and when the opportunity to study them in the Manchester area arose it soon became obvious that they could be understood only in terms of the cotton industry, just as those of South Wales had to be related to the coal trade. Various national factors like, perhaps, the rate of interest, peace or war, and so forth clearly affected building everywhere : but in the last resort the demand for a building is a function of local conditions.

This presents a serious challenge to the econometrician. If he attempts to relate the level of aggregate building to some national indices of production, income, population structure and rent then he has to consider whether he is interested in providing some descriptive equations which give a good fit and may possibly be useful to predict the national total, or whether he is seeking equations that purport to be behavioural. In certain circumstances a single set of equations may fulfil both of these functions, but if the aggregation is at a level differing from the behavioural level then there is considerable danger of having a model that is satisfactory in neither sense. To take an extreme example we may think of a country consisting of an expanding town and a declining town, well separated and each having its own separate housing market. By obtaining data about population, incomes and so on, in each town, one could build two meaningful models, which would possibly be quite different from each other, one for each town. These models could be built around testable behavioural assumptions and, at the same time, provide a useful basis for prediction of the course of building in each town. Now let us suppose that the only data available consist of aggregates for the two towns put together. It would still be possible to make assumptions of a behavioural kind, relating aggregate demand to aggregate income, and so on, but a number of snags would arise. The obvious one in this case is that whereas the one town has a building programme related to its expanding population, and the other town has a programme affected by its declining population, the aggregate volume of building has to be explained in terms of an aggregate set of stationary population data. Clearly, in such a case, the model may relate building to other variables in quite an adequate way, and may even predict : but it is no analysis of what is happening, and if the pattern of growth changes, so that, for example, neither town grows but every available aggregate behaves as before, then the amount of building predicted by these aggregates, taking no account of the cessation of internal migration, is likely to be seriously out. There are other even more serious objections to formulating econometric explanations at the wrong level of aggregation, some of which are mentioned in later chapters. The only point we need note here is that such explanations are especially likely to break down when the inter-regional balance is changing, and that in any case they are unlikely to provide an adequate analytical explanation even if they do result in a good fit.

On the other hand, it was soon clear that, as far as building was concerned, the statistics necessary for a thorough econometric investigation just did not exist at the local level. This was 'the Shadow'. Where a town had annual population data they turned out to be either post-census extrapolations or based on a count of houses. Only Glasgow had anything purporting to be useful as an index of rents for an adequate period. Trade-union unemployment statistics and data on wage-rates could be used to measure incomes, or at least to indicate their movements, but large gaps still remain in the list of available series. In South Wales one can use coal production, coal exports, coal prices, wages, marriage-rates, birth-rates, Welsh emigration to America and one or two other series to build an interesting model of the course of building in that area, and there is nothing to prevent this from being an econometric model. But there is nothing to indicate the extent of annual immigration into the area, and little on the magnitude of investment, and many other variables that a proper analytical account would have to consider. Such an econometric model would be a pretty exercise, but of limited use.

A study of his manuscripts reveals that, although most of his draft chapters dealt with national aggregates, Weber was thinking along similar lines, and he gathered a great deal of data on regional differences. These were mentioned in the paper in which he published his New Index of House-Building.[4] They were also emphasised in a paper which he wrote with Cairncross, and had published posthumously, on building during 1785–1849.[5] A study of this paper prompted me to look back even further, and I turned to Ashton's account of cyclical fluctuations in the eighteenth century.[6] When I did so I intended just to read it, and to see if there was any sign of a building cycle as far back as then, but it soon became clear that more had to be done. Ashton was writing of the short cycle, and might, like other historians of trade cycles, have written off building as being rather different, but apart from being too good a historian to write off the different as uninteresting, Ashton reveals a long and affectionate interest in building ; and, although he does not speak of the building cycle as such, he does, in fact, give very clear and detailed accounts of what turn out to be classical eighteenth-century long swings. As I read these works, and supplemented them with other reading, I realised that a proper understanding of the building cycle would come not from using tools which were fashioned on the assumption that adequate statistics would exist at the right level of aggregation, but by studying their history as closely as possible and then by testing any resulting ideas with the aid of some model building. At this stage, perhaps, I should have read the history, built some models, published some theory and left it at that. But the lure of history proved too strong, and when, in order to crystallise my own ideas, I wrote up the story of the building cycles I realised that any model would seem naked and unreal unless clothed and vitalised with an account of what really happened. Each building cycle was unique. In a rapidly growing country each span of twenty years had features that the previous period had never conceived, and no single model could accurately describe the cycles of a century. Yet the study of these cycles, taken in order, revealed certain patterns and certain trends ; and it is impossible to appreciate these without going into the history of each. To present to the world of scholarship a historical account based so largely on secondary sources is little short of impertinence, or folly, when it is written by one who has no training in the subject. In mitigation, I must plead certain points.

The first is that whereas the only new material in the book consists of a large amount of statistical data covering building in certain towns between 1850 and 1913, and a few odd facts gleaned from building plan registers and other contemporary sources, there is a great deal of new interpretation and argument. While I have neither quoted from nor referred to everything that has been written on British building activity, I believe that I have read most of it. I cannot, of course, make the same claim of industrial, economic or social history, but here I have attacked the literature in a way that seemed most likely to reveal any comments that had been made on the relationships between building and the rest of the economy. In none of it have I come across any systematic attempt to identify and to explain the long cycles of the eighteenth century, to consider the evidence for the existence of a birth cycle and its impact on the economy, or to examine the impact of the physical limitations of the coal industry on our economy in the 1870's.

It is, nevertheless, possible that the deficiency is in my reading, and that all of these points are well known to professional economic historians. If this is so, I must fall back on my second defence, which describes a state of affairs for which both historians and economists must take some blame. Whereas many books and papers written by economic historians emphasise the role of credit, and of such factors as harvests and wars, economic theorists have strangely neglected them. Jevons, Hawtrey and Robertson (and especially the youthful Robertson) made notable contributions in this field. But the Keynesian and post-Keynesian analysts have been so concerned with manipulating aggregates, and producing bold theories in terms of a manageable number of well defined macro-relationships, that such awkward concepts as credit and shocks have slipped into the shadows of our thought, and create positive nightmares whenever they re-emerge. It is true, of course, that this focussing of thought on other matters has had its reward, but it has also led us into errors.

The startling, and sobering, fact is that the dichotomy between historians and theorists has stimulated very little obvious regret. Historians have continued to produce more and more facts, and have in many cases acquired valuable and detailed understanding of the economy : but they have rarely succeeded in communicating their findings to the theorists, who have been more inclined either to look at the current situation for their facts, or to pay respect only to statistical evidence. The vast wealth of qualitative data unearthed by historical research stands as an ever-growing pyramid of fact, in which the theorist shows little interest, partly because its builders talk only to each other.

This has become more and more apparent to me as I have worked on building. By reading what is known to most historians I have learned a great deal that is relevant to current economic problems and theory ; and because I have an interest in current problems and theory I have been able to quarry into history's pyramid with a purpose. The result is a new arrangement and interpretation of well known evidence, which will probably be of greater interest to economists than to historians. Quite emphatically, this is an economist's attempt to learn from history, and to pass the lesson on to other economists. It is not a book that is designed to tell the historian anything — even though it is possible that a few may find it of some interest. Probably the historians who do read it will disagree with the interpretation and theory that is presented here. If they do, then the ensuing discussion should not only add to our understanding, but it may also do something to bridge the gulf between disciplines that have too long diverged.

Chapter 2 surveys the course of building in Britain for the period 1700–1832. It presents no new data, but leans heavily on standard authorities. The only reason for including it is that it marshalls the evidence for asserting the existence of building cycles as far back as 1700, and in doing so suggests certain features of importance in their causation. One of these is that stochastic events, and especially harvests, were particularly important as determinants not simply of minor fluctuations but of major upswings and down-swings. This is a point which is new to no historian, but whose importance is too often overlooked by the economists of growth. The other, which historians once again do not seem to have com-municated adequately to the theorists, is that these stochastic events had importances that depended very largely upon our supply of short-term credit. The Usury Laws of the period were partly to blame for this, but, as we shall see, the importance of relating an economic shock to the strength of the economy is to be borne in mind even today.

Chapter 3 contains a theoretical account of the major forces identified in Chapter 2. It leaves a number of problems unanswered, partly because the proper place for the answers seems to be later in the book.

It is not until we look at the period after 1830 that we are able to say much about regional variations, simply because the necessary statistics do not exist until then. Even when they do become available, the statistics are tarnished by our inability to distinguish between bricks used for houses and bricks used for railways, but the work of Shannon and Matthews still enables us to examine the thirties and forties in some detail. This is done in Chapter 4, which also uses other data, much of it new, to develop further the idea of regional fluctuations in the fifties and early sixties.

This brings us to the boom that prefaced the Great Depression, which we examine in detail for South Wales, the Manchester area and London. There were important regional factors at work, and the purpose of Chapter 5 is to isolate these. On the other hand there were also national factors, and it happens that from about this time onwards there is a fair collection of national time-series. These are not always at the level of aggregation most appropriate to our study, but it is possible to draw certain conclusions from them, sometimes rather tentatively. Accordingly in Chapter 6 we look at some of these, including especially building costs and Weber's work on rents, but it is essentially a partial study, arising more out of the need to do one thing at a time than out of any belief that these forces worked in isolation. Another major force at work was population change, which is examined in Chapter 7. Having thus prepared the way, we are able to look at our whole period from 1700 to 1913, and especially the shorter period from 1870 to 1913, from a more balanced viewpoint, incorporating both regional and national factors, in Chapter 8. Some new points emerge.

The First World War ends the great period of growth in a Britain without appreciable economic control. Thereafter, rent control, if nothing else, alters the nature of our problem. Accordingly Chapter 9 draws together the major points already made and emphasises the essentials of our theory of building cycles in a free economy. It then looks briefly at building between the wars, to see to what extent the theory requires modification under rent control, local-authority activity, more conscious budgetary policy, and so on.

The story is continued up to the present day in Chapter 10, which goes on to look at the future. If our theories are true — and they seem to be compatible with fact — then there are certain points to be made about the future time-shape of building, and these are particularly important now that there is such concern about slum clearance. Briefly our problem is that of phasing the slum-clearance programme so that it moves inversely to fluctuations in the provision of additional houses. This is a problem which is related to the age-distribution of the existing population — a factor which is so often omitted from economic analysis. It is also related to the whole problem of urban land values, and consequently Chapter 10 contains a brief treatment of the theory of this subject. It ends with a peep further into the future.

Behind this analysis there is a great deal of basic research into the course of building in a large number of towns between 1850 and 1913. These and other raw data are described in some of the appendices. There has also been a certain amount of mathematical work, which is either included in the appendices or published separately. Other appendices contain slightly edited versions of parts of Weber's manuscript.

In its original form the manuscript of this book went a stage further. I cannot pretend that I have done more than suggested a theory, and attempted to provide supporting historical evidence. The theory is still unproven. The non-existence of statistical data at appropriate levels of aggregation prevents the application of adequate econometric tests. In an attempt to provide some kind of test, I embarked on a long verbal account of an elaborate simulation model. As it happened it soon became apparent that the model was too large for any existing computer, and that my account of it was most tedious reading. For these very good reasons it is now omitted. A simpler version, which can be used both as a test of the reasonableness of our theory and as a means of experimenting with policy, is now being developed with the assistance of Mr. J. R. Eaton of Manchester University and Mr. G. C. F. Capper of Keele University. This is described in a little more detail in Chapter 9, which also discusses the use of models of this kind. It has grown out of this book ; and the book is essentially a prelude to the model. If there is one single point of importance that has struck me it is that history provides abundant evidence that the economy is far too complicated for us to hope to gain much further insight into it by the continued application of the methods that have served us so well in the past. Once one starts to acknowledge the importance of capacity restraints, gestation periods, shocks and interactions of all kinds, then the problems of analysis become too great for the un-aided human brain. Fortunately we have computers, with whose aid we can transcend the barriers placed before us. We can build model economies far closer to historical or current reality than has hitherto been possible. The innovation in our resources calls for an innovation in our methods, as well as in the scale of attack. Our model is an attempt to innovate according to this maxim, and the present volume contains the historical justification for its structure. If it fails to work, it will be interesting to discover which of our assumptions is wrong, or what crucial factors have been omitted.

If, on the other hand, it does work, then as we explain in Chapter 9 we shall be able to use it for a number of useful experiments.

NOTES TO CHAPTER 1

1. B. Thomas, *Migration and Economic Growth*, 1954.
2. A. K. Cairncross, *Home and Foreign Investment, 1870–1913*, 1953.
3. J. Hamish Richards and J. Parry Lewis, 'House-Building in the South Wales Coalfield, 1851–1911', *The Manchester School*, vol. xxiv, 1956, pp. 289–301.
4. In *The Scottish Journal of Political Economy*, 1955. See below.
5. A. K. Cairncross and B. Weber, 'Fluctuations in Building in Great Britain, 1785–1849', *Economic History Review*, 1956.
6. T. S. Ashton, *Economic Fluctuations in England, 1700–1800*, 1959.

CHAPTER 2

A SURVEY OF 1700–1832

'ONE thing, for sure,' says Sir John Summerson in his *Georgian London*, '. . . London's growth has not been a matter of gradual and even incrementation, but of distinct waves of activity at intervals of roughly about fifty years.' This interval has had 'an obvious relation to the alternation of periods of peace and war, and a less obvious relation to the increase of London's population. Each burst of house-building had a character of its own. . . .'[1]

Such an assertion cannot but jolt the student of the later nineteenth century into considerable doubt and speculation. Although Thomas has taken the British building cycle back to the 1830's,[2] for which period Matthews also examined the phenomenon,[3] most attention has been concentrated on the years after 1860, and there is by no means universal agreement that Britain had a building cycle much earlier than this. Those who assert that there was such a cycle throughout most of the nineteenth century speak of a periodicity of not fifty but about twenty years. On the other hand, it is well known that in later Victorian times building in London followed a pattern quite different from that which existed elsewhere. What does Summerson's assertion suggest in the context of this knowledge? Does it mean that London had a fifty-year cycle ever since the Great Fire, or even earlier, while elsewhere there has been a twenty-year cycle since some time in the nineteenth century? Or does it mean that perhaps the whole country has had building cycles of some periodicity or the other for much longer than most people suppose? If the answer to either of these questions is affirmative, how must we modify our views of the growth process, and how can we explain these phenomena? The purpose of this chapter is to begin to answer these questions by surveying the course of building from 1700 to 1832. The dates are determined by the fact that our earliest useful statistics begin in 1700, while in the thirties we begin, for the first time, to have building statistics of a kind that allow us to look not simply at the country as a whole, or at just one or two different towns, but at a number of fairly well defined towns and regions. It happens that these terminal years also embrace the period covered by Summerson's book.

The wealth of fascinating information in this book goes well with Ashton's accounts of building and of economic fluctuations in the eighteenth century.[4] Ashton has obviously long had an affectionate interest in building and its place in an economy, and in his various works he provides not only a great deal of valuable insight and data, but traces in detail the annual changes in activity. Most of what we now relate for the eighteenth century has been obtained from one or the other of these sources, and there is probably not a single new fact in the whole of this chapter. On the other hand, Ashton has not been concerned with the building cycle, as distinct from the trade cycle. His interest has been in short-term fluctuations rather than in long swings. The new features of this chapter are the emphasis placed on a feature that has hitherto been neglected, and an attempt to extract from the writings of economic historians some points which have been inadequately appreciated by those who are more interested in economic theory.

Taken by itself, the statistical evidence for the existence of building cycles in eighteenth-century Britain is a great deal stronger than it appears to be, and when it is supplemented by confirmatory qualitative evidence it becomes very convincing. At first sight a confusion of timber imports, glass output and stained paper does not inspire much confidence. Ashton has relied most heavily on a series showing the imports of deal and fir timber, which is graphed in the Figure 2.1. There are, of course, grave deficiencies in the data. Timber can be stored from one year to another, and its imports are liable to the vicissitudes of shipping, of war and of fear of war. Different timbers were used for different purposes and came from different places, but when one was scarce another could be substituted. For this kind of reason the data for annual imports must be treated with caution, and no single figure taken by itself, unsubstantiated by other evidence, can be taken as proof of high or low activity.

Similar remarks apply to a second indicator used, in addition to timber imports, in the second half of the century. This is a series showing the output of glass (other than glass used for bottles) which is also graphed in Figure 2.1. Most of it was used for windows, but some was exported and some used in other manufactures such as beads and buttons. We must also keep in mind its use in glazing existing windows, and the fact that sometimes new windows were put into existing buildings, before we start drawing inferences about the level of building. It is probable, too, that in the earlier years the statistics had a very incomplete coverage. A third series used by Ashton, with considerable caution, is one showing the amount of stained paper (i.e. wall-paper) charged with duty. This, of course, relates to a material used only in luxury building, and is also influenced by changes in tastes and the need of replacement. The last fifteen years of the century and the first half of the next century can be described with more certainty by using figures for brick and

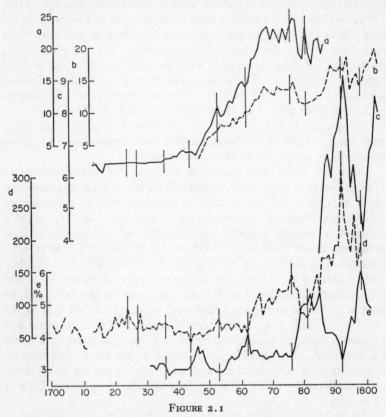

FIGURE 2.1

(a) Stained Paper charged with duty ('00,000 yds.). Excise years.
(b) Glass (excluding bottles, etc.) charged with duty ('0,000 cwt.). Excise years.
(c) Bricks charged with duty ('00 million). Excise years.
(d) Imports of Fir and Deal (£000).
(e) Yield on 3% Funds (reciprocal of average annual (July–June) prices). All based on Ashton.

tile production, and these, by moving more or less in harmony with a smoothed version of the timber import data do something to justify the use of this series in the earlier years.

There is a final statistical indicator, of a very different kind, that can be used from 1732. This is the Yield on Consols. The relationship between this and building was pointed out by Shannon [5] and has been described in some detail by Ashton. In the eighteenth-century building was very much affected by the Usury laws. Master-builders working in some of the building trades would employ other craftsmen to help them. Usually they obtained materials on credit, and borrowed enough money to pay wages and other charges by mortgaging the building during the course of its construction. Public works were also financed with borrowed money, sometimes raised through the issue of bonds. In London and many parts of the provinces the rates of interest on mortgages and bonds moved freely in steps of one-half per cent. Then as now, a rise in the rate of interest put up the cost of building, and consequently tended to cause a diminution in activity and — in an attempt to keep costs low — the use of inferior materials. In the eighteenth and early nineteenth centuries, however, a sufficient decrease in the price of Consols could cause the virtual cessation of building. The Usury Laws prohibited borrowers other than the State from offering, or lenders from receiving, more than 6 per cent until 1714 and more than 5 per cent subsequently. Once the yield on Consols had reached 3·5 or 4 per cent the rate of interest for building loans would normally tend to be at 5 per cent or above but this was forbidden. Various ways of circumventing the Usury Laws existed, but it was difficult to do so in a mortgage deed drawn up by a solicitor. Faced with the choice of, say, 4·2 per cent on Consols and only 5 per cent on a mortgage, the investor had insufficient incentive to turn from State-security to bricks and mortar. Thus, as the yield on Consols rose the supply of loanable capital just dried up, and building became not just more expensive but often impossible. In the provinces, where rates often tended to be a little higher than in London, the ceiling to activity imposed by the Usury Laws was probably reached a little earlier. In so far as some loans were raised locally, there were also local shortages of capital for other reasons. We shall use the Yield on Consols as an indicator in the confirmatory sense that when it is high we may expect building to be low, and vice versa.

Before examining these varied indicators, we must consider more precisely than has been done by other writers what exactly we mean by a cycle in an economic time-series. To help us to define a cycle we introduce the idea of nth order peaks and troughs. We define an nth order peak to be a value higher than all values within a span of n periods on either side, while an nth order trough occurs when there is a value lower than all others in a span of n periods on either side of it. It follows that, for example, a third-order peak implies a second-order peak. In order to determine whether a particular value is at a major peak or trough one therefore has to consider a total of up to $2n+1$ values. On the other hand, major peaks of order n can follow each other at intervals of $n+1$ periods. This is the series

    P   P   P   P   P

1, 2, 3, 4, 3, 2, 1, 5, 4, 3, 2, 7, 6, 5, 4, 13, 14, 3, 2, 7, 4, 3, 8, 4, 3, 2, 1

       T   T   T

the values marked P are clearly peaks of order 3, while those marked T are troughs of the same order. It will be seen that in this series there are two third-order peaks only four periods apart. It may also be seen that the third-order peaks do not always alternate with the third-order troughs. We shall now take the quite arbitrary step of defining a *cycle of semi-period n* to be a set of $2n+1$ values centred on an nth order peak and bounded by n^{th} order troughs. It is not suggested that all cycles must fall into this pattern. Those about a steep trend may never do so for anything but trivial semi-periods. We simply indicate a device that was found useful in a preliminary examination of the time-series for the eighteenth century.

The figures for timber imports are marred by two gaps early in the century, and by the fact that they do not stretch back into the previous century just those few years that would allow us to put the high values of the middle of the first decade into some perspective. They have been examined for peaks and troughs of various semi-periods, as explained in Appendix 1, by Mr. David Bugg. Naturally the number of peaks or troughs of a given order tends to fall as the order rises. An interesting point is that for this series it does not do so when the order rises from six to seven. The relevant dates are listed below, where it has been assumed that there was a high value in 1705, and that 1712 had a higher value than 1711. These are not crucial assumptions. The year 1727 is queried because the imports in 1729 were but barely higher than those in 1727. If the discrepancy is due to statistical error then 1729 must be classed as the trough. It will be noticed that these peaks and troughs alternate. It is shown in Mr. Bugg's appendix that the chance of this happening by accident is not high. Furthermore, there is a striking uniformity in the period from one trough to

Trough	Peak	Trough	Duration between Peaks	Troughs
c. 1698?	1705?	1711?		
c. 1711	1724	1727?	19	16
1727?	1736	1744	12	17
1744	1753	1762	17	18
1762	1776	1781	23	19
1781	1792	1798	16	17

the next. The extension of the semi-period to eight years excludes two of the peaks (1736 and 1776) but retains the listed troughs and so cuts out the alternation on which we have commented.

If we take the years we have just tabulated and consider them alongside our other statistics, it seems that most of them locate, at least to a reasonable degree of approximation, turning points in building activity. This is brought out by Figure 2.1, where the relationship with the turning points in the yield on Consols is strikingly apparent. The peculiar trends and other deficiencies of some other statistics shown in this graph make them less helpful in this respect, but after 1763 they are not too bad, while if one attempts to eliminate the trend influence by looking at deviations around it, the agreement for the earlier years is also considerable. The important question now is whether qualitative evidence confirms the suggestion that building moved in long swings with troughs approximately eighteen years apart throughout the eighteenth century, and on into the beginning of the nineteenth, where statistics of brick production enable us to be more confident about the course of activity. On this point it is encouraging to note that there is a close correspondence between the brick and timber figures during the years in which the two series overlap. For the rest, we may assert quite briefly that qualitative evidence does, on the whole, support the inference drawn from the statistics, as will become apparent from the following account of the long cycles we have just defined.

As far as we can see from the statistics, the first major fluctuation of the century had a peak around 1705. There had been a boom in house-building and the construction of waterways in the middle of the 1690's, but a set-back occurred, reflected in the suggestion of a dip in timber imports in the first few years of the next century. Whether the high figure for 1704, or the possibly higher one for 1705, indicates a major peak we cannot say, since possibly there was substantially higher activity only a few years before. We can, however, be certain that the years around this date saw a great deal of building, just as by 1710 there was a marked diminution. Ashton has marshalled some of the evidence for this assertion, but it is difficult to speak with any certainty about the reasons for the decline. Bad harvests led both to reduced incomes, in some cases, and to high food prices, which would reduce the demand for housing. The main causes, however, are more probably associated with the impact of war. The demands of the army and navy were considerable in regard both to man-power and to timber. The war also affected finance. Crises developed late in 1704, 1707 and 1710. Bankruptcies were high, and the Government, short of money, was seeking loans on such attractive terms that 'there was little incentive to put one's money into bricks and mortar'.[6] Summerson recorded a low level of building in London towards the end of Queen Anne's reign. However uncertain may be the peak of around 1705, there is no doubt that the trough of around 1711 marked the lowest level of building that the century had yet seen.

Just as we can be certain of the trough that began the next major cycle, so we can be sure of its peak around 1724, but the exact locations of this peak and the subsequent trough are not so definite. The coming of peace had brought both low interest rates and a renewed supply of labour and timber. It was estimated that the number of new buildings erected in the metropolis in 1716–18 amounted to a fifth of the number standing in 1695. Public works on road and river accelerated, not only because of the factors we have mentioned but also because of the tide of optimism that eventually brought with it the Bubble of 1720. When this arrived, building fell, but not heavily, and it soon recovered. Timber imports rose once again, but stock-piling makes the import peak of 1724 an uncertain indicator of the peak in building itself. Ashton cites evidence to suggest that building was active in London, Bath and Manchester much later in the twenties, but concludes that it 'seems probable that the prosperity came to an end in the second half of 1726, and that the crisis arising from the outbreak of war with Spain was the turning point'.[7] The improvement of 1728 was 'due to passing circumstances and not to any fundamental economic change'. The early thirties are well-chronicled as years of low building activity, and even the remainder of the decade saw only a gentle upswing, whose character we shall consider shortly. The great boom that began with the Treaty of Utrecht, marking the first well-established upswing of the century, and the first of Summerson's Georgian waves, had broken, and given way to a few decades of comparative quiet.

This building cycle, centring around the mid-twenties, is reasonably documented, and deserves a much more detailed study. We even know a little of the population movements of the time. The statistics are hardly the most reliable, but it appears fairly certain that the population of London had increased substantially since 1700, while the number of baptisms there had 'increased from the beginning of the century until 1724, when they were 19,370, and they decreased till they reached their lowest point, 13,571 in 1742'.[8] Thus births and building rose and fell more or less together, while burials began to increase on the building downswing, and continued to do so until they reached a peak figure of 32,169 in 1741. Crude figures of this kind, unadjusted for population level and age-structure, must be treated with reserve, but the broad movements are clear. Indeed, although the population of London 'was only kept up by immigrants who had passed the dangerous first years of life' and many of the elderly people moved out of the capital before dying, the crude death-rate was as high as 5 deaths per hundred of population in 1750.

Thus in considering building in London in that period we have to take account of a population that was increasing in the upswing of the cycle, and doing so both because of immigration and because of the increasing number of births. If this reflected an increasing number of marriages, then the demographic factor was even stronger in setting the level of potential demand at this time, when the availability of money, materials and men did something to convert it into supply. On the other hand, a very great deal of the building activity was luxurious, and influenced more by taste, fashion and wealth than movements of population. The proportion of building materials going into these luxurious dwellings must have been very great, and clearly there are dangers in interpreting the evidence. If, as is possible, both the statistics and the qualitative evidence are weighted in favour of the solid Georgian house, one must be careful not to try to explain the fluctuations in terms which may be more appropriate to hovels and cottages. In these latter terms, certainly, a substantial part of the explanation would be that the fall in births and high deaths of the late twenties, associated with bad harvests and costly food, reduced both the potential and the effective demand for houses; but we have no knowledge of the extent to which our data are concerned with the houses of the kind which would be so affected. Perhaps it is for this reason that Ashton has eschewed the demographic factor, and argued that the downturn was due to the familiar process 'by which the deflexion of an unduly high proportion of income to the creation of capital goods creates tensions that must lead to recession'. Certainly, as he points out, during this cycle there was an inverse relationship between building and overseas trade. In very many ways, the cycle that brought in the Georgian age is a feast for the researcher: but we must leave it, to move onwards.

The next major fluctuation, if we accept the classification of major peaks and troughs given in the table above, consists of a halting, gentle, barely perceptible, rise until 1736, and then a decline to the second-lowest level of the century in 1744. At best it must be thought of as of minor interest compared with the building cycle we have just examined, and some may be inclined to doubt its right to a place in the list of cycles, although, as we shall see in a moment, there are good reasons for including it. The few years around 1736 saw timber imports almost as high as those of the mid-twenties. Ashton points out that at this time 'a good part of the City was rebuilt and many dwellings converted into warehouses',[9] while Summerson refers to it as a 'rather dim period' in which 'expansion slowed down almost to a standstill' while 'a period of consolidation and gradual rebuilding in central areas began'.[10] On the other hand, there seems to have been good reasons for the decline that followed even this modest boom, for quite apart from the speculation associated with the generally rising trade, the strain on credit and the minor financial crisis that came with the outbreak of the War of the Polish Succession, there seems to have been substantial empty property. Some time around 1739 there was a reference to 'at least fifteen hundred houses now uninhabited in St. Martin's and other adjacent parishes' [11] which were to be rebuilt. It was a time when much of London was literally falling down, and as leases expired landlords took the opportunity to reconstruct. Possibly the houses were empty because of the state that they were in, but there is no doubt that the times showed all the symptoms of the depressed times so much better documented later in the century, when empty houses spread their heavy melancholy with the speed of successive bad harvests. Ever since 1726 births had been falling and deaths increasing. Bad harvests in 1740 and 1741 added to the disaster of war. Though prices rose, wages often fell. Bankruptcies and riots became common. It was not a time when the demand for houses for either the working class or the merchants was likely to be high. Ashton detected signs of recovery as early as 1741 itself, and spoke of 1743 as a year in which 'everything points to general prosperity', but the timber import figures were unaffected, possibly because the high cost of food deflected money from housing. In 1744 deaths were twice as numerous as births in London. The outbreak of war in the same year, and the Jacobite Rising of the next not only caused the yield on Consols to rise sharply, but also underlined the fact that this was no time for investment in property.

The rising yield in Consols from 1737 to the late forties, and the well-established relationship between this yield and building both in the later statistics and in reasoned explanation, is one reason why we should not ignore the cycle we are now considering, or dismiss it as spurious. If one looks at the pattern of the fluctuations in the yield on Consols for the rest of the century, one finds it difficult to believe that 1737 was not a major trough in this series, and that this more or less coincided with a major peak in building, especially since what we have of the yield series before that year suggests a downward movement to parallel the slight rise in timber imports.

The trouble with this particular building cycle is that it was on a long downward trend. It is, indeed, the only instance of one.

With the coming of peace in 1748 there also came a revival in home and foreign trade. Investment was made more attractive by the lower rate of interest, and the even cheaper money associated with Pelham's conversion of the public debt gave the final stimulus to activity in 1751. Probably the glass-duty statistics are not to be relied upon very heavily in their early years, but the spectacular rise certainly owes something to the generally increased building activity of the time. Quite apart from anything else, physical deterioration ensured that the long period of idleness would end before much longer, while there is evidence that these years saw a housing shortage in London.[12] It is, however, evidence that points to a shortage of fairly substantial houses, rather than houses of all classes and kinds. In other parts of the country, too, there was now activity, much of it in the nature of improvements.

In this upswing the aggregate level of building seems to have lagged behind the rest of the economy, and the same is true of the peak, and the downswing. Before timber imports reached their highest level in 1753, lower activity had set in in other sectors of the economy, including exports. The peak year itself saw a bad harvest, followed by riots in 1754. Money remained cheap, but building fell, probably simply because the onset of fresh bad times after a decade of uncertainties had caused a fall in demand, which manifested itself in a larger number of empty houses, falling rents and, consequently, reduced activity. When, in 1755, war broke out with the French in America, there was something of a panic. Ashton has suggested that one of the major causes in the collapse of the boom may have been over-investment in building. It seems to be a most plausible suggestion. The next eight years saw a series of small cycles about a falling trend, as far as timber imports go, while the glass and stained-paper series continued to rise but less steeply than formerly. With the corroboration of the rise in the yield on Consols and abundant qualitative evidence, there is no doubt that these years saw much reduced building activity. Yet a vast volume of public work was in progress, in the shape of canals, roads, iron-works, bridges and hospitals. Wages and prices were rising, as were births and population generally. In the late fifties there is abundant evidence of prosperity. Why, then, was there no upsurge in building?

The answer seems to lie in the shape of the graph showing the yield on Consols, which stood at 4·2 per cent in 1762 compared with 2·9 per cent in 1754. To some extent this rise was due to the un-settled international situation, and the demands of the armed services, but the factors creating prosperity, such as the heavy public investments, were no doubt also hampering the expansion of house-building, by creating a scarcity of capital. Then suddenly, in 1763, imports of deal and fir timber leap to their highest level for forty years, and the whole course of the economy seems to change. The building cycles are no longer about a more or less horizontal trend. Now they are undulating around a very positive upward path. In some respects the boom was perhaps no more spectacular than that of fifty years before, and it is, indeed, with this earlier boom that Summerson has compared it. The imports of timber in the first Georgian boom rose from £33,000 to £93,000 in thirteen years, which is a greater proportional rise than that from £56,000 in 1762 to £142,000 in 1776. On the other hand, the timber imports in the trough-to-trough period 1762–81 exceeded by 50 per cent the imports in any previous period of twenty years. Growth had appeared with a vengeance.

Without a more detailed analysis of these years it would be foolish to be too confident about any explanation of this sudden change in trend : but of one thing there seems to be little doubt. The great upsurge could come only when there was abundant credit. The Yield on Consols reveals that in the late fifties and early sixties the monetary position was tightening, but then with the end of the war, the yield fell sharply, rates of interest declined, and mortgages were easily obtained. We have already suggested that the credit scarcity in the late fifties prevented the expansion of activity at a scale that the comparative prosperity of those years, and the zeal for public works, warranted. Meanwhile births were rising and the death-rate falling, so that a marked increase in population was swelling the potential demand for houses. This pent up demand was suddenly liberated by easy money, and impinged with the force of a flood upon supply. Peace also liberated men and materials. In London and elsewhere buildings shot up at incredible speed, and sometimes fell down as quickly. Bricks were often made out of earth excavated for the foundations, mixed with ashes and refuse, warmed on the spot, and built into walls just one brick thick. Daily there were accounts of half-built houses tumbling down, and in 1765 a cart was loaded with bricks so fresh from the furnace that it caught fire. Equally valid at this time was a remark made in the *London Chronicle* in 1774 :

The builders and the work of their hands seem to have exerted their utmost to rival each other whether the builder or the building should first tumble into decay and ruin; the first frequently failing before the walls are half up, and the latter falling before it was finished.[13]

On the other hand, these years also saw Summerson's second wave of substantial building, and the whole upsurge was to some extent in response to the 1760 Act for widening and improving the City streets, and similar improvement measures. There was also great activity on bridges, canals and harbours, which were built to last in the same way as the substantial houses of the Golden Age.

There was probably another factor at work on the side of demand. Little is known of internal migration at that time,[14] and it seems to be an impossible task to trace the year when a large-scale migration to the towns really got under way. By the eighties many of our large towns were already growing at alarming rates, and the inflow of agricultural labour to the centres of industrial activity led to a vast amount of house-building, as we shall see in more detail shortly. If one examines the course of industrial production during these years it seems fairly safe to assert that although the increase of the eighties was more spectacular, there were also substantial developments in the sixties which must certainly have demanded higher urban labour forces than had existed ten years previously. The high demand of the sixties must have owed something to the increased pace of migration into the towns. Probably this inflow was more marked in the mid-sixties, just after the Peace of Paris, than later, when the post-war boom broke and employers found themselves oversupplied with both labour and fixed capital. Yet timber imports, although lower than they had been, were still at very high levels, and soon rose further before peaking in 1776. It seems likely that the building of the later sixties was largely of a kind other than working-class housing. The demand for public works and for the Adelphi could not have been much affected by any temporary inability of the new industrial workers to translate their potential demands into effective demands ; but the builders of these edifices were probably able to proceed more easily because of the increased supply of un-skilled labour, and even of skilled men of certain kinds.[15] This superior kind of building must also have done something to boost employment, and so to bolster the fortunes of the consumption industries. It was possibly this that acted first as a stabiliser and then as an accelerator, setting off the increased investment of the later sixties.

Labour became less abundant, and was made even less so by the restoration of the American export market in 1770. More prosperous times, aided by the creation of many private banks, increased the demand for houses once again. Within two years the Ayr Bank collapsed after speculations at home and abroad had impinged upon it. Money in Scotland became so scarce that building ceased,

B

and the Bank of England courageously met the crisis when it came south of the Tweed. Builders and contractors collapsed, yet both glass production and timber imports remained high, while in London houses were still being erected at great speed. Confidence, never very low, soon rose enough to enable activity to rise again, aided by the additional funds made available for home investment by the decline in overseas trade that came with the deterioration of our relations with American colonists. 'America and France must tell us how long this embarrassment of opulence is to last', wrote Horace Walpole,[16] and soon they did. The cost of war not only caused substantial increases in the duties on glass and stained paper, but uncertainties of war restricted the timber supply. Building costs rose, and so did the cost of money. Early in 1778 the yield on Consols passed the critical stage. Borrowing became impossible and building virtually ceased. The next year, depression saw more than 1100 houses unoccupied in the City of London. Not until 1785 was it once again possible for building to take place on borrowed capital.[17] These lean years for the builder were lean for almost everybody, for taxes were high to pay for the expenditures and loan charges connected with the war. Both taxation and government expenditure moved inversely to building almost as convincingly as did the yield on Consols, to which they were related.[18]

The imposition of a light tax on bricks in 1785 probably did little to affect the level of building, but certainly provides us now with a valuable index of activity from that depressed year until the middle of the following century.[19] It is an index that moves so similarly to the timber import series that it also adds to our confidence in the latter as an indicator of building. In the mid-eighties both of these series were shooting upwards, as building rose on newly available borrowed capital to meet the demands of the growing population, and the growing industrial towns, and to make up for the quiescence of the recent past. The whole country was bursting into industrial production, and in the cotton area the expansion was so rapid, and the demand for credit so great, that the use of small bills of local acceptability mushroomed at great speed. Everywhere there was optimism, prosperity and growth. There was also speculation.

As so often happens in such times, the over-expansion of credit was not based entirely on either sound or honest principles, and in 1788 banks failed and the crash came. In its origin it was a regional crash, but its repercussions were felt elsewhere, for the cotton area was large and composed a substantial part of demand. In the cotton area itself building of houses and factories almost certainly declined, if the experience of better-documented later regional set-backs is any guide, but aggregate activity seems to have paused, rather than fallen. In the twelve months ending in the middle of 1790 the production of bricks was higher than ever before. By then the crash was for most people well into the past, and the textile industries were working at their highest ever level, supplying both home demand and an expanding foreign trade. Better crops and rising incomes stimulated the purchase and production of all kinds of consumer goods.[20] Aided by still falling interest rates, the boom continued on its course. Refugee capital from France encouraged the yield on Consols to decline further. Country banks continued to expand, financing building and construction of many kinds. Expenditure on roads, river navigation, canals and similar works increased at a phenomenal rate.

Such rapid expansion was bound to cause strain. Raw material prices rose, and labour became scarce as men flocked from the land into canal cutting. Masons were in short supply. Wages rose. Credit became stretched to snapping point. The economy was as vulnerable to crisis as a tired man is to illness, and two events dealt the blow. The political situation in Europe led to foreign sales of British Funds and to a falling exchange rate. At the same time, a wet summer led to a poor harvest, and to the need to purchase foreign grain at a time when already there was a substantial drain on bullion, both overseas and to provide coin during a time of high employment and high wages. Even without the threat of war, the crisis would almost certainly have come. The explosive charge lay in the heights to which the economy had soared and the strains it had placed on its resources. If war had not acted as the trigger, the wet summer would probably have done so. Cunningham long ago emphasised that the bad times of this decade were 'connected with the progress of the industrial revolution' and 'were in some ways an anticipation of the troubles caused by the railway mania'.[21] It did not need much to bring a succession of commercial failures and a cumulative tightening of credit. When war came in February 1793, manufacturers lost their supplies of working credit, and their ability to pay wages. Unemployment was heavy, while the bad harvest made the price of grain high. Marriages and births both declined, and the effective demand for housing dried up at the same time as the supply of credit for their construction. Brick output fell by 40 per cent in two years, and in came the Speenhamland bread scale. Except for a brief rally in 1796, the decline continued until 1799, although in Scotland, where it had been more rapid, it halted earlier.[22]

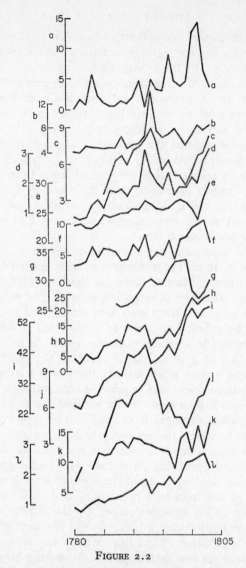

FIGURE 2.2

(a) Wheat and Wheat Flour Imports, G.B. ('00,000 quarters). *B.H.S.*, pp. 94–95.
(b) Index of Bankruptcies, G.B. (1913 = 10). Hoffmann.
(c) Bricks charged with duty, E. & W. ('00 m.). *B.H.S.*, p. 235.
(d) Value of Imports of Deals and Fir Timber. U.K. (£'00,000). Ashton, p. 188.
(e) Baptism, E. & W. ('0,000). *B.H.S.*, p. 28.
(f) English Patents Sealed ('0). *B.H.S.*, p. 268.
(g) Index of Beer Production, G.B. (1913 = 100). Hoffmann.
(h) Index of Output of Cotton Yarn, G.B. (1913 = 100). Hoffmann.
(i) Index of Industrial Production (excluding Building), G.B. (1913 = 100). Hoffmann.
(j) Repeat of (c) above.
(k) Imports minus Re-exports, G.B. (£m.). *B.H.S.*, p. 281.
(l) Domestic Exports, G.B. (£m.). *B.H.S.*, p. 281.

We have just suggested that the decline in building came about
when two exogenous factors — weather and war — coincided with
a strained credit situation which had arisen as part of the process of
expansion, and that this coincidence was sufficient to bring about a
crisis as the sudden increase in the demand for credit associated
with these exogenous factors shattered the delicate balance that
prevailed. The precise mechanism implied in this account must be
left until the next chapter, but we may note that this brief survey
of the history of the eighteenth century is built around a new interpretation of the importance of harvests, wars and credit. Briefly it
is that a good harvest, or some other favourable shock, is likely to
have a profound impact on the demand for housing and other forms of
investment if there is an abundance of credit, while a bad harvest
or a war is likely to have its most serious effect if it comes at a time
when credit is in any case strained. This thesis, whose theoretical
validity will be defended later, is central to the theme of this book
and has been derived from a more detailed examination of the major
fluctuations we have just reviewed. We shall now look at the first
two building cycles of the nineteenth century with the same ideas
in mind.

Measured from trough to trough the first of these cycles lasted
from 1799 to 1816, and covers some of the most complicated years
in this study, for wars, blockades and harvests combined to make the
impact of exogenous factors particularly important. The data for
the period have been assembled by Weber and Cairncross,[23] and
further information is given by Gayer, Rostow and Schwartz,[24]
although these latter authors were not concerned with long cycles.

When, after the crisis of 1797, the Bank found itself able to
pursue an easier monetary policy there was no shortage of claimants
for the funds it made available. A sustained boom in foreign trade
encouraged people to think in terms of industrial investment and
continued migration to the towns. In 1796 and 1797 the price of
wheat was about 30 per cent lower than it had been in 1795. The
improvement in real wages and nourishment led to a higher marriage-
rate, a higher birth-rate and a lower death-rate, in the way that it so
often did in eighteenth-century England, and this rise in population
and family creation increased the demand for housing. Abundant
credit allowed an expansion of supply. A few bad harvests led
to what was almost a famine situation in 1800–1, but by now
industrial investment was proceeding apace, and tided the construction industry over these difficult years, when the marriage-rate was
once again low. Harvest improvements were just around the corner,
and as grain prices fell so the number of marriages rose by over a

third between 1801 and 1803, while baptisms went up by a quarter. It is a rise that is evidenced not only in the total statistics for the country as a whole, but also in the official returns for parishes spread over the length and breadth of the land.

It was not simply the price of wheat that was responsible for this phenomenon. There was fierce investment activity in all sectors of the economy. Between 1796 and 1800 as many as thirty-five steam engines were introduced into cotton mills, and a large invest-ment took place in the woollen industry. The war had encouraged the erection of blast furnaces, whose numbers rose from 121 in 1796 to 221 in 1804. Docks were under construction in London and elsewhere, and in the Manchester area a score of factories were under construction in the summer of 1802. This rapid industrial progress was affecting the demand for housing both because of the income effect and because of the movement of people into the towns. Such internal migration, allied to natural growth, was bound to lead to a high volume of house-building when incomes allowed demand to become effective, and the monetary situation allowed supply to meet it. Of the 1,623,000 houses recorded in England and Wales in 1801, some 57,000 were unoccupied; but the number of families exceeded the number of houses by well over 300,000.

The lower price of wheat was not, of course, a blessing for every-body, and by 1803 there was considerable agricultural distress both amongst the larger farmers and amongst those who sold but little. Probably it also hit landlords of agricultural lands, in the sense that they would have their rent withheld.[25] At this time 'the extension of farm acreage constituted a principal outlet for new investment',[26] and consequently the good harvests must have had a significant impact on the supply of funds available for other purposes, including the provision of houses. The outbreak of war in May of that year, and the bad effect on trade, resulted in a more general depression. and the bad harvest of 1804 raised once again the price of grain, Brick output fell a little, yet on the whole money wages advanced more rapidly than the cost of living [27] for a few years, and demand for houses remained high. Even the trough year in marriages, in 1805, saw more weddings than any year of the previous century, and the impetus given to demand was such that the sharp rise in the yield on Consols between 1802 and 1804 was associated with only a hesitation in the upward course of brick production. It is as much an indication of the high level of activity reflected in a strong bargain-ing position, as of the futility of the Combination Acts to hold down the forces so tragically erupted in France, that it was possible to write in 1806 :

it is now a Confirmed thing that a Bricklayer, Mason, Carpenter, Wheelwright, etc., shall have 3s. per week higher Wages in Leeds or in Manchester, than in Wakefield, York, Hull, Rochdale, and adjacent Towns, it is in order too that Bricklayers and Masons' Labourers at Leeds shall have 2s. per week extra — no Workman will dare deviate from these Terms.[28]

By then there had been something of a trade revival, but soon the mercantile war between Napoleon and Britain compelled a complete reorientation of our trade. For two years it more or less stagnated, while the cotton industry was so affected that on January 3rd, 1809, the *Manchester Mercury* carried an appeal for subscriptions for the relief of the poor, beginning with the words 'Perhaps never before has the distress of the poorer classes in Manchester been greater . . .'. Building slightly declined. Frustrated commercial instincts found some outlet in the flotation of new companies and country banks. Towards the end of the decade the course of the Iberian Peninsular War opened trade with Latin America, adding to the prosperity that came from the renewed trade with the United States, and from 1808 building rose again from its minor recession. Labour shortages appeared, and the demand for capital expanded rapidly. The war and investment in South America exaggerated our capital exports, and it was against this background that the demands of home development continued to swell. Enormous increases in the Bank's accommodation to private borrowers took place against a declining reserve, and the country banks further strained the credit structure. The yield on Consols continued to fall, and a major crisis developed as our capital resources proved insufficient to meet the competing demands of war, foreign trade, home construction and the 'phrenzy of speculation'. In September 1810, *The Manchester Mercury* reported one of the country bank failures as an extension of 'the pecuniary embarassments for some time past felt in the metropolis'. The reaction was inevitable, with depression and heavy unemployment as the outcome, especially in Lancashire and around Birmingham. Bad trade led to lower wages and unemployment, and effectively reduced the demand for housing as assuredly as the creation of surplus capacity ended the period of industrial expansion. A single issue of *The Manchester Mercury* in 1812, despite heavy demands upon space due to its war despatches, reported riots in Bristol, Truro, Leeds, Macclesfield, Stockport and Birmingham as high potato prices added to the misery of depression. The Census of 1811 shows that in England there were 2,012,000 families occupying only 1,678,000 houses. In Middlesex as many as 222,000 families were squeezed into 130,000 houses. Over the whole of England and Wales, the number of houses had increased by 216,000 in ten years, representing a percentage increase of fourteen, which was just about the same as the rate of population change. But in Lancashire the population rose by almost a quarter, while in Merionethshire it hardly rose at all. Internal migration of this scale means that the supply of houses must increase faster than the population if demand is to be satisfied, and in the first decade of the century this did not happen. Against this enormous potential demand, output continued to fall. However great the potential demographic demand, once the credit crisis had come few were left with the means of making their demand effective, and there was, in any case, little credit to support further supply.

A general business revival from about 1811 to 1815 did little to alleviate the distress, which was to some considerable extent increased by the Anglo-American war of 1812–14. Loan-financed government expenditure remained heavy until 1816, emphasising once again the inverse pattern of government expenditure and building. The turning of foreign exchanges in our favour in 1814 might have helped the monetary situation, but a vast amount of speculative investment in stocks of commodities, with which to flood the soon to be liberated European market, absorbed all available funds. Expectations exceeded reality, and in 1816 there was severe unemployment as stocks were run down. Pressure on credit eased, and the Yield on Consols fell a whole point. Probably because of the fall in wheat prices, the marriage-rate had risen between 1813 and 1815, but the combination of the recent severe distress and the continued, if lessened, scarcity of credit prevented any immediate increase in building to meet the potential demand. As peace came, agricultural and commercial distress coincided and brought a fall in the marriage-rate at a time when considerations of age structure would have led one to expect it to remain at a high level.

It remains to mention one interesting suggestion about the location and kind of house-building of these war years. Summerson has pointed out that the shortage of Baltic timber and the high taxes on building materials had an adverse effect. 'Buildings in London dating from between 1793 and 1815 are therefore relatively scarce.' [29] The building cycle we have just examined was probably coloured more by working-class houses and less by luxurious architecture than any we have so far examined.

This was certainly not true of the next, which is the last for us to examine in this chapter. Every building cycle had features of its own, sometimes due more or less to accident, sometimes to the processes of institutional and technological evolution. The cycle that peaked in 1825 differed from its predecessors in a number of important respects. It was the first in the period we have studied to be more or less unaffected by war or the fear of war. It is true that the aftermath of war permeated the whole economy for several years, and that the volume of building that had already occurred since 1800 was probably a good deal less than it would have been if war had not intervened. In this and other ways the past bestowed its legacy, but economic expectations had now to give little place to the chance of international upheaval, even though the chance of internal upheaval was often considerable. In place of one exogenous factor had come another. On top of this, in the very year in which brick production leapt to its peak, the last legal fetter on the emigration of the British workman was removed. With the New World beckoning those who sought opportunity, or even survival, and a transport revolution about to reduce the rigour of the journey, free factor movement was beginning to bring a new variable into the economic system.

Peace brought speculation and disaster, but even in the darkest year births exceeded burials by over a hundred thousand. The second decade of the century saw the population grow by over two million souls, representing an increase of nearly a sixth. Partly because of differing age and sex structure, and partly because of migration, the towns grew more rapidly than the countryside. The ever-growing population provided a persistent and incipient boost to demand, and where it was augmented by migration even the year-to-year changes must have made perceptible impressions on the demand for houses and other goods. The increase in trade that came in 1817 was inevitable once the immediate causes of the recent collapse had blown themselves out, for in the past six years natural increase alone had added three-quarters of a million people. Emigration alone could allow trade to remain at low levels for long ; and in 1817 large-scale emigration was not possible.

For the first two years after the war, wheat prices rose sharply and the marriage-rate fell, but from 1818 onwards these movements were reversed until 1821 or 1822. The price of wheat was halved in under four years, and the number of marriages increased by a seventh. Times were still bad, however, and measured in the stark terms of how much wheat the money would buy, Poor Relief rose steadily between 1817 and 1822. Meanwhile building rose to a minor peak in 1819, when for the first time the annual output of bricks exceeded a thousand millions. In 1821 came a minor trough, before an even mightier surge continued the long upswing which began with the end of the war. With all the inaccuracies that there must be in these annual series, there is considerable danger in attempting to rely too much on the precise location of the peaks in

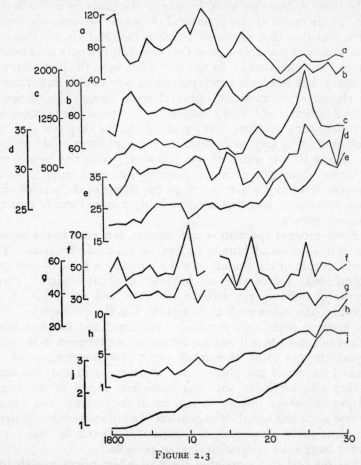

FIGURE 2.3

(a) Average price of Wheat, U.K. (shillings per imperial quarter). *B.H.S.*, p. 488.
(b) Marriages, E. & W. ('000). *B.H.S.*, p. 28.
(c) Bricks charged with duty, E. & W. (m.). *B.H.S.*, p. 235.
(d) Index of Beer Production (1913 = 100). Hoffmann.
(e) Index of Copper Production (1913 = 100). Hoffmann.
(f) Imports minus Re-exports. Computed Values (£m.). *B.H.S.*, p. 282.
(g) Domestic Exports. Computed Values (£m.). *B.H.S.*, p. 282.
(h) Index of Cotton Yarn Production (1913 = 100). Hoffmann.
(j) Index of Pig-iron Production (1913 = 100 for Pig-iron and Steel). Hoffmann.

the various series, but it is fairly clear that even if it did not actually decline, building must have paused in the early twenties. Other series tell a similar tale for other sectors of the economy, as is shown in Figure 2.3, which reveals that the pattern of building between

1815 and 1822 was more similar to that of imports than to that of certain other sectors of the economy. On the one hand, those factors which both call for and allow an increase in house-building, namely a growing population and a reasonable prosperity, are also likely to result in increased imports of food, just as bad times will lead to less house-building and reduced imports.[30] On the side of industrial building it is clear that when output is booming the demands for raw materials and for new buildings are likely to rise. The minor cycle lasting from about 1816 to 1822 reflects relationships of this kind, but, in addition to this, the import cycle was heavily affected by speculation which was a principal cause of the minor crisis that temporarily reversed the direction of the economy. It is tempting to examine the matter more fully, and to attempt to determine more precisely the mechanism involved, but to do so would take us too far from our main purpose which is to examine the major cycle on whose upswing this was but a ripple which seems to have left some industries quite unaffected. The Hoffmann series[31] for the production of pig-iron and steel rose continuously from 1817 to 1827, while copper ore production did not dip until 1823, even though the production of copper itself saw a sharp fall between 1817 and 1819. These movements are, of course, all to be taken in the context of a rapidly rising trend, but this applies to building and to imports as well as to copper and iron. The factors that were strong enough to cause some variables to move contrary to trend in other cases were clearly either unimportant or countered by other factors.

The early twenties, however, soon saw an enormous boom, short-lived in itself, but which should properly be considered in its entirety as the last stage of the major upswing that began in 1816 or 1817. The serious disturbances of 1819 were followed, the next year, by a sharp fall in living costs and a mild revival in trade.[32] The working classes of the textile counties were reported as enjoying 'regular employment at liberal remuneration'.[33] The price of wheat had been falling ever since 1817, and although 1821 marked a trough there were many signs of a basic buoyancy in the economy, not the least being the amount of railway building going on and the fact that every year from 1818 to 1821 saw an increase in the number of marriages and births. Indeed the number of marriages in 1821 was 101,000 compared with but 88,000 in 1817. On the capital market there were idle savings. Falling prices had reduced the amount of money tied up in trading stocks, or otherwise necessary to finance a given turnover of goods. They coincided with increased output, but the industrial plant that had expanded in the previous decades was capable of providing even greater outputs than those demanded by the home market. Manufacturers and investors sought new outlets for their goods and money, and Central and South America attracted both.[34] The situation was given a further buoyancy by the resumption of cash payments, and the decision taken in 1819 that the Bank should pay off all of its small notes with gold by 1823, while the country banks should withdraw their small notes by 1825. The Bank itself acted quickly on both scores. It sold securities and cancelled its small notes two years before its deadline, while, in order to meet the situation that it expected to arise in 1825 it continued to buy gold. The critics, especially those with agricultural interests, were filled with consternation, and fear of deflation. Under their influence Parliament enacted, in 1822, that the country banks should have an additional eight years' grace. With its reserves now at a level far higher than the immediate situation seemed to require, the Bank expanded credit on all sides. With abundant funds, a rising population and generally good conditions the climate was favourable for a further upsurge in building. 'Docks, railways, gas and water companies, and, above all, foreign governments and mining companies came for funds to London on an unprecedented scale.'[35] The desire to have a rich yield encouraged not only hazardous investment but also ludicrous speculation. Credit knew no restriction as optimism ousted prudence, and investment forged ahead. The Bank offered advances on mortgages.[36]

It was a boom that contained within it its own undoing. High activity in the United States brought increased orders to the textile and iron industries at a time when home demand was already high.[37] Industrial capacity, straining to produce more, had to be expanded at a time when every sector was competing for labour and materials. Food prices, which began to rise in 1823, were soon followed in their upward surge by non-agricultural prices. To the accompaniment of bitter strikes, money wages rose and added to the inflation. Late in 1824 speculation in imports became feverish. Raw cotton imports rose from 149 m. lb. in 1824 to 228 m. lb. in 1825. Speculation in foreign mining shares was quite as bad. To the strain on our resources of labour and materials was added a strain on our supplies of credit. In the money market as elsewhere there was full employment, soon to prove unstable. Inflation and speculation in imports had two almost coincident consequences. At home there was the inventory phenomenon, as we became overstocked, and the market broke. In the field of foreign trade, the exchanges turned against us because of our rising prices and excessive imports, and gold left the country. The Bank restricted credit at a time when speculators could not meet the obligations they had incurred when prices and interest rates were low. As the Usury Laws forbade interest charges above 5 per cent, the price mechanism of the money market failed. Loans were not forthcoming, and liquidity could be obtained only by holders of paper claims or by selling commodities at severely discounted prices. The rush for cash caused Sir Peter Pole, Thornton and Company, who held the accounts of forty-four country banks, to close their doors. Mining speculators, who had relied upon easy credit and rising share prices for the wherewithal to pay further instalments were but some of the victims in the flood of bankruptcies that followed.[38] An excessive supply of easy money in 1822–3, and the absence of credit restriction in late 1824 had encouraged speculators of all kinds to plunge headlong into a fire that need only have burned their fingers. Of the 624 joint-stock companies formed or projected in 1824–5 over a third never got round to issuing shares, while by 1827 only 127 of them existed.

Between 1826 and 1832 industry had almost unrelieved difficulties. In 1827–8 there was some slight recovery, but neither this nor the rally in textiles and exports of iron that came in 1830 lasted. The year after the crisis saw a sharp fall in money wages only partly countered by the lesser decline in retail prices. Imports of almost every kind fell, or at best rose more slowly, while it was foodstuffs and raw materials rather than manufactures that helped to swell our exports. Railway building slackened, and foreign loans disappeared completely until 1829. During 1828–31 poor harvests forced the purchase of foreign grain, and some payments were made by the sale of the recently acquired foreign securities.[39] In 1830 a recovery in textiles led to labour shortages in some trades, but the outlook was too unsettled for it to last. Agitations for the Reform Bill added to uncertainty. Funds were withdrawn to Paris and elsewhere, causing pressure on the money market. In America a minor crisis reduced the demand for our exports, and the year of the Reform Act began perhaps even worse than any of those that immediately preceded it. It marked the trough of a building cycle.

This is but a sketchy outline of the boom and its crisis, and so far little has been said about where building fits into the picture. With such a wealth of statistics it is tempting to seek an explanation based on the order in which the various series had their turning points, but although this technique has its merits it is doubtful whether there is much to be gained by using it at this juncture. Apart from considerations of errors in the statistics themselves, we have to remember that annual data have too long a time interval for a satisfactory analysis of turning points, while the monthly data that are available for this period are few and bedevilled by seasonal

factors. Furthermore, a detailed analysis of the causes and consequences of building fluctuations has to be done at a level of aggregation appropriate to the geographical extent of the market. Sequences
of turning points in prices, production, population and building in
the Manchester area can tell us something about causation in that
area ; but if we apply the same technique to national aggregates we
may obtain an 'explanation' that is valid for no single part of the
country as is demonstrated in Appendix 2. The final judgement
must come from other sources.

Certain relationships involving the national aggregates have
already been pointed out, but there are others to be mentioned, not
necessarily valid for short-term fluctuations, but which stand out
clearly for the major upswing and downswing of the cycle. Broadly
speaking the upswing of building, from a trough in 1816 to a peak
in 1825 was matched by a downturn in exports, as is shown in Figure
2.3. As building declined between 1826 and 1832 exports showed
a long-term upward swing. A similar inverse relationship existed
between building and emigration. In the twenties emigration
statistics were far from reliable,[40] but the available figures from
both British and American sources all indicate that emigration fell
from 1820 to 1824 and then rose to a peak in 1832. The Emigration
Act of 1825 undoubtedly had some effect, but it is interesting to
note that even at this time the link observed by other writers, for
later years, between exports, emigration and building seems to have
been fairly firmly established. Another long cycle showing an
interesting similarity to the building cycle in this period, as in some
other periods, is the beer-production cycle. We shall have more to
say about these and other similarities later on, but meanwhile it may
be useful to look at what data we have for building in these years, and
to consider the role played by this industry in the drama of the times.

It is not possible to disentangle house and other building with
much precision. It is, however, clear that the building industry as
a whole saw an enormous boom in the early and mid twenties,
and then a sharp decline, with a pause towards the end of the decade
before another fall. The peak of 1825 probably existed in both
house and factory building. The numbers of cotton mills in the
Manchester area were noted by Baines as follows.[41]

	Number	Addition in 3 Years
1820	66	
1823	72	6
1826	92	20
1829	95	3
1832	96	1

These figures show clearly that 1823–6 contained the peak of industrial building in an area which was the heart of manufacturing England. It is recorded that some mills were in fact left half-completed in 1825. The erection of blast furnaces also reached a peak in this year, although the continued building of railways ensured that the decline was less abrupt : [42]

	Number of Blast Furnaces erected in England and Wales
1824	18
1825	22
1826	20
1827	12
1828	17
1829	5
1838	2

Clapham reports a great deal of dock-building in the years 1824–6.[43] Evidence that this year also saw a peak in house-building is not quite so definite, but it remains strong. Clegg's *Annals of Bolton* refer to 1500 houses and many public buildings being erected in and around the town during 1820–5, while 1826 was noted as a year of distress.[44] In St. Helens the demand for accommodation was so high by 1821 (due largely to immigration) that 'house-building had become a most profitable form of investment', and in 1824 the First St. Helens Building Society was formed.[45] Yet two years later, in 1826, the town was in the depths of a severe recession, and it was possible to erect a glass factory 'on the most advantageous terms' by taking advantage of the consequent cheapness of labour and materials.[46] London had also witnessed a house-building boom, arising both from the incessant flow to the Metropolis and from an outward movement into suburbia. 'The greater merchants had gone first', wrote Clapham. 'They had long been going westward, or southward to Clapham and Denmark Hill. The lesser followed. Then the shopkeepers began to move. The spell of business activity in 1824–5 was accompanied by wholesale suburban migration, even to as far as Brighton. In the inner suburbs speculative builders were at work.[47] This and similar evidence all tends to support the suggestion that both house and industrial building reached a peak in 1825. The decade 1821–31 saw a net increase of 444,000 in the number of houses in England and Wales, compared with but 309,000 in the previous ten years. It was an increase in housing stock of over one-fifth. For the first time in the century, the number of houses actually increased at a faster rate than the population. This does not, of course, imply that the same was true in the larger towns. Both population and housing grew at very different rates in different places. Indeed in the south of England, where workers were sometimes reluctant to move to the industrial north, and preferred their existence to be at the mercy of the overseers rather than journey to a new way of life, landlords, tired of helping to support them, sometimes pulled down their cottages to persuade them that the cotton area, for all its remoteness and urbanisation, had distinct advantages.[48]

We have already seen that in London there was a good deal of speculative building, and there is abundant evidence that this existed elsewhere.   Wherever, in fact, a town was growing at all rapidly there the speculative builder was likely to be found, often providing 'houses of the lowest description' [49] which nevertheless were not infrequently better in many ways than the farm cottages that had been vacated.   Their main, and overriding, deficiency was that, unlike farm cottages, they were huddled so closely together ; and the problems of inadequate ventilation and sewage increased rapidly as the fields receded from the centre of the town.   Many houses were built by industrialists for occupation by their immigrant labour force, while by 1825 about two thousand houses had been erected or purchased by building societies, of which well over 250 are known to have been founded by that date.[50] Building clubs and societies thus accounted for about one house in a thousand, but this is to underestimate their importance in many ways, for they tended to be concentrated in the most rapidly growing towns of the north and the Midlands, where, by encouraging people to save for a house of their own on favourable terms, they not only hoped to provide houses but also helped to mould the character of the provident workman.   Some of the clubs were so unfortunate or so mismanaged as never to erect a single house, while a large number of these essentially very local institutions suffered in the crash of 1825–6.   Other houses were built on orders received from owner-occupiers or speculative landlords who saw a house as a solid source of assured income, or even of capital gain.

The growing population, abundance of credit, and upward trend in prosperity are ample reasons for the upsurge in both house and factory building, and no further or more detailed reasons need be sought at present.   It is, however, of some interest to attempt a brief assessment of the importance of house-building on the economy as a whole, and then to explain why total building subsequently declined, paused, and declined again to its trough in 1832.

During the decade 1811–21, brick production in England and

Wales amounted to 8590 million bricks, while in the next decade it was 12,300 million. The net increases in housing stock in these decades were 309,000 and 443,000. It is, of course, absurd to suggest that all bricks went into houses, or that all houses contained bricks, but if we accept, as a very rough measure, the suggestion that house-building fluctuated more or less as the production of bricks, we may attempt a rough estimate of the numbers of houses built each year. It may be noted that the ratio of bricks produced to net addition of houses is almost identical in each decade, being 2777 in 1811-21 and 2775 in 1821-31. The lowness of this ratio alone confirms that many houses were built of other materials, but its remarkable equality seems to warrant our next step.

The years 1817-25 saw the production of 10,280 million bricks, being just half of the total for the two decades. We may assume, in view of the facts just noted, that the same years saw the erection of about half of the houses added to the nation's stock over the same period. Accepting this as a very rough guide we may suggest that the upswing of the building cycle possibly saw the erection of between 350,000 and 400,000. One could argue about the validity of this estimate, but, as we shall see, it does not very much matter.

We may also take a sum of about £100 as being a reasonable estimate of the cost of a house.[51] This means that the cost of providing the houses built in the upswing may be put very roughly at between £35 m. and £40 m. spread over nine years. This compares with a million pounds or so spent on railways completed by the end of 1825. It also compares with the £372 m. capital required by the 624 joint-stock companies formed or projected in 1824-5. If one wishes to estimate the value of houses erected in these two years, one has to keep in mind that building prices were then above average. On the brick production basis and at a price of perhaps £100 per house the cost would come to about £14 m. This was, by any considerations, a very substantial sum but trivial compared with the claims of the joint-stock companies. Gayer, Rostow and Schwartz write that in the years 1821-5 the public 'was induced to export enormous amounts of capital in government bonds' and that 'These bonds, in the amounts actually paid up, constituted the largest single category of new investment which can be estimated for the period'.[52] The total amount of capital actually paid for these bonds came to £37 m. over 1821-5 and to £24 m. during 1824-5. It is perfectly clear that, even if our estimates are seriously out, the construction of houses absorbed less capital than did foreign loans, even though the amounts were still very considerable.

This analysis also shows one reason why house-building had to decline once the crisis came. Credit was required on a substantial scale: and it was not forthcoming. Increasingly bad times, as testified by the increase in poor-relief, and the decline in beer production, and substantiated by the upswing in emigration, undoubtedly reduced the effective demand for housing, and in many places newly-built houses must have been left tenantless. Conditions would have to improve sufficiently not only for most of these to be reoccupied, but also to persuade prospective builders that there was a reasonable prospect of a sustained improvement before another surge of development could be expected. Eventually population increase alone would see to this: but for some years at least the incentive to build was braked by caution, even when empty property had not put it into reverse.

As plausible an explanation as any of the peak and downswing in industrial building is given by Gayer, Rostow and Schwartz.[53] They suggest that around 1823 a typical firm might have been approaching the full capacity of its existing resources. Accumulated profits and increasing optimism, both generated by past success, combine with this pressure on existing plant to bring about an expansion. Other firms, acting under the same stimuli, do the same. The new plant built between 1823 and 1825 does not immediately become effective, and not until the mild recovery of 1827–8 is it fully utilised. Then it is found that the expansion of the whole industry has lowered the price, and even working at full capacity produces a loss. The answer is to use existing plant more efficiently, and to innovate rather than to expand. Not until the early thirties did rising demand (due partly to a fall in food prices) turn loss into profit and encourage further investment in building. 'The period of relative quiescence in new construction (e.g. 1826–32) represents the interval necessary for the secular increase in demand to "catch up" with the previous extension of plant.' Furthermore, 'Whether long-term investment was financed out of previously accumulated income or out of current income . . . it is evident that it precluded new long-term commitments on the same scale in 1828 as in 1825. . . . This process was, of course, reinforced by the decline in commercial and industrial profits, the fall in the value of new investment, by bankruptcies, and other phenomena of severe depression. . . . Thus on both the supply and the demand sides of the market for long-term investment, reasons can be found for a type of periodicity longer than that for business cycles as a whole, i.e. including minor cycles.' The important point for us to notice is that 'bankruptcies, and the other phenomena of severe depression' played their part; and it is in this way that a credit crisis had its impact, converting an inventory downswing into a major fall.

NOTES TO CHAPTER 2

1. Sir John Summerson, *Georgian London*, 1945. References are to the Pelican revised edition, 1962. This quotation comes from page 24.

2. Brinley Thomas, *Migration and Economic Growth*, 1954, *passim*, especially chapter xi.

3. See Chapter 4 below.

4. See especially T. S. Ashton, *Economic Fluctuations in England, 1700–1800*, Oxford, 1959, and his papers, 'Some Statistics of the Industrial Revolution in Britain', *The Manchester School*, vol. 16, no. 2, 1948, pp. 214–34 and 'The Treatment of Capitalism by Historians' in F. A. Hayek (ed.), *Capitalism and the Historians*, London, 1954. Most of the facts in the part of this chapter that deals with the eighteenth century, and for which no source is given, come from one of these three works.

5. H. A. Shannon, 'Bricks — A Trade Index, 1785–1849', *Economica*, N.S., no. 3, August 1934, pp. 300–18.

6. Ashton, *Economic Fluctuations*, p. 91.

7. Quoted by Ashton, p. 92, from Summerson, *Georgian London*.

8. Quoted from the work of Mrs. Dorothy George by Ashton, *op. cit.*, p. 144.

9. Ashton, *op. cit.*, p. 95.

10. Summerson, *op. cit.*, p. 111.

11. Quoted by Summerson, *op. cit.*, p. 111.

12. Summerson, *op. cit.*, p. 112.

13. Quoted by Mrs. D. George, *London Life in the XVIIIth Century*, 1925, p. 345.

14. Evidence that labour migration was affecting house-building in St. Helens in the late sixties is provided by T. C. Barker and J. R. Harris, *A Merseyside Town in the Industrial Revolution: St. Helens 1750–1900*, Liverpool, 1954. In 1768 a colliery owner of St. Helens advertised for twenty men, offering to provide them with lodgings if they came from far afield, and with cottages in six months' time. He continued to build cottages for his workers for at least three years (*op. cit.*, pp. 35, 44, 170. See also pp. 78, 140).

Dr. Saul informs me that the number of houses in Liverpool was 3700 in 1753, 4200 in 1760, 6340 in 1773 and 8148 in 1790. The period 1753–1773 thus saw an increase of nearly 70 per cent in the number of houses. The population, being 18,400 in 1750, 23,600 in 1760 and 34,000 in 1770 seems to have increased by a slightly greater proportion. The number of empty houses in 1773 was about 6½ per cent of the total which, as Dr. Saul conjectures, suggests that building was perhaps not very high just then, or at any rate, was due for a fall.

See also the work of Deane and Cole mentioned in Chapter 7 below.

15. To some extent this is confirmed by the fall in the real wage-rate of building craftsmen shown for this period by E. H. Phelps-Brown and Sheila V. Hopkins, 'Seven Centuries of the Prices of Consumables, Compared with Builders' Wage Rates', *Economica*, xxiii, 1956, pp. 296–314.

16. Quoted by Mrs. D. George in *Johnson's England*, i, p. 167, and requoted in Ashton *op. cit.*, p. 100.

17. Ashton, *op. cit.*, pp. 101, 131, 165. The fact that timber imports rose in

1783 and 1784 tends to confirm that it was capital that was holding back development. Some of the increase may have been due to the freeing of shipping, and a decision to take advantage of high stocks in timber-producing countries.

18. See Figures 2.1 and 8.1. I am grateful to Mr. R. C. O. Matthews for drawing my attention to this point.

19. H. A. Shannon, *loc. cit.*

20. Witness the production of beer, candles and soap.

21. W. Cunningham, *The Growth of English Industry and Commerce in Modern Times: Part II, Laissez-Faire*, Cambridge, 1907, p. 691.

22. See A. K. Cairncross and B. Weber, 'Fluctuations in Building in Great Britain, 1785–1849', *Economic History Review*, 2nd series, ix, 1956, pp. 283–97.

32. *Ibid.*

24. Gayer, Rostow and Schwartz, *The Growth and Fluctuation of the British Economy, 1790–1850*, Oxford, 1953. Further references to this work will be denoted by G.R.S. A great deal of unacknowledged factual material has been taken from this work.

25. See J. D. Gould, 'Agricultural Fluctuations and the English Economy in the Eighteenth Century', *Journal of Economic History*, xii, no. 3, 1962, pp. 313–14, for this and a number of other interesting points. Professor S. B. Saul drew my attention to this paper.

26. G.R.S., p. 59.

27. G.R.S., p. 59.

28. G.R.S., p. 82 quoting a statement made in J. L. and B. Hammond, *The Town Labourer*.

29. Summerson, *op. cit.*, p. 154. In April 1794, additional duties had been imposed on bricks and materials used for glass-making. Ashton says 'if the Legislature had sought to deflect resources from building to the purposes of war, it could hardly have found a better instrument. Probably, however, it thought only of revenue'. *Op. cit.*, p. 103, n. 65. The fact remains that 1800–15 saw a well-marked cycle, so that presumably, if there was little activity in London, there was a good deal somewhere else, which is, indeed, confirmed by Census returns.

30. Unless, of course, the 'bad times' are due to bad harvests and high wheat prices, when imports of wheat will tend to rise, causing an adverse flow of funds and a possible tightening of credit.

31. Walther G. Hoffmann, *British Industry, 1700–1950* (trans. W. O. Henderson and W. H. Chaloner), Oxford, 1955. We refer to the 'iron and steel' series because this is its name. At that time, of course, the product was simply iron.

32. G.R.S., p. 169.

33. Quoted in G.R.S., p. 154.

34. See G.R.S., pp. 182–5.

35. G.R.S., p. 171.

36. G.R.S., p. 203.

37. G.R.S., p. 172.

38. On this point see G.R.S., p. 432.

39. G.R.S., p. 219. Foodstuffs were not exported on a large scale, but they were of increasing importance.

40. G. R. Porter, *The Progress of the Nation*, 1838, provides evidence of this.

41. G.R.S., p. 553.

42. G.R.S., p. 230.

43. J. H. Clapham, *An Economic History of Modern Britain: The Early Railway Age*, Cambridge, 1930 (2nd edition), pp. 5–6.

44. *Annals of Bolton*, Bolton, 1888, pp. 78–79.

45. T. C. Barker and J. R. Harris, *A Merseyside Town in the Industrial Revolution, St. Helens, 1750–1900*, Liverpool, 1954, p. 170. See Chapter 4 below for further data on early building societies.

46. *Ibid.*, p. 205–6.

47. *Op. cit.*, p. 41.

48. A. Redford, *Labour Migration in England*, Manchester, 1926, pp. 77–78.

49. The 1831 Census Report (vol. ii, p. 895) says that Cardiff's population increase in the previous ten years was due to the ' number of families who have deserted the neighbouring villages, through the depressed state of agriculture, and now reside in houses of the lowest description, built by speculators for their accommodation '.

See also a very interesting paper by John R. Kellett, 'Property Speculators and the Building of Glasgow, 1780–1830', *Scottish Journal of Political Economy*, vol. viii, pp. 211–32, which emphasises the question of land ownership.

50. This information may be found, *inter alia*, in Seymour Price, *Building Societies: their Origins and Functions*, London, 1958, where a photograph appears of the twenty houses still constituting Club Row, in Longridge, erected in 1793. One is reminded not only of earlier less substantial building in London, but also of Ashton's description of building in Liverpool. 'Houses were run up rapidly, and many of them were flimsy structures, the outer walls of which were only 4½ inches in thickness. On December 5th, 1822, some of them were blown down. . . .' (Ashton in Hayek (ed.), *op. cit.*, p. 44). The builders of Liverpool at this time (I dare not fail to admit it) were usually Welshmen. For further descriptions of housing and house-building see Ashton in Hayek (ed.), *op. cit.*, and Clapham, *op. cit.*

51. It is difficult to guess this figure. Newspaper advertisements of the times show that many of the working class cottages cost £50 or even less. But there were many sizeable houses being built at greater cost, while one cannot exclude from the calculation of an average figure the extravagance of Georgian architecture. I am inclined to feel that perhaps £100 is rather on the high side, but no important point rests on its accuracy.

52. G.R.S., p. 189.

53. G.R.S., pp. 553–9.

CHAPTER 3

STOCHASTIC FACTORS, POPULATION AND CREDIT

W E have now looked rather briefly at the course of building over a period of 130 years. Despite the structural change around 1760, this long period can be thought of as a whole for certain purposes. International migration was never large, steam transport did not exist, and the Usury Laws were very important. The years after 1830, however, have to be viewed differently. The growth of railways and the steamship changed the whole pattern of trade and migration, and created new possibilities in urban and overseas development. Contemporary institutional changes emphasised the changing character of investment. Rarely can an economy have changed so fundamentally over such a short period as did the British economy between 1820 and 1840. This alone, justifies a pause in our narrative, while the appearance of regional building statistics in the thirties makes it convenient for us to sum up our analysis so far, before embarking on an examination of regional differences.

If we look back over the last chapter we may be struck by the fact that while every building cycle was stamped with its own characteristics, each had a great deal in common with others. In this chapter we shall emphasise these common characteristics, and indulge in a little speculation. Our aim is to describe certain forces at work, rather than to present anything like a complete theory or a model.

The idealised 'typical' building cycle of the earlier part of this period, combining the most common features of the actual cycles, may be described as follows. In a period of depressed real wages that has followed several years of rising activity there is little building. Forced to keep within their means, people are living — at any rate in the towns — in shared accommodation, and there is probably a large number of empty houses. Manufacturing industry is at a low ebb, possibly because of previous over-production, and the low level of real wages does nothing to revive it. There is very little investment of any kind, and what there is takes place cheaply. For some time past most savings have been loaned to the Government, possibly for purposes of war, and other savings have probably been hoarded. The low level of activity and wages has resulted in a decline in most imports other, perhaps, than corn. The birth-rate is lower than it was in more prosperous times.

Putting aside the effects of peace and war, which will be examined later, it seems that this rather melancholy state is most likely to be terminated in one of two ways. Either some foreign country increases its demand for our exports, or a good harvest increases domestic spending power and reduces our need to import. The two cases have much in common, for the increased demand for our exports will lead to a rise in activity and real wages in at least one

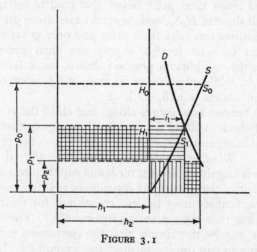

FIGURE 3.1

sector of the economy, which will in turn stimulate other sectors, while the flow of foreign funds in payment for our exports will improve the balance of trade, provided our income propensity to import is not too high. Having noted this, and remembering that in a detailed analysis we should have to examine the income elasticities of demand for imports and domestic goods more fully, we shall consider the consequences of a good harvest.

The immediate effects of an increased supply of home-produced corn are a fall in the price of corn and a reduction of corn imports. Some of the consequences may be examined with the aid of a set of diagrams. We may imagine a very inelastic demand curve D. In reality the shape of the curve at very high prices might be different from that shown in Figure 3.1, but this is a matter we need not now consider, since our task is to examine the effects of a good harvest rather than of a famine.

Let h_1 denote the extent of the previous harvest, which fails to satisfy demand except at exorbitant prices. This is a politically dangerous situation and the Government (which we suppose to exercise a rigid control over imports) has no choice but to allow corn to be imported. The poor harvest ensures that high prices will be paid, and a foreign supply is readily available. We shall denote the foreign supply curve by S, such that at price p_0 foreign farmers are willing to supply an amount $H_0 S_0$. In a perfectly knowledgeable market, imports would amount to $H_1 S_1$. If they exceed this then either the price is maintained at p_1, and corn goes into store for the next year, or importers make a loss (possibly offset by a subsidy), or home farmers lower their price below that paid to foreign farmers. If imports fall short of $H_1 S_1$, and no stocks exist from previous years, then home farmers can raise their price and only government interference or an inelastic foreign supply can then prevent further imports. In the equilibrium position shown, home farmers receive an income $p_1 h_1$, while currency of an amount $i_1 p_1$ is exported. The total bread bill comes to $p_1(h_1 + i_1)$.

If a good harvest now comes along, and all of the corn is put on the market (which is likely in a competitive agricultural economy) then the total home supply h_2 may exceed $h_1 + i_1$ — the previous total consumption. Whether conditions abroad have shifted the foreign supply curve is largely irrelevant, for home supply now satisfies home demand at a price that leaves the consumers well fed and contented. However, the farmers may be less contented, for their income of $p_2 h_2$ may be less than their previous income $p_1 h_1$. The result of the good harvest may be not simply that the consumers get more corn without having to pay foreign farmers the amount $i_1 p_1$, but also that they pay less to home farmers. The general result is that the balance of payments is (in the first instance) better by $i_1 p_1$, consumers generally are better off by having an amount

$$p_1(h_1 + i_1) - p_2 h_2$$

to spend on other things despite their increased consumption of bread, and farmers are better off by the (possibly negative) amount

$$p_2 h_2 - p_1 h_1$$

The gain to the community is equal to the reduction in imports, but its distribution between farmers and non-farmers depends on the price fall as well as on the size of the harvest. If we suppose that the supply of home corn in this analysis is the supply after farms have provided for their own needs, then we can think of the farmers and consumers as two distinct groups. The gain to consumers may be written as

$$(p_1 - p_2)(h_1 + i_1) - p_2(h_2 - [h_1 + i_1])$$

which is the difference between the areas of the two horizontally shaded rectangles in Figure 3.1. The gain to home farmers is given by the difference between the area of the two vertically shaded rectangles, which may be written as

$$- [(p_1 - p_2)h_1 - p_2(h_2 - h_1)]$$

The net gain to the community is the total area that is shaded in only one direction.

We now have to examine the effects of these changes. To do so, we may divide consumer demand into four categories: corn, house-room, other home-produced goods, and other imported goods. The elasticities of demand for these commodities have to be considered. That for corn has already been discussed, and those for home and foreign goods present no difficulty: but the demand for house-room requires further attention, partly because the demand consists of two parts. We have to consider demands on existing accommodation, and also the demand for new accommodation. In addition there is the very important point that people are more inclined to improve their accommodation in good times than to reduce it in bad times. Provided he is not starving, a person will put up with considerable deprivation before he will take his family into a smaller house, possibly to share it and certainly to lose comforts. This is especially true if he is already dissatisfied with his existing accommodation. On the other hand, if this dissatisfaction is intense, then while a small fall in his income may have no effect on his demand for house-room at existing rents, an even smaller rise in his real wages may result in a decision to seek an improvement, especially if he believes the rise is likely to last. In the same way an increase in rent may cause few people to move out of existing tenancies, while a general fall in rent may cause a large expansion of demand.

This irreversibility is shown in Figure 3.2. We consider the existing stock of houses to be fixed at the amount S. The level of rents is r_1. At existing real wages the number of houses occupied at this rent is n_1. An increase in rent will cause only a small fall in demand, so to the left of P the demand curve slopes steeply, but a decrease will see a much expanded demand, shown by the flattening of the curve to the right of P. A rise in real income causes the demand curve to shift (and, of course, perhaps to alter slightly in shape) in such a way that the kink remains at its original abscissa as on the curve D_2. If it shifts so that the existing stock of houses is insufficient to supply the new demand, then rents rise towards r_2. There is, however, a substantial degree of friction here. Rental contracts will prevent the rents of existing tenancies from increasing by the full amount for some time, and the additional payments of tenants to landlords will be somewhat less than $r_2 S - r_1 n_1$. We may denote the addition by $\lambda(r_2 S - r_1 n_1)$ where $\lambda < 1$. Before all of the empty houses have been let, speculative builders, and possibly other people, have begun to increase supply. Prospective new tenants, aware of this, have refused to pay inflated rents for the few remaining

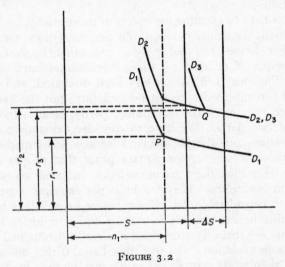

FIGURE 3.2

empty old houses, preferring to wait for a better bargaining time when the new houses are ready. We may envisage a new equilibrium situation, created by the building of an additional ΔS houses, and having a new average rent of r_3. Some empty houses remain, and the demand curve now assumes an elbow at Q instead of at P. If there is a very great deal of new building, compared with the income shift in demand, then rents may fall.

But this simple analysis does not tell the whole of the story. Before going further we have to examine several other aspects of the problem.

The first of these is that an increased real income affects the demand for houses not only because existing households seek better accommodation, but also because the marriage-rate rises. Throughout the eighteenth and early nineteenth centuries, when a period of depression was terminated by a good harvest, the marriage- and birth-rates rose, as we have already illustrated in our text and show further in our chapter on Population. This creation of new house-holds at an increased rate has an important effect on the total demand for house-room, and especially on the marginal demand for existing empty or newly-built houses. A subsequent diminution of incomes cannot be expected to restore the total demand to its old level unless it is so severe that the newly-weds emigrate. Furthermore, if the increase is substantial and lasts for a few years there is likely to be some sign of an echo-effect a generation later. We shall return to this.

The second point is that even if farmers' incomes fall, the total effect of a fall in corn-prices must be to increase the demand for houses, because of the asymmetrical income elasticity. Even if farmers and non-farmers are equal in number, a redistribution of income from the one group to the other will, according to the above analysis, tend to have a greater expansionary effect on demand for housing by the non-farmers than a contracting effect on the demand by farmers. When one also considers that the redistribution in favour of the consumers is at the expense of foreign farmers as well as home farmers, and that in any case the demand for farmhouses is not quite the same as that for other houses, the above assertion becomes even more convincing.

We now have to recall the effect of the new prosperity on demand for goods other than corn and houses. In what follows 'goods' should be interpreted in this sense. It seems that the demands for both home-produced and imported goods may be expected to rise. This need not immediately be the case unless certain assumptions are made. If a fraction μ of non-farmers' increased income goes on goods, while farmers who have lost the positive amount $p_1 h_1 - p_2 h_2$ react by reducing their expenditures on goods by a fraction ν of this amount, then the total expenditure on goods changes by

$$\mu(p_1 h_1 - p_2 h_2) + \mu p_1 i_1 - \nu(p_1 h_1 - p_2 h_2)$$
$$= \mu p_1 i_1 - (\nu - \mu)(p_1 h_1 - p_2 h_2).$$

If $i_1 = 0$ so that the good harvest follows not a bad one but an adequate one, while $p_1 h_1 > p_2 h_2$ so that farmers' incomes fall, then since, on the above reasoning, we must expect $\nu > \mu$, this expression is negative and so the total expenditure on other goods falls (in the first instance at least). If, however, $i_1 > 0$, implying that the good harvest follows an inadequate one, then the above expression may be written as

$$\mu p_1 i_1 \left[1 - \left(\frac{\nu}{\mu} - 1 \right) \left(1 - \frac{p_2 h_2}{p_1 h_1} \right) \frac{h_1}{i_1} \right].$$

In this, the second curved bracket must be a positive proper fraction, since $p_1h_1 > p_2h_2$. The first curved bracket is also positive but may exceed unity. The same is true of the ratio $\frac{h_1}{i_1}$. This means that the whole expression may become negative, especially if $v \gg \mu$, if $p_1h_1 \gg p_2h_2$ or if $h_1 \gg i_1$.

The first of these inequalities concerns the farmers' marginal propensity to reduce his expenditure on goods when income falls, and the non-farmers' marginal propensity to consume goods when income rises. Because of the irreversible element in expenditure on housing, there is also an irreversibility here, which prevents us from talking simply of non-directional propensities to consume. We have seen that we must expect $v > \mu$. The point now is that if this difference is large then the total expenditure on goods may fall, since farmers are reducing their demand by more than non-farmers are increasing theirs.

The second inequality shows that this may happen not only because of differences in the farmers' 'backward' marginal propensity to consume and non-farmers' 'forward' marginal propensity, but also because the farmers may have suffered a severe fall in income, which will be reflected by a low value of p_2h_2/p_1h_1.

Finally, we see that if the good harvest follows a year in which imports were low, so that the national gain is small, then the redistribution of incomes may lead to a reduction in demand for goods. If, however, the good harvest follows a really bad harvest, the stimulus to trade generally is likely to be positive, since in this case $\frac{h_1}{i_1}$ is likely to be fairly low, while p_2h_2/p_1h_1 is also likely to be low. The non-farmers have their home purchasing power increased by the amount they used to spend on foreign food, and any reduction in demand that arises from internal income redistribution has to be set against this.

Even if the immediate effect of a fall in corn prices is to raise the demand for houses but to reduce the net demand for other goods, the secondary effects may still operate the other way as far as goods are concerned. The increase in building activity will in itself provide incomes and exert certain demands, and these will tend to stimulate the whole of the economy. Furthermore, if the above assumptions do not hold, and the effect of the harvest is that people as a whole spend more on goods and only the same amount on housing, then once again a general upswing will appear and at some stage in this some of the increased incomes will certainly go into purchasing house-room. There seems to be no escape from the conclusion that a harvest improvement that follows a particularly inadequate harvest must inject new life into a depressed economy.

So far, however, we have not considered the international side of the picture. The expanding economy may require imports, and the loss of British incomes by foreign farmers must affect our own exports, possibly to a very serious degree. If, however, we have been in a typical depression period, brought on to some extent by a balance of payments crisis, aggravated by bad harvests, and possibly coinciding with a certain degree of over-production, then not only will the heavy unemployment result in low labour costs and prices, but also some other country is bound to have an unusual amount of British currency. Provided there is no war to hinder trade, it is difficult to see how the people in this other country can long continue to ignore the opportunity of buying cheaply with a currency of which the country has plenty, especially if our products are of a kind that are needed. Even, indeed, if there is no good harvest in Britain to kick our economy into life, there seems inevitably to be an export boom round the corner, and it is noticeable that in fact our economy was several times invigorated by such booms coinciding, more or less, with improved harvests. The harvest improvement would almost immediately result in a reduced flow of sterling to foreign countries, and this would, after a certain time, tend to reduce the demand for our exports. But the rising home demand would also require increased quantities of imported raw materials, and one effect of this would be to stimulate overseas demand for our goods, both because of the balance of payments factor and in the usual multiplier way. Eventually, of course, when idle capacity becomes fully utilised and prices begin to rise, exports may fall as they become too dear, but this is a long run consideration. In the short-run there are the conflicting consequences of our importing less corn, but more raw materials.

There is little point in pursuing the algebra of this problem here. We shall simply assume that, for reasons such as those we have just suggested, the economy starts on an upward movement which includes an increased amount of house- and industrial building. Our problem is to consider why building should now embark not on steady growth, nor on a sequence of oscillations conforming closely to the conventional trade cycle pattern, but on a series of long cycles, transcending the trade cycle, and having a period of something like eighteen years.

There are several possible explanations, and the paucity of statistical data makes it difficult to choose between them. Perhaps the true explanation embodies them all. Two of the explanations are well known, while a third has received less attention. We shall now consider these in turn. A fourth, with an emphasis on wars, will be considered in a later chapter.

There is little doubt that demographic factors are of some importance in determining the timing of building fluctuations. In the period before 1830 international migration was not on a very great scale, and for the moment we shall consider it to have been non-existent. A theory giving international migration a major role

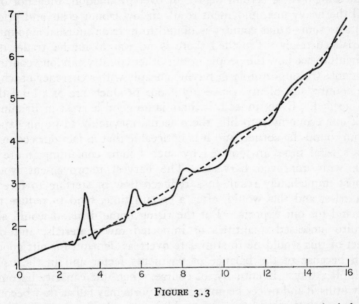

FIGURE 3.3

The vertical scale measures births, in arbitrary units, in the hypothetical case described in the text. Each horizontal division represents 10 years, the whole span being 160 years.

will be developed later in the book. When we speak here of demographic factors we mean those arising from natural increase, from the age and sex distribution, and from internal migration. There are hardly any reliable statistics for any of these during the period we are now considering, although we present some analysis of what does exist in Chapter 7. In the present chapter we shall begin by considering that a temporary bulge in births is normally likely to lead to another bulge about twenty years later, when the bulge babies begin to beget babies of their own. This echo of the original bulge will tend, from a biological point of view, to be very diffused, partly because not all of the first births occurring to parents born in the same year will occur in the same year, and partly because of births of children beyond the first. We have illustrated this in Figure 3.3, which begins with a reasonably steady rise in the annual number of births. The numbers occurring in the first forty years were chosen in order to give a steady upward trend shown by the broken line. Subsequent births were calculated by assuming that every thousand persons born in year t gave rise to a total of 1300 babies, born between year $t + 18$ and year $t + 40$, with the distribution given in the following table, which is, of course, purely fictitious.

Date	Births	Date	Births
$t+18$	1	$t+30$	45
19	3	31	40
20	7	32	35
21	29	33	30
22	80	34	25
23	200	35	20
24	250	36	15
25	190	37	10
26	120	38	6
27	80	39	3
28	60	40	1
29	50		

We then disturbed this growth, by imposing the initial decline, the upswing, and the second decline and minor upswing shown by the solid line at the left of the diagram. The effect of this on subsequent births begins eighteen years after the first year of the disturbance, and ends its first phase forty years after the end of the disturbance: but by then grandchildren from the initial disturbance have already begun to appear. It is seen that the effect dies out, or becomes difficult to recognise, fairly quickly.

As it is stated here, this is a purely biological phenomenon. When we take economic factors into account it seems that the dampening of the echo may be less severe than this account suggests. There is no point in attempting now to follow through all the economic consequences of an increase in births, taken in complete isolation, for a whole generation, but it is clear that, whatever else may happen (short of catastrophe or high emigration), a births bulge will result immediately in increased demands, but only slowly in an increased labour force. Whether that increased labour force adds effectively to production depends on a number of factors, although it is fairly certain to make labour cheaper than it would otherwise have been unless the demand for labour resulting from the increased demands of the increased population exceed the additional supply of labour, which is highly unlikely. If times are bad when these bulge babies reach marital age, then the severity of the times will be reflected in unemployment and low real wages, and they may be more severe simply because of the bulge in young workers which is more precisely predictable than a bulge in marriages. As a consequence, marriage and parenthood will be delayed until a good harvest or an export boom results in an increase in real incomes, when marriage will become a practicable proposition. Almost at once the postponed marriages of the hungry years will take place, with a sudden rise in the demand for houses, and in the birth-rate. Instead of beginning slowly eighteen years after the first bulge began, the echo will begin suddenly rather later; and the later it begins the more pronounced it will be. This need not always happen. It may be that times are good when the bulge babies reach the age of parenthood, in which case people may marry rather young, and pull the echo to the left: but even when food prices are at a more or less normal level the increase, over a short period, in the number of workers is likely to tend to make each worker poorer, and so there seems to be built-in bias towards hard times. If food happens to be dear then the echo is very likely to be postponed and shortened.

There is, then, some reason for believing that the echo of a single bulge in births may be less dissipated than one would expect upon purely biological grounds. We shall later see that there may be other forces at work, tending to concentrate the echo even further. Without suggesting that this results in anything like a regular births cycle, we may at least say that a boom in marriages and births will result in a *potential* echo about twenty years later, and that while earlier and intervening fluctuations may also be having some part of their effect at the same time, if economic conditions change in favour of the workers at the right time the potential echo may result in a considerable upswing in marriages and births. If this is so, then any economic consequences of a rise in these rates are likely to show a similar resurgence.

This, however, is no more than a tendency, albeit an important one. Another tendency is for internal migration, from country to town, to be a function of age-structure and population pressure. It is, indeed, probably in this way that a bulge in births is likely to have one of its major impacts on housing.

Without implying that every favourable turn of fortune arises out of a good harvest, we may conveniently pursue an analysis that is based on such an event. We have already seen that a good harvest following a succession of bad ones will be beneficial to the non-agricultural sector but possibly detrimental to farmers. Since this is so, we may expect the increase in the birth-rate to be largely an industrial phenomenon, although it would be wrong to ignore the possibility of a harvest improvement benefiting all sectors of the community and resulting in a general rise in the marriage rate. Even in this case, however, the greater benefit is likely to be derived by the industrial sector, where the real incomes increase as the result of falling bread prices.

Because of the relative gain of the industrial worker over the agricultural worker, there will be a tendency for some people to move out of farming into the factory. Furthermore, the generally better times, arising at least in part out of the increased demands made effective by the rise in real incomes, will swell the demand for industrial labour, and possibly do so to a degree that results in a rise in money wages, thus emphasising the poor lot of the farm labourer. As the extent of the inequality tips the scales in favour of migration, the demand for urban accommodation rises, and it does so not only because of the trek to the towns but also because of the increased marriages and births taking place within the towns themselves. How long this state of affairs lasts depends on many factors we have yet to examine, but it is clear that up to a point it will be carried forward by its own momentum, as the stories of urban prosperity seep back to the farms, and the multiplier effects of autonomous expenditures drive the economy onwards. It is a point we shall examine more carefully shortly.

This coincidence of a rise in the birth-rate with an upswing in building is important, and especially when we recall that both of these are largely urban phenomena. Within a few years many of the bulge babies will have died, but even so, the rise in the birth-rate will generally result in an increase in the number of ever more hungry mouths to feed.

It is difficult to know at what age a child begins to earn his own keep, or even at what age his needs are most in excess of his earning power, and it is certain that this age has altered considerably since the days when children began to earn almost as soon as they could walk. Let us, however, suppose for the moment that the excess of needs over earning power rises until the child is (say) ten years old. In order to maintain his standard of living, a worker needs a steadily rising income during this period. If times are booming, this may be possible, but otherwise it is unlikely, and if things become bad they become doubly so, for falling incomes will coincide with rising needs. Migration into the towns will dwindle, the birth-rate will fall, and

C

on both accounts the demand for urban houses will decline. This diminution in building activity will add to the distress, and point to a cumulative downward movement in which the urban worker, no longer prosperous, may return to the land, or even emigrate (if this is allowed and possible). If our assumption, that a child's needs exceed his earning power by a maximum amount when he is ten, is correct, then ten years after the births bulge begins two conflicting forces begin to operate. The children, by becoming effective additions to the labour force, are tending to make labour more abundant and so to reduce the average, and perhaps the total, reward to labour. At the same time, the families containing those children tend to become better off, provided that some work exists, for a greater share of the total wage-bill now goes to them. If there is high unemployment this is irrelevant, for the child is likely to remain unemployed, but if things improve, then for these families there will be a substantial gain, especially if there are several children per family.

It is important for us to realise that at the moment we are not attempting to say why times may become good or bad. We are concerned simply with emphasising the rather obvious, but often forgotten, point that if times become bad when there is an abnormally high number of young children then very severe poverty is more likely, with all the demand implications that this entails; whereas an improvement in conditions when there is an unusually large supply of young workers will be of very considerable benefit to the families concerned, even if it may, at first, be of less benefit to individual workers than it would otherwise have been.

Let us now suppose that such an improvement does come about, after a period of strain associated with an unusually large number of young families, during which the prime concern of parents has been the provision of food. It is likely that in order to keep above the subsistence level, they have let many comforts fall below standard. If there has been some temporary improvement in the economy that has resulted in higher incomes, then probably the additional money will have been spent on more food and such things as clothes that can be bought out of more or less current incomes. Before people with a young hungry family move into a larger house they wish to be fairly sure that they can afford to remain in it for a substantial time. Six months in a bigger house means little compared with six months' good feeding and some new clothes. There is abundant contemporary evidence to support the statement that this was an important feature of consumer behaviour in the early nineteenth century.

When the improvement in conditions coincides with the existence of a new young labour force, then the families of these new workers will see an assured rise in income — for no change of fortune can seem more certain than the existence of two, three or four earners in place of one. Even if times soon deteriorate, now there are greater chances of there being *some* income, while the unemployed young worker can to some extent fend for himself, and so be less of a burden. By now, too, older children will have emphasised the inadequacy of their housing, and so the need of a larger house becomes more apparent at a time when the additional number of workers in the family makes it more practicable for something to be done about it. It is true that these young teenagers may be getting married in seven or eight years' time, but that is a long time for cramped living, and the parents may reasonably argue that by using their children's earnings to help pay an increased rent — or even subscriptions to a building club — then they are paving the way for their own comfort later on, when marriage will remove some of their sources of income, but still leave them better off than they were when they reared their infants.

This means that a favourable change in industrial fortune occurring about twelve or fourteen years after the onset of a boom in births is likely to see a sharp increase in the demand for houses. The swollen demand stimulates the economy, and helps to ensure its own prolongation. If it lasts for a few years, then young marriages may add to the demand. Here, indeed, is one of those economic factors that tend to reduce the dissipation of the echo in births. When the new babies arrive they add to potential demand, but detract from its effectiveness by requiring, above all, expenditure on food.

There is, of course, great danger in an analysis of this kind, which emphasises just one side of the story and completely omits reference to many important factors. We must think of it in these terms — as an indication of tendencies towards a cyclical movement in building, and not as an attempt to prove that a good harvest, through causing a boom in births, gives rise to a building cycle of eighteen years' duration. The fact is that if births have a cyclical element, then whatever the economic impacts of a births-bulge may be, these too will tend to be cyclical. Whether such a cycle exists in births will be examined in Chapter 7.

Another possible partial explanation of the building cycle lies in the long period of production, the sluggishness of the industry and the stickiness of rents. On this argument a temporary recession in trade need have little effect on building for the following reasons.

A building is essentially a long-term investment. It also requires a long time between the planning stage and its completion. If, during this gestation period, the economy turns downwards one effect may well be to make labour and other costs cheaper. A half-completed building is no use to anybody, and provided the builder can reasonably believe that the recession is short-lived he may consider it more profitable to complete the building, and even to embark on further buildings, at a time of low costs, than to wait until there is a queue of tenants and also a queue for materials or skilled labour. If it is left empty for a short while he will not be unduly worried, for what he loses on rents he gains on costs. The reduction in labour costs and material prices has not been followed by a fall in rents, largely because of the contractual element in the rents of existing tenants, and there is every reason to believe that the new houses, built more cheaply, can be let at the old rents or, perhaps, eventually at higher ones. If the houses are being built by an employer for eventual occupation by his immigrant labour force, then he has the added incentive of wishing to be ready with housing to attract that new labour as soon as the next trade boom gets under way, and this is especially true if one of his prime motivations is to capture an increasing share of the market. Factors such as these may well tide the building industry over a minor recession, especially if it is more or less restricted to a single area or industry. The possibility of regional differences is one that we shall consider later.

As the building boom develops so it assumes a character and impetus of its own. As each house is built and occupied, so the attractions of solid investment become apparent; and the profits to be made out of building operations, out of speculative building and selling, and out of appreciation of land values attract still further. Craftsmen set up as master-builders, and in the larger towns a vast number of people in one way or another become responsible for launching a flood of projects, large and small, each based on the belief that there is a large unsatisfied demand for houses, and on the hope of profit. The first in the field succeed, and their profits encourage others to follow suit, until, with a startling suddenness, it is overdone. Houses remain empty for longer, rents stop rising, and may even begin slowly to fall, and further building ceases to be an attractive proposition. Many of the houses will have been built with borrowed money, and the inability of the builder to rent or to sell them leads to his bankruptcy. In a severe case of overbuilding, possibly made apparent by some other crisis which reduces both confidence and real incomes, the number of bankruptcies may be large; and many years will have to elapse before building firms once again begin to rise, as the shadow of speculation leading to ruin slowly ebbs into a past generation.

This approach to the building cycle has been written up by a number of authors,[1] and we shall not deal further with it now, especially since in a sense it anticipates points that can be made more easily later in the book. It is, however, necessary to mention it in order that we may make our final point.

An increasing amount of building or trade requires, under any ordinary circumstances, an increasing amount of short-term credit. A builder may not be paid until the whole building is completed, and at best he is likely to be paid only when substantial portions of the work have been done. Meanwhile he has to find labour and materials. Sometimes he may obtain the latter on credit from the manufacturer, who in turn has somehow to pay his current expenses before being paid for his product, just as the builder cannot escape his current wage-bill. Whether the builder obtains credit through the trade, through private means or directly through a bank, it is certain that at some stage in the credit chain substantial reliance is placed upon bank credit by somebody or the other, but this is not essential to the argument. An increasing amount of activity, involving larger labour forces and more purchases of materials will require more credit. Whether doubling of activity requires double the amount of credit is debatable, but it is clear that when a boom develops, and prices begin to rise and scarcities to appear, there is a strong tendency to buy more and more into the future, and this means that at that stage of affairs a small increase in activity may lead to a large increase in the desired amount of short-term accommodation. This is a point made by Pigou:

. . . it is significant that, at all events in some industries, as the tide of profits advances, credits do in fact tend to become both larger and longer. Some sorts (though not all sorts) of collateral, being of higher price, will command a larger advance, and, when no collateral is employed, A, looking optimistically on B's prospects, will regard with less critical eyes his request for credit. Thus, Sir Sydney Chapman observes: 'The longer the period of good trade, the further is forward buying drawn out and the more involved do traders become . . . under the pressure of demands crowding in in the face of only slightly elastic production.' Moreover there is reason to believe that, in nearly all industries in times of boom, there is an enormous increase in forward buying against informal promises to pay. . . .[2]

At this stage our argument goes back to harvests and other stochastic events. The exact impact of any exogenous influence on the volume of investment, or other activity, depends on a number of factors that are not exogenous, and perhaps the most important of these is the volume of credit.   If there is plenty, a favourable harvest will not only result in increased demands for houses, consumer goods and industrial investment, but the availability of abundant funds will enable this boom to take place.   If, on the other hand, it is very difficult to get a short-term loan, then the increased demands will not call forth a parallel increase in supply, but will be more likely to lead to an inflation, with possibly severe consequences. The favourable harvest may result in an improved balance of payments, which will tend to ease the credit situation, and it may lead to new optimism of a kind that will ease it further; but these are factors that will be more powerful if there is already abundant credit. An unfavourable harvest has to be viewed similarly.   If there is plenty of credit then the reduction in demand due to the unfavourable turn of events will be softened by the ease with which construction can be undertaken, which will encourage people to take a long-term view and perhaps to build for future profits at a time when costs are low, as described above.   But if credit is strained then the effects of an unfavourable harvest may be catastrophic.   Falling income- and marriage-rates reduce demands for both houses and consumer goods.   Builders and others who have bought on credit may be left with no means of paying their debts at a time when, because of the tightness of the situation, creditors are pressing for repayment, having more concern for their own liquidity than confidence in the future.   Bankruptcy is imminent.   The bad harvest, leading to an outflow of gold, strains the credit situation further, and once the pyramid of credit totters there is no telling how far it may fall.

The particular importance of this feature is underlined when we relate it to the population factor.   Almost all economic activity involves some form of credit, in the role of a catalyst.   As activity increases so the desirable amount of credit will increase, so that the economy may function smoothly.   Some activities require more credit than others, and probably none requires so much as building, in which the long period of production compels the builder to pay his wage-bill before he himself gets paid, while when the building is finished a great deal of capital is tied up irretrievably.[3]   If there is a building boom, the drain on credit will increase partly because of the greater level of general activity that is associated with it, partly because building requires so much credit, partly because of increased forward buying, and partly because the high profits that make industrial building desirable also attract towards share-purchase and speculative investment some of those funds which would otherwise have been available for short-term loans.   So far as there is any substance in the suggestion that we may frequently expect a building boom about twelve years or so after the onset of bulge in births, so, it seems, we may expect a period of strained credit to come a few more years later.   The economy becomes vulnerable to shocks, and when the crash comes any tendency for the echo in births to make itself felt has to fight against the poverty of the times.   When these improve the delayed marriages may be quite substantial.

Other factors should be mentioned.   If a time of boom activity is characterised by heavy home investment in preference to overseas investment, and of heavy imports in order to satisfy both our invest-ment requirements and our income-elastic demands for consumer goods, then this, tending to lead to an adverse balance of payments, acts as a brake on the banks' powers to create credit.   In the building cycles we have so far examined there was a more drastic brake on activity, in that the legal ceiling to interest rates was able to curtail the supply of credit very effectively, and very suddenly, and we have seen how this affected building.   In this connection we have to note that an adverse factor, causing a rise in the rate of interest, would have a more profound influence on building if the rate was already near the maximum legal rate, for in such a case building would be more likely to cease through the termination of credit supplies. The Usury Laws made the combination of stringent credit and adverse exogenous factors a more certain deterrent to building rather than a more potent one.

The fact that stochastic events have to be taken in the context of the credit situation is important.   The fashion in econometric work is to think of stochastic factors as being normally distributed and having a purely additive influence, but there seems to be an argument for making the influence of any given stochastic event a function of the supply of credit, or of the supply of credit expressed as a fraction of the demand for credit.   There may also be an argu-ment for making the influence multiplicative rather than additive: perhaps it should be both.   To emphasise the importance of thinking in these terms we have built, with the aid of Mr. David Bugg, a model of a multiplier-accelerator economy involving an inventory cycle, in which stochastic events have influences depending upon the credit situation.   The model is described fully in Appendix 3.   An interesting point that emerges from it is that when stochastic events are introduced in this way they alter not only the cycles, but also the trend around which the cycles grow.   Even if good shocks and bad shocks are equal in number, the worst that a bad shock can do to investment is to stop it — unless it is a war that actually destroys it — while a good shock may cause considerably more than doubling in investment provided the capacity and resources are available. This is a preliminary result, but it certainly seems that we are possibly assuming too much if we argue that shocks balance out in the long run. It may well be that if, instead of being added almost as an afterthought, they are worked into the system in the way in which they actually affect it, then quite different results will be obtained.

This chapter has emphasised the importance, in a subsistence economy,[4] of harvests and other shocks, of the age-structure of the population, of credit, and of internal migration. A full appreciation of this last requires some regional studies to which we now turn.

NOTES TO CHAPTER 3

1. Apart from the works mentioned elsewhere in this book, one should see K. Buckley, *Capital Formation in Canada, 1896–1930* (Toronto, 1955), and A. F. Burns, 'Long Cycles in Residential Construction' in *The Frontiers of Economic Knowledge*, Princeton, 1954.

2. A. C. Pigou, *Industrial Fluctuations*, London, 1927, p. 40.

3. This point is developed in Chapter 9.

4. We use this phrase to mean an economy in which often the consumer has little money left after buying his food.

CHAPTER 4

REGIONAL DIFFERENCES, 1832–1864

So far nearly the whole of our statistical material has consisted of national aggregates, and it has not been possible for us to compare the courses of building in different regions. Now, however, this becomes possible, in a very inadequate way. From 1832 to 1849 there are regional figures of brick production, while for the second half of the century there is information about house-building in an increasing number of towns. As we shall shortly see, the data are marred by many deficiencies, but they still provide a great deal of interest. Before saying anything else we may usefully glance at the nature of the data, and the regional differences that emerge.

The brick figures have been discussed at length by Shannon, and the national totals were used in our earlier chapters. From 1829 there are figures for the fifty different centres on which tax collection was based, and these provide ample evidence of regional differences, as is shown in Figure 4.1. On the whole the collection centres covered well-defined localities, and the bricks were mostly used in the centre that produced them. Shannon has used this fact in his analysis of the differences, and has emphasised that the use of bricks in railway-building, which was proceeding unevenly over the country, can account for a substantial part of the differences.[1] Matthews went a stage further. Noting that only two important collection centres (Uxbridge and Norwich) showed the twin peaks of 1836 and 1840 that are so apparent in the national total, he divided the various series into two groups — Group A, consisting of those whose major peak in the period 1832–43 came before 1839, and Group B, consisting of those whose major peak was in or after 1839. 'The result that emerges', says Matthews, 'is rather curious, and provides a good example of the uncritical use of economic aggregates. In both groups there was a strong rise up to 1836 and a falling off in 1837–8, though both the rise and the fall were more rapid in group A — which incidentally is the smaller of the two groups. But in 1839–40, while group B was rising to a peak that made that of 1836 look a trifling affair, group A showed no rise whatsoever but merely continued the mild decline that had begun in the previous two years. Finally, in 1841–2, the rate of decline in group A increased and output in group B at last turned down.' [2] Thus while almost every centre had low brick output in 1842–3, before rising to a peak some time around 1846–8, the pattern in the thirties varied considerably.

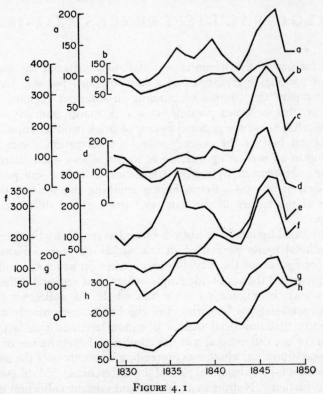

FIGURE 4.1

Index of Brick Duty charged in the following areas (1829 = 100):

(a) England and Wales	(e) Manchester.
(b) London.	(f) Rochester.
(c) Surrey.	(g) Leeds.
(d) Liverpool.	(h) East Wales.

Based on *Returns of Brick Duty*, B.P.P., especially in 1839, xlvi (329); 1846, xxv (82); 1847–8, xxxix (168); 1849, xxx (218); and 1850, xxxiii (112).

For what those bricks were used we cannot be absolutely certain. Certainly in the thirties a large proportion of them must have gone into increasing the national stock of houses by almost half a million houses, but the increased brick output of the forties saw a lower net addition to the number of houses. To some extent this probably distorts the picture of actual house-building, for substantial numbers of dwellings were demolished by the railway-builders, who were more active in the forties than in the thirties. The building of about 4,000 miles of railway in a single decade could not, however, have involved the demolition of something like an additional 150,000 houses, which is the scale of activity that would have been necessary if the gross output of the forties was to equal that of the thirties. Where the railway bulldozed its way through a town whole streets were sometimes demolished: but the actual mileage requiring such drastic reconstruction was small. There were probably more hedges than houses on the demolition schedule, and a large part of the brick output of the forties went into building the railways themselves.

Yet a considerable problem remains. The peak of 1840 has been attributed by both Shannon and Matthews to railway-building. 'The regions where brick production rises most pronouncedly in those years [1839 and 1840] — the home counties, the north-east and parts of the west country — were those where railway building was active,' writes Matthews,[3] who goes on to observe that brick production appeared (on an aggregative basis) to lag a little behind railway-building at this time. 'What the figures do not tell us, and what it would be interesting to know,' he continues, 'is whether the rise in 1839–40 was entirely due (directly or indirectly) to railways or whether in those districts — including the metropolis — in which the boom of 1836 had been relatively little felt, *house*-building continued to rise, or at least did not fall, until the depression set in in 1841–2. It seems not unlikely that this was the case, for the rise up to 1836 had been in many places fairly mild and did not lead to any very violent reaction in 1837–8; but we cannot say more.'

Actually a little more can be said because of some data provided by Cairncross and Weber.[4] These show that in certain parts of London, at any rate, house-building fell from a high level in 1831 to a much lower level for four or five years, before rising rapidly in the late thirties and early forties, as shown in Figure 4.2. It looks as if Matthews's conjecture about the metropolis is correct. The brick index for the London collection district, whose boundaries differed from those for which the housing data exist, peaked in 1840, and then hovered for a few years before declining, as is shown in the same Figure, where the difference between the London index and the national index is clearly revealed. Cairncross and Weber also look at Liverpool, where there was a housing boom in the early forties. Here the really interesting point is that there was a much more pronounced boom a few years later due to the combination of a huge immigration of Irish into the city, and a vast amount of speculative building inspired by the desire to make hay before the much-needed first Building Bye-Law of 1846 obscured the sun. It is a clear example of calamity in Ireland affecting the fortunes of the major port of immigration, at a time when local legislation (which was designed to deal with a problem that previous immigration had helped to create) was acting in the same direction.

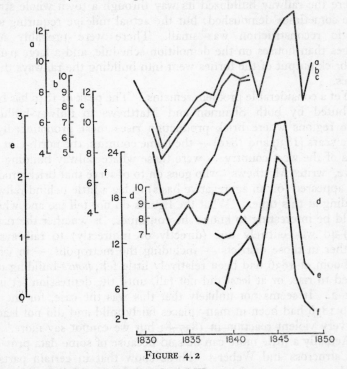

FIGURE 4.2

Indices of the following, all based on C. and W., pp. 290–3:

(*a*) Duty paid on Bricks, London (1840 = 10).
(*b*) Bricks produced in London (1840 = 10).
(*c*) New houses in London (1840 = 10).
(*d*) All new buildings other than houses, erected in a number of London districts (1840 = 10).
(*e*) Duty paid on Bricks, Liverpool (1840 = 1·0).
(*f*) Houses built in Liverpool (1840 = 10).

This first Building Bye-Law came just a year or two before a spate of others, based on model bye-laws issued by the Central Board of Health. Once a town had reached a certain size, no building could be erected without the plan having been approved by the local board, guided by its Surveyor. Many local authorities have records showing details of the plans approved, and these form the main source of our information about building after 1850. Since, however, a local board was set up only after an area had attained a certain degree of urbanisation, and since, even then, they did not always preserve their records, there are very few towns for which we have been able to obtain information about the fifties. Weber circulated the Librarians and Town Clerks of a large number of the larger towns but obtained data for any part of the earlier fifties only for Liverpool, Birkenhead, Bradford, Hull and St. Helens. Figures for Cardiff exist from 1851, and for two other South Wales towns (Newport and Aberdare) from 1855. In the Manchester area we have data for Manchester itself, Ashton-under-Lyne and Bolton. Similar data for towns in the North-East have lately been collected by Kenwood.[5] Some of this information is graphed in Figures 4.3 and 4.5, but care has to be exercised in its interpretation, as may be seen from the following account of the actual data recorded.

When a plan was submitted a note was usually entered in a register, describing the building and giving the name of the building-owner, the builder, or sometimes simply of an agent. Every so often, usually once or twice a month, a committee met to consider these plans and the decision was recorded. In most cases, reliable records stopped at this stage, even though many registers contained columns for recording the dates on which construction commenced and on which building was completed or final inspection carried out. Consequently, although for some towns there are series showing the numbers of buildings actually erected, or commenced, for most towns the series show simply the number of planning approvals given.

This means that the data have many deficiencies. A building could be anything from a hut to a town hall, while a plan could relate to a hundred houses, a mill or a new drain. Such heterogeneity makes any series headed simply 'buildings' or 'plans' of very dubious worth. Fortunately, however, several authorities have records that allow the extraction of data relating simply to houses, which, despite the variation in their size, do provide a more homo-geneous group. In almost every case we have been able to make tolerably certain that the house series relates either to houses erected, or, if it is derived from planning approvals, to the numbers of houses rather than to the numbers of plans. This matter is discussed more fully in Appendix 4. The Figures show the series adjusted for boundary changes. The data in Appendix 4 are unadjusted.

Industrial building is even more heterogeneous than house-building, and here the number of buildings planned or erected means little. Indeed, in some cases where it was possible to supplement examination of registers by examination of the plans themselves it was found that industrial plans described as 'extensions' to large mills might consist of nothing more than the addition of a single water closet, or, on the other hand, of an extension far larger than the original building.   For one or two towns tolerably meaningful series

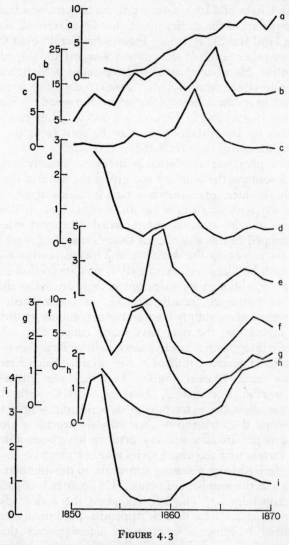

FIGURE 4.3

Houses erected or planned in the following areas. Allowances have been made for boundary changes. See Appendix 4.

(a) Hull ('oo).	(d) Ashton-under-Lyne ('oo).	(g) Cardiff ('oo).
(b) Liverpool ('oo).	(e) Swansea ('oo).	(h) Bradford ('ooo).
(c) Birkenhead ('oo).	(f) Newport (Mon.) ('oo).	(i) Manchester ('ooo).

exist for industrial building, and we shall refer to some of these later on. In any case, an increase in the number of plans passed does betoken some kind of change in activity, and can sometimes be usefully interpreted as an index of entrepreneurial expectations. If many people embark on small projects it may be a better indication of a widespread revival of confidence than the erection of a vast mill by one man. On the other hand, the passing of a local bye-law, or the extension of a sewage system, could have a similar result. Usually one can draw safe conclusions about industrial building only if one can examine the plans themselves. At this stage both the plans and the researcher tend to crumble.

The data graphed in Figure 4.3 show quite clearly that several areas had a high level of building in the early fifties, just as others saw very little activity. In Birkenhead there was the barest ripple to celebrate the Year of the Great Exhibition, but in all the other towns for which we have at all reliable data, a different story must be told. In Cardiff the number of approved plans for houses and shops was higher in 1851 than in any other year for another quarter of a century. Whether this year marked a peak we cannot say, but certainly 1854 marked a trough, at a fairly high level, before another substantial peak in 1856 led to a deeper trough in 1863. In Swansea, 1851 was again a year of high activity preceding a decline to 1856, while the second peak occurred in 1858. In Bradford house-building rose from its high 1851 level to hit a peak in 1852. It remained high in the next year, but then fell drastically, to reach its trough in 1861. Activity in Hull was slight in 1852, but fell continuously until 1855. In Liverpool house-building in 1850 was at its lowest level since records commenced in 1838, but it rose to a definite, if minor, peak in 1852, before falling somewhat again until, in 1855, it began a second minor cycle initiating a broad upward movement that peaked in the early sixties. A definite peak occurred in the year ending April 30th, 1853 (and therefore in the building year of 1852), in Manchester, while a steep fall two years later led the way to a trough in 1859–60. Ashton-under-Lyne, with its highest figure for plans approved in 1851, seems to have had a similar pattern. There was a marked peak in 1852 in the total number of plans, of all kinds, passed in Preston.

Taken in conjunction with brick data, which in some cases seem to show a trough in 1848, these pointers suggest that the early fifties saw some increase in the level of house-building, peaking in 1852. Further credence is lent to this view by an examination of Maywald's [6] index of building costs, and also by the figures for timber imports. Although building wages seem to have remained fairly steady during the early fifties, the costs of building materials rose sharply from a trough in 1851 to a peak in 1854, as did Maywald's index of total costs. While this is not by any means conclusive evidence of a rise in activity it is at least corroborative. More conclusive, perhaps, are Cooney's figures for lathwood and mahogany imports.[7] The lathwood series, which is broadly correlated with brick production in the thirties and forties, falls from a peak in 1845 to a trough value of 8,750 fathoms in 1849 as is shown in Figure 4.4. The following year there was a rise to 12,195 fathoms, and then comes a year for which we have no figure. However, in

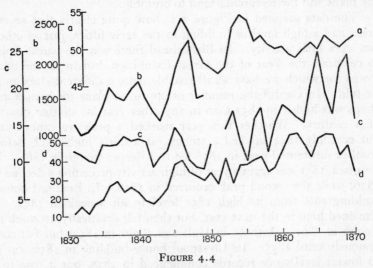

FIGURE 4.4

(a) Index of Building Costs (Maywald) (1930 = 100). *B.H.S.*, p. 240.
(b) Bricks charged with Duty, G.B. (m.). Shannon.
(c) Imports of Lathwood, U.K. ('000 fathoms). Cooney (1), p. 268.
(d) Imports of Mahogany, U.K. ('000 tons). Cooney (1), p. 269.

1852 the imports totalled 14,110 fathoms and then, in 1853, they peaked at 16,671, before falling to a trough in 1855. Imports of mahogany showed a roughly similar pattern, having a peak in 1846, a trough in 1849, a recovery in 1850, an even lower trough in 1851, and then a sudden upsurge to the highest value recorded before 1860, in 1852. We have remarked before that timber import figures are subject to many vicissitudes, and the 1853 imports were affected by speculation prior to the Crimean War, but taken along with the data we have on costs, and our knowledge of the course of housebuilding or planning in a handful of towns, they certainly conform with the suggestion that a short-lived spurt in activity took place in the early fifties. We shall shortly see other evidence of this.

For the later fifties and early sixties the data on house-building are more abundant. Apart from the addition of Merthyr Tydfil

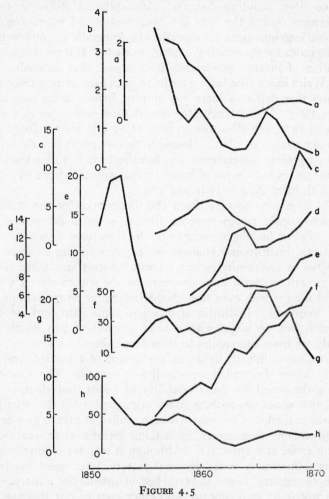

FIGURE 4.5

Houses erected or planned in the following areas. See Figure 4.3.

(a) Merthyr Tydfil ('oo).   (f) North-East England (1901–10 = 100).
(b) Aberdare ('oo).   (Kenwood).
(c) Bolton ('oo).   (g) London ('ooo).
(d) Birmingham ('oo).   (h) South Wales Coalfield (1901–10 = 100)
(e) Manchester Region (1901–10 = 10).

— then the largest Welsh town — its neighbour Aberdare, and New-port, which, with Cardiff, imported ore and exported their iron and coal, we also have data for Bolton, St. Helens and Birmingham.   All of these series are derived from house plans approved, and are graphed in Figure 4.3 or 4.5. They provide abundant evidence for the assertion that building behaved differently in different towns. Furthermore, when the data for Manchester and its environs are combined into one index (as described in Appendix 4) and compared with the index for the South Wales towns we find that there is a strong suggestion of inverse movements from about 1855 onwards. The South Wales index rose from 35·2 in 1855 to peak at 48·9 three years later and then fell to a mere 7·9 in 1863 before rising to a minor peak in 1867. The Manchester conurbation index was at a major trough in 1857, and then rose to peak at 61·4 in 1863 before falling to a minor trough in 1866. Alongside this we may place the equally strong opposing movements in Bradford and Birkenhead. In London[8] the broad course of building was upwards from 1856 until 1868, with brief dips in 1861 and 1864.

It is time now to turn from this description of the statistical sources to consider some reasons for the regional differences they reveal. Before looking at some of the local features we may usefully note certain institutional changes which were having an impact on the degree of uniformity in our growth. Sometimes, when talking about growth, we tend to concentrate on the spectacular at the expense of the gradual, even though the latter may be more important in the long run. Institutional changes come into both of these categories, but we begin with a brief account of two which were certainly far from spectacular in their beginnings.

It is always difficult to define the extent of a market, and particularly when the traded commodity is money. The finance of building depended on the availability of funds, but there is little information about where these funds originated. On the other hand there was at least one movement which tended at first to give certain areas advantages over others, by making investment in local house-building easier and attractive. Although it was not of anything but marginal importance in the national picture, until quite late in the nineteenth century, it was nevertheless of substantial importance in certain towns by mid-century, and since part of our thesis is that differences of this kind were important in the determination of the national level of activity we must pay some attention to it. The building society movement appears to have begun in Birmingham around 1775, when this town of some eight thousand houses was rapidly expanding. Ketley's Building Society, like all of its immediate successors, was a terminating society. Its purpose was to receive subscriptions from its members, and to use these, as they accumulated, to provide houses for the same people.[9] Once this had been done, it closed its activities. Usually the subscription in such clubs was between five and ten shillings a month, and the funds were invested as compound interest. Procedure varied, but usually there was a draw, and those whose names were called first had the right to the first house. The lucky ones thus received their houses, built with an advance from the communal chest, when they themselves had paid very few subscriptions. Others had to wait several years. Running expenses were met from fines for such offences as failing to attend meetings, and sometimes out of profits made by auctioning the right to the next advance.

The important point about these societies from our point of view is that they provided a new and specific source of funds. They had the purpose of providing a fixed number of houses as cheaply and as speedily as possible, before winding up. A monthly subscription of six shillings invested at 5 per cent compound interest would amount to £72 in fourteen years, and this may be taken as the approximate time that an individual would have had to save, at this rate of interest, before being able to build his own house.[10] It is unlikely that the number managing such unaided saving would have approached the number who did so with the aid of the discipline and encouragement provided by societies of this kind. Under the terminating society arrangements, if there were about twenty-five members the first house could be provided before the first year was out. The member occupying it would have to continue to pay his subscription throughout the life of the society, and interest on the sum borrowed from the date of the advance to the date of winding up. Thus those who had their houses first paid more in interest. Those last in the queue paid out less than the actual cost, receiving their reward for waiting from those who were first.

Several other societies soon opened in Birmingham, and the north soon followed. London does not seem to have had one until the Greenwich Union was founded in 1809, one year after the first recorded Scottish society. By this time some of the societies were already markedly different from the pioneers. Possibly under the influence of the first English savings bank, founded in 1799, some of them now had members who were more concerned with saving than with building. Indeed they sometimes had no wish at all to build, but were prepared to invest their funds in the societies in the belief that their capital was secure and that the rate of interest was attractive. Thus housing developed its own local capital market, which had to compete with nationally known consumers of capital but had many intrinsic advantages, not least being that the local saver knew the calibre of the people to whom he was lending, and could easily inspect the bricks and mortar that his money was financing. This was particularly important when we remember that despite the rapid growth of country banks at the beginning of the nineteenth century there is little evidence that they made advances for house-building.[11]

In 1836 the movement was given a considerable fillip by an Act relating to Benefit Building Societies which placed them under the relevant provisions of the Friendly Societies Act, thereby exempting them from being charged with stamp duty on shares, and providing them with legal recognition and the supervision of the Registrar of Friendly Societies. Two years later the Lords of the Treasury issued a set of model rules. Partly under these stimuli, the number of societies rapidly grew. Not all were well run, and some had such faith in the magic of compound interest that they died of its potions. Yet by 1846 nearly two thousand societies had registered with the Chief Registrar, some of them having as many as 250 members. One of the difficulties besetting even the best-run society was that over a period of years possibilities and current desires often deviated from initial intentions, and many troubles arose out of this. In addition, after the first few years in the life of a society it some-times happened that people who would gladly have joined were put off by the prospect of having to pay the back subscriptions. To overcome these difficulties, some societies began to augment their original schemes with new schemes, destined to provide a further supply of houses to new members, overlapping with the scheme already in existence, and economising by being able to share in the experience and material benefits accruing to the pioneers. The path to the permanent society was being forged. The idea here, pub-lished in 1847,[12] was that instead of being content with providing a fixed number of houses, a building society should think of itself as a medium for channelling the savings of the masses into a permanent supply of new houses. It was no longer a case of people putting up their own money in order to provide their own houses, but with people in various localities providing their own markets for housing finance; and to begin with these were essentially local, even though they grew into national markets.

In the decade that began with this scheme, another two thousand societies were registered. Not all of them were permanent, but it is of some interest that despite the rail speculation and the bank failures of 1847, of the permanent societies that were founded in the period 1846–56 no fewer than 137 reached their centenary, weathering all the storms that tore at weaker branches of financial institutions during panics, disasters and wars. To some extent this was because even then people saw that their savings were tolerably secure. Another factor was that about this date insurance companies began to woo the borrower, presenting attractive schemes for house purchase with life insurance. Even more important was the stark need of houses in the ever-expanding towns and cities, either for new population or to replace the slums that even then presented major problems. The ninth annual volume of the *Building Societies' Directory and Almanac* of 1854 listed over 400 building societies in London and over 500 in the provinces. There were 85 in Manchester, 61 in Liverpool, 22 in Birmingham and 12 in Sheffield.

The importance of this development, from our present point of view, is not simply that here was a new means of canalising savings into housing, but that the movement was particularly strong in certain areas, emphasising once again the regional variations in the supply of capital and credit. The people of Manchester who banded themselves into societies for the building of houses for their own occupation supplied their own funds from their own savings: and if housing had not proceeded, it is highly unlikely that those savings would have provided credit for builders elsewhere. It is, indeed, not unlikely that the savings would just not have existed. The building clubs and societies were a stimulus to saving, in that the first house, soon provided for the one lucky member, aroused envy, ambition and determination in the hearts of other members. Their numbers were small: but in some places at least they were exerting a powerful, if marginal, influence.

Another development was in the field of labour organisation. In 1832 the Operative Builders' Union was formed, with aims extending deep into syndicalism.[13] Robert Owen led the builders against the masters of Manchester, who were considered to be evading promises made to the workers. The masters retaliated by requiring their employees to sign 'the Document' declaring their intention of boycotting the O.B.U. For four months bricklayers, masons, carpenters and joiners were on strike, and another strike broke out in Birmingham. Out of this discontent came a remarkable, if abortive, idea, for in September of 1833 the Builders' Parliament met in Manchester and formed the National Building Guild of Brothers. This Guild was to erect buildings itself, and to look after its members' welfare by various means including that of building 'superior dwellings' and other buildings for their own use at times when public demand was slack. Unfortunately for the movement, idealism and revolutionary sentiment slept ill with efficiency, and the movement flopped. In 1834 the builders held aloof from the Grand National Trades Union. The strikes or lockouts that had lasted so long in Birmingham, Leeds, Worcester, Nottingham, Manchester, Liverpool and Preston petered out. The Document won the day. The remainder of the thirties saw little effective action, and it was not until 1844 that there was appreciable recovery. In the next few years building workers became better organised, largely under the leadership of Richard Harnott who, in 1847, moulded the Operative Stonemasons into a Union which looked not backward to the good old days, but forward to shorter hours and better treatment.

The full force of these changes in labour organisation was not felt until later in the century, but it is useful to keep this movement in mind. To some extent the strikes of the early thirties explain the low output of those years, but one cannot help but feel that, as so often is the case, the common worker struck at a time when, just because his grievance was bad, his chance of success was poor. If he had struck in 1823 and left many contracts half completed, he might have won: but then times were good. On the other hand, the building trades were moving towards a national unity, and a grievance in one area could lead to an increased willingness to strike in many other areas. Thus although local differences continued to exist, the movement towards unity was a force that tended to reduce regional differences in some respects. Despite this it is possible that the insistence on the national application of conditions that might be more appropriate to some regions than others at times tended to perpetuate other differences. A nationally agreed wage-rate could be so much above the customary level in some places, where demand was not as high as elsewhere, that it might cause building activity to fall even lower in these areas.

There were, of course, many other institutional changes. Our purpose is not to give an account of them all, but rather to indicate how those forces which initially might exaggerate regional differences could in time become unifying. This was true of both the building society and the trade union movements, and it was equally true of the much more spectacular railway-building. The piecemeal creation of railways was bound to impinge upon different parts of the country in different ways. The main economic impacts of railway-building and operation are well known, but it is too often forgotten that they were felt unevenly over the country. John Bull acquired his new look a garment at a time. The liberation of credit through a reduction in the size of stock that became possible when transport facilities improved did not happen everywhere all at once; nor did the multiplier effects of railway investment. Once the railways were more or less completed, and smoothly running, then the whole country was brought closer together, and they tended to reduce the regional differences. But during the long period of construction their consequences often underlined, or even created, discrepant fortunes.

A final point in the causation of regional differences is a consequence of regional specialisation, which was already well-established by the 1830's. The industries that dominated the principal regions were all highly competitive, and particularly prone to the familiar problems of over-production and the inventory cycle. A point that is sometimes overlooked is that the timing of the inventory cycle in a particular industry depends partly on exogenous factors, such as public demand, and partly upon technical considerations such as the length of time that is needed in order to expand the capacity of the industry in response to changes in demand. However much the exogenous factors may affect several industries in the same way and at the same time, these technical considerations may vary from one industry to another. As new capacity takes a shorter or longer time to come into being, so the upswing of the inventory cycle may be short or long, and regions that are dominated by different industries may consequently have different phases of fortune. Further reasons for regional differences may be found in differing sources of supply, and the different locations of customers. Once again, however, we come against the seeming paradox that what begins by emphasing regional differences may end by reducing them, for as regions develop their specialisms so they become more dependent on others. Price variations in a single region impinge upon the fortunes of many other regions, while the prosperity of the workers in a region affects the demands for products from all over the country. On the other hand, these effects are all of a secondary nature, and take time to become noticeable, especially when they are buffered by merchants. Furthermore, the adverse impact of a change in demand from one part of the country may be countered by a favourable change in demand from another place, so that these secondary effects are less certain in their aggregate. It is important to keep in mind that at times, at any rate, regional specialisation may tend to propagate similar patterns of activity, even though it is more usual for them to lead to diversified fortunes.

We shall now look at the way in which building activity was related to the rest of the economy. For the period before 1850 our emphasis will be on the total level of activity, with occasional references to local details, but then, as our material improves, we shall shift our attention to two regions, one specialising in coal and the other in cotton. In order to trace the various relationships we must once again look at the broad course of the economy, starting from the trough that followed the peak of 1825. We have already seen that the post-crisis depression was long and widespread.

There is little doubt that the immediate cause of the upswing in 1833 was the good harvest, operating in the now familiar way. Once again an exogenous shock had done the trick, liberating the steadily increasing pressure of demand that came with a growing population and the gradual absorption of the excess capacity created in the previous boom. In the cotton industry higher output required further investment. The marginal efficiency of capital was again at a respectable level, profits could be expected to rise, and manufacturers could view the future with more confidence. Already railway-building was forging ahead, as the result of earlier decisions inspired by the exemplary success of Liverpool and Manchester. It not only exerted a multiplier effect on incomes, but also exuded an atmosphere of confidence encouraging to general industrial investment. With both the need to invest and the encouragement to do so, manufacturers needed only money. Their meagre profits of recent years could sometimes provide little of this, but at hand were the resources of the banks. Need, encouragement and finance combined to set industrial investment on an upward path, and there is little doubt that in some areas there must have been an upsurge in house-building. Import prices rose, and speculation caused a brief if severe bulge in late 1833 in the gentler upward trend that otherwise endured until 1836. Speculation in Spanish securities rocked the boat in 1834, but new banking legislation in the United States led to an increased demand for our exports and helped to restore our equilibrium. As the United States became responsible for the purchase of nearly a quarter of our exports, and exchanges turned in our favour, the credit situation eased in 1835.

It was, however, but a temporary respite. At home expansion had been encouraged by joint-stock banks competing with each other to give credit. Railway speculation accounted for projects costing £74 m. between 1833 and 1837.[14] The coal and iron industries saw heavy investment, foreign loans were floated, and large amounts of credit were given to United States traders. The sight of prosperity and profits had lifted expectations out of the restraint of reasoned caution, and sensible expansion gave way to mania. Late in 1835 share prices, especially rails, soared wildly. (Fig. 4.6.) While British labour and credit were so fully employed that further expansion was bound to be difficult, and certainly discouraged, the American President ordered that in future public lands should be purchased not with notes but with gold. British reaction was sharp. The Bank raised its rate, and refused to discount American bills. Orders for imports were cancelled and American cotton prices fell to a third of their former level. At the same time, orders for British goods were cancelled by American merchants, and the consequent unemployment occurred at a time

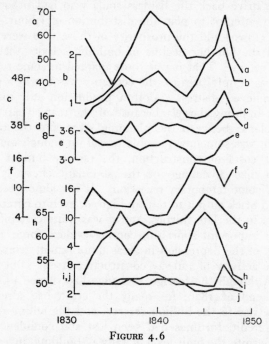

FIGURE 4.6

(*a*) Average Price of Wheat, U.K. (shillings per imperial quarter). *B.H.S.*, p. 488.
(*b*) Bricks charged with Duty, G.B. ('000 million). Shannon.
(*c*) Index of Beer Production, G.B. (1913 = 100). Hoffmann.
(*d*) Index of Bankruptcies, G.B. (1913 = 10). Hoffmann.
(*e*) Yield on Consols. Shannon.
(*f*) Bullion Reserve (£m.). G.R.S., pp. 267, 296, 329.
(*g*) Index of Railway Share Prices (1840 = 10). G.R.S., p. 437.
(*h*) Rousseaux' Index of Share Prices, quoted from Thomas (1), p. 289, where the average of the 1884 and 1896 values is taken as 100.
(*i*) Maximum Bank Rate.
(*j*) Minimum Bank Rate.

when wheat prices were high partly because of a naturally poor harvest and partly because the preceding low prices had resulted in less wheat being sown. A certain degree of ensuing depression was inevitable. Bankruptcies rose, the consumption of beer and tea fell, and brick output, reaching its peak figure of 1640 millions (in Great Britain) in 1836 fell to 1511 millions in the following year. Severe unemployment was recorded in many parts of the country, especially those with industry dependent on the flow of exports to the United States, whose imports of British goods in 1837 were but a third of those the previous year. Whereas only a little while before the Poor Law Commissioners had been sponsoring migration from the agricultural south to the industrial north, removal orders now operated to drive back the hapless souls who had become victims of this early attempt to plan the distribution of labour. Both the flood to the towns and the prosperity of those who were there had halted, and the familiar decline of building activity that comes at such times set in. That it was more marked in some regions than in others was simply because the economy was not in a position of utterly unrelieved distress. Cotton production still rose, and so did railway-building, largely because of the many years that were bound to elapse between the planning stage and the completion. As long as it was somehow possible to call up enough money to pay the current costs of construction, the railway builder was more inclined to take advantage of the abundant cheap labour than deterred by some temporary recession. It was almost certainly this that enabled brick output to remain high, or even to climb higher, in some places in the late thirties, and it was quite certainly this that acted as an important short-run counter-cyclical force, minimising the severity of the depression in areas quite remote from those that enjoyed the activity of railway construction itself. But it was not enough. Although the foreign exchange had turned in our favour before the end of 1836, for many the crash had already come. Despite the rise in the bullion reserve, and the falling market rate and easier credit, fortunes had been lost and confidence was still shaken. Despite the high level of railway-building, investment was falling, especially in manufacturing industries. Bad harvests raised the price of wheat from 53s. per quarter in January 1838 to 74s. in August, to reduce even further the demand for manufacture and the money available for rent. Even the completion of current railway construction was hampered by the inability of share-holders to pay up on the shares they had called some years before. Continued pressure on profit margins, and a falling off in exports to America, clearly decreed that industrial investment should also fall. When the need to import grain continued, and coincided with banking difficulties on the continent, leading to excessive exports of bullion, the bank and market rates rose sharply, and the new credit crisis, cutting at investment, robbed the economy of its remaining, if tottering, sector of high activity.

This story of the main events in the economy during ten years is closely reflected in some rather scrappy statistics for certain towns in the Manchester area for this period. For the neighbouring textile town of Ashton-under-Lyne, there is a useful series showing the number of depositors in the local savings bank, along with the total deposits held. Although this town is especially well documented, like almost every other town it has no annual building data for these early years. The diversity of experience in neighbouring towns in the fifties and sixties does not allow us to place much confidence in comparisons of building in one town and savings in another, but if we exercise a certain restraint something interesting may emerge from a comparison.

At the beginning of the thirties the last of the empty factories built in the boom that broke in 1825 were being filled with machinery, and a new wave of factory construction was under way.[15] An 'enormous' number of new mills was being built in Yorkshire in 1833, attracting labour that required housing, so that at times it seemed as if 'entire villages' were 'just out of the hands of the masons'.[16] In Stockport 'it was reckoned that a thousand families would be required from outside for the mills' built in 1833–4.[17] The curtailment of Child Labour under the 1833 Factory Act aggravated the incipient shortage of labour, and contributed further to the need for houses in the industrial areas. In the cotton districts the need was so apparent that 1835 and 1836 saw 'a great speculative boom in cottage-building'.[18] There was also a good deal of mill-building.[19] In short, the peak of 1836 must be attributed largely to more or less coincident factory- and house-building in the textile areas, and to similar, more widespread (and less spectacular) up-swings in other parts of the country. Even when the peak was passed, as in 1837 and 1838, activity in some areas remained high, and although some of this can be attributed to railway-building, there remained a considerable amount of mill investment. Whether there was much house-building we cannot say.

In 1830, when the textile depression was near its trough, the Ashton-under-Lyne Savings Bank had 69 depositors with average savings of £189.[20] The total deposits thus came to £1310, compared with the £18,327 standing to the account of 831 depositors in 1843. This rapid growth in the total saved was due partly to the growth of the town and partly to the growth of a habit and it would be easy to read too much into annual changes. For example, the average deposit fell from £207 in 1831 to £167 in 1834. These years also saw a fall in beer production in the Manchester area, as we see in Figure 4.7, and it is at least arguable that saving was less easy in this area and that the rise in brick production was, at this stage of the boom, associated with non-house-building. On the other hand there was, as it happens, a great deal of house-building in and around Manchester in or shortly after 1833, and the fall in average deposit may possibly be due to the influx of small savers (for the number of depositors rose from 106 to 206) or to the withdrawal of funds from the bank to build houses. Yet, despite such ambiguities, two years stand out clearly. One is 1836, when brick output was at a peak and beer production just declining. In this

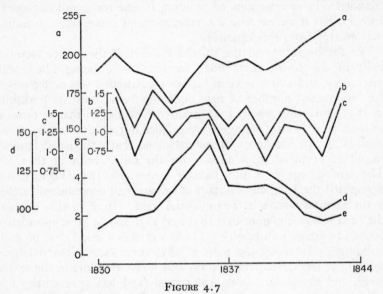

FIGURE 4.7

For the Ashton-under-Lyne Savings Bank (see note 20) :
  (a) Average deposit (£).
  (b) Proportional change in the number of depositors.
  (c) Proportional change in the balance owing to depositors.

For the Manchester area :
  (d) Malt used by Brewers, Victuallers and Persons Licensed to sell Beer, in the Manchester Collection Centre ('0,000 bushels) (see note 20).
  (e) Duty paid on Bricks in the Manchester Collection Centre (£0,000) (see Figure 4.1).

year the number of depositors was 361, compared with 269 the year before. Total deposits were £7150, compared with £4937, and average deposits £198 compared with £183. The following year, 1837, saw the addition of only 14 depositors, and total deposits increased by a mere £35. The average deposit fell. Brick production hovered half-way down its slope. 1838 saw a slight rally, but 1839 saw a fall in both total and average deposits, as well as in the number of depositors. The temptation to interpret 1836 as a year of peak prosperity, and 1839 as a year of severe depression (or change of fortune), is strong. It was in 1840 that brick production fell from its plateau half way down the decline that had followed 1836, and beer production dipped sharply.

How the boom of the early thirties had broken is not difficult to see. The full employment of labour and credit, due in part to the increasing amount of building and construction going on in certain parts of the country that was absorbing not only local resources but also such surplus resources from elsewhere as were mobile between areas, alone created shortages that must have made building more costly. At the same time came the joint impacts of the U.S. crisis and a bad harvest. Manufacturers were hit and employment fell at a time when food prices were rising. Increasing competition squeezed at profit margins. In 1839 Bolton was described as suffering distress. There were many unemployed, and, in November, Greater Bolton (whose 1841 population was 33,600) had over a thousand empty houses. In fact, an eighth of the rateable value of property in the township was untenanted. By 1841 there was severe general distress, especially in the textile areas. How this had been staved off, and possibly (in the long run) made more severe when it finally came, by railway-building, with its long ponderous projects has already been described. It was a time of bankruptcies and high emigration, with no inducement to build for habitation or production. Empty houses abounded as people, no longer able to afford dwellings of their own, moved to share with others,[21] to return to less depressed parts, or to quit our shores. Factories stood idle, and some mills at Gorton, three miles from Manchester, employing 830 persons and built for over £120,000 were sold for £26,100.[22]

The last few years of the brick production series underline its ambiguity as an index of building during the thirties and forties. Between the censuses of 1831 and 1841 the number of houses in England and Wales increased by 516,000, while 13,370 million bricks were produced. But between 1841 and 1851 the number of houses increased by only 314,000 despite the fact that the output of bricks during the part of that period — 1841-9 — amounted to 12,670 millions. Rising brick output coincided with a very sharp fall in the net increase in houses. Changes of definition, and demolition for the increasing amount of railway-building, make the figures for net increases rather poor indicators of the actual level of building, but it certainly seems that in the forties there was less house-building than in the thirties, and that the mighty peak in brick output that ends this useful series was associated largely with the creation of railways.

The history of the forties hardly needs repeating, but it so well illustrates the roles played in growth by speculation and exogenous circumstances that it seems worthwhile to devote a few pages to it, especially since it is our aim to introduce these features into our theory later in the book.

Even before 1842 was out, some signs of improvement were visible. Whereas exports to most parts of the world were still falling, those to Europe continued to rise, and the fall in the total volume was negligible. Brick production, shipbuilding and railway-building were all at low levels, as were the production of both consumer and producer goods, while bankruptcies were at almost double their level of four years earlier, but the bullion reserves were high and rising, and by the end of the year were higher than at any time since 1833. Credit was once again easier. Import prices were slowly falling, and a good harvest brought down the price of wheat. In the U.S.A. confidence was reviving, and our exports to this and other markets started once again to rise. An even better harvest in 1843, a large conversion of debt that lowered the rate of interest still further and increased the supply of funds available to industry, and a further expansion of exports due partly to tariff reduction, partly to treaties and partly to increasing foreign prosperity, provided a 'happy coincidence of blessings (which) induced a mood of confidence that knew no limit'.[23] Production rose in almost every sector of the economy, causing the fuller employment of both labour and existing capacity. As the mills of the previous boom began to prove insufficient, new ones were built, but already a great railway boom had begun, not in statistics but in the minds of men. In 1843 only 5 railway Acts for new lines were passed, but in the following year the number passed was 26, a figure almost as high as that of the previous peak in 1836. In addition, there were 22 Acts for the extension and completion of existing lines. Passed in 1844 they indicated but intermediate stages in investment processes which in some cases began with decisions taken in 1843 or earlier. Rising prosperity had not only generated additional supplies of capital, but also encouraged the utilisation of such supplies as had accumulated in the lean and unattractive years. 'Unemployed capital' stated Mr. Gladstone in February 1844, 'abounds to an almost unprecedented degree.' Its investment would, without doubt, 'take a direction towards the extension of railways'. It was, in fact, already doing so, both at home and abroad (for British methods, materials, money and men were already employed in France and Belgium), but it was in 1844 itself that capital authorisations took their great leap from £4 m. to £20 m., almost as great as that of eight years before, but trifling compared with those to follow. Railways, despite the lengthy time needed for their construction, brought good rewards when soundly managed, and captured the imagination of investors of all kinds.

Unfortunately, imagination and caution rarely go together. Railway promotion and share holding offered glittering rewards, but frequently brought ruin. Too often the shares were but partially paid on issue, and the purchasers had to find further instalments as the months and years went by, often at unexpected times. Speculators, offering bearer scrip, aggravated the danger that an investor might find himself called upon to pay out more than he had. Sometimes, in order to attract further capital, dividends were paid out of existing capital before a penny had been earned, and thousands of people were drawn deeply into impending disaster.[24] In the earlier years of the boom money was easy, and when the Bank Act came into force in September 1844, separating the Issue Department from the Banking Department, the latter proceeded to compete with the commercial banks, aggressively campaigning for opportunities to increase its private discounts, at a time when railway speculation was already rife. The railway share price index, standing at 100 in June 1840 but averaging only 86·4 in that year, averaged 121·3 in 1844, and in July of 1845 hit the peak level of 167·9.[25] By then the ordinary processes of speculation were causing some hardening in the money market, which was aggravated by the requirement that private and joint-stock banks should make deposits on behalf of the railway share subscribers with the government agents. In July 1845 Parliament decided that the cash deposit should be increased from 5 per cent to 10 per cent. 'Legislative interference was the occasion, not the cause, of the collapse that followed: investment had outstripped the actual supply of investible funds. Many purchasers refused to take up their allotment of shares; those who paid in full had to limit their expenditure in other directions; income was being sacrificed to capital, and the commodity market as well as the share market declined.'[26]

Figures 4.6 and 4.8 show that the next few years were marked by strangely conflicting movements, as the shadows of reality fell unevenly over the blaze of activity that, born in the boom now broken, still gathered strength. A poor harvest in 1845 had no serious effect on the price of wheat because of the stocks remaining from the bountiful 1844. Not until after the bad harvest of the following year, and a second failure of the potato crop, did the price of wheat begin to rocket. The fear of a cotton shortage drove up its price late in 1846. Generally rising prices tended to coincide with falling exports. Production of consumer goods dwindled. But in producer goods the tale was different, for the ponderous

machinery of railway legislation, and the persistence of committed
investors meant that even after the crisis of 1845 railway-building
continued to rise. The capital authorised in that year came to
£60 m., compared with the previous maximum of but £23 m.: yet

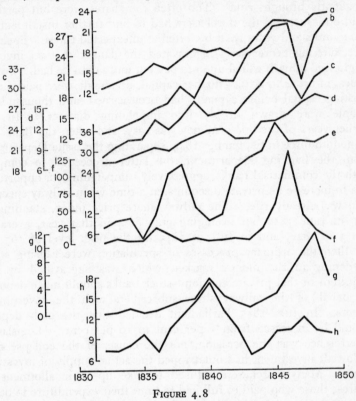

FIGURE 4.8

(a) Index of Industrial Production (excluding Building), G.B. (1913 = 100).   Hoff-
    mann.
(b) Index of Cotton Yarn Production, G.B. (1913 = 100).   Hoffmann.
(c) Index of Output of Consumer Goods Industries, G.B. (1913 = 100).   Hoff-
    mann.
(d) Index of Output of Producer Goods Industries, G.B. (1913 = 100).   Hoffmann.
(e) Index of Patents Granted, G.B. (1913 = 100).   Hoffmann.
(f) Railway Capital Authorised (£m.).   G.R.S., p. 437.
(g) Miles of Railway Built (?U.K.) ('oo).   B.H.S., p. 225.
(h) Index of Shipbuilding, G.B. (1913 = 100).   Hoffmann.

in 1846 the figure shot up to £133 m., and even though it fell to a
modest £39 m. in 1847, and to only £4 m. by 1849, actual new
mileage opened rose from 595 in 1846, through 780 in the following
year, to a peak of 1191 in 1848, three years after the crisis.   This
delayed construction boom exerted huge demands on the iron and

brick industries, both of which expanded their outputs to 1847, but in the iron industry both prices and employment turned in 1845. It was an industry with a vastly expanded capacity, still growing and changing so rapidly that it needed rapidly increasing orders if it was to work at full blast.   Despite increased railway-building and increased exports of iron, hardware and cutlery (in both volume and value), the demand was not sufficient to meet the potentialities of new plant, and the percentage of iron-founders unemployed rose from 3·9 in 1845 to 19·3 in 1846.   The following year saw only a slight improvement.   To such distress came the further aggravation of high immigration from a starving Ireland, helping to make 1847 a year of general acute poverty, to which a second financial crisis, due partly to a further calling up of share deposits and partly to grain imports, made a considerable contribution.   In the textile, mining and building trades 1846 had seen 'a spate of post-crisis strikes'[27] as employers sought to take advantage of their opportunity to use the end of labour scarcity in their fight with the Unions, while the onset of less prosperous times encouraged workers to think afresh of their grievances.   In many parts of the country there was neither the incentive to expand capacity nor the prospect of letting houses, as incomes fell, jobs disappeared, and people emigrated.   Builders became abundant.   R. J. Saunders, a Factory Inspector, reported that there was depression in many trades 'arising from a fear lest there should be a scarcity of food, and from the effect on the money market of the railway speculations'.[28]   Emigration, which had fallen below its 1841–2 levels, rose again.   Almost everywhere, nothing but the massive inertia of railway-building broke through the halt that the credit crisis called, and the first great wave of emigration began.   In 1848 a third of the iron-founders were out of work, as the demands even of the railway industry began to fall at a time when foreign crisis impinged on export orders.   Not until late in 1848 were there signs of recovery, when 'clear evidence of revival appeared in the northern textile districts'.[29]

   Yet even at this stage, despite the evidence of the statistical indices, building of one kind remained high in the London area at least, as is testified by a letter that is worth quoting at some length. Printed in *The Builder*, in October 1848, it spoke of The Building Mania:[30]

No one who has recently travelled with his eyes open in search of a home, a friend or a little fresh air, in the environs of this overgrown metropolis, can have failed to observe that houses are springing up in all quarters for the reception of the ever-increasing population of densely-populated London.   In the vicinity of other large cities, especially if they

D

boast the advantage of a railway, the same observation will have been made. There is no lack of brick and mortar, east, west, north and south; our cities are extending themselves into the country. Money is scarce; the whole nation is in difficulties; but houses spring up everywhere, as though capital was abundant — as though one-half of the world were on the look-out for investments and the other half continually in search of eligible family residences, desirable villas, and aristocratic cottages, which have nothing in the world of the cottage about them except the name.

Houses, we may say, spring up everywhere in the outskirts of our great towns. A suburb, in these days, is one congeries of crude brick and mortar. It is the most melancholy thing in existence. Streets, squares, crescents, terraces, Albert villas, Victoria villas, and things of the same inviting character, stand up everywhere against the horizon, and . . . beseech us to take them.

You may get a new house, of almost every conceivable pattern, and at any conceivable price down to £60 p.a. You may take your choice according to the length of your purse, of 'noble reception rooms' and 'rest parlours'. But you must have some length to accomplish even this latter. There is a boom of aristocracy in the parlour with folding doors. We only build, now-a-days, for the *gentry*. If a man has a little land, or a little money, or a little speculativeness or a little unemployed timber, or a number of unemployed workmen, he straightway buildeth a villa. The villa mania is everywhere most obtrusive. You would smile, perhaps at the vulgarity of the thing, if it were not for the certainty that the enterprising villa-builder must be building his gesture to death. Fortune must grow upwards, even more rapidly than they are growing downwards in these days, before all these splendid visions of wealthy tenants can be realized. Indeed, when we come to consider the number of pursy citizens that it will take to populate these snug suburbs, we are absolutely lost in wonder to determine where they can all come from.

You may talk about 'signs of the times' but there is not one more surprising than this. As it was asked with reference to the astounding array of good husbands, fathers, citizens, etc. whom we meet in monumental existence in our churchyards, where all the bad ones were buried, so we are disposed to ask in these days, when we contemplate the number of houses in course of erection for the rich, where are the poor to be housed? One would think that there was no increase of population, lower down than the classes which rejoice in £500 a year, or that there was something of so cumulative a character in the times that every man must needs be on the look-out for the means of expending a larger income than he has heretofore had facilities for scattering abroad. But there is a fatal error in all this. An age of progress it may be but not of financial progress. Retrenchment is the order of the day. We are fain to live over our shops. The trade of London is not men on the lookout for splendid suburban villas. There are enough and more than enough already in existence — unfurnished houses which we shall not soon see furnished — shells which will not speedily be ready for occupation. But the poor want dwelling places. Whilst we are exhausting our ingenuity to supply our villas with 'every possible convenience' we are leaving our working classes to the enjoyment of every possible inconvenience, in wretched shells to which men of substance would not consign their beasts of burden.

It is a letter of some importance, for it emphasises that differences existed not only between regions but also between different kinds of housing. We shall later have further evidence that sometimes the course of villa-building differed considerably from that of cottage-building. It also reminds us of the speculative element that was so strong in building, and which made it so especially vulnerable to credit crises. Another writer made the same point :

The builder no longer works for his customers but for the market. Like every other capitalist he is compelled to have finished articles in the market. While formerly a builder had perhaps three or four houses building at a time for speculation, he must now buy a large plot of ground . . . build from 100 to 200 houses on it, and thus embark on an enterprise which exceeds his resources twenty to fifty times. The funds are procured through mortgaging and the money is placed at the disposal of the contractor as the buildings proceed. Then, if a crisis comes along and interrupts the payment of the advance instalments, the entire enterprise generally collapses. At best, the houses remain unfinished until better times arrive; at the worst they are sold at auction for half their cost. Without speculative building, and on a large scale at that, no contractor can get along today. The profit from just building is extremely small. His main profit comes from raising the ground-rent, from careful selection and skilled utilization of the building terrain. It is by this method of speculation anticipating the demand for houses that almost the whole of Belgravia and Tyburnia, and the countless thousands of villas round London have been built.

The writer was Marx. The facts came from the Report of the Select Committee on the Bank Acts, Part 1, 1857.[31]

We have already mentioned the paucity of data on building in the fifties, but despite this the evidence summarised in Figures 4.3 and 4.5 indicates fairly clearly that there was considerable activity for a few years between the great railway peak of 1848 and the Crimean War in 1854. Most of this evidence is for house-building, but there is other evidence that the peak was paralleled in industrial investment. As we shall shortly see, the course of house-building around Manchester echoes pretty faithfully the course of investment in the textile industry, while house-building in South Wales bears a striking resemblance to what we know of investment in the coal industry. Before considering these matters further we may take a quick glance at some of the salient features of the years, so that we shall be in a better position to assess the importance of the pattern that is beginning to emerge.

The depression of the late forties was uneven in its incidence, for, apart from anything else, some export demands were still high. The volume of cotton exports was higher in 1848 than in 1847. Generally there was high unemployment, dear corn and falling incomes, and this meant a fall in domestic demand. But some raw material prices were also lower, while the bank rate, which had reached 8 per cent in October 1847, was down to 4 per cent when 1848 began, to 3 per cent before it ended. With rising overseas demand, a moderate fall in prices, a low Bank rate and a still rising population, there was considerable inducement for the industrialists to view the future with some hope even if, for the ordinary worker, the prospects seemed bleak. Between 1848 and 1853 the value of our exports almost doubled, and so showed a more rapid rise than at any other time in the nineteenth century. It was most spectacular in the case of foodstuffs whose value rose from £2·1 m. in 1848 to £8·4 m. in 1856. During the same period, total exports increased from £52·8 m. to £115·8 m. Exports of finished manufactures and metals increased appreciably.

This rocketing overseas demand was due largely to the discovery of gold, first in California (1848) and then in Australia (1851). Maritime industrial Britain was, of all countries, the most able both to produce and to carry the goods that the newly rich communities, expanding with huge inflows of immigrants, urgently demanded. The whole economy was stimulated, and much of the gold that flowed in soon flowed out again to pay for our own imports. Even so, real wages rose and credit was abundant. Bank rate hovered between 2 and 3 per cent from November 1848 until June 1853, and stood at 2 per cent for most of 1852. There was a pretty general boom in investment and, as we have seen, there is evidence that this included a boom in house-building which in some areas was of large proportions.

We can obtain some interesting insight into the relationship between building and the rest of the economy by looking at the cotton industry during this period. More than any other, it had set the pace of the economy during the first half of the century. By 1850 it was beginning to give way to the iron industry, partly because of the demands for machinery exports made possible by our foreign loans. For all that, it was still very much an expanding industry, and an important feature of its expansion in the fifties is that it was breaking into new markets. In 1831-5 India imported an annual average of just over 14 million lb. of cotton piece goods from England, compared with its own production of 360 million lb., but by 1856-60 — a quarter of a century later — India's own production had fallen to 295 million lb. while its imports from England had increased over eleven-fold. The industry's general rate of expansion was less rapid than this: but the total exports of piece goods doubled between 1840 and 1850, and doubled again by 1860.[32]

This remarkable growth was made possible by an expanding labour force and increased mechanisation aided by other innovations both managerial and institutional. The joint-stock Acts helped the introduction of the newest machinery, and it is partly this that explains how productivity was able to increase. In the three years centred on 1845 there were 190,000 workers operating an average of 100 spindles each. Output per spindle was 27 lb., and output per worker 2700 lb. Fifteen years later, on the eve of the Cotton Famine, 248,000 workers looked after 120 spindles each. Output per spindle was 30 lb., and output per worker nearly 3700 lb. The average wage-cost per lb. of yarn was 2·1d. in 1860, compared with 2·3d. in 1845, while for cotton goods the average wage-cost per lb. fell from 3·5d. to 2·9d. in the same period.[33] Thus production increased faster than wages in both the spinning and the weaving and manufacturing side of business. The total horse-power in the industry more than trebled in the fifties, while the total employment rose from 331,000 to 452,000. Machinery was not, in any long-term sense, displacing the worker, but rather was so increasing the possible output per worker that the overall demand for labour was increasing even though the death of backward firms often created local un-employment. Increasing productivity had its parallel in an increased demand. Home trade rose in the fifties from £17·6 m., to £23·2 m., but exports rose from £28·3 m., to £52·0 m., and the multiplier effect on the British economy was instrumental in providing the growth that followed. In particular we have to remember the huge demands on the iron industry for textile machinery that came at a time when home railway construction and maintenance were running at high levels, when the iron ship was on its way in — thereby increasing not only the demand for iron but also the speed and cheapness with which migrants and merchandise could travel the seas — and when industrial and transport developments in Europe and America were demanding British labour, capital and materials.

The investment boom in the Lancashire cotton industry began

with the post-1848 recovery, and reached its first peak in 1854, as is shown by the following table.[34]

| | New Factories | | | | Additions | | | |
	Cotton	Woollen Worsted Flax, etc.	Silk	All Textile	Cotton	Woollen Worsted Flax, etc.	Silk	All Textile
1851	88	123		211	43			89
1852	109	95	20	229	29	39		69
1853	130	101	20	255	37	34	3	74
1854	156		64	318	33			49
1855	87	86	16	195	4	15	1	21
1856	123	87	31	247	22	13		36

Based on *Reports of Factory Inspectors, Accounts and Papers*, 1852–3, vol. xl; 1854, vol. xix; 1854–5, vol. xv; 1856, vol. xviii; 1857 (sess. 1), vol. iii.

In 1851–2 there was a dip in exports, but at home there was a boom. Raw material prices were rising only slightly, but cloth prices rose more rapidly. Profits rose, interest rates were low and the incentive to invest was so high that factories were built more rapidly than they could be supplied with machinery.[35] We have already seen that around this time the Manchester area also witnessed a house-building boom. Some of the indices are shown in Figure 4·9.

Late in 1853 the tide began to turn. Price inflation had appeared in most industries. Bad harvests and the threat of war drove the Bank rate up to 5 per cent, making investment less attractive. The Australian market was overstocked, and this was but one manifestation of the over-production that had occurred, far outstripping demand. As each mill-owner scrambled for as large a portion of the growing market as he could get, capacity and output expanded so much that the market was not big enough. At the same time, organised labour, knowing that production and profits were rising faster than wages, pressed for a higher reward and the great Cotton Strike began. It was estimated that 50,000 workers withheld their labour. Whether it was, in economic terms, a justified strike is doubtful, for the 'profits' contained the returns on a vastly increased amount of capital, but it is certain that the strike was a foolish one. It came at a time when the mill-owners were eager to see overall production lowered and the strikers played the masters' game. Total output during the year was, in fact, higher than ever before, but the rate of increase was much slackened. The number of building plans approved in Preston, where the strike began, fell by 50 per cent and the Manchester area saw a severe fall in house-building, due partly no doubt to the reduced need of providing for new labour, partly to the strike reducing workers' incomes and their effective demand for housing, partly to the Bank rate (which was at

5 or 5½ per cent throughout 1854) making house-building less attractive, and partly to the credit scarcity which the Bank rate reflected. Industrial building in the textile area reached its peak in this year, but it is interesting to note that the peak in additions to existing buildings came in the previous year. This may be an aggregation phenomenon, or it may reflect the tendency for 'additions' to represent smaller projects than 'new factories', and consequently the shorter completion time involved. In any case, 1855 saw the figures of both additions and new factories at marked troughs. It was a period of falling cloth prices but rising raw cotton prices. The number of unoccupied factories rose, but building continued, rising in 1856 to a level not far short of that in 1853. Hughes has argued[36] that it was a case of the weaker firm going to the wall, and leaving room for the expansion of the efficient. Although profits were low, production was not, and hopes were reasonably high for those who had the will and knowledge to turn innovation and its new tests of efficiency to their advantage. Even so, there remained an excess capacity which was probably bigger than it might otherwise have been simply because expectations were high.

The Crimean War affected industry in various ways. Some were hit badly, but the iron industry and some textile industries benefited from military orders and innovations. An explicit reference to the impact on housing in Bradford is given in Appendix 5. On the cotton industry, the impact was mixed. When peace came, exports rose, but home demand fell, partly because of the direct effect of the cessation of military orders for cotton goods, and partly because of the indirect multiplier effects of the cessation of orders for other manufactures. Expectations were so thwarted that in 1857 the cotton industry was working short-time. Despite the continued upsurge in America, and the second spurt in our exports in 1856–7, home prices were falling and there was no marked revival in domestic investment. Bankruptcies, which had been at a trough in 1853, were now beginning to become frequent again, for although there was abundant credit it was available only at high interest rates. Speculation was again exacting the surrender of caution and cash in exchange for ill-secured promises, and bankers were foremost in favouring high yields to the low-risk securities which paid so poorly. This was true not only of British companies, for there was investment too in the mighty U.S. railway schemes. In the first half of 1856 the Bank rate fell gradually to 4½ per cent, but autumn brought a sharp rise to 7 per cent. The following year saw the same pattern, but now conditions were tighter and the fall in the earlier part of 1857 took the rate no lower than 5½ per cent.

Into this strained atmosphere came the news that some of the American rail bond-holders were not to receive their interest. The bond-holders foreclosed and associated banks collapsed. The result was the October crisis in America, and the collapse of British discount houses associated with the American companies. Bank rate rose to 10 per cent to protect the reserve which had fallen to a mere half million pounds. The 1844 Act was suspended, and only by an excessive note issue was it possible to save the country from a greater disaster than that which actually beset it. 1858 saw severe distress, but at this critical moment various factors — not the least being the fruits of our heavy investments in India and the Colonies — came to our aid by giving the textile industry a second injection of high demand. Again there was the prospect of falling raw material prices, and higher profits. A Bank rate as low as $2\frac{1}{2}$ per cent by the end of 1858 favoured further expansion, and the inventory cycle of the early and mid-fifties gave way to another, in which investment was being accelerated by the integration of spinning and weaving under one roof. The Indian boom, the absence of full-scale competition from abroad, the cheapening of supplies and a low rate of interest brought about a new boom exceeding that of 1850–4. One firm which 'in 1856 . . . would not have valued their concern at above 5/- a spindle, yet, in the next two years . . . made in each year an amount equal to 20 per cent on the capital employed'.[37] To such prosperity was added the influence of new company legislation, simplifying the process of investment. Whereas eight new joint-stock companies were registered in the English cotton industry in 1856, and only another eleven during 1857–9, the first year of the new decade saw 45 registrations and in 1861 there were 63 — a number exceeding the total formed in the next ten years.[38] The total number of cotton-factories rose from 2210 in 1856 to 2887 in 1861, while house-building, at its trough in 1857, rose in sympathy as both population and incomes responded to the prosperity of the region. The key variables are graphed in Figure 4.9.

It ended with the Cotton Famine, originating in the American Civil War:

> Oh dear! iv yon Yankees could only just see
> Heaw they're clemmin' an' starvin' poor weavers loike me.
> Aw think they'd soon settle the'r bother, an' strive
> To send us some cotton to keep us alive.[39]

But 'yon Yankees' were not the sole cause of the acute distress so indelibly printed in the history of the cotton towns. The years before had been too good, and the industry had once again over-expanded and over-traded, this time with an even greater use than before of credit. It was not the only industry to expand in this way, and the increasing scarcity of credit is reflected in the gradual

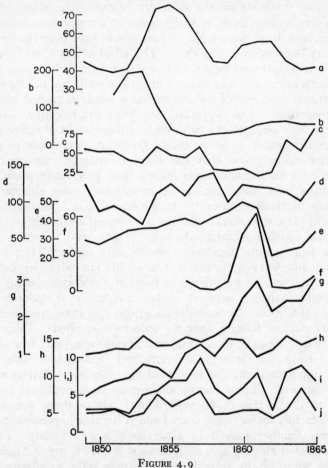

FIGURE 4.9

(a) Average Price of Wheat, U.K. (shillings per imperial quarter). *B.H.S.*, p. 488.
(b) Manchester Regional House-building Index (Appendix 4).
(c) Emigration from G.B. to U.S.A. ('000). Thomas (1), p. 282.
(d) Index of Bankruptcies, G.B. (1913 = 100). Hoffmann. See *B.H.S.*, pp. 245–6.
(e) Index of Cotton Yarn Output, G.B. (1913 = 100). Hoffmann.
(f) Number of Joint Stock Companies registered in the English Cotton Industry, Farnie, p. 497.
(g) Cotton Exports, G.B. ('00 m. lb.). Ellison, table 1.
(h) Exports of Finished Iron and Steel Goods, U.K. (£'000). Thomas, p. 293.
(i) Maximum Bank Rate. %.
(j) Minimum Bank Rate. %.

increase of the Bank rate from 3 per cent in January 1860 to 6 per cent by mid-November and to 8 per cent the following February.

D 2

It was just unfortunate that the cotton industry, so over-stretched and with profits already on the wane, was the one most dependent for its raw materials on the Southern States. The shock of war and its implications came to the industry at a time when credit was strained, and stocks were high. There would have been the familiar inventory depression in any case. The effect of the Civil War was to make it deeper and larger, and to enrich those who could profit from rising prices at the expense of those who could not be employed. The general economy of the country as a whole remained buoyant and prosperous. The depression was local and selective. Manufacturers with large stocks, who might otherwise have suffered the usual consequences of an inventory downturn, were able to profit from the rising prices that the Famine brought. Brokers who worked on a commission basis reaped their percentage profit, and speculators lined their pockets by anticipating price changes and financing blockade-running.[40] In Liverpool and Manchester, the centres of the cotton market and the commercial and credit organisation from which Lancashire drew its finances and to which all of Europe paid tribute, handsome profits were made.[41] But in the spinning and weaving towns it was a different tale. In Ashton-under-Lyne, and its neighbouring town of Stalybridge, along with their satellite villages, only one worker in eight was at work full-time in May 1862, while 36,000 out of its 67,000 operatives were working for three days or fewer a week.[42] 5000 were stopped. Taking the cotton districts as a whole we find that in this same year, over 18,000 persons emigrated, some to America and Australia,[43] while 4000 found employment in the neighbouring counties. Marriages and births declined. These factors alone must have exercised a sharp effect on the course of house-building: but to them was added another factor, for as wages ceased and it became impossible to pay the rent, families moved to share each other's houses. Empty houses existed side by side with serious overcrowding.[44] Building societies were hit in several ways. Funds were withdrawn, and investors failed to maintain their payments. At the same time the demand for loans fell sharply, and existing borrowers defaulted on repayments.[45] Landlords lost rent.

Both house- and mill-building fell. In the different towns of the cotton area, specialising in different work and affected to different degrees, building declined at different times. We have precise data for few, and these relate chiefly to plans which do not always locate the actual downturns in activity with the certainty one would seek, but there is abundant evidence of a sharp fall in activity in house-building in 1862 and 1863 in the manufacturing towns. Yet in Manchester itself the number of houses actually erected rose from 352 in the year ended April 30th, 1861, to 662 the following year, 652 the next year, and to 861 in the year ending in April 1864. The poverty of the mill-worker and the prosperity of the 'city' was even thus apparent.

It is not surprising that the Famine also reduced the amount of mill-building. Around Blackburn in the autumn of 1862, 40 new mills were 'ready, or nearly ready, for starting . . . when trade revives'.[46] Elsewhere, too, the Famine caught building at its peak and sharply cried halt. The number of new joint-stock companies in the industry fell from 63 in 1861 to 3 in 1862, and except for 1865 (when it rose to 12) the annual figure remained below ten for the remainder of the decade.

Yet there was room for optimism. One effect of the Famine was to solve the problem of inventory stocks in a way that brought profit to several manufacturers, and these, knowing that labour was cheap and that times would improve, were able to use the lull in activity to advantage. By 1863 the mills left half-completed at the beginning of the crisis were being worked upon again, existing establishments were being modernised and orders for new mills were placed. It was not a great building boom, but there seems to have been a substantial amount of industrial building, arising out of low labour costs and high expectations, while house-building remained low (except in the prosperous city) simply because wages did not allow the rent to be paid, and the direction of migration had been reversed. The three towns of Ashton-under-Lyne, Stalybridge and Dukinfield embarked on the joint construction of reservoirs for the purpose of improving the water supply and providing work for the unemployed.[47]

This account of the economy of the cotton region has indicated some of the ways in which industrial and house-building are geared to both the fortunes of local industry and the movements of the national economy. We now look very briefly at South Wales which was seeing the coal-mining industry encroaching upon the importance of the iron industry, and then at London, before pulling in some threads.

In 1850 the magnet of the South Wales labour market was undoubtedly the iron industry of Merthyr Tydfil. It was, however, an industry that was producing a diminishing share of the nation's increasing output. Whereas the Welsh make of pig-iron in 1847 was 720,000 tons, representing over a third of the U.K. output, by 1852 it had fallen by about 3 per cent, and amounted to a mere quarter of the U.K. production.[48] This proportion was maintained throughout the fifties, but by the mid-sixties its make of 1,100,000 tons was only 19 per cent of the nation's total. The coal industry, on the other hand, though producing less than a seventh of the country's total in 1854 was slowly increasing its importance. Although closely related to each other, in that about 15 per cent of the nation's coal went into the production of iron, and the growth of rail transport and the iron ship made demands on both coal and iron, the two industries sometimes had differing fortunes, due partly to the greater price flexibility of coal. The South Wales productions of pig-iron and coal are shown for the period 1854–65 in Fig. 4.10.

There is no need to analyse the determinants of building in this area as closely as those of building in Lancashire, because in fact much of it would be repetition. Both of these industries were more sluggish in their response to demand changes than was the cotton industry, and consequently the character of the inventory cycle was different, but once this is appreciated the analysis is much the same. The slow reaction of output to demand resulted in violent price movements, bringing large profits and encouraging investment.[49] This was especially so in 1853–4, before 1866 and in 1872–4. We have house-building data for only Cardiff and Swansea before 1855, and these show steep declines from 1851 (the first recorded year) to 1854 and 1856 respectively. On the other hand these ports were not mining towns, and although most of their trade was geared to coal and iron, there were more local factors — such as dock construction — still important in affecting the demand for new houses. Aberdare, a town to the west of the Merthyr Tydfil, provides some slight evidence of what was happening in the early fifties in the coal areas themselves, for its first recorded housing figure (for 1855) was higher than at any subsequent time before 1914, and it is not unreasonable to infer that probably the actual coal-mining areas saw a housing boom around the years 1853–4. Aberdare also saw housing booms in 1864–6 and 1873–4, both of them coinciding with the investment booms (over a wider area) just mentioned.

On the other hand, there are reasons for not expecting too great a correlation between house-building and investment in coal mining. Sinking a mine could take several years, and changes in demand were more likely to be reflected in price changes, and so in wage changes, than in immediate changes in output. The same tendency arises from the fact that a mine is one of the few examples of a plant whose capacity slowly increases as it is used, at least until it nears exhaustion or technical difficulties arise. As the maze of underground tunnels grows, so, up to a point, can employment and output grow, without any appreciable investment. Thus the demand for houses, depending upon the growth and income of the labour force, can hardly be expected to echo the pattern of investment as faithfully as in the cotton region.

For this reason it is interesting to notice that the South Wales

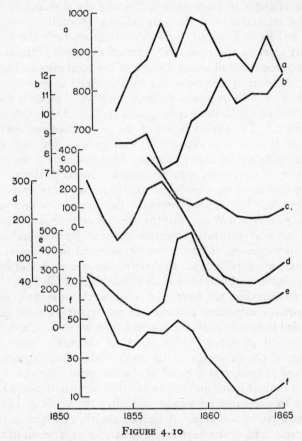

FIGURE 4.10

(a) Pig-iron Output, South Wales ('ooo tons). *B.H.S.*, p. 131.
(b) Coal Output, South Wales (m. tons). *B.H.S.*, p. 115.
(c) House-building in Aberdare. Appendix 4.
(d) House-building in Cardiff. *Ibid.*
(e) House-building in Swansea. *Ibid.*
(f) House-building Index for South Wales Coalfield. *Ibid.*

housing index, for all its defects in the early years, arising chiefly from its inadequate coverage, moves in much the same way as coal wage-rates. These tended to fall around 1853, but then to rise until the crisis of 1857, when another decline set in. A spurt in activity, increasing the demand for labour, saw a rise in wage-rates in 1862 which continued until late 1866. The end of the Franco-Prussian war inaugurated a boom that saw a very large increase between 1869 and 1873.[50] A glance at Figure 4.5 shows that this description could be applied almost as well to the course of housing.

These changes in wage-rates, reflecting the demand for labour, which was attracted from the surrounding agricultural areas, from Ireland, and from England, were dependent on both the home and the export sides of the economy. Actual exports of British coal in 1855 accounted for well under a tenth of the total output, but almost a half of the output was absorbed by the metal industries. These were influenced by overseas demand both in that they made the machinery that made the exports, and in that they exported their own produce. The export boom of the late forties and early fifties saw a doubling in our exports of iron goods, and so, approximately, a doubling of that particular foreign demand for coal. A recession in 1854–5 gave way to another boom peaking in 1859, and a hesitant upswing that began in 1862 rose more speedily later in the decade. We cannot measure the precise impact of these movements on South Wales, but the general picture indicates clearly that, directly and indirectly, overseas demand for coal and iron was exerting an increasing influence on the demand for colliers, on coal wage-rates, on migration into the coal-fields and on house-building. This is a matter to be examined in greater detail later on.

The relationship we have just suggested must not, however, obscure equally important factors. In particular we must note that the recorded booms in coal investment began when the Bank rate was low and credit abundant. The boom of the early fifties, arising largely out of the demands of the metal industries, expanded both capacity and output, but the end of the Crimean War saw a decline in demand both at home and overseas. Excess production and rising stocks led to pressures on wages, and after the crisis of 1857 there were substantial reductions. A similar position existed in the iron industry, and it has even been argued that the depression in the iron trade in 1857 was the origin of the commercial crisis. Certainly, with its high stocks it was in no position to stand up to a monetary crisis. Hughes has usefully summarised the contrast with cotton in the remainder of our period:[51]

New investment in coal and iron did not revive substantially until the early 1860's when rising prices again prevailed. In the period from the end of the Crimean War until 1860 capacity created during the boom of the early 1850's, together with war-time investment, seems to have been mainly sufficient to provide for current demand. This differed from the experience of textiles, where 1858–60 saw a renewed expansion of capacity.

It would seem to follow from this that considerable excess capacity existed in iron and coal by 1856. The decline in investment in iron and coal after 1855 helps to account for the weakness of effective demand in 1856–7, together with the 1858 depression and the uneven recovery of 1859–60. Excess capacity had to be utilized in iron and coal before the domestic economy's expansion induced another increase of prices and investment in those industries in the early 1860's.

The conclusion that emerges from this comparison of the two regions is that the time-shapes of building differed for three distinct reasons. Exogenous factors exerted different effects, as was certainly the case with the Cotton Famine. The reaction to common influences was different, due partly to the actual structure of the industries. And finally, while an increase in demand for textiles led fairly speedily to increased capacity and employment, and so affected the demand for housing partly through a fairly rapid expansion of the labour force, in the coal industry the first impact on housing was through higher wages of existing workers. The impact through the immigration of additional workers was lagged and less spectacular.

When we look at London, which was dominated by no single industry, we have a somewhat different picture. We have already quoted some current views on the behaviour of house-building in the metropolis at the end of the forties. There is also evidence that there was another period of fairly high activity in the middle fifties. Tooke and Newmarch speak of the 'enormous extension of building enterprise in London in 1853–55' which 'drew to the Metropolis its undue proportion of workmen'.[52] But it was overdone. In *The Builder* of January 31st, 1857, a letter blamed the depressed state of the London building trade upon the high prices of provisions, and the large amount of war-taxes.

A very large number of houses in and around the suburbs of London are finished, and fit for occupation; but the supply is greater than the demand, not that London has been depopulated . . . the population is still increasing, but the cause lies here. The war has enhanced the price of provisions . . . these must be obtained at every other sacrifice. The working man who formerly had two or three comfortable rooms, at the present time makes shift with one. Many of the middle class give up their houses and take apartments. . . .

There had, of course, been a large amount of speculative building in the trade, which had made it vulnerable to any decline in demand, such as that which would come through a rise in the price of food. It was argued in the press of the day that the level of building was

low because capital could be employed in more favourable investments[53] and because the building operatives, insisting on higher
wages and shorter weeks, were driving up prices too high, but
these are factors that have to be taken in the context of current
demand. If this had been higher, then other forms of investment
might not have been so much more favourable.

It is at this time that Cooney's series of data for Surveyors' Fees
begins,[54] and it seems reasonable to infer that in fact it begins in a
trough. In 1858 *The Builder* lamented that 'the check . . . still
continues', but as Cooney's index shows an upswing was on the way.
In July 1863 a short article had this to say, as it described the high
activity in London and elsewhere:

> Many important works are in progress at the present time. Although
> the chief lines of railway have been completed, there are still in course of
> construction branches and extremities which give employment to a large
> army of work-people; besides there are the metropolitan lines, the Thames
> bridge and embankment, and the gigantic main drainage works. In the
> centre of the City an almost entire rebuilding is going forward; in places
> which are noticed by few wayfarers, important buildings are being raised,
> at an immense cost. In the suburbs acres of ground are in these summer
> months being built upon; and in all directions spacious and substantial
> churches, chapels and schools are being erected. Nor are these great
> operations confined to the metropolis, for in nearly all the chief towns a
> wonderful extension is going on.

So was reflected the general prosperity of the times, for the
Cotton Famine had little impact on the general economy. 'Iron and
steel' production rose about a steady trend throughout the fifties and
early sixties, with only very minor dips in 1858 and 1861, and a very
minor peak in 1864. While 1860 and 1861 were years of low iron-ore
production, there had been a substantial rise by 1864, and bankruptcies were comparatively few. Shipbuilding was rising, railway-
building was high, and share prices more than doubled between 1859
and 1864. After the depression of 1857 most of the country was
now full of optimism and energy. Commercial treaties, company
formation and expanding markets spelt prosperity, and it was to this
that the 'wonderful extension' was due. But it also created strain.
Indeed the general tone of the economy was so far from depressed in
the early sixties that bad harvests and the need to import corn once
again proved a serious embarrassment to our reserves. In an attempt
to overcome the Cotton Famine purchases were being made from
India, Egypt and Brazil, and these had to be paid for with specie
rather than manufactures. Thus bad harvests and the cotton
famine called heavily on our reserves at a time when expansion was

requiring more and more credit. The Bank rate rose. Further drains were due to the withdrawal of gold by France to pay for public works, and by the United States to pay for war, while relief in Lancashire must also be added to the bill. By May 5th, 1864, Bank rate reached 9 per cent compared with 2 per cent in July 1862, while the building industry was reeling under a cannonade of strikes, coming this time when labour was so scarce that it was necessary to allow shorter men into the army than hitherto.[55]

This brief study of different regions is useful for several reasons, and probably the most important of them is that it emphasises not only that the course of building differed in different regions — which we were able to observe from the brick index — but that within a region both local and national forces were at work. A good harvest would tend to stimulate building in the manner already described. Essentially it would be a national influence. Everywhere corn would be cheaper. But its secondary effects would differ between regions, for different goods are made in different places, and have different income elasticities of demand. A booming economy never grows evenly, while affluence may kill an industry as easily as it may make one.

A general overseas expansion would have only a partially similar effect, for clearly the principal impact would be felt in those regions producing the goods that were in highest demand as exports. Here the need for labour would soon rise, and the processes already familiar from the above account would take place. The prosperities of these regions would have secondary effects throughout the economy.

The effect of war could be even more varied, in that regions with industries geared to war needs would be stimulated while others might find difficulties arising out of raw material or other shortages. Quite apart from this, war would also have an effect on the credit situation.

Credit for house-building was raised largely on a local basis, but the national picture, and such factors as the level of Bank rate, had their influence. This is a matter that we shall examine in more detail later. For the time being it is sufficient to note that usually, but not always, a credit crisis left its mark in all areas, both by drying up the supply of short-term loans available to builders and by so reducing the pace of the economy that the demands for the products of almost every industry declined, so that employment tended to fall and depression to set in.

Thus even national or international events had differing consequences in different regions. The local factors were even more

divergent.   Different industries had different histories and characteristics.   Their production periods differed and their inventory cycles
were quite special to them.   Labour disputes, upsetting both
production and incomes were often confined to a particular region,
while innovations were introduced at different times.   Briefly, the
outcome of the interaction of these forces may be summarised in the
statement that when the demand for a region's product increased so
that new labour was needed, or when the prosperity of existing
workers increased so that they could live under better conditions, a
local housing boom would set in provided that materials and credit
were available at reasonable prices.   The boom would cease in one
of two ways.   On the one hand the local demand might become
exhausted because of a cessation of immigration, a wage-reduction or
over-building leading to empty houses.   On the other hand the
combination of house and industrial investment coinciding in their
upward swings in many regions might, after perhaps quite a long
time, so strain the structure of credit that some exogenous event
would lead to a credit crisis, and the reduction of building almost
everywhere.[56]   Above all we have to keep in mind the importance, in
a subsistence economy, of the price of food.   The consumption
decision was essentially a two-stage decision, with an allocation of
residual income after essential food had been bought.   This point,
implicit in so much historical writing, and explicit in the letter we
have quoted, must form an essential plank in any adequate theory
of growth and building cycles.

NOTES TO CHAPTER 4

1. H. A. Shannon, *loc. cit.*

2. R. C. O. Matthews, *A Study in Trade-Cycle History, 1833–42*, Cambridge,
1954, p. 115.

3. *Ibid.*, p. 116.

4. A. K. Cairncross and B. Weber, 'Fluctuations in Building in Great Britain,
1785–1849', *Economic History Review*, vol. ix.

5. Weber's data were incorporated in an index of house-building covering two
towns in 1851, and increasing to six by 1856 and thirty-four by 1900. B. Weber,
'A New Index of Residential Construction and Long Cycles in House-building in
Great Britain, 1838–1950', *Scottish Journal of Political Economy*, vol. ii, 1955, pp.
104–32.

The data for South Wales appear in J. Hamish Richards and J. Parry Lewis,
'Housing-Building in the South Wales Coalfields, 1851–1913', *The Manchester
School*, vol. xxxiv, 1956.

Manchester data, and a general revision of other material, appears in J. Parry
Lewis, 'Indices of House-Building in the Manchester Conurbation, South Wales,

and Great Britain, 1851–1913', *Scottish Journal of Political Economy*, vol. viii, 1961, pp. 148–56. The compilation of the indices is described further in Appendix 4, which also gives the data for some of the towns. See also A. G. Kenwood, 'Residential Building Activity in North-Eastern England, 1853–1913', *The Manchester School*, May 1963.

6. K. Maywald, 'An Index of Building Costs in the United Kingdom 1845–1938', *The Economic History Review*, s.s., vii, 2, 1954, pp. 187–203.

7. E. W. Cooney, 'Long Waves in Building in the British Economy of the Nineteenth Century', *The Economic History Review*, s.s., xiii, 2, 1960, pp. 257–269.

8. E. W. Cooney, 'Capital Exports and Investment in Building in Britain and the U.S.A., *Economica*, N.S., xvi, 1949.

9. Seymour J. Price, *Building Societies: their Origin and Function*, London, 1958. Most of my data on building societies have been taken from this work. A new book is E. J. Cleary: *The Building Society Movement*, London, 1965.

10. The Droylsden (Manchester) Building Society (1792) was to build houses for £63. The Amicable (Birmingham) was to build at a cost not exceeding £80. It had twenty-seven members and a subscription of 5s. per fortnight. (Price.)

11. L. E. Pressnell, *Country Banking in the Industrial Revolution*, Oxford, 1956. pp. 339–40.

12. The scheme was due to Arthur Scratchley, a mathematician employed by a life assurance society.

13. R. Postgate, *The Builders' History*, London, 1923, is the most useful source of information on this subject.

14. These years embrace the period of authorisation rather than of completion. See G.R.S., pp. 257-8.

15. Matthews, *op. cit.*, pp. 131, 134–5.

16. Redford, *Labour Migration*, p. 41. The use of 'masons' here underlines that many houses were built of stone, especially in the north.

17. *Ibid.*, p. 87.

18. Matthews, *op. cit.*, p. 115.

19. See, for example, G. F. Foster (ed.), *Ashton-under-Lyne*, Centenary Volume published for the Borough Council, 1947, especially p. 32. A similar volume for a town adjacent to Ashton-under-Lyne is J. W. March (ed.), *Stalybridge*, 1957, containing much fascinating data. Probably detailed researches in the copious archives of these towns would reveal most useful information on the course and determinants of building.

20. The data are as follows:

	1830	1831	1832	1833	1834	1835	1836	1837	1838	1839	1840	1841	1842	1843
(a)	1310	2197	2053	3055	3447	4937	7150	7185	9510	7933	10,281	12,948	11,628	18,327
(b)	69	106	109	166	206	269	361	375	486	423	530	632	546	831
(c)	189	207	188	184	167	183	198	192	196	188	194	205	213	221

(a) = Balance owing to depositors (£). (b) = Number of depositors. (c) = Average deposit (£).

Years ending November 20th, except for first 'year' which began in August 1829, and so lasted approximately 15 months. Based on data in *The First Report on the Large Towns*, 1844, Appendix, p. 82.

The data for malt used by brewers and others comes from *British Parliamentary*

Papers, 1831-2, 223, xxxiv (27) ; 1833, 95, xxxiii (183), etc. These papers contain malt data for a large number of centres. On the whole they conform fairly closely to brick production data.

21. Matthews, *op. cit.*, p. 117. A great deal of vivid description exists in a variety of places, but perhaps the most outspoken is to be found in F. Engels, *The Condition of The Working Class in England*, 1844. English translation by Henderson & Chaloner, Oxford, 1958. See also William Cooke Taylor, *Notes of a Tour in the Manufacturing Districts of Lancashire, in a series of letters, etc.*, London, 1842.

22. Factory Inspectors' Report, September 1841, p. 7.

23. J. D. Chambers, *The Workshop of the World*, 1961, p. 161.

24. *Ibid.*, pp. 56-7, 112.

25. G.R.S., p. 331.

26. Chambers, *op. cit.*, p. 162.

27. G.R.S., p. 339.

28. Report, May 1846, pp. 16-17.

29. G.R.S., p. 340.

30. A copy of this letter was found in one of Weber's files.

31. Karl Marx, *Capital*, vol. ii, pp. 233-4 in the edition published by the Foreign Languages Publishing House, Moscow, 1957. Book II, chap. xii in other texts. Marx cites the Select Committee Evidence, Questions 5413-18, 5435-36.

32. T. Ellison, *The Cotton Trade of Great Britain*, 1886, p. 63.

33. Ellison, *op. cit.*, pp. 68-69.

34. Based on Reports of Factory Inspectors, Accounts and Papers, 1852-1853, vol. xl; 1854, vol. xlx; 1854-5, vol. xv; 1856, vol. xviii; 1857 (sess. 1), vol. viii.

35. J. R. T. Hughes, *Fluctuations in Trade, Industry and Finance, 1850-1860*. Oxford, 1960, pp. 76-77. A great deal of this chapter is derived from this book.

36. Hughes, *op cit.*, p. 83.

37. G. F. Foster, *op. cit.*, p. 43.

38. D. A. Farnie, *The English Cotton Industry, 1850-1896*, 1953, M.A. Thesis in Manchester University Library.

39. From a poem by the Stalybridge poet Samuel Laycock, quoted by Harry Jones in *A Short History of Stalybridge*, printed in J. W. March, *op. cit.*

40. W. O. Henderson, *The Lancashire Cotton Famine, 1861-65*, Manchester, 1954, pp. 14-15.

41. *Ibid.*, p. 2.

42. Foster, *op. cit.*, p. 44.

43. Henderson, *op. cit.*, p. 117.

44. *Ibid.*, p. 19.

45. Price, *op. cit.*, pp. 138-9.

46. Henderson, *op. cit.*, p. 18.

47. March, *op. cit.*, p. 53.

48. Hughes, *op. cit.*, p. 155.

49. J. H. Morris and L. J. Williams, *The South Wales Coal Industry, 1841-1875*, 1958, p. 79.

50. *Ibid.*, p. 218.

51. Hughes, *op. cit.*, pp. 182-3.

52. Tooke and Newmarch, *A History of Prices*, London, 1838-57, vol. vi, p. 175.

53. See *The Builder* in January–February 1857.

54. *Loc. cit.*

55. *The Builder*, June 11th, 1864.   See also May 14th, 1864.

56. See my papers, 'Building Cycles: A Regional Model and its National Setting', *The Economic Journal*, vol. lxx, September 1960, especially pp. 532–4, and 'Growth and Inverse Cycles: A Two-Country Model', *The Economic Journal*, vol. lxxiv, March 1964.

CHAPTER 5

SOME REGIONAL ASPECTS
OF THE SEVENTIES

THE Great Victorian Depression[1] is a subject on which every-body who looks at the nineteenth century seems to have a view of his own. One of the few common observations is that building rose to a peak in the mid-seventies, a few years after other industries had turned down, and then tumbled into a trough from which it did not emerge until the early nineties. Various explanations of this pattern have been put forward, some of the more convincing hingeing upon the inverse building cycle theory associated with Cairncross, Cooney and Thomas,[2] at which we shall look in later chapters. In this chapter we examine building in certain regions, as a prelude to a more detailed study of the later nineteenth century. In doing so, we begin to reach certain tentative conclusions of our own.

We begin by looking at the fortunes of different industries and the course of building in different towns. The regional differences which we have noticed for earlier periods continued to exist in the seventies, as is demonstrated by Figure 5.1. Here we see the pattern of house-building in several towns, which have been arbitrarily selected from those for which data exist. Bolton had its major peak in 1869. Bradford had a plateau throughout the early seventies, and was almost a perfect inversion of Burton-upon-Trent whose peak came so late in the decade, but not as late as London's which was 1881. On the other hand, several towns exhibited more or less coincident peaks in the mid-seventies. An adequate explanation of these points would involve detailed studies of each town. For this chapter, we shall content ourselves with looking at Glasgow and London, and continuing our examination of the cotton and South Wales coal regions. By doing so we shall be able to develop further ideas about the relationships of regional building activity to the national aggregate, and (in particular) to the course of the Great Victorian Depression.

We have seen that the earlier building cycles were intimately

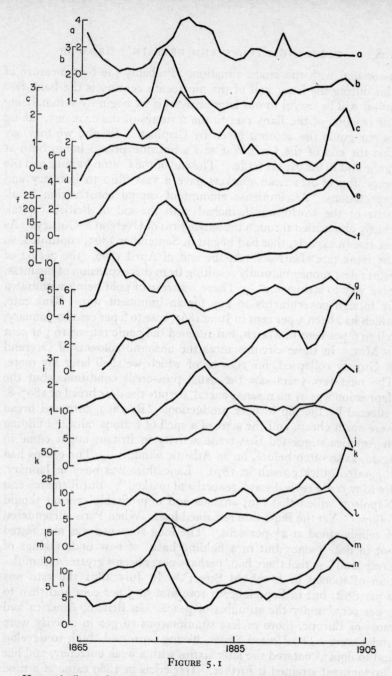

FIGURE 5.1

Houses built or planned in the following towns. See Figure 4.3.

(a) Burton upon Trent ('oo).	(e) Glasgow ('ooo).	(i) London (o,ooo).
(b) Birmingham ('ooo).	(f) Salford ('oo).	(j) Cardiff ('oo).
(c) Liverpool ('ooo).	(g) Bolton ('oo).	(k) Merthyr Tydfil ('o).
(d) Bradford ('ooo).	(h) Rochdale ('oo).	

House-building indices (1901–10 = 10) for the following areas.

(l) South Wales Coalfield. App. 4.   (m) Manchester Conurbation. App. 4.
(n) North-Eastern England. Kenwood.

associated with the credit situation. Probably the best measure of this during the latter half of the nineteenth century is the Bank rate and it will be useful to our later analysis if we begin by summarising the reaction of the Bank rate to the fortunes of the economy, taking as our guide the account given by Clapham. Briefly, we may say that the end of the Civil War saw a not unexpected boom both at home and in the export trade. The end of the Cotton Famine and the reopening of American markets gave a vast fillip to industry and expectations. An immense amount of capital construction in all parts of the world was launched with the aid of British capital, chiefly channelled through the single firm of Overend & Gurney. As the rise in exports, that had begun in September 1865, continued, so the Bank rate also rose. At the end of April 1866, 'the period of rather dear money naturally resulting from this expansion of business, gave way to stringency'.[3] There was fear of gold being withdrawn by foreign governments to pay for an imminent war. Bank rate, which had been 3 per cent in June 1865, rose to 8 per cent by January, fell to 6 per cent in March, but reached the panic rate of 10 per cent in May. In these circumstances the unsound colossus of Overend & Gurney collapsed, for reasons of which we shall later say more. The next few years saw the usual post-crisis conditions, but the depression was by no means general, despite the dear bread of 1867–8, reflected by the dip in beer production. 'By 1869, corn and bread were again cheap, and the start of a spell of furious railway building in America suggested that trade activity in Britain might come in again, as so often before, on an Atlantic wind. . . .   The omens had suggested quick growth in 1870. Lancashire was busy in January. By May trade revival was "general and marked". But Bismarck and Napoleon willed that (an) anxious and unprofitable' period should follow.[4] Yet the Bank rate remained low. When Paris surrendered it calmly stood at $2\frac{1}{2}$ per cent. The long suspense was manifested not in dear money but in a holding back 'of new undertakings of every kind', so that there had 'perhaps never been a greater accumulation of money in Lombard Street'.[5] In July 1871 the rate was 2 per cent, but in September it rose first to 3 per cent and then to 4 per cent, under the stimulus of peace. In Britain, America and most of Europe, more or less simultaneous surges in activity were under way. The United States, having borrowed 'both to develop and to fight',[6] entered the later sixties with a weak currency, and her development strained it further. Her crisis in 1869 came at a time when the Franco-Prussian war was influencing Britain and Europe, while her post-crisis recovery coincided with the impetus of peace in Europe. Her railway-boom continued, and Atlantic immigration, which had fallen sharply in 1868, rose once again to reach a level in 1873 higher than any for twenty years. At the same time, she bought vast quantities of manufactures from Britain, largely on credit. In Germany there was a major boom, especially in the iron industry and building, and land speculation was rife. How some of these factors affected the British economy will be considered shortly, but their combination with internal affairs had an effect which is usefully summarised in Figures 8.2 and 8.3, which show the remarkable leap into activity, and the severity of the reaction after 1873. In May of that year, Austria's boom collapsed, and further collapse and liquidation spread throughout Europe as both confidence and demand were weakened. Possibly the full effect of this on Britain would have been fairly severe in time, but time was not allowed, for in September came news of a crash in New York, arising largely out of excessive railway-building and speculation. The direct effect on the Continent was heavier than in Britain. In November the combined withdrawals of gold by America, France and Germany — because of their internal troubles — and the drawing on Bank deposits by British bankers drove the Bank rate up to 9 per cent, which 'worked perfectly and very fast'.[7] By the year's end it was down to 4½ per cent. There was a banking reserve of over £12 m. 'There had been losses and failures but, as yet, nothing extraordinary or discreditable.'[8] Except for building, the whole economy had turned downwards. By June 1874, the rate was down to 2½ per cent, and although it rose to 6 per cent before the year was over, from January 1875 onwards it fluctuated between 5 per cent and 2 per cent right up to the time, in October 1878, when the discreditable happened, and the City of Glasgow Bank collapsed. The rate, which had been rising steadily from 2½ per cent in May, and was put at 5 per cent in August, rose to 6 per cent, and within six months was down again to 2 per cent. The downturn in the national aggregate of house-building, and in most individual towns, came at a time of low Bank rate, between the crisis of 1873 and the Glasgow crash of five years later. It was not a shortage of credit that caused building to fall from its lofty peak in the seventies.

The key industry of the period is the coal industry, and a brief examination of it, especially in the South Wales area for which we have housing statistics, sheds useful light on a number of other problems. Between 1850 and 1900 United Kingdom coal production grew from 56 million tons to 225 million tons — a quadrupling of output in half a century — while exports of coal, coke and bunker fuel grew from a mere 4 million tons to 58 million tons.[9] In the middle of the century the main demand for coal arose from our own iron industry, but before the century was over it was steam power, in industry and on railways and ships throughout the world, that exerted the real influence.   It was, indeed, the export of coal, more than of any other commodity, that enabled our total exports to grow at all in the last quarter of the century, as is clearly shown by the following table:

	U.K. Coal Production	Exports of Coal, Coke and Bunker Fuel	Value of all Exports	Value of Coal Exports	Col. (4) as per cent of Col. (3)
	Million Tons		£ Million		%
1850	56	4	71	1	2·0
1860	80	8	136	4	2·7
1870	110	14	200	7	3·4
1880	147	24	223	11	4·8
1890	182	39	263	24	9·0
1900	225	58	291	48	16·6

Based on a table in D. A. Thomas, 'The Growth and Direction of our Foreign Trade in Coal during the Last Half-Century', *J.R.S.S.*, September 1903.

Throughout the whole period coal exports rose with a steadiness that at first appears remarkable to one who is used to looking at graphs of industrial fluctuations.   'Four out of every five of the last fifty years show an increase on the preceding year,' wrote D. A. Thomas in 1903.   'Only in one instance, 1877, has the decline shown in any year amounted to over 5 per cent, and then but to very little more.'[10]

The same smooth growth is exhibited by coal output, and has its origin in the inflexibility of production on which we have already commented.   Fluctuations in demand were reflected in price changes in the short run and in supply changes in a long run so long that the annual figures are almost free of any semblance of a cycle.   To sink a new coal mine and to put it in working order took several years, especially if it was deep, and once it had been sunk it had to be kept working if subsidence, water and collapse were not to win the day.[11]   Once capacity had been expanded, in sluggish response to an increase in demand possibly already dampened by rising prices, there was every incentive to use it and to produce, even if prices and profits fell.   When output did fall it was usually the result of labour disputes.[12]

This long period of gestation in the coal industry had a consequence that is not always appreciated for it was this, more than any other factor, that drove up the price of coal, and thereby the price of iron and other products in the boom of the early seventies.   The mechanism of price adjustment in terms of inelastic supply tells only part of the story, for coal wages were related to coal prices, and as scarcity drove them up together, and colliers became better off, they restricted their output.

When, for example, in 1870 the average declared value of coal was about 9s. 6d. a ton, the average output per person employed was 321 tons; but when the price had risen to 17s. in 1874, the average output fell to 235 tons. In South Wales the decrease was from 320 tons to 222 tons.[13] As the price of coal rose, existing workmen produced less, thereby raising both the labour cost and the average overhead-costs of each ton. By expanding the labour force to work the mines to capacity once again the overhead-costs per ton could be restored to their earlier level, but the wage-cost would be higher, and capacity output would be available only at higher prices. In fact, the supply curve shifted to the left, and only the rightward shifting of demand maintained output at its earlier level. Eventually, expanded capacity, by lowering prices, would also lower wages and increase productivity until the next expansion in demand.

The violence of these price changes in coal is seen from the fact that, for example, the index of average declared value of coal exports based on 1886–90 as 100 stood at 103·3 in 1866–70, at 181·5 in 1871–5, and down at 100·6 in 1876–80. The price per ton rose from about 9s. 6d. in 1871 to £1 os. 6d. in 1873. The enormous construction booms, and especially the railway booms, that erupted all over the industrial world around 1870, impinged on the coal industry chiefly through their demands for iron, whose manufacture consumed a third of the nation's coal output. A single ton of pig-iron needed two and half tons of coal. Despite improved techniques that consumed less coal, the iron industry could not obtain all that it required, because of an inelastic supply and an expanding demand for coal as a fuel for steam power. As coal prices rose, both the raw material and the labour costs of the iron industry rose, for the two industries were similarly located and competed for the same men, and the huge demands enabled the increased costs to be passed on as increased prices. A great deal of new capacity was built, but the more there was of this the greater was the competition for men and, above all, coal, and prices rose further. Eventually they rose so much that buyers, many of whom had already had their demands at least partially met, and were feeling the strain of investing in an economy whose costs were rocketing, began to hold off, and the profits of iron began to fall. 'Early in 1873,' writes Rostow,[14] 'before either of the great financial crises of the year, the turning point in iron had appeared. In January "prices are rising for the present, but as new business is not active the stronger tendency is due rather to deficient supply than to increased demand". Puddling furnaces in the north and in South Wales were blown out in January and February; the demand for finished iron was "not as good as expected" in April. Export orders for finished goods were being held off in the hope of a fall in prices: lower prices are still looked for and concessions continue to be slowly made. By the end of the year the demand for railway iron had fallen off sharply, the pressure on coal supplies had relaxed.' The price of coal fell as rapidly as it had risen, wages more slowly adjusted downwards, and the capacity that had been increased to meet a rising demand had to be kept working — if it was not to deteriorate — at almost full-steam. The demand for railway iron ceased, both because of less new construction (although replacements were very important) and because of the use of steel, whose demands on coal were less. On the other hand there were other demands, which did not decline. The use of metals by the engineers was maintained, and if steel had ousted iron in the manufacture of rails, iron had replaced timber in ships. Although the output of pig-iron fell by a tenth in 1874, it rallied in the following year, while output of steel in that year was three times its level in 1870. The Hoffmann index of pig-iron and steel production stood at 21·7 in 1860, 31·3 in 1869, 39·9 in 1872 and 39·8 in 1873. The next year saw a dip to 36·9, but then it rose to 39·5 and in 1878 was at its highest level to date, of 41·8, after which it dipped sharply for a couple of years. This growing activity was allied with greater efficiency and fuel economy, and so its impact on coal was not as great as it might have been, but the transport revolution, especially at sea, was well under way, and although the increased output of coal could be sold only at lower prices and sometimes with cut-throat competition, total output continued to expand with but very brief and very minor recessions.

The coal area in which we have a special interest, partly because of its housing data and partly because of a factor about to emerge, is South Wales. In 1850 it accounted for about an eighth of our total coal exports, in 1870 for almost a third, and in 1880 for two-fifths, when it at last overtook the north-eastern coalfields.[15] Its output was growing rapidly, as is shown by the following table :

	U.K. Output of Coal	S. Wales Output of Coal
	Million Tons	
1860	80	10
1870	110	14
1880	147	21
1890	182	29
1900	225	39

Its growth in the sixties was about as rapid as that of the United Kingdom coalfields generally, and for much the same reasons, for although it was even then recognised that certain Welsh coals, by being virtually smokeless, had marked advantages, especially to H.M. Navy, the northern coalfields protested vigorously against any attempt to let this influence buying and it was not until 1872 that Welsh coal won its victory at sea.[16] It came just in time, for the prosperity of the iron-works in the Welsh hills was severely hit when the post-Franco-Prussian War boom ended. In place of a single home industry as its main customer, came the world demand for steam coal, and it was this that henceforward exerted the main influence on the price of South Wales coal and miners' wages. Not all South Wales coal was smokeless or for export. In 1875 over two-thirds of the United Kingdom's tin-plate works, and half of their copper-smelting plants, were in this region, and consumed the coal that was mined locally, but even these industries had a large export demand. Taken as a whole, whether as a supplier of steam-coal or as a supplier of coal for home consumption in industries that were largely orientated towards foreign markets, South Wales was essentially more dependent on foreign demand than on any area whose main concern was the home market.

As in the period examined in the last chapter, the volume of investment in the coal industry increased as rising demand drove up prices and (initially) profits. The aim was not simply to invest up to the point where, in the short- or medium-run, net profits were made at some minimum acceptable rate, but also (in many cases) to maintain or to increase one's share of a market which one knew to be expanding in the long-run: but when this investment, in the hands of competing entrepreneurs, proved unprofitable in the short-run it was curtailed. Often it must have been undertaken in the knowledge that before it was completed prices would fall and profits become paltry, but the desire to be ready with existing capacity for the next boom was strong, and current profits could be used to provide it, even if bad times might intervene.

The quantitative data on investment are poor, but it is known that there was a great deal of activity in 1866 and 1872–4.[17] Prices were rising in 1863–5 and 1870–3. The actual peak of prices in South Wales came in January 1874. Figure 5.2 shows the course of investment as measured by the formation of limited companies in South Wales, excluding those known to be primarily concerned with iron manufacture, and compares it with the price of coal. Broadly speaking, the course of house-building followed suit, with a suspicion of a lag. In Merthyr Tydfil there was a peak in 1873, a sharp

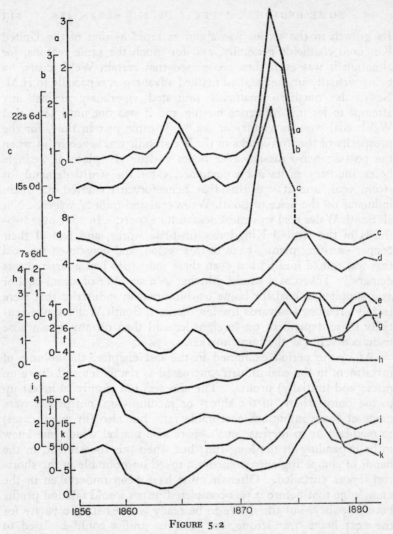

FIGURE 5.2

(a) Nominal Capital of Limited Companies registered in South Wales, excluding those concerned with iron manufacture (£m.). Morris and Williams, p. 151.

(b) Number of such companies ('o). *Ibid.*

(c) South Wales Coal Price. Until 1875 the graph shows average selling price per ton of colliery-screened coal, f.o.b. at Cardiff. Morris and Williams, p. 81. From 1875 it shows the price per ton of steam coal, f.o.b. as recorded in S. Wales audits. Based on Finlay Gibson, pp. 172-3.

(d) House-building Index for South Wales Coalfield (1901-10 = 10). Appendix 4. House-building in the following towns. See Figure 4.3.

(e) Merthyr Tydfil ('oo).   (f) Cardiff ('oo).   (g) Mountain Ash ('o).

(h) Aberdare ('oo).   (i) Swansea ('oo).   (j) Llanelly ('o).

(k) Newport (Mon.) ('o).

Note that while the diagram shows adjusted data (see Figure 4.3), the text refers to movements in the raw data.

decline for two years, an isolated high value in 1876 and then another three years of low activity.   Aberdare, the mining town next door that supplied high-grade steam coal, had a well-defined peak in 1874, a gradual decline for two years, and then a sharp drop to a level just above zero from which it did not begin to recover until the mid-eighties.   Another mining town just south of Aberdare, Mountain Ash, had a sudden peak in 1873, a two-year dip, and another larger peak in 1876; while Llanelly, further west and supplying the local metal works, peaked sharply in 1875.   The remaining towns for which we have data are ports rather than mining towns (although Llanelly was also a substantial port).   Cardiff had a peak in 1875, as did Swansea, but Newport's peak came two years later.   Taking the aggregate of these towns, we obtain a peak in 1875, but we may note that there was a tendency for the peaks in the mining and metal towns themselves to have peaks in 1873 or 1874.   Since, in any case, these figures relate to planned building, one cannot always be very certain of what happened, but it looks as if, except for purely local factors, building ceased, or at least paused, as soon as the falling demand for coal had reduced prices, wages and migration to the coalfield.   The numbers employed in South Wales coal-mining, put at 73,300 in 1874, fell slightly in 1875, but in 1876 dropped sharply to 67,500.   The trough came the next year, and it was 1882 before the peak of 1874 was passed.   The minor boom that then was evident can be identified as in Figure 5.3 with a slight rise in the price of coal, a rise in wages and marriages, a new demand for houses, and a building boom which in some parts of the coalfield was quite substantial,[18] as can be seen in Figure 5.2.

We shall draw certain conclusions from this account of the South Wales coal industry and its relationship to house-building, but it will be useful if we look at another region, before doing so.

The Manchester cotton area has some interesting similarities with South Wales.   It supplied both home and foreign markets, and although one sometimes thinks of cotton as one industry and iron and coal as two, the degree of interdependence between the South Wales industries was probably almost as high as that between cotton spinning, cotton weaving and the manufacture of finished garments. There were, however, two vital differences.   The period of gestation was much longer in coal than in cotton, and it was easier to close a mill than to close a mine.   In textiles supply as well as price adjusted to demand.   We must remember at the outset that spinning and weaving were being conducted more and more by separate enterprises, and that these two branches of the cotton industry tended to have different locations and sometimes different fortunes.   Weaving

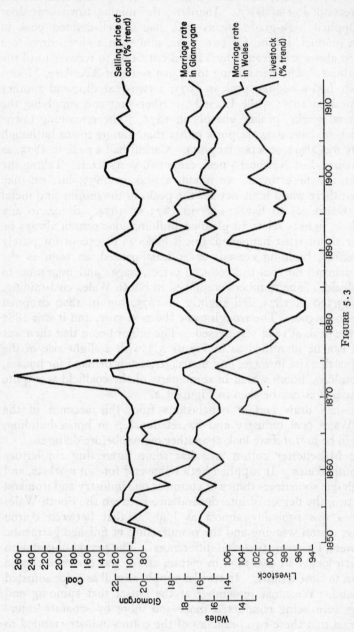

FIGURE 5·3   Reproduced by courtesy of Professor Brinley Thomas from Thomas (2), p. 24.   The livestock graph shows the deviations from trend of the amount of live-stock on Welsh farms.

was always the first to feel a depression. The position of the spinners could be satisfactory while that of the weavers might be 'going from bad to worse'. It was cheaper to put up a loom than a batch of spindles, and possible to weave profitably on a small scale. The ease of entry into weaving led to keener competition than in spinning, and to a more rapid disappearance of profits. Furthermore the multitudinous weavers had few markets, while the spinners had many. The weaver had often to buy his yarn in a firm market but to sell his cloth in a weak one.

So long as the manufacturer keeps his looms going he must have yarn, no matter what the price, but in dull times, when demand is small and stock large, he must, if he wishes to sell, take the best price the buyer of calico can be persuaded to give. Eventually, he may be compelled to stop his looms. Thereupon will follow a diminished demand for yarn, which, if it continues long enough, will cause spinners first to reduce their prices and then to curtail production. Simultaneous 'short-time' amongst both spindles and looms will lead to a reduction of surplus stocks, and by-and-by bring about a revived demand, first for goods and then for yarn. During the first portion of the revival manufacturers will do better than spinners; but when the whole of the looms have got to work the spinners will once more be able to make their own terms as to price.[19]

Local specialisation was not confined simply to spinning or weaving. Different mills, and eventually different areas, tended to specialise in different qualities as well as in different operations. Technical innovation sometimes meant that one locality prospered while another suffered. In the early eighties, for example, the districts around Oldham and Ashton-under-Lyne were booming because they had developed their mule twist business. Mule was cheaper than warps made from throstle yarns. Keen competition had reduced costs, but had also reduced prices, and the manufacturer who made most cheaply survived at the expense of the old-fashioned throstle spinners. These were located largely in Burnley, Rossendale and Rochdale, and so we see those areas experiencing less happy times than those that Oldham saw.[20] For reasons such as these we must not assume that even within the cotton area there was a uniform pattern of growth any more than in South Wales. Nor was all the technical change reflected in building. An increase in the number of spindles in Oldham between 1860 and 1867 saw not a single new mill.[21] Furthermore, the size of mills was changing. Some evidence of these factors is provided by the following table[22] which shows that the percentage increase in the number of spindles far exceeded that in the number of spinning mills. The same was true of looms and weaving mills. The table also shows that a smaller

E

proportion of the mills was performing both operations.   It is clear that one must not expect data of mill-building to reflect changes in

	Number of Mills		Number of Spindles (million)		Number of Looms (000)	
	1850	1878	1850	1878	1850	1878
Spinning	834	1159	9·1	28·7	—	—
Weaving	278	765	—	—	50·9	234·5
Spinning and weaving	573	597	11·1	15·5	198·7	280·4
Total (U.K.)	1932	2674	21·0	44·2	250·0	514·9

capacity with any high degree of fidelity.   They seem, however, to be more likely to reflect changes in capacity demand for labour as is shown by the following table,[23] in which the last row suggests that

	Spinning Mills		Weaving Mills		Mills combining Spinning and Weaving		U.K. Total	
	1850	1878	1850	1878	1850	1878	1850	1878
No. of spindles per mill	11,885	24,738	—	—	20,131	26,022	10,857	16,532
No. of looms per mill	—	—	183	305	364	468	128	192
No. of hands per mill	114	138	113	146	332	354	171	180

employment per mill was not changing as rapidly as the amount of machinery.   On the other hand the table takes no account of changes that possibly occurred in this ratio in the intervening years.

We have already seen that the fifties witnessed such an increase in capacity that in some respects the Cotton Famine had its advantages.   Ellison wrote that the 60 per cent increase in the number of looms between 1850 and 1861

led to a considerable over-production of cloth, especially during the last three years of the period, and to a serious diminution in the profits of manufacturers.   It gave rise also to a gigantic amount of over-trading with the Eastern and other markets, from the disastrous effects of which the shippers were saved only by the enforced reduced production occasioned by the cotton famine.[24]

On the other hand, the impact on the workers of this overproduction, and of the Famine itself, was disastrous.   The distress was at its worst in November 1862, when almost a quarter of a million operatives were out of work and over 160,000 working short time. Ellison estimated the loss of wages at that time to be running at the rate of £170,000 per week in the cotton industry alone, and to have

been as high as £50,000 even in May 1865.[25]   In the four years
ended Lady Day, 1865, the total expenditure in Lancashire by the
Guardians and Relief Committee came to almost £3½ million.   The
loss of trade amounted to roughly £70 m., although many mill-
owners profited from stock appreciation.   Yet, if we are to believe
Samuel Smiles, these years of poverty for many were also years of
thrift for the more fortunate.   Self-help prevailed, and in 1864
Smiles extolled the virtues of building societies, describing their
membership in glowing terms:

There are also exceptional towns and villages in Lancashire where
large sums of money have been saved by the operatives for buying or
building comfortable cottage dwellings.   Last year Padiham saved about
£15,000 for this purpose, although its population is only about 8,000.
Burnley has also been very successful.   The Building Society there has
6,600 investors, who saved last year £160,000, or an average of £24 for
each investor.   The members consist principally of mill operatives,
miners, mechanics, engineers, carpenters, stonemasons, and labourers.
They also include women, both married and unmarried.[26]

The end of the Civil War was not entirely beneficial to the
cotton industry, and profits were further reduced by the impact of
the Overend and Gurney crash, which had a substantial part of its
origin in the volume of construction going on around London at
this time.   In an attempt to recoup profits manufacturers tended
to over-produce during 1865–9, and although output did not soar
to the dizzy heights of 1860, the textile areas saw a minor boom in
house-building as fuller employment increased effective demand.
Figure 5.4 shows that house-building also reflected (with a short lag)
the slight dip in textile activity of 1869, and then it rockets upwards
as the cotton industry entered on one of the most prosperous periods
in its history.   The seventies began with Great Britain's consumption of cotton rising from its average for 1865–70 by over a quarter,
while the United States and the Continent also saw spectacular, if
rather lower, increases.   The interruption of Continental output
during the Franco-Prussian War led to an abnormal demand for
English products, and especially for English textiles, while the
American railway mania, which commenced in 1868, driving up
the demand for iron and coal in a way we have already noted, contributed to a rapid inflation, in which not only wages and prices, but
also profits rose.   Stimulated by these exceptional profits, the cotton
industry expanded output still further, and with the expansion came
a boom in mill-building and another in house-building.   We shall
shortly look at certain aspects of these booms a little more closely.
    In 1872 the tide began to turn.   English merchants had already

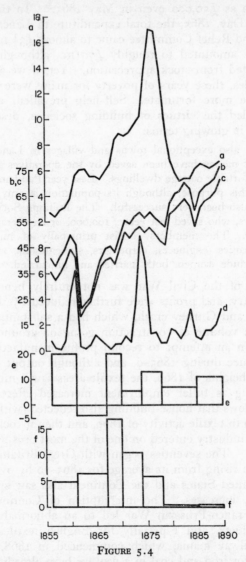

FIGURE 5.4

(a) House-building Index. Manchester Conurbation (1901–10 = 10). Appendix 4.
(b) Index of Production of Cotton Yarn, G.B. (1913 = 100). Hoffmann.
(c) Index of Production of Cotton Piece Goods, G.B. (1913 = 100). Hoffmann.
(d) Number of Joint-Stock Companies registered in the English Cotton Industry.
    Farnie, p. 497.
(e) Average Annual Increase in Cotton Looms, U.K. ('00). B.H.S., p. 185.
(f) Average Annual Increase in Cotton Spindles, U.K. ('00). B.H.S., p. 185.

spoken of 'excessive stocks and unremunerative prices'[27] and this alone was tending to arrest the rise in production.   In the same year the French and German industries began to recover from the war, and their home production soon began to oust the expensive products of British inflation, especially after the annexation of the Alsatian spinneries by Germany resulted in a mill-building boom in France, thereby increasing the total Continental capacity.   How credit crises in America and other countries affected the demand for British goods is a subject we shall consider more carefully in a later chapter, but we must also mention here that the failure of Jay Cooke and Company in 1873 halted the American consumption of cotton for two years; and Britain, at a time when not only rising prices were reducing demand, took advantage of the fall in cotton prices to increase output.   France and Germany did the same, and soon the whole of Europe's cotton industry was burdened with heavy stocks and unprofitable prices.   Investment slowed down, or even ceased.   In 1875 the Eastern trade was disorganised by financial failures, and when hopes and output revived in 1876, gloom descended quickly as bad harvests and other factors reduced demand.

The fifties had seen heavy investment in looms but in the later sixties it was chiefly in the spinning sector that investment took place.   By 1874 the balance of the industry was back to its 1850 level of roughly one loom to 85 or 90 spindles.   After that year came a pause.   There was, of course, a certain lag.   Indeed, between 1874 and 1878 over two and a quarter million spindles came into operation but most of these had been 'projected or started in 1874'.[28]   Mill-building had been overdone, as the supply of yarn now exceeded the demand, affected as it was by bad harvests, commercial depression and other factors we have just described.   'Prices ran so low that dividends became things of the past, and losses, calls and forced sales of shares, matters of everyday occurrence.'

Ellison's statement that mill-building boomed in the early seventies and fell sharply in 1874 or 1875, remaining at a low level at least until 1878, conforms with the impression given by Figure 5.4. This shows the annual numbers of joint-stock companies[29] registered in the English cotton industry, and the average net additions to spindles and looms over certain periods.[30]   It seems to be a reasonable representation of investment in the industry, but clearly no great accuracy can be claimed for it in this respect.   Substantial peaks revealed in 1861 and 1874 measure intentions rather than activity, and should not be taken as certain evidence that actual investment peaked in those years.

We have already seen that in the fifties and early sixties,

house-building in the Manchester area was closely correlated with investment in the cotton industry, and we may now examine the relationship for this later period, remembering that there were substantial variations within the area we are considering. By 1870 the number of towns in the Manchester area for which we have house-building statistics had grown to a dozen, and another ten were added before the decade ended. The index of house-building based on this growing number of towns, and described in Appendix 4, reveals a minor boom in the late sixties, with a slight dip in 1871 before soaring to a mighty peak in 1876–7, and then declining sharply to remain at a low level until the mid-nineties. It is tempting to argue that house-building therefore continued for two or three years after the decline in mill-building, but our statistics do not warrant this conclusion. The peak in house plans in Salford came in 1875 when nearly 3000 houses were approved. This was also the year when industrial plans reached their peak in that area. In neighbouring Eccles the peak figure of 340 houses in 1874 coincided with the maximum number of 16 industrial plans. Bury had an industrial peak in 1875 and a housing peak in 1877. In Bolton, with its unusual pattern, the main peak came in 1869 in both housing and industrial building, while the secondary housing peak of 1876 came a year before the industrial peak, which was heavily influenced by non-textile building. We have already explained that the industrial plans data leave a great deal to be desired, but when we look at what we have for individual towns in the Manchester area the evidence does not suggest any uniform lag in either direction. When we recall the fundamental problems of determining lags from absolutely reliable annual data, it seems better to make no firm statement other than that. In any case, we must remember that the towns covered by the Manchester Index in this period do not include the whole area, and, for a few critical years, exclude Manchester itself. It is possible that a more complete coverage would shift the peak. If we look at the indices for the sub-conurbations around Manchester (also described in Appendix 4) we find that peaks occurred as shown below: but we have to bear in mind the incomplete coverage.

Ashton-under-Lyne and District · ·	1877
Bury and District · · · · ·	1877
Oldham and District · · · ·	1877
Rochdale and District · · · ·	1875
Salford and District · · · ·	1875
Bolton and District · · · ·	1869, 1876
Altrincham and District · · ·	c. 1869, 1877
Stockport and District · · · ·	1878

One could argue that the Stockport peak in 1878 was an isolated year on a downward trend that began in 1875. This table emphasises the point already made about the varying prosperities within the industry, and that Oldham and Ashton boomed at a time when Rochdale was feeling the pinch, not only because of the factors mentioned but also because of heavy rates arising from the erection of a costly magnificent town hall and extensions to its waterworks, poor railway facilities, and the collapse (in 1878) of a local private bank.

Appendix 6 describes a rather unsatisfactory index of house-rents in the Manchester area, which is very difficult to interpret but confirms that some time between 1874 and 1876 the housing market underwent a marked change of fortune. A Manchester man, Mr. Samuel Ogden, giving evidence before the House of Lords on behalf of the promoters of the Ship Canal Bill, pointed out that the depression of trade had forced landlords to lower rents. Many works had closed between 1874 and 1884, especially after 1878. They had employed over 12,000 hands, many of whom had migrated to other places, leaving streets of empty tenements and houses, many of which were dilapidating. So great was the combined effect of sharing and migration that in 1881 the number of unoccupied houses in Manchester and Salford exceeded the number of inhabited houses in adjacent Stockport.[31] It is not surprising that the empty cottage was not often advertised in the *Manchester Guardian* in these days.

The decline in the cotton trade had hit Manchester with a vengeance, and the vast expanse of empty houses reflected the diminished incomes of the manufacturer, the worker and the land-lord. Many of these landlords were cotton operatives themselves. By the 1870's the more skilled workmen were 'almost middle class in their way of life, with large investments in house property, their pianos in the parlour, their trips to Paris and the continent'.[32] This is probably something of an exaggeration, but it is certainly true that many skilled workmen were small property owners. Men of this kind sometimes lost both their earned income and their rents. Others lost heavily through the building societies. By 1870 these had grown so much that Liverpool alone boasted over 200, with some 60,000 members. In Manchester there were over a hundred, while Oldham had 66 with a subscribed capital totalling £800,000.[33] The difficult times of the mid-seventies caused withdrawals of funds, and failure to keep up payments. Rumour was often more devastating than fact. The Manchester societies were not involved to any extent in the City of Glasgow Bank Failure, but it was said that they were, and heavy withdrawals occurred. Some politics played a part.

In 1878 the cotton strikers were exhorted to withdraw their deposits from building socities so that mill-owners would be unable to borrow from them in the hard times they were about to experience. For these and other reasons some societies felt it necessary to deduct as much as a fifth from deposits in order 'to get straight', or to lend against unsound security. A witness before the Royal Commission of 1885 felt that they would need twenty years 'to recover from the position of 3 or 4 years ago'.[34]

Even so, by the time the Commissioners sat the cotton industry itself had undergone another boom. From the building point of view it was not important, and its impact on the housing index is little more than a ripple in a mighty trough, but it has some interesting features which we may note before passing to an examination of quite exceptional developments in the Oldham part of the cotton area.

Between 1878 and 1883 there was a gigantic rise in world cotton consumption. At the beginning of the seventies the total consumption in Europe and America was just over 6 million bales per annum. In 1878–9 it stood at 7·2 million, but its average over 1881–3 was up to 9·6 million. The markets of the world had at last absorbed the surplus stocks, and the industry could expand again. As always, it was the manufacturing side that felt the improvement first, and the export demand for yarn came later than the demand for goods. The looms were again at work before the spindles, 'and although the latter shortly followed, the former, for a little time, kept ahead, and thereby laid the foundation of the unsatisfactory state of trade which ruled in 1882–3'.[35] There were other reasons for this 'unsatisfactory state', which Ellison describes in later pages[36] and need not detain us here. It is sufficient to say that by the end of 1883 'looms began to be stopped, either voluntarily, or through bankruptcy, or in consequence of strikes against reduced wages'.[37] These were not the times for house- or mill-building. Perhaps the most interesting point is that although other countries had also had troubled textile trades, this boom of the early eighties reflects one of the many ways in which Britain was beginning to lose its supremacy. While, in the sixties, British consumption of cotton had risen by 15 per cent, compared with a slightly smaller rise on the Continent and one of only 11 per cent in the United States, between 1871 and 1883 British consumption rose by 25 per cent, compared with 75 per cent on the Continent and no less than 111 per cent in the country to which our own impoverished textile workers were migrating in such large numbers.[38]

Before concluding this survey of building in the Manchester area we must note the growth of investment in the Oldham area,[39] which was of tremendous importance to the whole cotton industry. In 1858 the Oldham Industrial Co-operative Society launched the Sun Mill, at first as a manufacturing company, but within a few years, as a spinning company. All the share and loan capital of this joint-stock co-operative venture was to bear 5 per cent until spinning began, the interest to be added to the fixed stock.[40] The security was paid up share capital, and the rules seem to have been borrowed from the Rochdale Co-operative Manufacturing Society. It began to spin in 1861, and was soon hit by the Famine. In 1862 it was refused a mortgage of £10,000 on a new mill, and in 1865 the balance sheet showed a deficit of over £11,000. Such was the subsequent prosperity that by the end of 1866 a dividend of 5s. per £5 paid up share was declared. Subsequent dividends increased until, for the quarter ended June, 1871, as much as 40 per cent was declared.[41] Other companies were by now hot on their heels, and the early seventies saw a mania of co-operative company flotation in and around Oldham. In the two years 1874-5, 45 companies were floated in Oldham itself, with a nominal capital of nearly £2,700,000, accounting for three million spindles. Many of the 140 companies floated elsewhere were in the immediate neighbourhood of this remarkable town. The shares were held by all sorts of people. Before 1873 the working class was estimated to have owned at least three-quarters of the capital then invested in the local spinning companies — about £750,000. There were hundreds of people earning well under £2 a week each with hundreds of pounds invested in their local mills. By March 1874 'there could not have been fewer than 10,000 persons holding shares in Oldham'.[42] The importance of this widespread thrift is emphasised by the fact that these co-operative mills were the most modern, enterprising and efficient. By the mid-eighties the seventy-one limited liability mills in this district contained 'almost as many spindles as there are in either France, Germany or Russia . . . and about one-third of the total at work in the United States'.[43] The spinning industry of Britain was rapidly becoming concentrated into one small district, in which almost every man knew more about every aspect of cotton 'than most private employers had ten years ago'.[44]

Yet it is a remarkable fact that the guiding lights in much of this development — and this is especially true of the later years which we have yet to consider — were not textile men, lawyers or bankers, but architects. Joseph Stott was one, who held 6619 shares in 21 Oldham companies at £5 apiece.[45] These were launched between 1863 and 1892, and he himself helped to promote four of them.

The typical procedure was for an architect, a landowner, and a few other people to launch a society. The bulk of the funds came, in the earlier days, from local people. The architect was often a director, and often received a fee for his professional services. It was not unknown for him to resign after a few years and to launch a new society, with a new plan and a new fee. Many Oldham mills have remarkably similar designs. Other prominent promoters were textile-machinists, who sometimes gave large credit on machinery, for Oldham was the main centre in the world for the construction of spinning machinery.[46] These are matters which had important consequences on the course of mill-building early in the twentieth century, but for the moment we must remain with the seventies.

Much of the capital was not fully paid up, and the crisis of the mid and late seventies was consequently all the more keenly felt. Ellison lists twenty-three of the largest mills, each containing 70,000 or more spindles. 'In the first half of 1876 the quarterly dividends on the shares of these mills ranged from 5 to 30 per cent, in the third quarter from 5 to 20 per cent, and in the fourth quarter from *nil* to 13 per cent. In 1877 the dividends gradually disappeared. . .'[47] In 1878 only one of these larger mills declared a dividend. The other twenty-two were in the red. The palmy days of 1875 and early 1876 had attracted a great deal of capital from elsewhere — much of it withdrawn from overseas — and by 1877 only half of the capital was local working class. Nevertheless the heavy calls on unpaid-up share capital in 1877–9 hit the workers very badly, and many of them lost the whole of their hard-earned invested savings. They quickly learned their bitter lesson, and switched (when they could) to savings banks at $2\frac{1}{2}$ per cent and cottage property and building clubs at 5 per cent. By 1885 only $7\frac{1}{2}$ per cent of mill employees were shareholders in cotton-spinning concerns, and 'cotton operative shareholders in the cotton mills where they worked themselves were probably not 2 per cent of the shareholders in those mills'.[48] We thus have the phenomenon of workers saving, investing in their own industry, and drawing high dividends which were usually re-invested. They stimulated not only industrial building but also house-building, more through migration into the area than through an income-elasticity of demand. When capacity and building had been overdone, and they lost both their jobs and their savings, they migrated, or moved together, and left surplus houses. But when better times came they retained their thrifty habits and now facilitated house-building by supplying funds.

At this stage we may draw some interesting comparisons between the cotton industry and the coal industry. In both cases the industry was particularly vulnerable to reductions in overseas demand, largely because a number of circumstances, including the Franco-Prussian War, had led to abnormally large exports. But it was the inelastic supply of coal that contributed most to the general inflation, and drove up the prices of our manufactures at a time when our markets were already being jeopardised by the revival of Continental production. The world-wide investment boom brought benefits to Britain because of her industrial supremacy, but her capacity to produce iron and coal were inadequate to meet these enormous demands without upsetting the whole economy. First came inflation, with its soaring profits and its incentives to expand capacity. By the time that capacity had been expanded, inflation had helped to make it unnecessary, partly by pricing British products out of the market, and partly by so increasing investment costs that the various foreign financial crises were made more inevitable. If the great boom of the early seventies had been more subdued, if the Franco-Prussian war had not pushed British industry into the fool's paradise of a temporary near monopoly as a supplier of manufactures and iron[49] and if the supply of coal had been more elastic, the whole course of the later seventies and eighties would have been smoother, and the building cycle in the cotton and coal areas might have known neither the mightiness of 1876 nor the despondency of the early eighties.

Welsh coal and Manchester cotton cannot tell the whole tale of British building, and we have a great deal to learn from London and Glasgow. Cairncross has examined the Scottish city with the aid of data of a kind and quality that exist for no other.[50] In particular, he found annual statistics of empty houses, and series for the average rents of both occupied and unoccupied houses. These and other data for the period 1860–85 are shown in Figure 5.5. There was a fall in the amount of building in the early sixties, followed by a rise which became very sharp around 1870. The number of plans passed paused in its upward flight in 1874, but then leapt to a peak in 1876, after which there was a sharp fall reaching a trough in 1883. On the other hand, the annual increase in the total number of houses reached its maximum in 1874, declined substantially, and rallied to a secondary peak in 1877. Since there was a great deal of demolition proceeding at this time, it is not reasonable simply to assume that the proportion of plans not acted upon was higher in 1876–7 than in the earlier years, but this is a possible partial explanation that has to be kept in mind. The building of houses by railway companies, and other bodies that proceeded by private Act of Parliament and needed no local planning permission has also to be remembered. Whichever set of statistics is taken to represent actual activity, there is no denying that 1878 saw a great deal less than the preceding year, and masons' hourly wage rates which had doubled between 1864 and 1877 fell sharply by a third.   The same year saw the beginning of a long decline in the average rents of unoccupied houses, echoed a year later by the onset

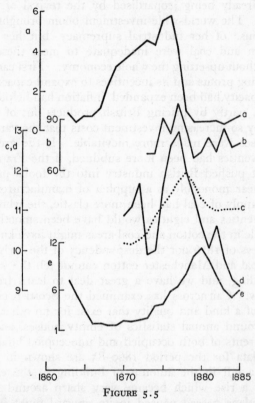

FIGURE 5.5

(a) House plans approved, Glasgow ('000).   Cairncross, pp. 16–17.
(b) Average cost per room, Glasgow (£).   Ibid.
(c) Rents of occupied houses, Glasgow (£ per annum).   Ibid.
(d) Rents of unoccupied houses, Glasgow (£ per annum).   Ibid.
(e) Percentage of houses empty at Whitsun, Glasgow.   Ibid.

of a long but less severe decline in rents of other houses.   Whereas in 1876–7 the average rents of empty houses exceeded those of occupied houses by about 10 per cent, in 1878 they were almost the same, and by 1885 empty houses had an average rent about 18 per cent lower than that of occupied houses.   Ever since the boom began the proportion of empty houses had been rising.   In 1874 it rose steeply, from 2·54 to 3·99 per cent.   In the next two years it continued to climb, reaching 4·91 per cent in 1876. Then, as the second building peak exerted its effect, it leapt again in 1877 to 6·48 per cent, there being nearly 2000 additional empty houses on the market in that year. Thereafter, the rate of building slackened, the number of occupied houses actually fell (as did the total number of all houses in 1883–4) and the proportion of empty houses rose to exceed 11 per cent in 1880. Although the severe fall of 1878 came in the year when the City of Glasgow Bank also cracked, there is little doubt that the downturn in demand had already begun.

Cairncross's analysis of the data is an essential part of his larger examination of the relationship between long cycles in building, migration and foreign trade. This is a matter to which we have so far paid little explicit attention, even though it has frequently been in the background. Soon we shall have to turn to it, but there are good reasons for deferring this matter until we have traced the detailed movements in building as far as 1913. We shall then be in a better position to look back over the whole period, and to make such generalisations as our data seem to warrant. Consequently, instead of presenting Cairncross's argument in any detail at this stage we shall remark that his basic findings are compatible with the story of South Wales and Manchester. He found a 'fairly close agreement between shipbuilding activity and the demand for house-room, and the violence of the fluctuations in the one can be read in the others'.[51] The unemployment and wage-cuts in a slump cause a fall in marriages, migration and the number of occupied houses. On the other hand, these factors all affected demand rather than supply, which Cairncross felt to fall off, 'if anything . . . at the peak of a boom'.[52]

Finally, we turn to London, whose building fluctuations seem to have little in common with the rest of the country at least until the close of the century. A more or less steady boom can be traced from the mid-fifties, when annual statistics become available, right up to 1868, after which there was a sharp drop to a trough in the early seventies, and then a new boom peaking in 1881. Figure 5.6 shows that there is absolutely nothing in the course of London building statistics to hint at the crisis of 1873 or the downturn in building activity that occurred around 1876 in other parts of the country.

Our examination of the Manchester area and South Wales suggests that a principal determinant of building was the prosperity of local industry, exerting its impact through rising wages and immigration. Since London had no dominant industry whose fortunes can be traced it is difficult to examine the same thesis here.

Yet this is not as unfortunate as it may seem, for on reflection one has to concede that house-building in London in the latter half of the nineteenth century was motivated by totally different forces than those that operated elsewhere; and it must be partly for this reason that the peaks and troughs are so differently timed. In his classic paper on Urban Housing Problems, read to The Royal Statistical Society in 1918, J. Calvert Spensley drew attention to the inverse relationship that existed between new house-building and the percentage of houses that stood empty. As he pointed out, there was a certain lag, which is shown in Figure 5.6 The trough in empty property, coming in 1876, preceded the building peak by four years, while the maximum figure for empties occurred in 1884, six years before building reached its nadir. The next low point in the index of empty property came in 1898, while building showed a double-peak in 1899 and 1901. In 1910 the vacancy rate began to fall, and Spensley felt that this was evidence that, if war had not intervened, London would have had a building boom, to which, indeed, the slight increase in building during 1913 bears some testimony. He did not carry the analysis of this inverse relationship very far, being more concerned with the period after 1900, which was better documented, but it is clear that he had in mind a mechanism similar to that advanced by Cairncross for Glasgow. When empty property reached a certain minimum percentage, the normal movements and growth of population ensured that building would be profitable. But as building proceeded, and eventually overtook demand, so that empty property became more abundant and rents began to fall, so it would become less profitable. The reduction of building activity would reduce local incomes, and if the rise in empties was in any case partly due to a more general distress in the area one might expect this vacancy rate to go on increasing for a few years, even though building was at a lower level. The matter is discussed further in Chapter 6.

One of the participants in the discussion of Spensley's paper was H. H. Gordon, whose concern was with the causation of the long cycle revealed by Spensley's data. He had plotted a graph of London's population, which revealed no reason for the time-shape of building, but when he broke down London into its regions he found that 'as regards the growth of London there were material points occurring both in 1876 and in 1901 which seemed to have some bearing' on the problem he was examining. In 1876, he said, the population of the central area of London began to decline, for the first time, while in 1901 the population of London County also fell. What, he wondered, was the cause of this? He presented his answer, and there is no record that anybody believed it. Spensley's reply was little more than polite, probably because Gordon's presentation was muddled. He had ignored entirely the lag we have just mentioned, and referred to 1876 as a turning year in building rather than in empties. But, even if his presentation was inadequate, his basic point was probably correct. It was clear to him, at least, that the building cycle was a transport cycle. He had graphed the number of journeys performed in London as a whole, both on an absolute and on a *per capita* basis, and had found distinct upward

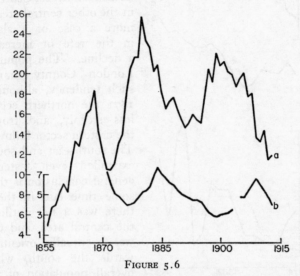

FIGURE 5.6

(a) Surveyors' Fees for New Building in London (£'ooo). Cooney (2), p. 354.
(b) Empty Property in London (%). The graph shows the percentage of water-rates lost through 'Empties, bad debts, etc.' Spensley, *op. cit.*, p. 210.

jumps in both 1876 and 1901, which was just what he had expected. 'At the present time,' he continued, 'when the old horse tramway is as dead as a Dodo, it seems hard to believe that it played a most important part in accounting for the shape of the diagram. But in point of fact it is true. In 1876, after many years when there had been no change whatever in traffic conditions, there began the development of horse tramways, and within a few years the old, despised horse tramway had created a new volume of traffic which was larger than that aggregated in two generations before by railways or omnibuses.'[53] In 1901 came 'another revolution' associated with electric tubes and tramways. It was these transport revolutions that held the key to the building cycle. Spensley agreed that it needed looking into, but felt that his dates matched the graph of empty property rather than building, which, indeed, they did.

One cannot say that London's annual population data are very reliable for the seventies. If, because of this, one is less ambitious and looks simply at the Census years, one finds that the population of Central London reached its peak in 1861.[54] This was also the peak Census year for North Central and West Central, while in the other central areas it was more a case of a slackening in the rate of increase than a decline. The population of London County showed no such tendency, although after 1871 the northern sector rose less steeply, and from 1881 the eastern sector followed suit. The south-east and south-west expanded even faster. The general conclusion is that from some time late in the sixties there was a net outflow from the central area, and that this was eventually orientated towards the south, while the overall population of London County increased with every decade.[55]

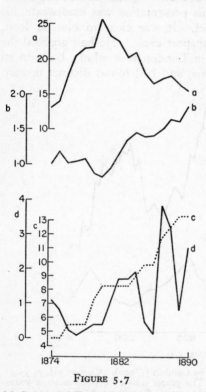

FIGURE 5.7

(a) Surveyors' Fees for New Building in London (£'000). Cooney (2), p. 354.
(b) London Tramways: Million Passengers per mile. *London Statistics*.
(c) London Tramways: Miles of Tramway. *Ibid.*
(d) London Tramways: Additional Passengers (millions). *Ibid.*

The journey statistics used by Gordon were not specified, but as his emphasis was on the horse tramway in the seventies we may usefully look at those shown in Figure 5.7. These represent the annual increments in the numbers of passengers carried by horse tramways, and seem to bear little relationship to house-building. There is, however, something to be seen if we divide the number of passengers by the number of miles of tramway. The resulting statistic has obvious imperfections, but it is interesting to observe that in the period of increasing building activity this ratio had a slight downward trend, which became reversed at about the same time as building hit its peak.   It would be easy to read too much into this, and a proper analysis would have to look at the more detailed statistics of travel on different routes.

The theory of the relationships between house-building and transport developments contains a number of alternatives.   If we have people living in great density on top of some central industries, then the building of a single railway to the outskirts may lead to house-building near its outer terminus, and the increase in building will lead to an increase in travel.   If the families who move into these houses have children a few years below working age, then ultimately the number of passengers is likely to swell further, and to do so before there is a marriage-bulge to augment the demand for houses.   The incentive to building provided by the new railway may be so great that additional services are provided, or new extensions made.   On the other hand, if the building is speculative it may be overdone, and if a railway is built into a wilderness, where speculative houses are provided, there may be both empty houses and empty carriages.

A second possibility is that in a large overcrowded city, industry becomes more dispersed — perhaps because of high rents and rates at the centre.   It may, indeed, even go to the outskirts where the local population cannot provide a labour force.   This certainly happened in Lancashire where many towns sprang up around mills that had migrated into the country where land was cheap.   In such a case workers may either leave the centre of the town and go and live further out, causing a boom in building, or they may — if transport is available — travel every day.   Thus we have a case in which the provision of a railway line may reduce the inclination to build, rather than increase it.

Fortunately, we have a fair amount of information about the development of London's transport.   The more general information has been conveniently summarised by Rasmussen,[56] while more detailed remarks on the relationship between building and transport in a southern suburb of London are provided by Dyos, in his invaluable study of Camberwell.[57]   Two major innovations in London's transport system came in the mid-fifties, when a building boom was just beginning.   In 1854 the building of the first underground railway was sanctioned, while in 1856 the London General Omnibus Company bought up 600 of the omnibuses being run by smaller companies and introduced co-ordinated, efficient and cheaper services.   The policy of population dispersal that had been advocated, if not actively pursued, at least since Elizabethan times was given an opportunity to work by these new services, and in 1861 an Act was passed requiring the North London and Metropolitan Railways to run the workmen's trains a day in each direction at fares not exceeding a penny a mile. Three years later the Board of Trade was empowered to require any railway to provide cheap workmen's trains. The next important legislation was in 1870 when local authorities were given powers to grant (or to withhold) concessions to companies wishing to operate tramways:

If a private company were to construct a line it had first to obtain the sanction of the local authorities in each of the areas through which it had to pass. . . . If a concession were granted, it was only valid for 21 years. At the end of that period, the town had the right to buy the entire plant and all the stock at the appraised value, regardless of the revenues of the company at the time. The result of this arrangement was that the company had to earn as much as possible in the 21 years allotted to them . . . The local authorities (sometimes) obliged the companies to keep the streets in repair, to build public lavatories, or whatever else they might need (in return for the privilege of carrying passengers). . . .

It is easy to see that under such conditions the tramways had to follow *after* development. No line could be constructed unless it were absolutely certain to pay. While the Underground and the omnibuses went ahead and opened up the way for new quarters, the tramways appeared later in districts already invaded by the Builders.[58]

The point made by Rasmussen, that tramways were not primarily concerned with gambling on the development of new areas is important, and tends to detract from the explicit point made by Gordon. But it does not indicate that tramway development had no impact at all, or indeed, that such impact as it had, tended to increase or to decrease the amount of building. It is a point on which only detailed local studies can shed light, and here it is fortunate that we have the study of Camberwell by Dyos. Between 1835 and 1862 the only public transport available in this area was the omnibus. The closest point of Camberwell was a mile and a half from the city, and even in 1860, only the better paid clerk or artisan travelled by bus rather than on foot. Many 'ambitiously sited new estates remained bus-less' and were saved only by the railway. By the 1860's 'the deserted stations which merely punctuated the route to more distant destinations' had attracted their first suburban customers, and suburban railways became sound economic propositions. 'A high proportion of the tangled lines proposed to Parliament in the little mania of railway promotion in London in the 1860's were suburban in character, and it was in the years 1862 to 1868 that Camberwell became one of a new ring of railway suburbs.'[59] The initial invasion of the suburb by the railway was due to a struggle between two companies for the Dover traffic, which resulted in a 'sudden rash of London termini' but 'their construction must also be reckoned as extravagant gestures in the courtship of potential City and suburban travellers'. The line opened in 1866 between London Bridge and East Brixton, with four new stations in Camberwell, was certainly part of a scheme to connect the City and the West End with the suburbs.

This outburst of feverish activity in railways had its parallel in house-building as it became possible, and in some cases socially desirable, to live along the route, building houses well away from the cramped slums and decaying villas of Central London. Fascia boards at local stations advertised the houses of the speculative builders, to whom the railways bestowed the benefit of rapidly appreciating land values. *The Builder* asked where the rise in rental values would stop.[60] Effective unionism in the building trades combined with high activity to drive up wages, and scarcity of materials drove up prices. In 1865 the London building operatives claimed higher wages on the four grounds that these had been granted in other parts of the country, that house-rent had risen because of demolitions (due largely to railway-building), that prices had risen and that the masters could afford to pay more.[61] Less than three months later the *Building News* published details of wage-rises for operative bricklayers of between 4d. and 1s. a day, with reductions in hours of between $1\frac{1}{2}$ and $3\frac{1}{2}$ hours a day, in thirty-two towns throughout England.[62] The average return from investment on house property was being quoted as between $7\frac{1}{2}$ and 10 per cent.[63] Eight tenders for the erection of a dozen houses in Kensington ranged from £2,188 to £3,970, the cheapest having allowed £500 for old materials and the dearest only £200.[64] In March of 1865 a building society was ready to advance £10,000 on freehold or lease-hold property for up to fifteen years, at 5 per cent interest on the balance. It had already advanced more than £370,000.[65] In May of the following year it was prepared to offer advances of up to £20,000, and its total advances had passed the half-million mark.[66] The advertisement appeared exactly one week before Overend & Gurney collapsed. It is interesting to read the comment of the *Building News*, in which these advertisements had appeared, in its first issue after the crash:

The late financial crisis differs from many former ones, in that it has been chiefly caused by the exaggerated speculation of great houses connected with the building trade. The difficulties of Messrs. Peto and Betts assisted to draw down the house of Overend, Gurney and Co. . . . It is clear enough . . . that the operations of (Peto and Betts) have been the chief cause of the troubles that have recently arisen in the building trades, so far as the prices of materials and workmen's wages are concerned.   The price of labour in the metropolis has during the last twelve months risen 10 per cent, chiefly in consequence of Messrs. Peto's works upon the London, Chatham and Dover Railway, and their engagements elsewhere have tended to raise the price of labour in various parts of the country. . . . The ruin that has fallen upon speculative builders is very great, and not only have the employers of labour been made to suffer, but the holders of shares in their schemes have been sufferers also. *The Times* calculates the loss from this source at between 130 and 140 millions between present prices and those at the beginning of the year.[67]

With this testimony before us it is difficult not to associate the London building boom of the sixties, and its collapse with the development of the railways.[68]   When the collapse came, and the Chatham Company was put in Chancery for five years,[69] further expansion of railways was halted, and fares had to rise.   The stimulus to suburban development wilted, rents fell[70] and houses did not rise again until the oppressive load of tight money lightened, and the railway companies became solvent.   That the peak in house-building came a little after the crash is almost certainly due to the completion of certain works already begun,[71] and the fact that a large number of development leases required the erection of a specified number of houses within a specified period.   In 1870 reasons for the financial collapse of 1866–7 were still being quoted in *The Builder*.   One letter referred to 'a reckless employment of a super-abundant supply of actual and spurious capital' as a principal cause, and a letter signed 'T. L. D.' advocated a massive public building campaign, along with reduced building wages.   Correspondence about the usefulness of reduced wages as a means of stimulating building soon became eloquent and contradictory. While the papers of the time bore ample evidence of the building boom in other parts of Britain, there were for a few more years constant references to distress amongst the building trades in London, and not until 1875, when building in other parts of the country was nearing its peak, did any real recovery set in.

This greater boom of the seventies can be analysed in much the same way as that of the sixties.   Again transport developments played an important part, but by now the speculative builder was probably even more important than before.   Some of these were large, and well organised; others were small-scale opportunists. Dyos presents a table showing the size distribution of house-building firms in Camberwell in 1878–80, when the boom was at its peak.[72] Of the 416 firms about a quarter 'had so few resources as to have been capable of building no more than one or two houses, even on the very crest of the boom'. Half of them had six houses or fewer under construction. On the other hand, almost a third of the 5670 houses built in these twelve years were put up by fifteen firms, each of which built over sixty houses. The activities of some of these firms were detailed by Dyos, who concludes that probably 90 per cent of all the house-builders in Camberwell were building on speculation, 'and practically all the remainder were building under contract for some other builder or small capitalist whose venture was usually equally speculative'.

Under these circumstances, excessive building was almost certain, and it is significant that there was an increasing amount of empty property in the late seventies. By the early eighties things had been so overdone that 'the suburbs were glutted with new but tenantless houses'. Rents were lowered to attract tenants, often without avail, and further railway extensions were advocated.[73] But by then almost the whole of the country, except indeed South Wales, where another boom was just beginning, was complaining of the same thing. In Birmingham there were over 5000 empty houses of the artisan class reported in early 1884,[74] while in Newcastle 'there has lately been great depression in the shipping and other trades, and thousands of men have been thrown out of work, with the consequence of the heads of families having little to spend in procuring accommodation'.[75] Exactly the same factors helped to cause the continued rise in the proportion of empty houses in London. At a time when this proportion was at its peak, overcrowding was worse than ever. One reported instance was of a six-roomed house occupied by six families, with as many as eight persons eating and sleeping in a single room. Rents were so high that in parts of London almost four-fifths of the poor population was estimated to be paying more than a fifth of their incomes in rent, while nearly a half were paying between a quarter and a half of their incomes.[76] The rent of a two-roomed tenement was quite likely to be as high as 6s. — or even higher, while a coster-monger or hawker would earn less than double this if he secured a full week's work. A dock labourer would not be much better off. The reason for the empty property was simply the high fraction of total income that the rent represented. The Royal Commission of 1885 emphasised that there were several factors aggravating this situation. Basically there was — despite the level of empties — a housing shortage, especially as far as the poor were concerned. The suggestion that 'all information tends to show that London is still overbuilt', made by *The Economist* in 1888[77] ignored the fact that the empty houses could all have been occupied if rents had fallen, or

wages risen, sufficiently.   Extreme poverty still compelled people to
live near their work, and so to drive up their own rents.   As railways
were built so property was demolished, and since the railways found
it cheaper to buy up cheap housing, it was the poor who felt the
pinch.   School-building, of its very nature to be found in crowded
areas, added to the demolition of a kind of house already in short
supply.   To make matters worse, middlemen sometimes made
handsome profits by taking commissions far exceeding the true rent
itself.[78]   In an attempt to overcome these problems the Royal Commission advocated an extension of Cheap Travel.   The empty houses
of suburbia were both too expensive and too remote for the poor of
Central London ever to occupy them: but if others could be persuaded to move, perhaps the poor could move into the houses they
vacated.   London had to filter outwards.   Perhaps Birmingham had
the answer, for here factories had moved to less populous parts to
make way for demolitions, and the work people had moved in their
wake.[79]

Some of our findings in this chapter are simply further examples
of relationships we have previously mentioned, such as that between
local house-building and local industrial activity, but some interesting
new points are, at least, suggested.   They cannot be asserted more
positively until we have looked at a number of factors that have
hitherto been almost neglected in this study.   We have, for example,
said little about international migration, or building costs.   But it
is not possible to look at a problem from all directions at the same
time, and before we embark on an examination of some of these
neglected aspects we can profitably put forward, in a very tentative
way, a few ideas that this partial analysis suggests.

Around 1870, the British economy leaned heavily on coal and
cotton, and the events we have already discussed led to inflated
prices, to over-production and to a collapse of foreign demand in
these sectors.   If this had happened in one sector or the other the
impact on our economy would have been less serious, just as, for
example, the Cotton Famine (which was, admittedly, a different kind
of crisis) left much of the rest of the economy buoyant.   But
America's attempt to recover after her Civil War, and the impacts
of the Franco-Prussian War, and its termination, so phased the
demands on Britain's resources that everything came together.   The
huge demands for coal, leading to inflated prices, contributed towards the dearness of our manufacturers; and the huge demands for
our manufactures increased the demands for investment goods, and
especially for machinery, thereby adding to the huge demands for
coal.   We have already suggested that if coal had been in more

elastic supply the consequences would have been easier. As it is, it seems that this great burst of activity operated through the inelastic coal supply to help to cause an inflation that was a notable factor in the ensuing credit crises that swept such a large part of the world. Why aggregate building in this country continued on its upward path after our foreign markets had broken is a problem we must defer. But we must point out that the rate of production was arrested in 1872, long before any noticeable British credit crisis. Our analysis of local factors has emphasised that while the general course of the economy had its impact on building, there were also a number of specific exogenous factors, such as, for example, the annexation of the Alsatian spinneries, exerting very appreciable influences on the fortune of industry, and the course of investment. In London the impact of the Overend and Gurney crisis was very marked, but elsewhere the general industrial expansion overrode its main effects. Possibly it was the reduction of building in London in the next few years that helped to support the London building boom in the later seventies, but we should keep in mind that this was geared very largely to transport development, which was influenced by a large number of factors, many of them (such as competition between companies) both intangible and important. The decline in building in most parts of the country arose from a falling off in industrial activity, even if it was rather delayed; and the delay in the decline served to lengthen the ensuing depression. When it did come, however, the decline liberated funds which (since there was, after all, some mobility of funds between regions) made the transport and housing developments in the London area all the easier, and all the more tempting, until here, too, they were overdone.

NOTES TO CHAPTER 5

1. We insert 'Victorian' to distinguish it from the Great Depression of the 1930's.

2. A. K. Cairncross, *Home and Foreign Investment, 1870–1913*, 1953; E. W. Cooney, 'Capital Exports, and Investment in Building in Britain and the U.S.A., 1856–1914', *Economica*, N.S., vol. xvi, No. 64, November 1949; Brinley Thomas, *Migration and Economic Growth*, 1954.

3. J. H. Clapham, *An Economic History of Modern Britain*, vol. iii, 1938 (reprinted 1951), p. 375.

4. *Ibid.*, pp. 377–8.

5. *The Economist*, 15.4.1871, quoted by Clapham, *op. cit.*, p. 379.

6. *Ibid.*, p. 380.

7. *Ibid.*, p. 383.

8. *Ibid.*, p. 383.

9. D. A. Thomas, 'The Growth and Direction of our Foreign Trade in Coal during the last half century', *J.R.S.S.*, September 1903, p. 2. This paper was

reprinted for private circulation.   Page references are to this reprint, of which I was loaned a copy by Professor Brinley Thomas.

10. *Op. cit.*, p. 29.

11. See D. H. Robertson, *A Study of Industrial Fluctuations*, 1915, reprinted London, 1948, pp. 15–17, and J. H. Morris and L. J. Williams, *The South Wales Coal Industry, 1841–1875*, 1958, p. 78.

12. D. A. Thomas, *op. cit.*, pp. 29–30.

13. *Ibid.*, p. 45.   Miss Margaret Williams has reminded me of the break in continuity of the data for employment in the coal industry (see Mitchell and Deane, *Abstract of British Historical Statistics*, p. 119). This would account for part of the apparent loss of productivity, but not for all of it.   In any case, the point is made by D. A. Thomas, on his general knowledge of the industry.   Its truth does not rest on the statistics quoted.

14. W. W. Rostow, *British Economy of the Nineteenth Century*, Oxford, 1948, p. 80.   Several of the facts about the coal industry are taken from this work.

15. D. A. Thomas, *op. cit.*, p. 60.

16. Morris and Williams, *op. cit.*, p. 39.

17. *Ibid.*, p. 79.

18. Brinley Thomas, 'Wales and the Atlantic Economy', *Scottish Journal of Political Economy*, November 1959, reprinted as chapter i of Brinley Thomas (ed.), *The Welsh Economy: Studies in Expansion*, 1962.

19. Thomas Ellison, *The Cotton Trade of Great Britain*, 1886, pp. 77–9.

20. *Ibid.*, pp. 34–5.

21. W. O. Henderson, *The Lancashire Cotton Famine, 1861–65*.

22. Based on Ellison, *op. cit.*, p. 72.   The 'Total (U.K.)' row refers to the number of spindles, looms or hands per mill in 1932 mills in 1850 and in 2674 mills in 1878.   The other columns appear to relate to England and Wales rather than to the U.K.

23. Based on Ellison, *op. cit.*, p. 72.

24. *Ibid.*, p. 77.

25. *Ibid.*, pp. 95–6.

26. Smiles, *Thrift*, London, 1875.   The quotation comes from pp. 123–4 of the Popular Edition of 1907.   Quoted without reference by Price, *op. cit.*

27. Ellison, *op. cit.*, p. 107.

28. *Ibid.*

29. D. A. Farnie, *The English Cotton Industry, 1850–1896*, M.A. Thesis (1953) in the Library of Manchester University.

30. Ellison, *op. cit.*, p. 77.

31. Ogden's remarks are referred to by A. Woodroofe Fletcher, in a paper called 'The Economic Results of the Ship Canal on Manchester and the Surrounding District', read to Manchester Statistical Society, 10th February 1897.   The comparison with Stockport is confirmed by the official Census figures.

32. Farnie, *ibid.*, p. 298.

33. Price, *op. cit.*, p. 189.

34. Royal Commission on Housing of the Working Classes, 1884–5, Questions 13897–13900.

35. Ellison, *op. cit.*, p. 78.

36. *Op. cit.*, pp. 297 ff.

37. *Ibid.*, p. 300.

38. *Ibid.*, p. 103.

39. A great deal of useful information is to be found in Fred Jones, *The Cotton*

Spinning Industry in the Oldham District from 1896–1914, M.A. (Econ.) Thesis (1959) in the Library of Manchester University.   See also Roland Smith, 'An Oldham Limited Liability Company, 1875–1896', *Business History*, vol. iv, 1961, pp. 34–53, especially for details of share ownership.

40. Jones, *op. cit.*, pp. 34–5.

41. Farnie, *op. cit.*, p. 109 and Ellison, *op. cit.*, p. 134.

42. Farnie, *op. cit.*, p. 261.

43. Ellison, *op. cit.*, p. 139.

44. Ellison, *op. cit.*, p. 138.

45. Farnie, *op. cit.*, p. 256.

46. Jones, *op. cit.*, p. 13.

47. Ellison, *op. cit.*, p. 136.

48. Farnie, *op. cit.*, p. 262.   See also Smith, *op. cit.*

49. It is true that continental producers exported little compared with Britain: but a little that is growing may still be serious competition.

50. *Op. cit.*, ch. ii.

51. *Ibid.*, p. 21.

52. *Ibid.*, p. 22.

53. *Loc. cit.*

54. *London Statistics, 1905–6*, London, pp. 24–5.

55. See also Cairncross, *op. cit.*, pp. 71–2.

56. S. E. Rasmussen, *London: The Unique City*, 1934.   Page references are to the abridged edition published in Pelican Books, 1960.

57. H. J. Dyos, *Victorian Suburb: A Study of the Growth of Camberwell*, Leicester, 1961.

58. Rasmussen, *op. cit.*, pp. 131–3.

59. Dyos, *op. cit.*, pp. 69–70.

60. *The Builder*, 18.3.1865.   See also *The Economist's Commercial History and Review, 1868*, pp. 37–8, on the rise of rents in 1863–5, and the subsequent decline.

61. *Building News*, 26.5.1865.

62. *Ibid.*, 4.8.1865.

63. *Ibid.*, 30.6.1865.

64. *Ibid.*, 10.2.1865.

65. *Ibid.*, 24.3.1865.

66. *Ibid.*, 4.5.1866.

67. *Loc. cit.*

68. See also *The Economist's Review, 1867*, esp. pp. 17–18.

69. Dyos, *op. cit.*, p. 71.

70. *The Economist's Review, 1868*, pp. 37–8.

71. *The Economist's Review, 1869*, said that in 1868 'the contraction of building operations and the suspension of many great undertakings have continued to depress the (timber) trade; and though our actual consumption is not materially lessened, the spirit of intermediate dealing has been wanting throughout the year'.

72. *Op. cit.*, p. 125.

73. *Ibid.*, p. 82.

74. Royal Commission . . . 1885, Q. 12399.

75. Royal Commission . . . 1885, vol. i, p. 23.

76. Royal Commission . . . 1885, vol. i, pp. 16–17.

77. *The Economist's Review, 1888*, p. 20.

78. Royal Commission . . . 1885, pp. 18–22.

79. Royal Commission . . . 1885, Q. 12398, 12594.

CHAPTER 6

COSTS, RENTS AND OTHER FACTORS

OUR account of the building cycle that reached its peak in the seventies paid little attention to the role of international migration. Other factors, such as building costs, were mentioned but briefly, and taken as it stands, Chapter 5 is by no means an adequate study of the boom that gave birth to the Great Victorian Depression. This is because, just as the programme notes to a symphony can talk only serially of different themes that are being played simultaneously, so the symphony of Britain's growth has to be described with an emphasis now on one aspect, now on another, and not until the separate themes have all been presented, as intelligibly as they can be when taken in isolation, can one stand back and listen to the whole, with all the forces interacting. So far we have concentrated almost entirely on two features. We have stressed the importance of regional variations, and the necessity of adequate supplies of short-term credit. But to say that our organ pipes have not always sounded at the same time, and that when they have in fact all blown together the mighty noise has sometimes whimpered out as the supply of wind has proved inadequate for so many simultaneous demands, is not to convey the pattern of the music. To do this, we have to get away from such detail, and view the whole — to change our level of aggregation, looking at the national picture, and then, finally, returning to some of the detail, so that both local and national forces may be more properly appreciated.

Building costs, levels of rent, empty property, housing standards, investment opportunities and migration of labour and capital are all matters with which we have so far dealt but inadequately. By the mid-eighties, however, some of these factors reach an importance which does not allow us to leave them lurking vaguely in the background any longer. The whole economy is, after all, an organism that never stands still, and factors that are trivial in one generation may dominate in the next. The period we are now surveying, from 1700 to 1914 can be divided very roughly into four overlapping and ill-defined periods. Until about 1760 is a period that saw fluctuations but no spectacular long-term overall growth, with little overseas migration, and internal migration directed almost entirely to London. The coming of the industrial revolution, and the growth of the factory towns, saw a leap in construction activity, derived largely from migration to these towns; it inaugurated a completely new trend and the second of our periods. During both of these an important element in determining the fortunes of the country was the harvest, with its repercussions on home prices, imports and the balance of payments. The Usury Laws operated with marked efficiency, as Shannon's famous article[1] so well shows. But in the third period, dating from the first of the railway booms, and steam transport, the whole economy was subjected to a new climate of interdependencies, communications and organisational changes just at a time when, as it happened, population pressure and transport changes made international migration on a large scale useful and possible, while the Usury Laws became ineffective and eventually ceased to exist. This third period merged uncertainly into the fourth, which may be taken as centring around the eighties. Shortly we shall examine it more carefully. For the moment it suffices to say that it was a period in which the increasing importance of other economic powers began to become apparent, when a complete change in our trade became noticed, and when the international flow of money and men was never more important. During this period the factors we have already examined still existed. In the major towns and regions there was still a close correlation between house- and factory-building and its general development. The importance of this approach in the nineties has been emphasised by Saul, who grouped all the towns for which data exist around the turn of the century according to their main industry or location.[2] We have also to keep in mind the rapid extension of suburban transport systems, to a time-schedule that depended on such varied factors as the growth of main lines (often because of inter-company rivalries), the whims of local landowners, and the optimism of local speculative builders. The influence exerted by transport development on building in London had its echoes in similar suburban development in and around other large towns, modifying the timing and location of building to a very large extent. Yet the more we consider these factors, the more we have to return to the movement of people, and to the resources and alternative uses of credit and investible funds. To put these into proper perspective we have to take a long-term view, spanning several building cycles. The most useful time to do this seems to be after we have very briefly surveyed the thirty years that remain before 1914. In doing so, we shall not attempt to emphasise once again the importance of regional differences, but rather to present just sufficient background for us to be able to embark on a fuller analysis, combining the broad movements of national aggregates and the behaviour of factors we have so far neglected, with the ideas we have already gleaned from our regional study.

Between 1860 and 1913 building described a large cursive M, as is shown in Figure 6.1, with a peak in the mid-seventies and

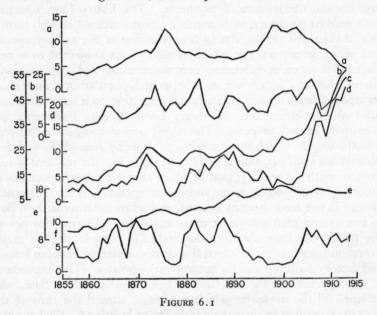

FIGURE 6.1

(a) Index of House-building, G.B. (1901–10 = 10).   Appendix 4.
(b) Gross Mercantile Shipbuilding, U.K. (£m.).   B.H.S., p. 373.
(c) Domestic Exports, U.K. (£'o m.).   B.H.S., p. 283.
(d) Net Income available for Foreign Investment, U.K. (£'o m.).   Feinstein, p. 119.
(e) Index of Real Wages (allowing for Unemployment), U.K. (1850 = 10).   B.H.S., pp. 343–4.
(f) Migration from U.K. to U.S.A. ('0,000).   Thomas (1), p. 282.

another period of high activity, showing as a double peak, around 1900. Broadly speaking other home-investment had much the same shape. We have already looked at some of the factors influencing the first upswing, and the timing of the peak in aggregate activity in the seventies. We have also noted that London, in particular, had a very much delayed peak, and we shall return to these matters before long, but it is sufficient now to note that by the mid-eighties building was at a low level almost everywhere, even if there were isolated local minor booms. Generally speaking, times were bad. Clapham summarised one aspect of the situation as having arisen because 'one of those pauses between equipment and re-equipment in Britain, coinciding with the close of a fierce spell of first equipment in America, had given the trade-union of the Boilermakers and Iron Shipbuilders three successive years (1884–6) in which on the average more than twenty per cent of its members were out of work'.[3] The next few years saw an improvement. In 1887 there was a slight temporary upturn in wholesale prices, and the next year brought in a fresh outburst of shipbuilding. Exports and foreign lending increased together, and by 1889 the demand for coal once again exceeded the capacity of the pits. Home investment, slowly rising at a time when foreign investment was especially attractive, so drove up the demand for capital that the discount rate rose eventually to 6 per cent in early 1890, but for all that the actual volume of investment at home was low, and in 1891 it slackened further.

The early nineties were years of many crises. 1890 itself saw a crisis in Argentina, and the Baring Crisis at home, as a company which had underwritten extensively in South American and other securities found itself unable to sell them before its own liabilities became due. 1893 saw disaster in Australia, and India was drawn in. Yet in the middle of all this, another disaster that was so far the greatest that had hit the building society movement, coincided with the actual upturn in building, and the beginning of a new boom.[4] Ever since 1874, when it became compulsory for building societies to submit annual accounts to the Registrar of Friendly Societies, a careful eye had been kept on their activities. The Baring Crisis, well-handled as it was through co-operation between the company and the Bank, sucked many smaller companies into its vortex, and contributed eventually to the fall of Portsea Island Building Society in 1892, which failed to repay its pressing depositors; but a few months later a giant crumbled. In 1868, Jabez Spencer Balfour, a man of good family and great gifts, had persuaded his fellow Nonconformists to line his pockets. His Liberator Building Society was 'to assist in the building of Nonconformist chapels and also to afford facilities to persons desirous of purchasing house property on equitable terms'. Not content with the usual means of advertisement and recommendation used to obtain depositors and borrowers, Balfour employed clergymen and people of all denominations who were in any way connected with temperance or thrift, as agents on a commission basis. This was not just a building society, but a virtuous one, and Sunday sermons could end not only with the usual collection, but with the additional collection of contributions. Far from the towns and the usual hunting grounds of the rival secular societies, Balfour's agents worked, taking savings from all classes of people, blessing them and receiving their commission. Within three years the assets of the society amounted to £69,000. Four years later, they had risen to half a million, while in another three years, just ten years after its birth in 1868, the assets of this society topped the million pounds mark. By 1880, it was the third largest society in the country, and Balfour was an M.P. But the Liberator was associated with a number of other companies, and its finance became shady. Land and property deals were financed without adequate cover, provided that they could bring an adequate capital gain to one or the other of the associated companies. Sometimes money was advanced on nothing more than a third mortgage. The ordinary business of the building society became less and less important. Balfour was not interested in lending money for either chapels or houses, but in making shady profits for himself out of the savings of the masses. By 1885 the total due from mortgages to the Liberator was over £2 m.; but the amount outstanding on advances of the kind normally made by building societies was a mere £330,000, from six hundred members. Seven years later, when the crash came, normal advances outstanding amounted to only £65,000 from just over two hundred members; and this is a measure of the extent to which the great Liberator was a true building society.

In 1892, when smaller societies were failing fairly often, a society of the Liberator's fame could not conduct such dealings with impunity, and rumours were circulating. There were heavy withdrawals from its funds and from those of two associated companies, the London and General Bank and the House and Land Investment Trust. In September the London and General Bank was compelled to suspend business. The same day the Liberator announced that it could repay its depositors only in rotation, and that afterwards it would repay its shareholders in the same way. A month later a compulsory winding-up order was made, and it soon disclosed that while the mortgage assets of this society amounted to £3,400,000 over 93 per cent of this vast sum was out on loan to three of Balfour's other companies, in not a single instance with any security better than a third mortgage. The total loss to the shareholders and depositors of the Liberator and its seven associated companies exceeded £8 m. Within a year the total membership of the building society movement fell from 640,000 to 590,000, and their assets from £51 m. to £43 m.

Perhaps if this disaster had occurred at a time when foreign investment was really attractive or when the credit situation had been tight, its impact on house-building would have been great; but in fact it occurred at a time when Bank rate was only 2 per cent, and in a way that shook confidence in building societies rather than in houses. Possibly if it had not occurred, the building society movement would have played a greater part in the nineties than it did, but the one indisputable fact is that house-building was already stirring itself out of its long despondent trough, and the two years of easy money that began late in 1894 were sufficient to lift it right up. 1893 was described as a year in which there was 'a state of suppressed energy' while 1894 revealed 'some stir' in public investment at home, but very little in overseas investment.[5] From 1895 to 1899 capital exports were 'inconsiderable', while exports of British produce were barely back to their level of 1890. A slight improvement in real wages and a steady improvement in employment was able to translate a potential demand for houses into a real one, at a time when money was abundant. 'Resources which might have gone abroad', wrote Clapham, 'were being employed to advantage at home, and a quick expansion of foreign trade and investment was proving less necessary to the general welfare of the country than those interested in them had supposed.'[6]

Late in 1896 the Bank rate of 2 per cent was abandoned, although it came down to this level again in 1897 for just a few months. Foreign trade continued to decline, and home investment saw a continued boom. The cotton industry was profiting as rarely before, and coal prices were once again rising. Then came the Boer War. Clapham has argued that it 'had only absorbed surpluses, [and] had not strained the country's saving capacity',[7] but it is precisely these marginal surpluses in total savings that make a great difference to the supply of short-term credit, and in any case the war was never argued to increase confidence in the future. The local builders in Edinburgh attributed the decline in building in that city, in 1900, to 'dear money' and 'restricted advances',[8] and there is little doubt that, whatever else may have happened, the war did have an effect of this kind. The Boer War loans of £43 m. in 1900 and £67 m. in 1901 must have hit building finance, and by the time that the war was over, foreign investment had again become attractive. The United States, Canada, South America, South Africa, Australia, indeed, almost the whole world, called out for capital and men, especially after 1905. At home, both nominal and real wages were stagnating, keeping down the demand for houses at a time when more or less stationary rents, and rising costs, made their supply less likely while fortunes were to be made abroad. But we have more to say about this in a later chapter.

Such is the broad background, and it has been impossible to

paint it without bringing an essential part of the 'long-swing' theory with its stress not only on migration, but also on the alternations of home and foreign investment.   This is a theory we shall shortly examine, but before doing so we must look at such matters as costs, rents and other related topics.

Until 1954 the commonly-cited index of building costs was that of G. T. Jones[9] but this has now been replaced by Maywald's index.[10] While this is a vast improvement on the pioneering one produced by Jones, it is important that we should keep an eye on some of its limitations.   Data on building costs are not easy to come by, and it is virtually impossible to obtain anything like comprehensive information for a single town or region.   On the other hand, while other information is available at a national level, certain vital data exist only for London or Glasgow.   Maywald has indicated that a principal deficiency in his index is that it 'omits any adjustment on account of technological changes in the building industry itself' even though technological change does 'affect the index insofar as it is reflected in prices of building materials', but the heterogeneity of the data is probably a more serious deficiency for it may, in fact, lead to more serious mistimings of turning points or distortions of short-term changes than the absence of allowance for technological change. It must, of course, be pointed out in all fairness to Maywald that, as he says, any index must be a compromise; and it is difficult to see how one could have improved on his efforts without stumbling across some unsuspected further data.

The principal changes in coverage during the nineteenth century are shown below:

1854: Lead prices change from those of English sheets to those of average computed value of imported lead.

1856: The iron 'B' prices change from those of British iron bars to the average declared export value of manufactured iron (bar, angle, bolt and rod).

1858: Scotch bars replace wrought-iron marked bars in the iron 'A' series.

1861: The timber price index becomes based on a different series of imported fir timber prices.

1863: Instead of using Laxtons' prices of stock bricks in London, being prices suitable for 'fair work' rather than market prices, a new series of brick prices in Glasgow is used.

1864: The lead prices introduced in 1854 (imported lead) are replaced by the London prices of English pig.

1870: The prices of window glass become import prices rather than export prices.

This list is as much a tribute to Maywald's ingenuity as it is a caution to the unwary. Except in the sixties the index is a reasonably faithful echo, as far as short-term fluctuations go, of Sauerbeck's wholesale price index, and this is itself some check on the reasonable nature of the index, which has the further advantage of usually behaving in the way one might expect from a knowledge of the course of building — which Jones' index did not do. In the sixties the general index of wholesale prices rises to a peak that has little or no parallel in the building costs index. Maywald offers a convincing explanation of this in terms of agricultural prices, and it seems more reasonable to accept this explanation than to attempt to ascribe the whole of the difference to the many changes in the composition of the index during this period. It is, however, important to keep in mind the fact that the geographical bias of the index is not constant. While several of the components are national, the brick prices were rather unsatisfactory London prices until 1863, and then rather more satisfactory Glasgow prices until 1900. We have already seen that building in these two cities behaved differently. Cairncross has looked at the relationship between building costs and other variables in Glasgow in some detail.[11]

Broadly speaking, we can say that Maywald's index of building costs declines in the late forties to a trough in 1851. Then it rises to a peak in 1854, due entirely to a rise in material costs. By 1856 half of this rise has been lost. Within a few more years wages began to rise, but material costs fall, rallying a little in the mid-sixties, just before the more rapid rise in wages that began in 1866. By 1870 the pace of wage-advances had slackened, but the feverish activity of the next few years, in so many parts of the world, drove up prices of building and other materials to a high peak in 1873. The ensuing fall, marked by slight rallies around 1880 and 1890, was accompanied by a sticky phase in wages, but the increasing activity of the later nineties saw both wages and material costs rise fairly sharply, and when peak activity was reached around the turn of the century, and the decline set in, wages levelled off, while material prices fell. All of this is shown in Figure 6.2.

Maywald's index of building costs includes the prices of materials and labour, but it does not include the rate of interest. The actual amount of interest paid by the builder on short-term loans made to him during the period of construction is, of course, a cost of production: but the variations in this from one year to another can rarely have equalled as much as three per cent of the total cost. A more important rate influencing the volume of building is the rate a landlord could get if he invested his money in some other solid

F

security, or the rate that a buyer would have to pay on a mortgage. It is not easy to measure these. One relevant rate whose course we have examined over a long period is the yield on Consols, but as the nineteenth century rolled on the inverse relationship disappeared, at least for a while. As is shown in Figure 6.2, the building upswing of 1860–76 had no parallel at all in the yield on Consols, and not

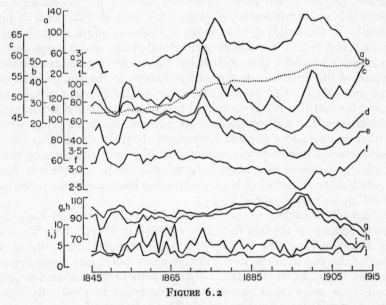

FIGURE 6.2

(a) (i) 1845–9. Bricks charged with Duty, E. & W. ('000 m.). *B.H.S.*, p. 235.
    (ii) 1856–1913. Index of House-building, G.B. (1901–10 = 100). Appendix 4.
(b) Index of Building Costs. Wages (1930 = 100) (Maywald). *B.H.S.*, p. 240.
(c) Index of Building Costs. Total (1930 = 100) (Maywald). *B.H.S.*, p. 240.
(d) Index of Building Costs. Materials (1930 = 100) (Maywald). *B.H.S.*, p. 240.
(e) Wholesale Price Index. (1867–77 = 100) (Sauerbeck). *B.H.S.*, pp. 474–5.
(f) Yield on Consols (%). *B.H.S.*, p. 455.
(g) Maximum Price of Consols (£).
(h) Minimum Price of Consols (£).
(i) Maximum Bank Rate (%).
(j) Minimum Bank Rate (%).

until we see the trough in the yield in the late nineties just preceding the downturn in building, about which we shall comment later, is there a suspicion of some relationship. This is not unexpected. The Usury Laws no longer applied, and in any case the supply of Consols was reduced after 1875 by the working of the Sinking Fund. While a high yield on Consols might reduce the comparative attraction of some other form of investment, these other forms were now able to benefit from the higher rates they could pay, and from an efficient market. At home and abroad new channels of investment existed. It is not surprising that the yield on Consols no longer serves as a reliable indicator of the stringency of credit. On the other hand, as we have seen in our account of the early seventies, the Bank rate had become an active, if muddled, instrument of policy, and to some extent its changes reflect judgements about the adequacy of credit, just as the rate itself tends also to affect the supply of credit.

From our point of view the Bank rate has the disadvantage of its volatility. There were, for example, no fewer than fifty changes in it during 1847–57. The year of peak production of bricks, 1847, saw ten changes, with the historically high rate of 8 per cent in October. Subsequent changes were traced in Chapter 4 where we noted a rate of 10 per cent in 1857, when building had had a minor boom but was not at any remarkably high level. Clearly the almost perfect inverse pattern of long cycles in building and the yield on Consols was not to be found with building and the Bank rate. On the other hand it is fair to recall that although a low interest rate is not, in itself, sufficient to cause a building boom, a high rate is a potent factor both in reducing the amount of activity when this is high and in restraining activity when it is already quite subdued. At any time of credit-shortage other than the most transient, one might expect the rate to be high.

If we look at the period from 1844 an interesting change of pattern emerges. Figure 6.2 graphs the annual maximum and minimum Consol prices and Bank rates, and compares these with building. The low price and high interest rates of 1847 are easily associated with the peak in brick production. The lower rates, and higher consol prices, of the early fifties continue the association with rising building activity, in the minor boom we have already noted. For a few years from 1854 the maximum rate rose steeply and the minimum rate was high. We have already seen that this was a time when credit was plentiful at a high price, and the peak rate of 1857 ties up with the crisis of that year. There was not a great deal of building, for reasons we have examined. The early sixties saw a slightly declining price of Consols and an uncertain, but generally low, Bank rate. Building was not particularly active except in the London area. The price of Consols continued to fall slowly until 1866, while the Bank rate reached its highest value of the decade in the same year, after reaching almost equally high rates in the preceding three years. It was a year of crisis, whose main impact on building was around London.

The sharp fall in the Bank rate to its 1867 value coincided with a rise in the price of Consols, while the subsequent rise in the rate, to its peak in 1873, which saw simply a horizontal trend in Consol prices, was associated with rising building in most parts of the country, but a steep decline in London. Both the inverse relationship between price and Bank rate, and that between yield and building, had become markedly less pronounced, and by the time that the aggregated house-building reached its peak in 1876, the Bank rate had been falling for three years. With only brief rallies it continued to fall until 1880. By 1882 it looked as if perhaps an upward trend had set in again, but in fact throughout the eighties the rate was never as high as 5 per cent for more than a few months at a time. For over four-fifths of the decade it was below this figure, and for well over half of the decade the rate was 3 per cent or lower. Towards the end of the eighties there were signs of an upward movement, but 1894 and 1895 saw cheap money which played an important part in encouraging the upswing in building. Very broadly speaking, the shape of the movements in the Bank rate was similar to the long cycle in building. The fall in the mid-seventies, preceding the fall in building, led to a more or less low level through the eighties, which culminated in a trough in 1894. The ensuing upswing is paralleled in the building graph, as is the downturn early in the next century: but the high rates of 1907 are not reflected in the curve of building activity.

The information available on the rate of interest charged on new mortgages is scanty. The following table presents some information assembled by Cairncross for rates charged by a variety of institutions in Glasgow, and some other data obtained by Weber for four of the major building societies. On the whole the Glasgow figures seem to move in the same direction as building during the period from the fifties to the nineties, which Weber interpreted as 'indicating that credit conditions, if anything, adjusted themselves to building activity rather than vice versa'. In the nineties a contrary movement is suggested, which he felt meant 'that in this period the trend of interest rates may have acted first as a contributory and then as a deterrent factor on building activity'.

It is convenient to quote Weber's remaining remarks, on the rates charged by the individual building societies:

The striking feature here is the rigidity of nominal rates charged. The Halifax Building Society apparently had only three changes in mortgage rates in the whole of the period from 1853 to 1913 and the range of the charge was no more than 4–5 per cent. The Temperance Permanent Building Society and another anonymous society in the south of England made only two changes in a period of similar duration and the range was only 6–7 and 4–5 per cent respectively. Nor are these changes ostensibly related to the timing of major fluctuations in building activity. Greater flexibility than is implied in these rates was, of course, attained by deducting bonuses or charging additional premiums of varying amount or for varying periods of time. In addition the length of the repayment period and the proportion of loans advanced could be varied — all factors which may significantly change the cost of ownership. In any case the

RATES OF INTEREST ON MORTGAGES, 1850–1913

	Rates Prevailing in Glasgow	Temperance Permanent Building Society	Halifax Building Society	Society A (South of England)	Society B* (South of England)
1850–5	$3\frac{2}{3}$				
1851				7	
1853			5		
1854		5 (plus varying premium)			
1855–70	4				
1859			$4\frac{1}{2}$–5 (less bonus)		Rates reduced from 6 to 5
1864				slightly less than $6\frac{1}{2}$	
1875					
1877	$4\frac{1}{2}$				
1878		5 (premium payable only for short fixed period)			
1881			$4\frac{1}{2}$–5 (no bonus)		
1885			4–5		
1889				6	
1890	4				
1896	$2\frac{3}{4}$–3	$4\frac{1}{2}$ (plus premium of 1%)			
1903		4 (plus premium of 1%)			
1904	$3\frac{1}{4}$				
1908	$3\frac{3}{4}$				
1912	4		$4\frac{1}{2}$–5		$4\frac{1}{2}$ (plus 1 for first five years)
1913					

* Records incomplete

administration of such individualistic credit instruments as mortgages must have meant at any time considerable deviations from generally laid down rules and practices.

Building society policy has nevertheless aimed for a wide measure of stability regarding interest payments. As a consequence adjustments to changing market conditions were carried out not so much with the aid of the price mechanism but by variations in the direct supply of funds. When capital resources were ample, interest on mortgages was not reduced but — given the demand — the volume of business was stepped up; and when funds were scarce business was restricted. Loan conditions might be tightened, loans on new houses might be substituted for loans on old and only high-class and safe properties might be entertained — but the rate of interest charged may not be affected. Under such circumstances the supply of capital may still play a more important role in the determination of the level of building activity than is suggested by movements of the rate of interest.

We have also to remember, of course, that the use of building society funds was still confined to a minority of cases, even though it was becoming more popular. Perhaps during 1901–15 the average number of houses financed by building society mortgages per annum was about equal to a quarter of the average annual supply of new houses, but many of these loans were, of course, made on old houses.[12] What rates were charged on privately negotiated loans, which were certainly very common, can be discovered only by systematic sampling of old contracts, and this has not been done.

Once we consider the cost of building, we have also to take account of the incomes arising from buildings, and this immediately presents us with the problem of examining rents. A certain amount of local data exists, but if we are seeking a series that can, in some way or the other, be of use in an argument about national aggregates, we have to turn to other sources. This is a task that was undertaken by Weber, whose account of a new index of house-rents for Great Britain, for 1874–1913, may be reprinted in its entirety.[13]

Most studies of the building cycle assign some importance to rent, but the degree and nature of the relationship is the subject of considerable controversy. Writing of the U.S.A., Long emphasised expectations of rental incomes as a main influence on the inducement to invest in houses, although he did not attempt to illustrate any empirical relationships.[14] W. H. Newman, who carried out an empirical analysis[15] failed to uncover any connection between rent and the building cycle in the U.S.A., but for the U.K., H. W. Robinson found that there were slight waves in the movement of rent about its upward linear trend, and that these agreed well with the long cycles of residential construction.[16] A similar relationship has been noted by A. K. Cairncross, who is more emphatic about the connection.[17] One of the reasons for this difference of opinion is that there is a paucity of suitable rent statistics over a long enough period. The object of this paper is to present a new index of house rents and briefly to examine some of the conclusions that it indicates.

The index of rent most commonly used in studies of the U.K. is A. L. Bowley's[18] covering the period 1880–1914, and based on data in the Second Fiscal Blue Book.[19] This series relates only to working-class

houses in London and twenty provincial cities and has, therefore, a
limited coverage.   The inclusion of rates makes the index somewhat unsuitable for many purposes, and the rather arbitrary method of allowing
for that part of rates which arose from improved services makes it less
useful than one would like it to be.[20]   A more important objection is that
the index is based on only six years, the estimates for the remaining years
being obtained by interpolation.

Cairncross's rent index appears to be based on the same basic source
in 1880–1900, but different figures have been used in 1900–13 and the
index has been carried back to 1870.[21]

An alternative index of house rent can be based on the statistics of
the Inhabited House Duty.   From 1874 the annual value and number of
all houses in Great Britain is given in the Inland Revenue Reports, and
an index of average rentals can be calculated by simple division.[22]   The
main advantage of using inland revenue statistics for the construction of
rent indices is that they are not confined to working-class houses · in
selected urban areas, and that they cover a much longer historical period.
One of their disadvantages is that changes in average rentals reflect not
merely changes in rent per identical unit but also changes in the size and
quality of the average house, but this difficulty has not been adequately
overcome in any index.   It is moreover a short-coming which, though it
affects long run trends, is probably never important enough to dominate
the pattern of fluctuation.

The main statistical difficulty in deriving annual average rentals is to
allow for the downward lag between re-assessment years, arising because
rent-reductions were allowed for in each year but rent-increases were not
taken into account until the next assessment.   To correct for this, we
extrapolated the figures for inter-assessment years to cover the year in
which the next assessment was carried out, and then assumed that the
difference between the value so obtained and the new assessment had
accumulated over the whole span between assessment years at a linear
rate.   Since the assessment years in England and Wales were not the
same as in the Metropolis the same procedure was carried out separately
for the two regions.   In Scotland the system in question amounted in
practice to an annual reassessment and no lag inhibits the figures.   The
method is essentially the same as that used by A. R. Prest and A. A.
Adams for their similar estimates for 1900–19.[23]   It was in fact deliberately followed so as to make possible a consistent set of estimates from
1874 to 1919.[24]

The description of the more detailed workings need not be repeated
here, since they are fully set out by Prest and Adams.   There is one
divergence, however, which must be briefly noted.   It relates to the
estimation of empty property which must be excluded from the total
housing stock.   No statistics of empty houses in England and Wales are
given in the Inland Revenue Reports before 1900.   They were therefore
estimated by applying the ratio of the number of empty houses to all

houses in London to the total of all houses in England and Wales.[25] This procedure is not entirely satisfactory as conditions in London have at times diverged from conditions in the rest of the country, but the error introduced into the total occupied housing stock is slight and the use of the series certainly produces more accurate estimates than would be attained by omitting to allow for changes in 'empties' altogether. The problem does not arise in Scotland as the annual value of empty property under Schedule A is available in the Inland Revenue Reports. Two adjustments were, however, called for. First the figures refer to net quantities and had to be converted to gross values — Prest and Adams multiply by a correction factor of 1·2. This figure was taken to apply in 1900 and gradually decumulated at a linear rate to 1·1 in 1874 in order to conform to the changed relationships between gross and net values over the period. The other adjustment corrects for the fact that the empty property allowance under Schedule A covers all buildings and not specifically residential structures. The proportion of the residential sector was estimated by applying to all 'empties' under Schedule A the average ratio in 1874–1900 of the total gross value of dwelling-houses to the total gross value of houses and messuages in Scotland.

In 1900 our index of average rentals in G.B. was chained to the similar index calculated by Prest and Adams. The absolute figures in 1900 agree very closely and compare as follows:

	A. R. Prest and A. A. Adams	B. Weber
Expenditure on house-rent	£ Mn. 129·51	£ Mn. 131·25
Number of houses, 000's	6925	7003
Average rentals	£18·70	£18·74

The diagram (Figure 6.3) compares the index with that of H. W. Singer,[26] based on the Schedule A statistics. This, as we have seen, relates to all structures other than farmhouses and some other minor groups. It also relates only to England and Wales. Inevitably its construction is rougher than ours, and the nature of the basic statistics militates against any attempt at refinement. We also show the course of house-building in Great Britain from 1856.[27]

Three points may be noted about the movement of rent. First, rents have for a period of almost 70 years followed an upward trend. This emerges particularly strikingly if compared with the movement of general prices. Singer's index of rent stands at approximately 85 per cent higher in 1910 than it stood in 1845 whereas neither wholesale prices nor building costs were significantly higher just before the outbreak of World War I than they were in the late 1840's. The explanation for this rise in trend is largely to be found in the improvement in quality and size of the average house.

Secondly, although showing a firm long-run rise, rents have nevertheless been 'sticky'. They followed a course alternating between long periods of stability and relatively steady advance unaccompanied by fluctuation other than in the rate of growth. Declines in rent were never sustained for longer than a year or two and were so slight as to be well within the margin of error. This absence of absolute declines may be attributed partly to the powerful upward trend — associated with the increasing size and improving quality of the housing standard — which tended to offset any downward force exercised by market conditions. Part of the explanation must also lie in the proverbial 'stickiness' of rents, arising

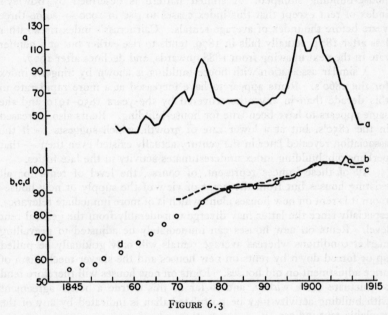

FIGURE 6.3

(a) Weber's Index of House-building in Thirty-four Towns. Weber (1).
(b) Weber's Index of House-rents. Appendix 13.
(c) Cairncross's Index of House-rents. Cairncross, p. 213.
(d) Singer's Index of House-rents. Singer, p. 230.

from the practice of long leases, long lets and the relative rigidity of the rent bargain.

Thirdly, the alternating movements of advance and stability have tended to conform closely to the various phases of the building cycle. Rents rose when building was on the increase and remained stable when building was on the decline. The only disharmony in this association in the period 1874–1913 occurred on the turn from the 1870's to the 1880's when rents apparently continued to expand for some years after the turn in building activity in 1876. Closer inspection of the figures shows, however, that almost half of the whole increase in rent in the period 1874–83 occurred in the two years of 1876–7, the peak years of building

F2

activity.   After that the rate of increase declined and what annual increments there were were slight.   It must be remembered also that house-
building continued to expand in London until 1881 and that almost a
third of the total annual value of house-property under the Inhabited
House Duty was located in the capital.   From the early 1880's to the early
1890's rents remained stable while house-building was depressed; and
from the middle 1890's to approximately 1902–3 rents rose while house-
building boomed.   Finally, rents again stayed stable in 1903–14,[28] while
house-building slumped.   A similar pattern is described by Bowley's
index of rent except that this index ceases to rise in 1900 — some three
years before the index of average rentals.   Cairncross's index rises rather
less after 1874, actually falls in 1879, tends to rise earlier but at a gentler
rate in the next upswing from 1888 onwards, and declines after 1907.

A similar association with house-building is shown by Singer's index
for the 1860's.   Rents appear to have increased at a more rapid rate in
this decade than in any other covered by the years 1850–1910 and the
same appears to have been true for house-building.   Rents also increased
in the 1850's, but at a lower rate of growth, which suggests — if the
association revealed later in the century actually existed even then — that
perhaps our building index underestimates activity in the late fifties.

All of these indices represent, of course, the level of rents for all
existing houses but from the point of view of the supply of new house-
room it is rent on new houses alone which is of more immediate relevance,
especially since the latter may diverge considerably from the general rent
level.   Rents on new houses can immediately be adjusted to prevailing
market conditions whereas average rentals will only gradually be pulled
up or forced down by rents on new houses and the slower mechanism of
price adjustment on old houses.   Rents on new houses will therefore tend
to fluctuate more widely, and so far as this is true a better agreement
with building activity may be postulated than is indicated by any of the
available rent indices.

It would, however, be wrong to think of rent as being the only
measure of income from property.   There is always the possibility
of capital gain through selling at an inflated price, and property
values reflect this, as well as such almost unpredictable variables as
site values.   This is another matter on which it is convenient to
print from Weber's unpublished papers:

The movement of property values can be illustrated by some scraps
of information on the average number of years' purchase offered for
house-property.   Some figures of this kind for a few individual years
covering the period from 1872 to 1907 have been compiled by W. Frazer
in 1908.[29]   They are based on houses sold by auction at the Glasgow
Faculty Hall and only a proportion of all transactions in the city is therefore
represented.   Few new houses are, moreover, likely to have been included.

AVERAGE NUMBER OF YEARS' PURCHASE OF HOUSE-PROPERTY SOLD AT THE
FACULTY HALL IN GLASGOW, 1872–1907

1872	14·3	1886	12·8	1901	14·9
1876	17·0	1891	13·0	1906	13·0
1881	13·5	1896	14·1	1907	12·1

The striking feature of the series is its resemblance to the long waves
of house-building. The two peaks in 1876 and 1901 stand out. A
trough is located in 1886 and there is a decline in 1906–7. The high
prices offered in 1876 are of special interest. An average of 17 years'
purchase was being offered for house-property in that year and this
compares to only 14·9 in 1901 and 12·8 in the trough year of 1886. In
the absence of a correspondingly greater demand for house-room it is
strongly suggestive of the prevalence of specially powerful speculative
elements in the boom of the 1870's.

An annual series of the average number of years' purchase of house-
property has been compiled by Cairncross from the Estate Duty Statistics.
It is available from 1895 to 1914 and represents the value of estates
passing at death. The valuations are consistently higher than the valuations in Glasgow, a fact which is probably explained by a small proportion
of highly valued properties sold at the Glasgow auction market. But
both series follow the same pattern of fluctuation. Property reached a
peak in 1901 when, according to the Estate Duty figures, 15·8 years'
purchase was being offered for house-property. After 1901 they declined
in each year, except 1906, to 1909, in which year property was valued at
13·2 years' purchase. In 1910 the trend was reversed and 14·4
years' purchase was being offered in 1914. But the recovery was apparently not sufficient to rescue the building industry from its continued
relapse.

It may be legitimately objected that rent and property prices cannot
by themselves be considered governing influences on building activity if
examined in isolation from building costs and the rate of interest and that
it is the movement of all these variables in relation to each other which is
of importance. An attempt has therefore been made to combine rents
and property prices respectively with building costs and the rate of
interest into two composite indices of profitability. The period covered
is 1872 to 1914 and the formulae used were

$$\frac{p}{c.i} \quad \text{and} \quad \frac{r}{c.i}$$

where p stands for property prices, c for building costs, i for the rate of
interest and r for average rentals. Some of the statistical shortcomings
adhering to these basic series have already been noted but it must be
stressed that the possible error which they introduce into the combined
indices will be magnified.

The formulae compare first property prices, and then rental income, with the return at current interest rates obtained by investing an amount equal to the current cost of building.

The year to year movements are not sufficiently reliable for any conclusions to be drawn but the variations in long run trend are more meaningful. On the whole they bear out the relationships with the phases of the building cycle already suggested by the indices of average rentals and property prices (Figure 6.4).   The index of profitability based on property values corrected for cost and interest, conforms to building activity. The alternative index, based on average rentals, moves more sluggishly,

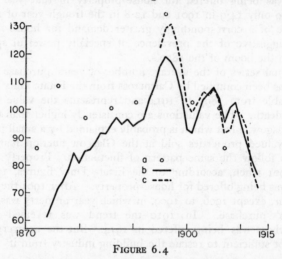

FIGURE 6.4

Indices of profitability of house-ownership, derived as described in text.   Series (a) uses Frazer's data printed on page 159, (b) uses Weber's Index of House-rents, and (c) uses Cairncross's series of the average number of years' purchase.

and in the period from 1874 to just before the turn of the century, variations in trend emerge only in the rate of growth.   To a very considerable extent this is due to the 'stickiness' of rents.   In all probability an index of rent relating to new houses alone — if available — would show either *absolute* rises and falls or at least significantly greater variations in the rate of growth.   As it is, the use of an index of average rentals for all houses tends to understate profitability in periods of use and to exaggerate it in periods of decline.

Whether rents and house values are compared directly with house-building activity, or whether they are first expressed in terms of cost, an empirical association with rent and property prices following a course consistent with being of causal significance appears clearly established. The absence at the same time of similar relationships between house-building, the rate of interest and building costs illustrates that if and in

so far as building cycles are initiated on the side of supply, it is the returns
to be secured by investment in houses rather than cost which is the
initiating factor.

What then have been the main influences determining the secular
fluctuations in rents and property prices? Variations in the direct process
of supplying new house-room has clearly not been a determining factor
since rents and property prices rose rather than fell when house-building
increased and remained stable or fell when building declined. Building
costs on the other hand were more important. They tended to follow
sympathetic movements to rent and property values even though they
fluctuated more and declined in building cycle downswings while rents
merely ceased to rise. Rising costs led to higher rents and property
values and falling costs at any rate helped to prevent a continuation of a
rising trend in rent and contributed to the fall in house-values. A similar
association of rent and house-values with the rate of interest can theoreti-
cally be postulated but since the empirical evidence only partly bears this
out one can only conclude that it was of a relatively minor character.
Finally, a close connection with long cycles in demand, as measured by
population growth, income movements or the vacancy rate, can also be
observed; and some force must be allocated to elements of speculation.

If, however, rents and house-values changed by virtue of corresponding
movements in cost, and changed *at no greater* rate than cost, the changes
need to provide no stimulus for house-owners and builders to change the
supply of house-room. A greater return will in that case merely be offset
by a greater outlay and no change in profitability will occur. In other
words variations in rents and house-prices need not, and are indeed
unlikely to, set off corresponding fluctuations in house-building if they
are the consequence of changes in cost.

The conclusion emerges that rents and house-values play a causative
part in building cycles only if the initial stimulus has come from changed
conditions not of cost but of demand. In that case, moreover, their
function is only to a limited degree causative and the ultimate cause must
be sought one stage further back on the side of demand. Building
activity seems to have been governed by rent and house-values, which in
turn were affected by building cost (in which case they may be discounted
as of causative significance in inducing building cycles) and conditions of
demand.

These conclusions of Weber's are essentially partial and preliminary. They were made in a draft chapter that preceded his
section on demographic factors, and the final few pages of his
manuscript indicate that the conclusions just quoted were liable to
modifications. For all that, they present a very reasonable, and
very useful, summary of a major aspect of the building cycle mechanism. By avoiding any reference to the dating of turning points, or
any attempt to establish whether the fall in building followed or

162   BUILDING CYCLES AND BRITAIN'S GROWTH

preceded the fall in rent, he also avoided the principal danger implicit in the use of time-series at the wrong level of aggregation, for clearly if we are to argue that, for example, falling rents caused diminished building, then we must speak of rents and building in a particular locality. Cairncross's analysis for Glasgow tells us a story that is based on a reasonably appropriate level of aggregation, at which the dating of turning points may be taken to have a real meaning in terms of causation: but it would be wrong to assume that the same sequence of events necessarily existed in all other towns. It would be even more wrong to assume that the sequences and patterns existing in the national aggregates existed and operated causally in any single housing-market. On the other hand, these national aggregates, and even the dating of their turning points, do have considerable uses, and certainly any relationship that appears to be revealed by them demands careful consideration and examination, preferably at the right level of aggregation — but this is not always possible, and then one has to take the relationship as suggested rather than proven.

Having made the preliminary surveys of the background in the later nineteenth century, and the course of costs, rates of interest, rent and other factors, we shall now look at the demographic factor, and embark on an account of the theory of inverse building cycles. We shall then be in a position to weave together these separate strands of thought.

NOTES TO CHAPTER 6

1. H. A. Shannon, *op. cit.*
2. S. B. Saul, 'House-Building in England, 1890–1914', *Economic History Review*, vol. xv, no. 1, 1962, pp. 119–37. See Chapter 8 below.
3. Clapham, *op. cit.*, p. 5.
4. The account that follows is based largely on S. J. Price, *op. cit.*
5. Clapham, *op. cit.*, pp. 28–9.
6. *Ibid.*, p. 30.
7. Clapham, *op. cit.*, p. 46.
8. *Master Builders' Association's Journal*, February 1900, p. 13, quoted by C. H. Feinstein on p. 279 of his Ph.D. (Cantab.) Thesis.
9. G. T. Jones, *Increasing Returns*, Cambridge, 1933.
10. K. Maywald, 'An Index of Building Costs in the United Kingdom, 1845–1938', *Economic History Review*, II, vol. vii, 1954, pp. 187–203.
11. *Op. cit.*, chapter ii.
12. H. Bellman, *Bricks and Mortar*, London, 1949, p. 147.
13. The account that follows first appeared in *The Scottish Journal of Political Economy*, vol. viii, 1961. It is a slightly edited version of part of a draft-chapter of Weber's incomplete thesis.
14. Clarence D. Long, Jnr., *Building Cycles and The Theory of Investment*, Princeton, 1940, p. 21.

15. W. H. Newman, 'The Building Industry and Business Cycles', *Journal of Business of the University of Chicago*, vol. viii, July 1935, no. 3.

16. H. W. Robinson, *The Economics of Building*, London, 1939, pp. 126–7.

17. A. K. Cairncross, *Home and Foreign Investment, 1870–1913*, pp. 214–16.

18. A. L. Bowley, *Wages and Income in the U.K. since 1860*, p. 121.

19. Cd. 6955.

20. One half of the rates was treated in the same manner as rent, while the other half was assumed to be payment for increased services and amenities, and was excluded.

21. A. K. Cairncross, *Home and Foreign Investment, 1870–1913*, p. 213.

22. Prior to 1874 the House Duty has only statistics of houses actually charged to Duty (annual value of £20 and over), and these form only a small proportion of the total housing stock. The House Duty is therefore of little use for this earlier period, but an indication of rent movements can be obtained from the statistics given under the Schedule A of the Income Tax. These relate to buildings of all kinds except farmhouses, railway buildings, gas works and some other minor groups, but even so they may be sufficiently reliable to yield a broadly accurate picture of trends in the residential sector. This is confirmed by the close agreement between results based on the Schedule A figures and the indices of house rent in 1874–1913.

23. A. R. Prest and A. A. Adams, *Consumers' Expenditure in the U.K. 1900–19*, Cambridge, 1954, pp. 92–7.

24. The estimates can be continued to 1938 on the basis of information given by R. Stone in *The Measurement of Consumers' Expenditure and Behaviour in the U.K.*, Cambridge, 1954, p. 221.

25. J. Calvert Spensley, 'Urban Housing Problems', *J.R.S.S.*, lxxxi, Part II, 1918. The figures are based on losses to Water Companies, arising largely from 'empties'.

26. H. W. Singer, 'An Index of Urban Land Rents and House Rents in England and Wales, 1845–1913', *Econometrica*, vol. ix, nos. 3 and 4, 1941, p. 230. The index was re-based to 1898–1903 = 100.

27. The graph drawn is of the index of house-building in thirty-four large towns, taken from B. Weber, 'A New Index of Residential Construction and Long Cycles in House-building in Great Britain, 1838–1950', *S.J.P.E.*, vol. ii, pp. 104–132. It is based on an increasing number of towns, from six in 1860 to seventeen in 1880 and thirty-four in 1900. The rent index appears as Appendix 13.

28. Prest and Adams' figures show a sharp peak in 1909 followed by a decline in 1910–1 to a level approximately the same as in 1908. This is not confirmed by any of the other indices and does not tally with what is known about the housing market of the time.

29. W. Frazer, 'Fluctuations of the building trade and Glasgow's house-accommodation', *Proc. Roy. Phil. Soc.*, Glasgow, 1908, p. 27. The figures have been reproduced by A. K. Cairncross, *op. cit.*, p. 31.

CHAPTER 7

POPULATION AND INVERSE
BUILDING CYCLES

THE variables we discussed in the last chapter are rather badly represented by regional statistics, but there are tolerably reliable series depicting their movements at a national level. In this chapter we look at population, both at a national and at a more disaggregated level, in an attempt to check some of the speculation of Chapter 3 against fact. Unfortunately the population statistics leave a great deal to be desired and we must proceed most carefully.

We may begin by drawing upon some of Weber's work on decennial increases in population and households. His data, derived from population censuses, are summarised in Table 7.1. He pointed out that as a rough approximation a steady increase in population might be expected to result in more or less steady increases, from one decade to the next, in the stock of houses, while fluctuations in the rate of increase of population, indicated by the second differences, should show some similarity to the pattern of building activity. How close this correspondence was may be judged from Figure 7.1, which graphs the second differences of population against the decennial increases in housing stock. Only in one decade — that of 1821–31 — is there a definite divergence in the direction of movement. It arises from the high population increase in 1811–21 which in turn is partly a reflection of the return and demobilisation of the armies serving abroad in the Napoleonic Wars. It derives from a population increase which is not of the same significance for housing demand as that arising from natural growth or from migration. Few new houses were required as the soldiers formed part of already existing households from which they were temporarily absent and into which they were re-absorbed on their return, while house-building in the first half of that decade was, as we have seen, hampered by war-time scarcities and stringencies.

In all the remaining decades — except perhaps the 1850's, for which period there is some doubt — the movements were in the same direction. Faster growth in population in the 1830's, the 1850's, and

1860's and 1870's, the 1890's and the inter-war period, was accompanied also by higher levels of building activity and greater net increases in housing stock. And slower growth in population in the 1840's, the 1880's, the 1900's and 1910's was similarly matched by lower activity in house-building [1] and smaller net increases in the housing stock.

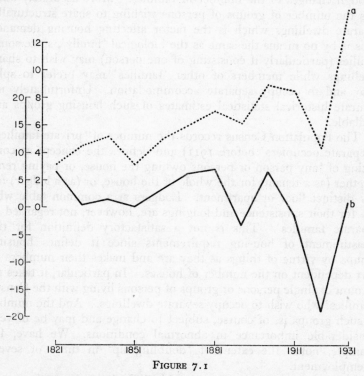

FIGURE 7.1

(a) Decennial Increase in Housing Stock, G.B. ('00,000).
(b) Inter-decennial second difference in Population, G.B. ('00,000).

The general agreement in timing of the fluctuations in population growth and house-building is unmistakable. Less satisfactory is the agreement in the degree of the movements. The slight fall of the population increase in the 1840's for instance could hardly, by itself, carry the whole burden of the explanation for the drop in the increase of houses. And the addition to population increase in the next decade is too small (a mere 31,000 compared to, for instance, 630,000 in the 1860's) to account for its rise. Nor can the boom of the 1920's and the 1930's be entirely explained by population growth — though it was a contributory factor. Other factors are clearly at work and it is the combined influence of all of these which determines the level of building activity at any given time. But the close connection with population growth suggests that the latter has been a force of predominating importance.

It may be argued that demographic influences affect housing demand not so much through changes in the number of persons as through changes in the number of families. More accurately still, it is the number of groups of persons wishing to share structurally separate dwellings which is the factor affecting housing demand. This is by no means the same as the biological 'family', since some families (particularly if consisting of one person) may wish to share dwellings while members of other 'families' may prefer to split away and to occupy separate accommodation. Unfortunately no accurate historical statistical estimates of such housing groups are available.

The Population Census records the number of 'private families' ('separate occupiers' before 1911) and defines the concept as consisting of 'any person or persons owning the house, or paying rent, whether (as a tenant) for the whole of the house, or (as a lodger) for any distinct floor or apartment. Lodgers at a common table who pay for their subsistence and lodgings are, however, not regarded as separate families'. This is not a satisfactory definition for the measurement of housing requirements since it defines housing groups by virtue of things as they are and makes their numbers in part dependent on the number of houses. In particular, it takes no account of single persons or groups of persons living with the Census 'families' who wish to occupy separate dwellings. And the number of such groups is, of course, subject to change and may be of very considerable importance in abnormal conditions. We have, for example, noted the extent of 'doubling up' in times of severe unemployment.

An attempt partly to overcome this difficulty and to estimate the number of families in a more useful form for housing problems has been made by the Registrar-General in the 1931 Census for each census year from 1861 onwards.[2] Three alternative indices based on the following assumptions were prepared: A, that the number of private families was the same as the number of married women; B, that widows and widowers under 65 years of age should be included; and C, that 10 per cent of all single males and females between the ages of 20–45 be further added. The C-estimate is the best approximation to the actual number of households in existence but it still neglects to take into account the number of single or family units wishing to double up. It may also be objected that the application to long historical periods of estimating methods involving rigid statistical assumptions can hardly avoid error, on account of the failure to take account of changes in the social and institutional background. Comparison of columns (3), (5) and (7) in Table 7.1 reveals that except at the time of the First World War, the second

TABLE 7.1

POPULATION AND FAMILY CHANGES IN GREAT BRITAIN, 1801–1951

Cols. (4)–(7) England and Wales only

(000's)

	(1)	(2)	(3)	(4)		(5)	(6)	(7)
	Total Population	Increases in Col. (1) per annum *	Second Differences of Col. (2) per annum *	Separate Occupiers	Private Families	Second Differences of Col. (4)	Private Families. Registrar-General's C-estimate	Second Differences of Col. (6)
1801	10,501			1897				
1811	11,970	146·9		2172				
1821	14,092	212·2	+65·3	2493		+46		
1831	16,261	216·9	+4·7	2912		+98		
1841	18,534	227·3	+10·4	not returned				
1851	20,816	228·2	+0·9	3712				
1861	23,129	231·3	+3·1	4492			4,219	
1871	26,072	294·3	+63·0	5049		-223	4,776	
1881	29,710	363·8	+69·5	5633		+27	5,391	+58
1891	33,028	331·8	-32·0	6131		-86	5,999	-7
1901	37,000	397·2	+65·4	7037		+508	6,959	+352
1911	40,831	383·1	-14·1	8005	7,943	+60	7,953	+34
1921	42,769	193·8	-189·3		8,739		9,046	+99
1931	44,795†	202·6	+8·8		10,233	+698	10,140	+1
1939	46,694	230·2	+27·6					
1951	48,841	182·7	-47·5					

* The figures are given per annum so as to render comparable the population increases in 1931–9 and 1939–51 with the increases in other periods.

† Registrar-General's mid-year estimate. Including H.M. Forces serving overseas and excluding Commonwealth and foreign forces in Great Britain.

differences in population increased or decreased in phase with the second differences in households. For all their limitations, our data on population are more reliable than the best available estimates of the numbers of families, and this similarity in the pattern of inter-decennial changes provides some justification for our continuing to use the former when theory suggests that, if we had decent estimates, we should prefer the latter.

But national totals of population can be but a crude indication of the national demand for houses, for people move and leave their houses behind. International migration clearly has its impact on decennial changes of population, but internal migration, which is a powerful factor in determining demand, cannot appear in changes in national aggregates. These are matters to which we must now turn, first, once again, for the purpose of interdecennial comparisons.

Weber used the not very accurate annual data on births and deaths provided by the Registrar-General since 1837 to estimate the decennial natural increase of population. Comparison with the inter-Census changes provided estimates of net migration, which are shown in Table 7.2. This table can be used to provide crude

TABLE 7.2

POPULATION CHANGES (000's), 1811–1931

	Average Annual Increase in Inter-Decennial Addition to Population		Average Annual Natural Increase		Average Annual Migration		Increases in Col. (2)		Increases in Col. (3)	
	(1)		(2)		(3)		(4)		(5)	
	G.B.	E & W	G.B.	E & W	G.B.	E & W	G.B.	E & W	G.B.	E & W
1811–21	65·3									
1821–31	4·7									
1831–41	10·4									
1841–51	0·9			209·5	−8·1					
1851–61	3·1	12·4		246·5	−32·7				37·0	−24·6
1861–71	63·0	50·8	326·9	285·2	−32·6	−20·6			38·7	12·1
1871–81	69·5	61·6	389·5	342·6	−25·7	−16·4	62·6	57·4	6·9	4·2
1881–91	−32·0		413·6		−81·8		24·1		−56·1	
1891–01	65·4		409·4		−12·2		−4·2		69·6	
1901–11	−14·1		458·7		−75·6		49·3		−63·4	
1911–21	−189·3		279·6		−85·8		−179·1		−10·2	
1921–31	8·8		258·8		−56·2		−20·8		29·6	

indications of the relative direct importances of natural increase and net migration in shaping the fluctuations in additions to the population. Except for the 1930's, net migration was always outwards, but from our point of view it is changes in net migration that matter at present. These are shown in column (5), which provides a comparison with changes in natural increase, printed in column (4). Only in the sixties and seventies of the nineteenth century were both natural increase and international migration changing in favour of a rising population. In all other decades, either natural increase accelerated at the same time as emigration, or it slowed down at a time when emigration also dwindled or — and this last occurred only in the decade of the First World War — natural increase was retarded and emigration increased, so that both forces slowed down the total growth of population.   This rough summary of the movements suggests that, with both forces working together and upwards, the sixties and seventies should have seen a large amount of building, while the second decade of this century should have seen little. Broadly speaking, this was so. We may also notice that between 1881 and 1911 there was a greater degree of conformity between column (1) and column (5) than between columns (1) and (4), suggesting that migration rather than natural increase was the dominant force in determining the fluctuations in population increase.

This approach of Weber's takes no account of the age-distribution of the population.   Feinstein[3] has made an interesting attempt to

TABLE 7.3

POTENTIAL DEMAND FOR HOUSES FROM POPULATION AGED 20–44
GREAT BRITAIN, 1871–75 to 1906–10

Estimated Demands for Houses (Thousands) through Population Change			Houses Actually Built (000's)	Difference (4) – (3)	
By Natural Increase	Lost by Emigration	By Actual Increase		Direct	Lagged
(1)	(2)	(3)= (1) – (2)	(4)	(5)	(6)
1871–75	444	64	380	477	97	—
1876–80	465	60	405	531	126	151
1881–85	591	193	398	402	4	–3
1886–90	617	163	454	389	–65	–9
1891–95	702	32	670	430	–240	–24
1896–00	730	13	717	691	–26	21
1901–05	670	114	556	714	158	–3
1906–10	697	210	487	538	51	–18

relate natural increase and emigration to the demand for houses by concentrating on people aged 20–44 years.   He used decennial data and certain reasonable — if slightly arbitrary — assumptions to compute quinquennial changes, and broke these down according to age-groups.   He then used his results to calculate the demand for houses arising from natural increase and migration, on the assumption that the operative part of the population was that aged 20–44. The calculations are summarised in Table 7.3, which differs slightly from Feinstein's, chiefly in the insertion of the last column which shows the difference between the demand in one period and the provision of houses in the next.   It will be seen that, except for the period 1876–80, the number of houses actually built was remarkably close to the estimated potential demand of the previous quinquennium.[4]

If one looks, instead, at the quinquennial changes in demand —
which Feinstein believes to be more relevant to an examination of
fluctuations in house-building — we have the following table:

TABLE 7.4

	Change in Potential Demand due to Population aged 20–44			Change in New Houses
	By Natural Increase	By Emigration	Total	
1871–75 to 1876–80	21	4	25	54
1876–80 to 1881–85	126	–133	–7	–129
1881–85 to 1886–90	26	30	56	–13
1886–90 to 1891–95	85	131	216	41
1891–95 to 1896–00	28	19	47	261
1896–00 to 1901–05	–60	–101	–161	23
1901–06 to 1906–10	27	–96	–69	–176

A similar pattern is revealed here. Except for the marked fall
(of 129,000) in houses built between 1876–80 and 1881–5 — corresponding to the large difference of 151,000 noted in the last column
of the previous table — there is a close agreement between the change
in demand between quinquennia and the change in building in the
overlapping inter-quinquennial period. It seems possible that if we
could have a finer breakdown of population changes, so that we
could examine the increases in, say, the age-groups 23–38, at annual
intervals rather than quinquennial ones, we would find an even closer
association between population change and slightly-lagged house-
building. But it is unlikely that this would get us away from the
exceptional behaviour of 1876–80.

Another factor of some importance, which the above analysis
cannot reveal, is internal migration. This has been examined in
some detail by other writers.[5] Another useful account by Weber
appears as Appendix 7. Here he divides the country into urban
and rural areas, and looks at the two sub-totals of changes in housing
stock, natural increase and migration. He concludes that although
there is little evidence of an urban housing boom in the eighteen
thirties, 'the major residential fluctuations under discussion are
essentially an urban phenomenon. Their urban character is
accounted for by internal migration.' Broadly speaking, we may
say that the findings suggest a *modus operandi* that is compatible with
our theory in Chapter 3, and our account of regional fluctuations
since 1832, but we shall say more about this matter shortly. Now
it seems time to look at the annual data, lest we rely too much on the
broad movements of inter-decennial change.

The unreliability of our early population data is almost proverbial,

and to use them is particularly perilous.   For all that it seems that
certain rather tentative conclusions can be derived from them, as
we shall now attempt to show.   In Figure 7.2 we plot the course
of baptisms recorded in England and Wales for 1780–1840, and of
births registered between 1838 and 1938.   The figure also shows
the course of marriages from 1755.   The main points to be borne
in mind when interpreting these data are that for the period before
1840 the figures come from an incomplete set of returns made from
Parish Registers; that some of the Registers were in any case inaccurate, especially in the early nineteenth century; and that for the
period between 1838 and the seventies the statistics provided by the

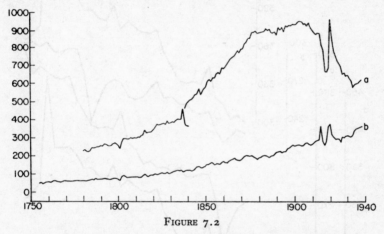

FIGURE 7.2

(a) (i) Baptisms, E. & W., 1780–1840 ('000). B.H.S., pp. 28–30.
     (ii) Births, E. & W., 1838–1938 ('000). B.H.S., pp. 28–30.
(b) Marriages, E. & W., 1755–1938 ('000). B.H.S., pp. 28, 45–46.

Registrar-General had an incomplete coverage.[6]   The break at
1838–40 is particularly unfortunate because of the suspicion it casts
on the trough in births in the early forties.

A question that we must now ask is whether, despite these serious
deficiencies, there is any evidence of the birth-cycle suggested in
Chapter 3.   Since our theory has led us to expect a bulge in births
to be echoed a generation later, with a precise dating dependent upon
economic factors, there is little point in assuming the existence of
a regular periodicity, and performing the usual statistical tests.
Instead we may look carefully at the graph.

We may describe the course of baptisms as rising in the middle
and later eighties, to a plateau in the nineties before a brief sharp
drop, a sudden rise, and then a gentle rise from 1803 to 1812.   It is
then that a sharper upward trend sets in — about twenty-eight years

after the earlier upsurge seems to have begun.   In 1823 or 1824 there
is some diminution in the rate of growth, which may be related, with
a little wishful thinking, to the plateau that began thirty years before.
On the other hand, it could also be related to the plateau that began
only twenty years earlier, just as the peak of 1837 may owe something

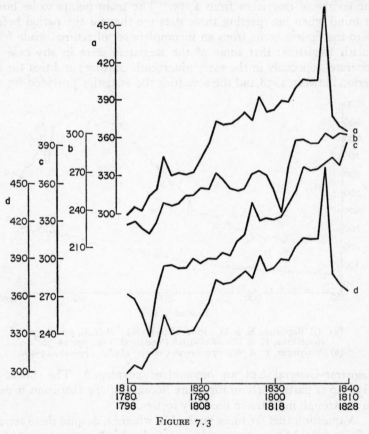

FIGURE 7.3

Baptisms, E. & W. ('000) : (*a*) and (*d*) : 1810–40.   (*b*) : 1780–1810.
(*c*) : 1798–1828.   *B.H.S.*, p. 28.

to the rising births at the end of the Napoleonic War.   The comparison is aided by Figure 7.3, in which the baptisms of 1780–1810
are plotted beneath those of 1810–40, while they appear above those
of 1798–1828, which in turn may be compared with those of 1820–40.
Taken by itself, this diagram hardly proves the existence of a births-
cycle — especially since it is difficult to choose between the thirty-
year lag and the lag of only eighteen years, unless one uses refined

statistical techniques which are of doubtful validity when applied to such dubious data.   On the other hand, it reveals a pattern which is not inconsistent with the suggestion of an echo.   If one wishes to do so, one can suggest that perhaps the low values of the early forties reflect the pause just before 1820, but these are treacherous wonderings when we think of the break in the data.   What does seem beyond contradiction is that between 1847 and 1878 not even the most partisan of chartists could proclaim the existence of a cycle even though the peak in the mid-eighties, and the subsequent dip, seem perhaps to be echoed about nineteen or twenty years later.

We shall have more to say about births very shortly, but first we turn to marriages.   Before 1840 these reveal fluctuations which

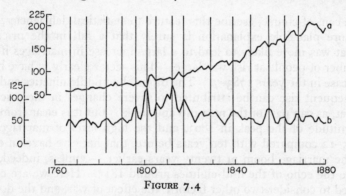

FIGURE 7.4

(a) Marriages, E. & W. ('000). B.H.S., pp. 28, 45–46.
(b) Price of Wheat (i) Winchester College. Shillings per Winchester quarter, 1765–70.
         (ii) U.K. Average. Shillings per imperial quarter, 1771–1880. B.H.S., pp. 487–9.

are almost perfectly mirrored in the course of births, but it is less easy to see any simple relationship in later years.   Close inspection reveals that the years marking the troughs in the minor cycles in marriages were usually years in which births also slightly declined but we can trace in the course of births the feeblest ripple to reflect the meandering of the rise in marriages.   What is much more easily seen is the close inverse relationship between the price of wheat and the marriage-rate.   As Figure 7.4 shows, this was especially so between about 1765 and 1820.   Thereafter the rising trend of marriages and the falling trend in wheat prices obscures the relationship, but if these trends are removed it remains fairly convincing at least until the late sixties.

This close inverse correlation between wheat prices and marriages also exists, of course, between prices and births until 1840, but there

is an important point to keep in mind. While changes in the price
of wheat indicated the direction of the change in marriages, the
magnitude of the changes often bore little relationship to each other.
For example, we may consider the following table, which is also
indicated in the graph:

	Wheat Price	Change		Marriages ('000)	Change
1779	34s. 8d.		1779	64	
1783	54s. 3d.	+ 19s. 7d.	1782	63	− 1
1786	40s. 0d.	− 14s. 3d.	1787	76	+ 13
1790	54s. 9d.	+ 14s. 9d.	1790	71	− 5
1792	43s. 0d.	− 11s. 9d.	1792	75	+ 4
1796	78s. 7d.	+ 35s. 7d.	1795	69	− 6
1798	51s. 10d.	− 26s. 9d.	1798	79	+ 10

One can, of course, ascribe this feature to statistical deficiencies, but
a more plausible explanation is surely that a fall in the price of
wheat was more likely to lead to a large increase in marriages if the
number of people at risk was large. This seems clearly to have been
the case in the years 1783–7. The dip in the middle nineties and the
subsequent rise can be attributed to severe changes in the price of
wheat, as can part of the next dip and peak. But it is clear from the
magnitude of the peak in 1803, and the high level of marriages in
1805–12 compared with ten years before, that here we have an echo
of the marriage boom of twenty years earlier — unless, indeed, we
place the echo of the mid-eighties around 1815. Here we are compelled to consider two other factors: the effect of war, and the death-
rate. It is clearly possible that the combined effects of harvest and
war, both affecting the price of wheat and the latter withdrawing men
into the Army and Navy, was to split the echo of the 1783–92 boom
in births into two parts, one coming rather early, during temporarily
favourable conditions, and the other later, after some interruption.
Indeed, the more one considers this, with all the graphs before one,
the more plausible it seems to be.

But surely, it may be asked, a falling death-rate might, by raising
the number of survivals to manhood, be responsible for a boom in
marriages that echoed no previous boom? This is certainly true,
but it requires an analysis of age-specific death-rates, which do not
exist for that period. The higher level of marriages in 1803–12 would
have required a considerable fall in the infantile and juvenile death-
rates between about 1780 and 1790. All we can say is that during
that decade the number of burials remained more or less constant —
perhaps slightly downwards — while population was rising. What
evidence we have suggests that the death-rate was falling, and it is
not unreasonable to suppose that the young benefited. Indeed there

is contemporary evidence to suggest that they did. It is therefore very likely that the rising marriage- and birth-rates had part of their origin in a more frequent survival to maturity: but this makes a population echo more likely rather than less likely.

The fact that the rising price of wheat between 1822 and 1825 saw no fall in marriage is partly because of the general prosperity of the times, and the full employment of labour at high wages; but it also suggests that there was a considerable number of people of marrying age. Here, it seems, may be a simple echo of the rather interrupted rise in marriages and births that took place between 1796 and 1803, with a subsequent brief plateau not only reflecting continued high prices during the less prosperous post-crisis times, but also the levelling of births between 1803 and 1812. But it was at a high level, and the fall in wheat prices, and the general recovery of the economy, came at a time when the boom in births of 1814–15 was still too near to account for the early years of the upswing, but may well help to explain the spread-out top of the marriage bulge in the thirties.

Enough has been said to show that the echo argument is plausible, but unproven. Yet when one considers the biology of it, there do not seem sufficient grounds for rejecting the hypothesis out of hand during this period. What now can be said of the fifties and sixties? The plain fact is that while marriages continued to fluctuate, and to respond to changes in the price of wheat, there is hardly any sign of this in the statistics of registered births. When one looks back one sees that even in the thirties the close correspondence between marriages and baptisms was upset, and the remarkable peak in the latter series, in 1837, seems to be explicable only in terms of an accumulation from the under-represented years that just preceded it. Either the newly married postponed their families, or baptisms were unusually late. This, admittedly, is speculation, but the only alternative is to accept without question not only the sudden breakdown of the natural parallel between marriages and births, but also the existence of an isolated high value quite atypical of all that came before. Does a similar explanation hold for the fifties and sixties? We know that registrations were far from perfect during this time, and that births were under-registered. What we do not know is whether in years of abnormally high births the amount of under-registration was also abnormally high. If, for example, a births boom was essentially urban, and registration in some of the rapidly growing towns was inadequate, then the national series might well fail to show fluctuations of the correct amplitude. What other explanations may there be?

There seem to be two possibilities worthy of consideration. One is that there was a change in habits. This could be manifested in two ways — either a delay in the first conception, so that the birth series would no longer have a component of first births almost synchronous with marriages, or there could be larger families, so that the first births would form a smaller proportion of the total, and so have less influence in shaping the graph. This second alternative is not unsupported by the statistics, for the decennial ratios of births to marriage rose progressively through the fifties to seventies: but the known deficiencies of the data do not allow us to rely on this evidence. The former alternative suggests that some form of birth control was becoming effective — in a way that postponed conception but not so generally or effectively that family size was reduced. This seems to be quite possible. Although coitus interruptus had long been practiced, this is a form of contraception whose effectiveness is subject almost entirely to the will of the husband, who is the least likely to be concerned about the burden of child-bearing. But in the middle 1820's Francis Place was distributing pamphlets which advocated other methods — much more under the control of the female. It is commonly agreed that 'although many thousands of these were distributed and the subject was discussed in many periodicals, this movement had no traceable immediate effect on the birth-rate'.[7] Yet it seems possible that it nevertheless had some effect on the timing of births. In the end, an effect on the birth-rate itself would wait upon a change in the attitude to family size — which is different from a desire to have fewer children in the early years of marriage.

The other interesting possible explanation of the absence of the marriage-cycle from the births data is that many people married and emigrated before becoming parents. If we look at the short-term fluctuations in the figures of immigrants into the United States from Great Britain (Figure 7.5) we obtain some light on this. The dip in marriages between the peaks of 1853 and 1860 saw a rise in emigration. On the other hand the minor cycle in marriages that peaked in 1866, and has no echo in births, was almost exactly parallelled in emigration, just as were the early years of the next upswing. It was a time when the Civil War was operating against the more normal determinants of migration, but it is nevertheless possible that in the pre-war years the emigration was largely of the unmarried — which helped to reduce the marriage rate — while in the post-war years it consisted largely of newly married, who became parents abroad.

These possible explanations of the steadiness of the rise in the statistics of births — deficient registration, birth-control, and emigration — are all rather speculative. Perhaps the best approach is to say that all of these three forces were undoubtedly present to some degree in this period, and make any interpretation of the data particularly difficult. It is also true that migration, at any rate, would impinge upon any tendency for there to be a births-cycle. We shall return to this point shortly.

When we come to the seventies the whole trend changes. In 1873 marriages peaked, hesitated for three years, and then dipped to a trough in 1879 which was at a lower level than an extrapolation of previous troughs would have suggested to be likely. The next peak, in 1883, was also lower, and not until 1900 were marriages at a level compatible with the earlier trend. The long bowl of building

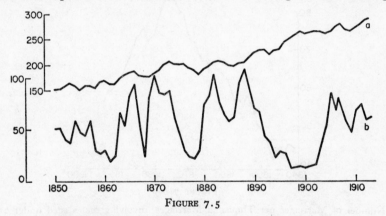

FIGURE 7.5

(a). Marriages, E. & W. ('ooo). *B.H.S.*, pp. 45–46.
(b). Immigration to U.S. from G.B. ('ooo). Thomas (1), p. 282.

in the Great Victorian Depression seems to have its counterpart here. But the remarkable feature is the complete change in the trend of births, which became almost horizontal, as family size diminished sharply. Many forces had combined in the previous thirty or forty years to change attitudes about large families. The decline of home industries, and successive Factory Acts, prevented the very young from being earners. Musgrove[8] has recently emphasised that, in addition, 'more children were surviving' and so becoming not only a greater cost, but a more certain cost. Since they were more likely to live, there was more point in educating them, and preparing them for adult life. Social conscience and the growing desire for education were also at work, and these tended further to postpone the day when the child would pay for his keep. Slowly new attitudes began to form, and then, quite suddenly, two forces combined to tip the scales, and to turn the trend of population. At a time when large families were already less desirable than previously, came the bad years of the late seventies and early eighties, to exaggerate the undesirability of new burdens.   At the same time, the Law once again became an instrument of propaganda, as Charles Bradlaugh and Mrs. Annie Besant reprinted and sold a book which had first appeared in this country over forty years before.   In less than four years after their trial, annual sales of the book in Great Britain rose from one thousand copies to two hundred thousand, and by 1891 over a million tracts giving contraceptive advice were sold in England and Wales.   Perhaps if this trial had come in better times its impact would have been less marked.   As it was, it advertised a solution,

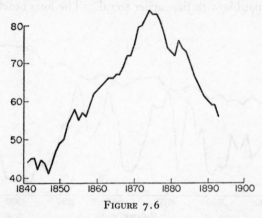

FIGURE 7.6

Number of Marriages per Thousand Marriages, involving males aged under 21, E. & W.   *Registrar General's Report*, 1890, p. xxx ; 1891, p. xxxvi ; 1893, p. xxxiii.

and the acceptability of an attitude, at a time when economic factors made it particularly desirable.   And with the change in the trend of births came a change in the whole trend of the economy, as we shall see in the next chapter.

Before leaving the subject of marriages and births, we may report on an interesting experiment.   There is some evidence to suggest that the age of marriage fell during the early part of the nineteenth century.[9]   By the early forties it seems to have been rising again, perhaps only briefly, for in 1847 the proportion of marriages involving men aged under 21 was at its lowest level — of 41 in 1000.   From then on the proportion rose, with just a slight hesitation in the late fifties, to reach a peak level of 84 in 1000 in 1874, after which a steady decline set in.   (Figure 7.6)   The average age of marriage stood at 25·6 years for men and 24·2 years for women in 1873, and rose slowly to 26·5 and 25·0 by the mid-nineties.

These average ages, of course, conceal the real magnitude of the changes as far as any births echo is concerned, for even in 1851 only a fifth of the men aged 20–25 were married, and a postponement of a substantial number of young marriages by a few years would have little effect on the average age of marriage.   For want of better data we may assume that in the mid and later fifties people were tending to become married around the age of 25.   To allow for some spread we may suppose, more precisely, that people marrying in the years t to $t+3$ were most likely to have been born between the years $t-30$ and $t-17$ — allowing most marriages to occur between the ages of 20 and 30.   If this was so, one might expect to find something interesting by comparing the total of marriages in a four-year period with the total of births in a longer earlier period.   Because only a little more than half of the people aged 25–30 were married, the limits we have just suggested seem to be a little too narrow. Accordingly Figure 7.7 plots the ratio of marriages in a four-year period t to $t+3$ with a weighted sum of births over the period $t-35$ to $t-16$, with the rather arbitrary weights given below :

t–16	1	t–26	40
t–17	3	t–27	29
t–18	6	t–28	20
t–19	11	t–29	13
t–20	20	t–30	9
t–21	30	t–31	7
t–22	43	t–32	5
t–23	52	t–33	3
t–24	54	t–34	2
t–25	51	t–35	1

These weights correspond to an average age of marriage of 25·84 years.   The Figure also shows the course of British immigration into the United States.

The difficulty in interpreting this graph is increased by the switch from baptisms to births.   To reduce the sharpness of the switch the series of baptisms was multiplied by a factor that reconciled the 1838–40 figures of the two series.   This is quite inaccurate, but since we are concerned chiefly with the shape of fluctuations it can be defended in this instance.   The main finding is that the resulting graph, of the weighted ratio of actual marriages to what might be thought of as marriage potential arising out of earlier births, has a broad shape in the middle of the century that is an interesting inversion of the curve of emigration.   This is emphatically not a comment on short cycles, but rather on long swings.   It suggests,

despite all the deficiencies of the data, that emigration removed those
who were about to be married.   It is a pity that the data are not good
enough for a more refined analysis.

We have already seen that emigration was important in determining the shape of population changes, and, on a quinquennial basis,
in fashioning demand for houses.   Cairncross and Thomas[10] have
been the main proponents of a theory that during at least part of the
nineteenth century transatlantic migration linked economies on
either side of the ocean.   Cairncross, prefacing his study of national

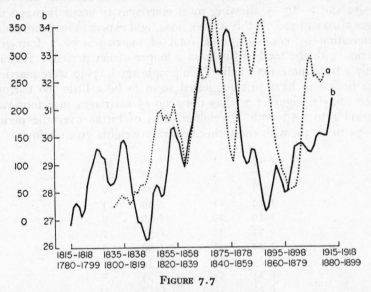

FIGURE 7.7

(a) Immigration to U.S. from G.B. ('000).   Thomas, p. 282.
(b) Rate of corrected marriages in overlapping periods of four years (beginning in
     1815–18), to the weighted sums of births in overlapping periods of twenty
     years (beginning in 1780–99).   See text, pp. 178–9.

cycles with a detailed examination of Glasgow, upon which we have
already drawn, points out that

The building cycle was little more than a migration cycle in disguise. . . .
As a rule, when emigration from Scotland was low, Glasgow grew fast;
when emigration was high, Glasgow houses stood empty and the building
industry was idle.   It was the prosperity of the Dakotas, so to speak, that
brought building to a standstill in Dalmarnock.[11]

Emigration was chiefly to the places to which capital was also flowing,
and when both of these outflows were low there was pressure on
housing accommodation and a surfeit of cheap money that enabled
this pressure to be relieved.   At the same time, 'distress sales of raw

materials and foodstuffs' came over the Atlantic, driving people off the land into the towns, and increasing the purchasing power of the workers, and their demand for housing. But when, as in 1904, 'the tide turned, carrying with it cheap money and a throng of tenants, the building industry all over Britain was left on the rocks'.[12]

We shall look further at some of Cairncross's views in the next chapter. His analysis was concerned chiefly with the period 1870–1913, when, he argued, migration was a link between inverse building patterns on either side of the Atlantic. This conclusion was also reached by Brinley Thomas, whose study embraced the years 1830–1950. Thomas's main interest is migration but, as he constantly points out, 'building is a branch of investment which reacts directly to changes in population'.[13] He observes that labour and capital migrated together, and explains that

Each wave of trans-Atlantic emigration was in essence a rural exodus. When capital exports to the United States were booming and home construction in Great Britain was languishing, surplus labour on the land tended to migrate to America instead of to urban countries at home; in the next phase when investment in Britain increased substantially the workers released from agriculture flocked into the rapidly growing towns and emigration declined. There was thus an inverse relation between internal and external migration. A wave of home construction drew on the agricultural reserve army for urban employment at home; and a wave of foreign investment drew on the agricultural reserve army for urban employment abroad.[14]

This observation is based on a detailed analysis of time-series for both sides of the Atlantic. For United States building Thomas relied for most of the period on Riggleman's series of the annual value of building permits *per capita* at constant prices.[15] This series goes back to 1831, but in its early years it is based on only a few towns. C. D. Long has shown, in constructing another building index beginning in 1856,[16] that later in the century building was sometimes booming in one town while it was feeble in another. For this reason we cannot place much reliance on Riggleman's series before about 1845. As it happens this does not seriously affect Thomas's conclusion, for his finding is that the series he uses do not support his idea of inverse swings for the period 1830–47. As far as the data go, 'building in the two countries seems to have moved in unison between 1830 and 1847'.[17] Even that, however, is a risky statement to make on the slender and incomplete data available. We have already noticed that in the building cycle that had its peak in 1825, emigration and building moved inversely, and although there is no evidence to suggest that building in the receiving

G

countries followed the path of immigration it must at least be admitted that the course of building must have been influenced, if only to a minor degree. Perhaps the wisest thing to say is that we do not know.

For British building Thomas uses a compromise synthesis of data that has received some criticism but is not as bad as it looks. The brick index ending in 1849 and Cairncross's 'Volume of Building' from 1870 are respectable indices. In an attempt to bridge the gap Thomas uses a series of railway miles opened per million of population. This bridge does not, of course, represent building, but it does tell us something about a major constituent of home investment. Unfortunately, it is marred by the long period of construction. A peak year in miles opened might arise some time after the peak in actual railway construction, or even before it. We must not, however, be over-critical, for Thomas's only real use of the railway data was to suggest a building-cycle trough in 1855, and a peak in 1863, and to substantiate the suggestion in Cairncross's series of a trough in 1871.

It is important to remember that a more accurate description of Thomas's thesis is that 'home-construction' — 'i.e., all kinds of structures (not only houses) in areas other than purely export areas'[18] — moved inversely to home-construction abroad. His building-cycle is, more accurately, a home-construction cycle. His use of railway-miles as an index of home-construction is very reasonable in this period, and its plausibility is enhanced if other components of construction show troughs in or near 1855 and 1871, and a peak in 1863.

The house-building data we have now collected relates to only a few towns in 1855. For what it is worth in these early years, the index combining the available data is compatible with the Thomas hypothesis, for it shows a steep fall from 62·4 in 1854 to 29·8 in 1855, 31·2 in 1856 and an absolute trough of 27·5 in 1857. We have already seen that factory building in the Manchester area was at a trough in 1855. Whether it was a major trough it is difficult to say because of the short period covered by the available data.

Some further check on 1855 is provided by Cooney's timber imports figures which have been examined in Chapter 4. These are not easily interpreted, especially since the war caused speculative buying. It is, however, difficult not to interpret the mahogany import figures as having major peaks in 1846 and 1862, and a major trough in the early fifties. The missing value in the lathwood series makes interpretation of these data most hazardous. On balance the data for timber appear to indicate a long cycle more or less inverse to the U.S. building cycle.

It thus seems that the use of railway-miles added has not led to a substantially incorrect location of the major troughs, and it has represented to some degree at least the boom of the early fifties. How correct was it in also locating a peak in 1863? We have just seen that the mahogany imports series has a peak in 1862. The lathwood series has its peak in 1865. In the Manchester area there was a house-building peak in 1863, but not one that can be referred to as a major peak. Some other towns reveal a similar pattern, although in South Wales building was then at a trough, for reasons (already examined) associated with the export trade in coal. On balance our housing data point to a minor peak in this year. Certainly they do not indicate any major peak between the middle of the century and the mid-seventies in our best available estimate of the national housing fluctuations. Yet mahogany imports tell a different tale, not very different from that of lathwood imports. Rather than reject the 1863 peak it seems more reasonable to suggest that there was a considerable boom in some kinds of construction at this time, but in housing it was not sufficient to allow 1863 to be described as a major peak. This means that our verdict on the existence of inverse construction cycles — as opposed to inverse house-building cycles — must be that for this period it hinges on the Civil War. It can be argued that there was a peak in 1863 (and there is strong evidence of one, except in the South Wales export sector) and that inverse-construction cycles are established. If this is rejected then we must enquire whether it is sufficient evidence for the rejection of a theory that is otherwise fairly acceptable. The Civil War not only reduced investment in America, but also had an adverse effect in Britain. The fact that a war-time trough appeared in the U.S. building-cycle and was followed by a possibly compensating upswing, at a time when the pure theory of inverse cycles required otherwise, is not necessarily sufficient to destroy a theory that was valid from the mid-forties to the late fifties, and from the late sixties onwards. When we consider that, in any case, there is strong evidence of some kind of British constructional peak in 1863, it seems better to let the theory stand, pending the assembly of further information.

Thomas argues that in the period before 1847 the United States was largely an extension of the British economy, leaning heavily on our capital, but affected only slightly by the trickle of emigrants. In 1847, however, 'the first great wave of transatlantic migration started',[19] and the kind of mechanism we have already described comes into operation. It is amplified by the inverse relationship between emigration and internal mobility, already noted. 'The expansive force of this induced investment' (in house-building) 'is more potent than the depressing effect of the foreign trade multiplier; hence the rise in real income a head relative to trend.'[20]

This simple statement of the theory is qualified. First we have to keep in mind that it is a broad statement and that the precise details of one cycle were not the same as those of the next. Secondly it must be emphasised Thomas considered the origin of the waves of emigration to lie in population pressure due to a birth-cycle[21] combining with the impact of innovation or calamity. Indeed, in this theory, population pressure is akin to a credit shortage in the system of Chapter 3, and any given adverse impulse is likely to produce a huge upswing in emigration if pressure is high but to have less effect if pressure is low. We have already noted some relationship between migration, births and marriages, but there is little point in attempting to establish exact mechanistic links. Population pressure may consist of a large number of young children, hungry and too young to earn, or of older people wishing to raise children but out of work, or of youths becoming old enough to work but unable to find any. Thomas usually used the term to describe the existence of a large number of people in their early and mid twenties, and established high correlations between emigration and birth-rates of a generation earlier for Europe and for Sweden.[22] But the point to keep in mind is that an increase in the number of people in this age-group may swell emigration for two kinds of reason. One is economic. The other is purely psychological — that it is the age when people think for themselves, feel that they must take steps to secure their future, and are able to act with independence and in the spirit of adventure. Migration of this kind has economic consequences, even if it has no economic causation. The other kind, arising out of a comparison of economic prospects at a time when families are being formed, may be much less willing, and dependent much more upon the relative states of the economies. While psychological emigration may be a fairly simple function of the number in an age-group, economic migration is not and depends on the interaction of many forces, including such shocks as wheat and potato prices or the glitter of rumours of gold. Before attempting a theory of building fluctuations, in which migration plays a part, we shall now make a brief survey of the eighteenth and nineteenth centuries, in an attempt to pin-point certain facts and ideas, and to comment on a few unsettled points.

NOTES TO CHAPTER 7

1. There is little *direct* evidence for a higher level of house-building in the 1830's and for a lower level in the 1840's (except for Liverpool). In the 1850's the level was low in relation to the 1860's and 1870's but it is not inconsistent with an *increase* in the net housing stock.

2. 1931. Census of England and Wales. *Housing*, vol. ii, chapter 5.

3. Feinstein, *loc. cit.* Brinley Thomas and Margaret Williams have recently questioned these estimates.

4. This was pointed out to me by Mr. D. Coppock.

5. Notably T. A. Welton, *England's Recent Progress: an Investigation of the Statistics of Migration, Mortality, etc. in the Twenty Years from 1881 to 1901 as indicating Tendencies towards the Growth or Decay of Particular Communities*, London, 1911, and 'Note on Urban and Rural Variations according to the English Census of 1911', *J.R.S.S.*, vol. lxxvi, 1913; A. K. Cairncross, *op. cit.*, especially chapter iv; Brinley Thomas, *Migration and Economic Growth*, especially chapter viii, and *The Welsh Economy*, chapter i.

6. See especially Phyllis Deane and W. A. Cole, *British Economic Growth, 1688–1959*, Cambridge (1962), chapter iii and the references therein cited.

7. *Royal Commission on Population*, Report, 1949, p. 36. Most of my data on this subject come from this report. See also Margaret Hewitt, *Wives and Mothers in Victorian Industry*, London, 1958, chapter vii, to which I was directed by Mr. Lionel Williams.

8. F. Musgrove, 'Population Changes and the Status of the Young in England Since the Eighteenth Century', *The Sociological Review*, vol. 11, 1963, pp. 69–93, which is well documented on this subject.

9. *Ibid.*

10. *Op. cit.*

11. *Op. cit.*, p. 25.

12. *Ibid.*, p. 36.

13. Thomas, *Migration and Economic Growth*, p. 33.

14. Thomas (ed.), *The Welsh Economy*, p. 6.

15. J. R. Riggleman, 'Building Cycles in the United States, 1830–1935' (unpublished thesis in the Library of the Johns Hopkins University, Baltimore).

16. Clarence D. Long, Jr., *Building Cycles and the Theory of Investment*, 1940.

17. *Migration and Economic Growth*, p. 175.

18. Quoted from a letter by Thomas to the author.

19. Thomas, *Migration and Economic Growth*, p. 177.

20. *Ibid.*, p. 178.

21. See, for example, *Migration and Economic Growth*, p. 157.

22. *Ibid.*, pp. 155–8.

CHAPTER 8

1700-1913: A SURVEY

BEFORE we attempt a more connected account of the period from 1870 to 1913, in which we can draw upon the observations made in the last few chapters, it will be useful for us to look back to the beginning of our period, so that we may underline certain ideas that seem to be of importance, and be in a better position to judge the nature of the forty or so years that preceded the First World War. Although we have been primarily concerned with building, our account of the British economy since 1700 has impinged upon a number of other subjects. To write a full, or even balanced, account of Britain's growth has not been our aim. We have tried, rather, to show how building has fluctuated during this time, and how these fluctuations have been related to other features of the economy. Not even this has been done adequately; and when the necessary original research for primary data has been done it is quite possible that a number of the points we have made will need modification, and that even before this stage is reached some of our bolder assertions will look better if thought of as tentative suggestions. This has been a Concerto for Construction rather than a Symphony of Growth, and it may well be that the soloist has sometimes blown too loudly.

Yet there is one point that the soloist has not been able to distort, and that is the basic rhythm. It has sometimes been asserted that there was no British building cycle before the later nineteenth century; yet the statistical evidence for the eighteenth century is quite conclusive. Quite apart from all other indicators, the timber figures show fluctuations which qualitative data confirm to be fluctuations in building at least in so far as the major fluctuations are concerned. Furthermore, these fluctuations are not just the product of a wishful gaze into the chartist's crystal ball, but are statistically detectable, and are of a character that is unlikely to have occurred by pure accident. The matching of the turning points with those in the yield on Consols, whose association with building activity has been made perfectly plain by Ashton, Shannon and others, adds further weight to our assertion that, whatever its causes or consequence, construction moved in long swings during the eighteenth century. We cannot, however, say to what extent this was housing, although my own feeling is that probably housing moved in much the same way as the timber index. This seems likely to be especially true, both because of the evidence we present in Chapter 2 and on more general considerations, from about 1760 onwards. Habakkuk has argued in relation to the early nineteenth century that house-building probably conformed closely to the trade cycle.[1] It is certainly a tenable argument, but there is not sufficient quantitative evidence either to prove it or to disprove it. Even if one accepts Habakkuk's reasoning in its broad terms, long swings could still have existed. We have seen that the direction of changes in house-building in the middle and later nineteenth century was usually the same as the direction of local trade activity, and in that sense house-building conformed with the trade cycle; but this is not to say that the magnitude of the change was the same. Habakkuk's reasoning is strictly applicable more to the direction than to the amount of change, and offers no convincing reason for discounting the suggestion that there were, at least, local building cycles of considerable duration, transcending the local trade cycles. Furthermore, as we argued in Chapter 3, there are substantial demographic arguments in favour of a house-building boom occurring when generally good times approximately coincide with the period when the population born in a birth-bulge that coincided with a previous building boom reaches marital age; and it is some time in between these dates, when the bulge-children are perhaps about seven or eight, that the ratio of food-requirements to earning power is probably greatest, and the ability to translate demands for housing into actual building most likely to be frustrated. Once one starts to take into account factors such as these, the suggestion that there were long cycles in these earlier years becomes more convincing, for seemingly sound reasons exist to support the interpretation of the time-series data.

In Chapter 2 we made a rather brief examination of these earlier cycles, and showed that the pattern of fluctuation revealed by the statistics agreed very well with the qualitative evidence of the time. On the other hand, most of this evidence concerned events in London, and a good part of our explanation of the earlier cycles hinged upon these events. We must now, in summing up, consider whether we have a distorted view of what happened. The limitation of our information to the London area is most serious in the first half of the eighteenth century, when the timber series exhibited its fluctuations about a more or less horizontal trend. We have suggested in Chapter 2 that this was a time when most of the internal migration was to London, and that the violent cycles around the upward trend

that erupted in the sixties had part of their causation in the flood of
people to rapidly growing towns. We may now look at this a little
more closely, in the light of research by Deane and Cole.[2] Triumph-
ing over the scantiness and inaccuracy of eighteenth-century population statistics, these authors have produced an analysis of natural
increase and migration, which, although primarily concerned with
trends, sheds interesting light on our own analysis of cycles.

During the first half of the eighteenth century the population
of England and Wales rose by less than a third of a million, but there
was a great deal of local variation in what was happening. In some
counties there was fairly rapid natural increases, while others had
enormous natural decrease. On top of these changes, came internal
migration. Broadly speaking, people swarmed like flies to London,
where they died like flies. The counties of Essex, Kent, Middlesex
and Surrey witnessed a net immigration from the rest of the land of
over 600,000 people — about double the total population increase
of the whole country. But during the same time, deaths so exceeded
births that the actual increase in population of these four counties
came to a mere 35,000. Broadly speaking, the agricultural counties
lost people to the industrial and commercial countries, and it is significant that not a single country from which there was not emigration
also saw natural decrease. Only Gloucestershire and Lancashire
had sizeable additions to population through both a net immigration and an excess of births over deaths. Both of these counties
had total population increases exceeding that of the four London
counties put together — 48,000 in the case of Gloucestershire and
79,000 for Lancashire.

Deane and Cole suggest that on the whole the growing towns
absorbed population from the nearby countryside, and the migration
into the towns of Lancashire and Gloucestershire may well have
exceeded the amount suggested by these figures, but it was clearly
never of the proportions reached by the flood to the Great Wen.
In its economic consequences, and especially in its demand for
housing, the arrival of a new immigrant is very different from arrival
of a new baby, while since the age structure of the immigrants was
almost certainly very different from that of deaths, a thousand of the
one would not just balance out a thousand of the other. Over a
long period, the impact of a thousand immigrants might be more or
less indistinguishable from that of a natural increase of the same size,
but the arrival of immigrants generally has a more immediate impact
than the arrival of babies or the prolongation of old-age, and it seems
likely that the time-shape of immigration into London was the principal determinant of the fluctuations in the potential demand for new

housing, even though the more or less static trend of house-building is to be ascribed to a more or less static population. There were, quite certainly, regional differences in the birth- and death-rates, and this means that probably there were regional differences in building activity; but London, which contained one in ten of the population of England and Wales, was subjected not only to natural changes (which we examined a little in Chapter 2) but also to the combined effects of inflowing adult migrants, and a colossal amount of rebuilding. Although an understanding of what happened in the Metropolis does not tell the whole story, it undoubtedly tells a good part.

The upsurge in the timber-import series, and the beginning of the first major cycle about an upward trend, which we have located in the early sixties, comes into the middle of the second period analysed by Deane and Cole. The years 1751 to 1781 witnessed a population increase of nearly 1,400,000 in England and Wales, compared with less than a quarter of this amount in the previous fifty years. This rapid change in natural increase has been variously ascribed to rising birth-rates and falling death-rates. Whether it was primarily the former or the latter is important from an economic point of view, but if the fall in the death-rate was largely a fall in the death-rates of infants then it is not of great importance. In any case it is not a matter for us to consider now, especially since there is by no means conclusive evidence or argument one way or the other. What does matter is that there was a rapid acceleration in the total size of the population, and that this was bound to invoke a rising trend in house-building. A steadily rising population need not call forth a rising amount of new accommodation. It is only when the actual increments of population are increasing that the volume of new building need grow. This condition was certainly satisfied in the eighteenth and early nineteenth centuries, and we need look no further to explain the upward trend.

Yet it was not the only demographic factor at work. Internal migration was assuming a new pattern. The drift to the South was beginning to become augmented on a sizeable scale by drifts to the Midlands and the North, which were incipient even in the early years. The total number of counties with a positive net immigration during 1751–81 was seventeen, compared with only thirteen in the previous period, but the contrast is greater when we look at actual values. London expanded at the same rate as before, while Lancashire became temporarily a slight net contributor to emigration, probably as people moved to Cheshire which was having an inflow. Warwickshire, which had had an average rate of net immigration of 2·2 per

G 2

thousand in the first half of the decade (compared with 11·4 for London), was now increasing on this account at treble this rate, as also was Huntingdonshire. The period of really rapid growth of the cotton area through migration was yet to come, but already towns other than London were developing at great speed, partly because of the immigration from the rural parts of the same county which the statistics do not show, and which was increased by the high natural increase of these areas. Liverpool and Birmingham had been growing rapidly throughout the century, but since they were minute compared with London their impact was small at first. At a time when London boasted more than half a million people, and its runner up was Edinburgh with a mere 35,000, rapid growth rates in smaller towns were to be expected. But by the end of the eighteenth century they were tilting the balance. Liverpool trebled its population between 1700 and 1740, and then increased more than fivefold by the first population Census. Birmingham grew about as rapidly in the earlier part of the century, and doubled its population between 1760 and 1801. During the same forty years Glasgow trebled its size, while this feat took Manchester a shorter period . . . from 1773 to 1801. 'It is true,' say Deane and Cole, 'that all these towns had passed the 20,000 level by 1760, but London was still the home of approximately four out of five residents in the large towns of Great Britain. By 1801 not many more than half of those living in towns of over 20,000 inhabitants lived in London.' The relative influences of natural increase and migration may be judged from the following table:

	1701–51		1751–81		1781–1801		1801–31	
	Nat. Inc.	Net Immig.	Nat. Inc.	Net Immig.	Nat. Inc.	Net Immig.	Nat. Inc.	Net Immig.
Middlesex	−456	464	−177	265	−18	185	132	397
Lancashire	37	42	116	−13	147	126	474	183
Cheshire	11	−3	42	13	35	−1	100	41
Warwickshire	15	12	24	29	51	−15	98	28
Northampton-shire	14	−14	14	8	15	−13	62	−16
All Counties	317	±693	1390	±487	1623	±473	4899	±837

In interpreting this table we have to keep in mind that the columns are for periods of different lengths. The 'All Counties' row represents the total natural increase in England and Wales, and the sum of the positive net outflows from each county (with Wales being treated as a single county). During the first fifty years almost exactly two-thirds of this total went to Middlesex, but in the next period the proportion was little more than half, while it dwindled further towards the end of the century even though it later revived, at a time when London was also experiencing positive natural increase.

But this table is concerned with county boundaries, and conceals the vast amount of migration into the towns. Even as it stands, it shows that the average net flow from counties per annum increased from just under 14,000 in the first half of the decade, to rather more than 16,000 between 1751 and 1781, and then to over 23,000 by the end of the century. Since the total population was larger, one would expect greater migration in any case, but the rate of migration was growing faster than population. The average population in the first half of the century was 6 million, while around 1790 it was about 8·3 million, which represents a rate of growth considerably lower than that revealed by a change from 14,000 to 23,000 in annual migration rates. The migration into towns was growing even more rapidly. When we keep in mind that, as we have already emphasised, building was likely to be influenced more immediately by migrants than by births, it seems very likely that while the long-term trend was the result of population increase, the more violent fluctuations in building were largely to be explained in association with fluctuations in migration to the towns. The great surge in activity that began in 1764, and the gigantic upswing of the eighties which so dwarfed it, are to be explained increasingly in terms of urbanisation superimposed on a rising population.

In Chapter 2 we emphasised the importance of the rising births and immigration into London in determining the upswing of building that peaked around 1724, and noted that in London at any rate births were less than deaths on the long downswing that followed. It was this that gave such feeble character to the next building cycle, peaking in the late thirties, which must be dignified with that title both in order to be consistent with our statistical definition of a major peak, and because of the confirmatory trough in the yield on Consols, to say nothing of qualitative evidence. Perhaps the rising births of the forties were to some extent an echo of the births boom in the twenties, but infantile and juvenile death-rates were so high, and so fluctuating, that it is very difficult to be convinced that this was the case, without any shadow of doubt. For all that, population was rising at the time of the third building upswing, and the death-rate had by then fallen so much that we can much more confidently ascribe to the subsequent movements a considerable element of echo. Although these conclusions were reached by the path indicated in this book, with its emphasis on cycles, they conform to a surprising degree with the summing up of Deane and Cole, reached by very different methods:

. . . it was in the second decade of the eighteenth century that the birth-rate apparently started to rise. But in the next decade both economic expansion and population growth seem to have been checked by a sharp rise in the death-rate which, if we are right, had comparatively little to do with economic conditions in England. It was only in the 1740's, when the wave of mortality ebbed, that the effects of the rise in the birth-rate made themselves felt in a new and unprecedented wave of population growth and economic expansion. This in its turn was followed by a further modest rise in the birth-rate and a continuing fall in the death-rate in areas comparatively remote from the major centres of economic growth, which laid the basis of a further advance in the 1780's. And when the full story comes to be told, it may well appear that at each stage in the process, the growth of population, itself produced by economic changes in the generation before, was one of the factors which drove the British economy upwards on the path of sustained growth.

But, of course, population is not the whole story. The importance of harvests has been adequately emphasised, and need occupy us no further, nor need the credit situation for these earlier years, because although it was very important there is hardly need to reiterate that population change, the credit situation, and stochastic events are the Punch, Judy and Hangman of our show. On the other hand, before we go on, we must consider the view that the fluctuations of the eighteenth century were largely the result of war — that building fell in war-time and rose in peace-time. This hypothesis can hardly be better represented than in Figure 8.1, which shows the course of net public expenditure on the Army, Navy and Ordnance, graphed against timber imports and other indicators of building activity. It is clear that, as one would expect, there was a close inverse relationship. It was not perfect, witness the low expenditure in 1737–8 and the low value of timber imports in those years, but broadly speaking when expenditure on the army and navy went up, expenditure on houses went down.

It would, however, be all too easy to dismiss the building cycle as a mere product of war and peace. The economic consequences of war were usually the removal of men, a shortage of various provisions including timber, high Government borrowing and an export of specie to pay our troops abroad. All of these operate in the same direction as far as building is concerned, and peace, which reverses these movements, must tend to stimulate activity. But we cannot ignore the other factors, some of which had very similar

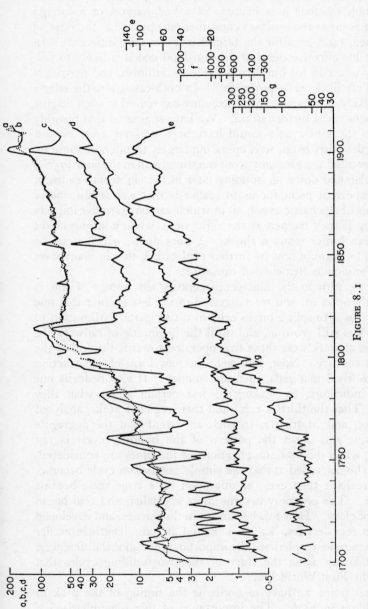

FIGURE 8.1

(a) Total Net Income, G.B. (£m.), 1700–1801.   B.H.S., pp. 386–8.   Total Gross Income, G.B. (£m.), 1802–1913.
   B.H.S., pp. 392–4.

(b) Total Net Public Expenditure, G.B. (£m.), 1700–1801.   Ibid., pp. 389–91.   Total Gross Public Expenditure, G.B.
   (£m.), 1802–1913.   Ibid., pp. 396–8.

(c) Army, Navy & Ordnance Expenditure, G.B. (£m.).   Ibid., pp. 389–91 and 396–8.

(d) Total Civil Government Expenditure, G.B. (£m.).   Ibid., pp. 389–91 and 396–8.

(e) Index of House-building, G.B. Appendix 4.

(f) Bricks charged with Duty (millions).   B.H.S., p. 235.

(g) Value of Imports of Deals and Fir Timber (£'000). Ashton.

consequences. If food is dear and specie exported, it does not matter much whether it is because of a bad harvest or a foreign expedition as far as the ordinary consumer (as opposed to the farmer) is concerned, (and even for the farmer it is not very different). In both cases his effective demand for non-food goods is likely to fall, the supply of credit for builders is likely to diminish, and marriages and births are likely to be postponed. In both cases, too, the effects are more likely to be severe if the economy has soared to such heights that it cannot stand further strain. We have suggested that possibly the peak of the mid 1720's would have been no later even without war. On the other hand, war, operating largely through its drain on specie, prevented the economy from bursting forth in the later 1750's, just as it clamped down on building later in the eighteenth century. But the important point for us to realise is that war is but one of many forms of stochastic event, all of which can have similar impacts on building if they happen at the right time, while a strong credit situation can buffer many a shock. A final point, which must be mentioned but cannot now be further explored, is that in many wars there are economic elements of causation.

When we turn to the nineteenth century the impact of war is immediately upon us, and we suggested in the last chapter that one of its effects was to split a births echo into two parts. Migration to the towns was still growing, and until the beginning of railways the main forces at work were those that operated towards the end of the eighteenth century. Now, however, the new form of construction activity absorbed materials, men and money. It also bedevils our statistical indicators, by making us less certain about what they describe. That the thirties exhibited their regional peaks, analysed by Shannon and Matthews, to such an extent that the aggregate peaked twice and upset the pattern of the building cycle is not surprising, when the new complications of the times are considered. Nor is it to be marvelled at that the simple population cycle becomes even less realistic than ever, as migration on a large scale became practicable. The economy became more specialist, and coal began its period of glory. How this became so in the thirties, and developed in the next few decades, has been treated at some length in earlier chapters, where we emphasised the importance of regional differences. Now we take up again the story of the two building cycles that preceded the First World War.

The first point we have to notice is the timing of the peak in house-building in 1876. The importance of this is emphasised if we look at Figure 8.2 which graphs Feinstein's estimates of home and foreign investment during the later nineteenth century.[3] 1876–7

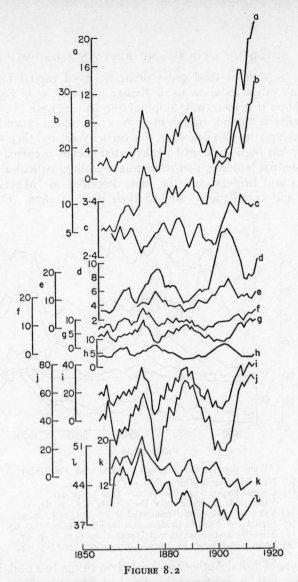

FIGURE 8.2

(All of the data for this Figure are taken from Feinstein and refer to the U.K.)
(a) Net Income available for Foreign Investment (£'o m.): p. 219.
(b) Total Investment (Net Domestic Fixed Capital Formation+Foreign Investment) (£'o m.) : p. 222.
(c) Ratio of Stock of Fixed-revenue-yielding Capital in £ (1912 and 1913), (excluding Building) to Industrial Income (Profits and Wages) : p. 228.
(d) Net Domestic Fixed Capital Formation (£m.) : p. 219.
(e) Gross Domestic Industrial Capital Formation as % of Industrial Profits: p. 220.
(f) Total Investment as % of National Income : p. 220.
(g) Foreign Investment as % of National Income : p. 220.
(h) Net Domestic Fixed Capital Formation as % of National Income : p. 220.
(i) Foreign Investment as % of U.K. Exports : p. 227.
(j) Foreign Investment as % of Total Investment : p. 227.
(k) Ratio of Industrial Profits in £ (1912 and 1913) to the Stock of Fixed-revenue-yielding Capital (excluding Buildings) : p. 228.
(l) Ratio of Industrial Profits to Industrial Incomes (Profits and Wages) : p. 228.

also saw a peak in total gross domestic fixed capital formation. Feinstein's estimates allow us to disaggregate this, as in Figure 8.3, which shows that mercantile shipbuilding had its peak in 1874, and was actually at a minor trough in 1876, while capital expenditure by railway companies also peaked in this earlier year, and then settled at a slightly less high level until a substantial decline occurred in 1878. But residential building, non-residential building, structural work to buildings and bridges, and the item described as 'Miscellaneous, Fittings and Installations' all had their peak in 1876.   Only loan

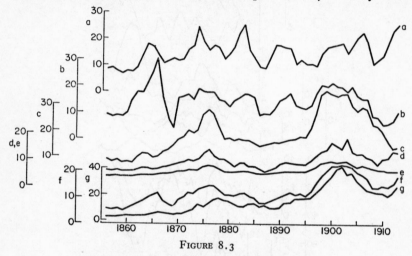

FIGURE 8.3

(All the data for this Figure are taken from Feinstein)
(a) New Mercantile Shipbuilding (£m.) : p. 86.
(b) Capital Expenditure by Railway (£m.) : p. 91.
(c) Value of U.K. Residential Building (£m.) : p. 82.
(d) Value of U.K. Non-Residential Building (£m.) : p. 97.
(e) Structural Work to Bridges and Buildings (£m.) : p. 97.
(f) Miscellaneous Fittings and Installations (£m.) : p. 97.
(g) Loan Expenditure by Local Authorities (£m.) : p. 91.

expenditure of Local Authorities carried on rising, to a peak in 1878, and it may well be significant that this had dipped in 1875.   Taking the picture as a whole we find that all recorded forms of private fixed capital formation peaked in the same year as our aggregate of housing. We have already seen that house-building in South Wales and the Manchester area had regional peaks in 1876, and that in both of these there was a close relationship between industrial activity and house-building.   The coincidence of so many investment peaks in the national aggregates in this same year tempts us to suggest that probably investments in industrial capacity and houses were booming together in most areas in the seventies.   Not every town had its peak in 1876 and in London it was several years later, but the evidence we have for individual towns confirms the impression created by the national aggregates, that industrial fixed investment and housing saw their highest activities at about the same time except in the Metropolis.

The location of this peak, preceding by two years the trough in American building, as shown by both the Long and the Riggleman indices, marks the time after which there is indisputably an inverse relationship between building on the two sides of the Atlantic. As we have already pointed out, the course of building in both countries was upset by the Civil War, and there is little doubt that Thomas erred in tentatively placing a trough in British building around 1870. An adequate analysis of these years calls for a thorough examination of the American and British economies on a regional basis, and there is little point in attempting here and now to decide on an explanation. It is a period of very considerable interest and difficulty, which is not made easier by our uncertainty about the course of births in the forties and early fifties, which makes an analysis of potential demand for housing on the basis of age-structure rather difficult. It is, however, clear that, whatever its exact shape through time, the rising trend in births and marriages warranted a faster rate of building in Britain than had been common in the early sixties, when a generally booming economy was braked by the poverty of Lancashire. The end of the Civil War was bound to liberate potential demand both here and in America. That emigration was high in the late sixties was partly due to the greater opportunities afforded overseas, and partly to population pressure.[4] Clearly, although it was high, it was insufficient to hold down completely the rising British demand for housing. Yet it seems that perhaps it was also insufficient to sustain the American boom with an adequate abundance of cheap enough labour. The few years of being in phase were, in fact, years in which American building was rising much less rapidly than it had been, while British building was taking off into a minor boom, and pausing after the Overend, Gurney and Company crisis, before a further, longer upsurge, during which the course of American building was undoubtedly downwards. The peak came, as we have seen, in 1876.

Yet long before 1876 the downturn in our economy had begun. When we looked at coal-mining and the cotton industry, we saw that for both of these industries the writing was on the wall in 1873. Perhaps our hindsight makes visible a warning that was less clear at the time. Certainly the fall in raw-cotton prices bolstered up the industry in 1874, and even after the failures of 1875 there were optimists around in 1876, though they were soon to become the victims of bad harvests.   Yet it is a characteristic of crises that people who fail to read the mural warnings usually do so because they are in a mood of buoyancy and optimism, rather than because the writing is obscure; and the fact is that although, by the end of 1873, none but the blind could have failed to see the bold letters of bad tidings, nobody read the words they spelled.   The transfer of £200 m. indemnity from Paris to Berlin had wrought havoc in the money market.   In America, where the mileage of railroads doubled between 1865 and 1872, the huge speculations, and a widely criticised monetary policy had brought down the house of Jay Cook and Company, terminating railway-building and the demand for British iron.   It did not require much imagination to predict that the excessive capacity of the British iron and steel industry would soon lead to losses and failures; especially since America was not alone in reducing its demands.   In the same direction operated the lull in shipbuilding, that followed the boom occasioned by the opening of the Suez Canal in 1869, and the augmented war-time capacity of the continental iron industries competed with our own.   The wave of crises that swept America and Europe in the early seventies has been described by Newbold,[5] who asserted:

there is very strong ground for supposing that what started off the great crisis which commenced in 1873 was the even more profound unsettlement of the short-term money markets by the movements of gold and the transfers of balances from France to Germany via London, the unique magnitude of the operations and their impact on a market that, strong as it was as a machine and made yet stronger in funds by the war, had never been intended to stand against a strain of this sort.

To this he added the American rail speculation, the technical revolution in the iron industry that made so much capital obsolete, and repudiation or default of debts by Turkey, Egypt and various South American countries.   Suddenly realities replace hopes, and

the ensuing shock to credit . . . carried away inevitably a great deal of quite genuine capital, whilst by dint of political manœuvring much fictitious value was carried over into the future.[6]

Yet the sum of these upheavals had, if anything, a stimulating immediate effect on home investment, for although the demand for iron had temporarily fallen, and the demand for coal was down, yet house-building was an attractive investment.   In the middle of 1873, *The Builder* had reported:

The building trade at the present time is perhaps receiving more benefit from the opening of the numerous new coal-fields than any other branch of industry, excepting, of course, the business of mining and sinking. Building operations are in many instances greatly retarded by the higher prices of labour and materials; and there can be no doubt that investors as a rule are turning their attention to other modes of utilising their capital than laying it out in cottages. Another matter highly favourable to building operations is the opening out of new coal-fields which are removed from the bulk of the population or in localities where existing property is fully taxed with occupants. This is just now especially the case in South Yorkshire, where more new schemes are being projected than ever before known in the history of the coal trade.[7]

But soon other influences were at work. In 1874 the diminished demand we have already mentioned led to falling prices. In 1875 'the commercial difficulties and failures, and the fall of prices which marked 1874 have been still more severe',[8] and this fall occurred in building materials as well as in others.

At the same time emigration had slackened, as the New World proved less attractive, and for precisely the same reason foreign investment also dwindled, leaving men at home to demand accommodation, and money seeking an outlet that was untarnished by the failures of foreign speculation and default. Here, in the shape of a rising potential home demand, and an abundance of money and rising real wages at a time of falling building costs — arising at least in part out of declining coal and other costs which had their origin in reduced foreign demands — lies the reason for our blindness to the warnings of the times. For the wood trade, 1876 was described as being generally prosperous, with advancing prices.

The greatly increased demand seems to be owing chiefly to the low price of money, and to the inclination on the part of capitalists to prefer investments in substantial property in England to foreign stocks. . . . As long as money continues cheap, this rate of consumption may be maintained, although it will probably result in building beyond the requirements of the population.[9]

This, indeed, is precisely what seems to have happened. Although the downturn of 1873 was largely due to foreign credit crises reducing demands for our exports, there was no severe British credit crisis. The Bank rate touched 9 per cent for a few days in November, but had fallen to half of this before the following month was over. Both short-term credit, of the kind needed for day-to-day building operations, and long-term loans of a kind that could finance the ownership of a house, were in easy supply. On most previous occasions when the economy had turned downwards it had done so at a time of tight money, and bankruptcies and disasters contributed to declining activity at a time when dear money, or completely unobtainable credit, made building difficult. But now this was not so. Even though our exports had fallen, the British economy was providing a more attractive home for the hesitant migrant than was America, in the throes of crisis, and easy money enabled his demands to be translated into actual buildings. The multiplier effects of this huge activity so cushioned almost the whole of the economy against the more severe impact of declining exports that there was further encouragement for industrial investment, aided, once again, by low costs and cheap money to augment the profits of the previous boom. That all of this was possible was due, essentially, to the abundance of funds. If the credit had not been available, house-building and other forms of investment could never have soared to the heights of 1876, when, as we have seen from previous chapters, it was overdone. Much of it was speculative, and inspired by the desire for a solid investment in bricks and mortar, without due regard for the possibility that there would be no tenants. Only continuing industrial expansion — not stagnation — could ensure that migration to the towns and rising wages would still sustain effective demand for housing; and only a colossal upsurge in home demand, or a revival of foreign demands, could provide an adequate reason for the expansion of home industrial investment and output. But the revival was not forthcoming, and the sheer magnitude of the boom made the reaction all the more inevitable, as excess capacity appeared almost simultaneously in industry and the housing market. The consequent decline in activity in each sector hit the other, and aggravated the downturn, made all the more severe in any case by the simultaneous depressions in coal, iron and cotton. If credit had been less abundant in 1874–6, so that some form of credit scarcity had led to an earlier downturn in building, the ensuing slump would probably have been less severe. As it was, a large amount of empty property was to weigh down the market for many years. Only, indeed, in London, with its special attractions for migrants and its competing railway companies catalysing the construction of houses, was demand still sufficient to absorb the swollen supply: and even there the amount of empty property was rising ominously, spelling over-supply. The rise in real wages in the eighties might, if the over-supply had been less severe, have stimulated building: but the amount of empty property gave an initial inertia that was not easily overcome, while many of the speculative builders who had fallen victims of the late seventies had neither recovered their finances nor been replaced by newcomers, eager to rush in when days were still dubious. By now, emigration was high, and foreign investment rising, as America and the Empire exerted their attractions. In the United States, where the advance in agriculture had halted in the early eighties, there was a 'consolidation' which 'took the form of town- and railway-building' and was 'financed largely by British capital and carried through with the help of British immigrants.'[10] It was a consolidation that had been 'held up in the seventies by monetary difficulties in America and distrust in London'. These were the very factors that had aided the British investment of the mid-seventies to a degree that demand did not justify. The ensuing reaction in Britain came at a time when America was recovering, and men and money again found it the more attractive side of the Atlantic. *The Economist* described 1883 as 'a year of disappointment' for the British economy, while 1884 was 'more disappointing still'. Worse was to follow, and the *Commercial History and Review* of 1887 had this to say: 'for the last five years we had to report the wood trade of London as being in a very depressed condition, but of none of those years was it necessary to give such gloomy accounts as of 1886'.[11]

Timber prices were falling, but despite this consumption was also on the wane.

The great demand for timber comes from the building trades, but with empty houses abounding, and as a consequence rents rapidly falling, there has been little to encourage the erection of new dwellings, and from such agricultural districts as London still supplies, the demand has fallen away comparatively to nothing. As the wood trade has always been the last to participate in any improvement in the general trade of the country, there is but too little reason to expect any immediate substantial change for the better.[12]

In America, on the other hand, new building was at a peak according to the Long index, and well on the way to one according to Riggleman. In Britain, the rate of profit on capital had fallen (with but a brief rally around 1880) since the early seventies, and it was abroad that eyes seeking handsome profits turned. Feinstein has analysed this decline in some detail, and has emphasised that while it was due to many factors, including the adverse effects of foreign competition on the prices of manufactured goods, the falling off in demand for iron and textiles, and the consequent vast surplus of capacity, this decline in profits was aggravated by the stickiness of wages, which meant that the distribution of industrial incomes was turning in favour of that section of the community that was least inclined to invest in British industry: for it was largely out of profits that new industrial investment still took place. One reason for the switch in investment from home to overseas was that there was less money to plough back. Investment was being undertaken less by people tied to their own firms and more by people who could view the whole field of investment opportunity in terms of security and profit rather than loyalty. These economic considerations were tipping the scales in favour of America.

1887 saw the beginning of a slight improvement in the home economy, as exports began to rise, and the coal industry to prosper. We have already looked briefly at these beginnings in Chapter 6. In 1888 emigration fell slightly from its high value of the preceding year, and so began a downward sweep that lasted almost unbroken until the century's end. Thomas has summarised the sequence of events, as revealed by the turning points in national aggregates, as follows:

The next phase was inaugurated by a change in the domestic sector — a fall in the index of empty property in 1885 ; 1888 saw a recovery in home investment, building and the general level of employment, accompanied by a downturn in emigration and American railway construction, after which came changes in imports, exports, foreign investment and American building.[13]

Although the full force of the building upswing did not impinge upon the economy until the mid-nineties, there is little doubt that its beginnings must be traced back to this period. There was no sudden revival but 'the hesitating, halting improvement which characterised the closing months of 1887 developed in 1888 into a distinct and well-sustained revival'[14] while 1889 was a year of 'gradual but steady progress'. The rate of profit on capital was rising, as is shown in Figure 8.2[15] and although wages were also on the upswing this was clearly better than if profits had been falling. Yet overseas investment had still to reach its peak, and did so in a year that saw the crisis in Argentina. So began the final decade of the century, with a succession of crises that included the Baring Crisis and the collapse of the Liberator. In making overseas investment less attractive, some of these helped to turn funds to the home sector, even if others turned them away from building societies. The rising profits on which we have already commented disappeared in the early nineties but soon returned at a time when wages were rising less rapidly, and so provided a much-needed source of funds for long-term industrial investment. 'Perhaps,' said *The Economist* in 1894, 'the most noteworthy feature of our trade in 1893 is the strength with which it resisted the series of extremely adverse influences. . . .' To some extent this was due to the tendency once again to look at home for opportunities. The British economy was basically sound, and ripe for expansion after almost a generation of stagnation. Although two and a half million people had left the country during the eighties, the total population was still rising, for natural increase in that decade was over four millions. As emigration slackened, due partly to changing fortunes overseas, people of house-seeking age and circumstances formed a larger proportion of the net increase in population. Some of these were the children born at the time of the previous housing boom. Meanwhile, the low level of building in the eighties had shaken out the housing market, and given the empty houses arising out of the previous over-building and subsequent distress time to fill. Rents were once again beginning to rise, even though, as Saul has pointed out,[16] in Birmingham at least they were still at very low levels in 1892 at a time when costs were high. But the potential demand was obvious, and for the speculative builder it was this, rather than the level of rents that really mattered. In industry the slow growth of demand, and depreciation over a long period, had absorbed surplus capacity. It needed only a favourable turn in prices, a rise in profits, and then, as was shortly to come, a plethora of cheap money, to turn the potential demands we have just indicated into active construction.

The most detailed examination of the course of house-building during these years has been carried out by Saul,[17] who examined activity in a large number of towns, and emphasised the existence of the kind of difference revealed by Richards and myself when we compared house-building in South Wales with the general index compiled by Weber.[18] Some of the data are graphed in Figure 8.4. The conclusion suggested by Richards and myself was that by this time the South Wales coal industry was more closely geared to the development of overseas economies, and their demands for Welsh coal, and to our export industries which, as was usual, were booming during a time of falling home construction, than to the internal demands of the economy. The point has been examined in more detail by Thomas, who presents a convincing case.[19] On the other hand, until Saul published his paper there had been no examination — other than Cairncross's work on Glasgow — of building in other towns, and it is clear that the experience of South Wales cannot be taken as typical of that of any other area. Indeed, the whole point is that it was quite different from that of other regions.

Before looking at the discrepant performance that inaugurated this century, we must make a few points about the background. The boom whose beginnings we have just traced, and which had as a major factor in its causation the demand arising from the new adults born in the preceding boom, was augmented by the influence of migration. Partly because of the less favourable turn in America,

and partly because of the greater prosperity at home which was due
in part to the increasing volume of building, emigration had declined.
Whereas the eighties had seen a low marriage-rate, and a high
emigration, there was now a high marriage-rate and a low emigration,
and these two factors operated in the same direction. Saul has
observed that although the net loss by migration was only 68,000 in
the nineties compared with 601,000 in the eighties, the natural
increase in population accounted for roughly three and a half million
in each decade, and that despite the age and marital structure of the
migrants 'it is hard to believe that migration of itself could account
for more than a small part of the wide fluctuations in house construction'.[20] This is a conclusion that seems to be questionable
for several reasons. First we must note that fluctuations in the
supply of additions of housing stock — i.e., in new building net of
demolition — should be related to fluctuations in the additions to
population stock — i.e., to the first differences of the data for natural
increase. If we do this, we find that between the eighties and the
nineties, natural increase fell by 36,000, whereas net emigration fell
by 533,000. The net increase in population in the nineties was thus
almost half a million higher than it was in the eighties and this was
because of the fall in emigration. Since the population was growing
more rapidly, one would expect the demand for new houses to rise.
The second point is that if we look not at population increase but
at the number of marriages, we find that in the nineties these
amounted to 2,393,000, compared with 2,047,000 in the eighties.
This increase in the marriage-rate, which was noted by Saul, implies
an additional demand for houses. There were a third of a million
more new married couples, even though, of course, we should take
into account the disappearance of married couples through deaths.
Since emigration was usually largely of people of marriageable age,
a substantial part of this increase in the number of marriages must
be attributed to the lower emigration. It is true that the number
of people of marriageable age was higher than it had been, because
of the high births of the early seventies, but if emigration had
remained high very many of these people would have gone abroad
before marrying. As it was, the number of marriages rose by a third
of a million, while the number of emigrants fell by half a million.
How much of the former is due to the latter is uncertain, but from
the point of view of our argument it does not matter very much.
The only relevant point at the moment is that these two statistics
are of very similar magnitudes, and that quite certainly some part of
the increase in marriages was due to falling emigration. It follows
that the direct effect of the falling migration on the demand for

housing must have been comparable with that of other demographic factors. Whether it was the main factor is not of very great importance; although it is quite possible that it was. A third reason for rejecting Saul's argument is that it pays no attention to the effect that falling emigration has on demand generally, and the supply of labour, which differs from the effects of natural increase. But even without this, the argument seems to fail on purely demographic grounds.

This effect of falling emigration on the demand for houses means that, since the fall was partly attributable to unfavourable events abroad, these events must be thought of as partial determinants of the course of British building. Another was soon to effect building in a different way. The high level of national activity drove up costs all over the country, and the Boer War came at a time when these high costs emphasised the need of ready advances. But even before then there had been clouds gathering in the sky of the century's Indian summer. The index of share prices, whose major fluctuations tended to predict those in the aggregate of housing activity, had leapt from a level of 90 in 1894 to 100 in the following year, to 121 in the next, and then to 133 in 1897.[21] It was an increase of 50 per cent in four years. But then it halted, and by 1900 had risen only three more points. Clearly there were some, at least, who felt that British industry was no longer the best place for investible funds, which is not surprising when one notes from Figure 8.2 that the rate of profit on capital was beginning to fall. For some years there had been anxiety about our export trade, which was hardly holding its own in the fight for foreign markets.[22] Soon building made the first of its twin peaks.

Although it would be wrong to attribute the dip entirely to the Boer War, we must certainly take it into account. The war had its effect both through its impact on confidence, which was weakening in any case if share prices tell us anything, and through its effect on the price of money. Feinstein quotes a correspondent of the Master Builders' Association, who wrote from Edinburgh in February 1900:

A very serious building crisis has arisen . . . the collapse has been brought about principally by dearness of money and the disposition of the banks to restrict advances over this class of security.[23]

As Saul has put it:

Changes in the availability of short-term funds could seriously affect the builder who had to borrow to see him through the period of construction. Especially to the speculative builder the problem was less one of cost than of actual 'drying up' of the supply of such money and this was reflected by a high short-term rate of interest. The stringency caused by the Boer War was the most obvious example of such a short-term fluctuation. Of 32 series originally calculated for this paper, whereas 26 showed increases of building activity in 1896, 1897 and 1898, in 1899 only 22 rose and in 1900 only ten. By 1902, 18 were rising again . . . in 1907 short money was again extremely tight and in consequence the following year saw only seven series rising. By this time, however, a sharp general depression at home had left money much easier, and, in 1909, 21 of the series showed building on the increase.[24]

But the Boer War was not the whole story, and Saul is probably correct in referring to its impact in terms of 'a short term fluctuation'. Even this was uneven in its incidence, for in Birmingham, which seems to have had a ready supply of money, and to have operated only slightly on credit, building boomed throughout the war.[25]   No doubt one reason for this was the demands made upon the local industries as a result of the war itself, stimulating employment and local incomes.   Saul has shown that when a depression in industry set in in 1903, there was already sign of surplus housing in Birmingham.

It is important for us to know to what extent this was an isolated phenomenon, and how it arose.   In 1901 the level of empty property was fairly high, as is witnessed by the Census returns, and Saul has shed some interesting light on the situation.   He obtained a measure of the rate of change of house-building around the turn of the century by dividing the number of houses built in 1901–03 by the number built in 1898–1900.   For each town that he examined he plotted this ratio against the percentage of empty houses in 1901. For twenty-six towns the ratio was above 100, showing higher building in the later years, while for twenty-five it was below this value.   There does not seem to be any relationship at all between the values of the ratio and the degree of empty property.   On the other hand, the same exercise carried out ten years later shows a very clear distribution of the points around a rectangular hyperbola, with high empties strongly associated with declining building, and low empties with increasing building.   This suggests that the state of the market was a more important influence in determining the course of building around 1911 than it was around 1901, and although the average level of empties was higher in 1901 than in the later year, it is clear that there were other factors more dominant then than later. In about a third of the towns considered, building was increasing at a time when the level of empties, exceeding 6 per cent, should have bade caution.   The principal disregard for caution came from the speculative builder, and the fact that the financial stringency of the Boer War lasted only for a short time, and so prevented anything like a major credit crisis, enabled him to continue his activities with only a slight pause. His supply outstripped demand.

But why was this so? What changes were taking place in demand? Were there forces tending to reduce it, or was it simply that it did not keep pace with the growing supply of new houses?

Since the level of empties was high in 1901 in many towns, we have to look at what happened before then to lead to this position. Without implying that this is the whole of the explanation we may note that in the years immediately before 1901 prices had been rising in this country, while both marriages and wages had passed their peak. This is shown quite clearly in Figure 8.4, and it is clear that as a consequence the high level of empties in certain towns in 1901 must be attributed not simply to a high level of building, but also to a fall in demand. As had happened so often in the past, falling marriages, falling incomes and rising prices coincided to reduce demand below the level that would otherwise have existed, and it is probable that if these three forces had not worked in the same direction then in some of these towns the level of empties would have been lower in 1901 than the Census recorded. The plain fact is that, quite apart from demographic changes, there was a deterioration in the lot of the worker.

Before we go further we must note an important and sometimes forgotten factor. Already we have drawn attention to the change in the trend of births in the late seventies, when rapid increase gave way to stagnation within a couple of years. By the turn of the century this rapid change must have been visible in the trend of the numbers of people approaching the age of marriage, and this was almost bound to mean that, quite apart from any additional disturbance caused by low wages or high prices, one would expect a fall in the number of marriages from about 1903 onwards. It also meant that in the earlier years the number of young workers had not been increasing at the rate that had applied formerly, and so the influence of juvenile incomes, which we have previously held to be important, was diminished, partly because they were increasing less rapidly, and partly because they were starting work later.[26] Thus the change in the trend of the birth-rate twenty or so years before was now bound to affect the demand for houses. Between them, the Education Acts and Mrs. Besant were changing the course of the economy.

To this diminution in demand that arose from birth control was added the influence of increased emigration. A boom was under way in American railways and building, and the outflow of labour took another of its upward flights as once again conditions abroad offered better prospects than those at home, and there was an

abundance of newly married couples to seek their fortunes. The
course of marriage, emigration, and American activity is shown in

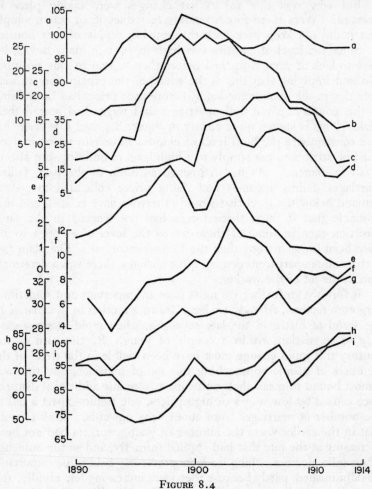

FIGURE 8.4

(a) Index of Real Wages in the U.K. (1914 = 100). Bowley, pp. 30, 34.
(b) House-building in London ('000). See Appendix 4.
(c) House-building in Manchester ('o). See Appendix 4.
(d) House-building in Birmingham ('oo). See Appendix 4.
(e) House-building in Glasgow ('000). See Appendix 4.
(f) House-building in Holiday Resorts ('o). Saul, p.121.
(g) Marriages, G.B. ('0,000). B.H.S., p. 46.
(h) Sauerbeck's Price Index (1867–77 = 100). Ibid., pp. 474–5.
(i) Rousseaux's Price Index (1865–85 = 100). Ibid., pp. 472–3.

Figure 8.5.   To dissociate these factors, and to relegate emigration
to a minor role, does not seem to be very realistic.   It is clear that

at this time building would have fallen, because of the falling number of marriages, and rising prices. But emigration added to the severity of the fall, and aided the rise in activity in America and elsewhere, just as eventually it helped to increase the marginal product of labour in this country, to improve the lot of the worker,

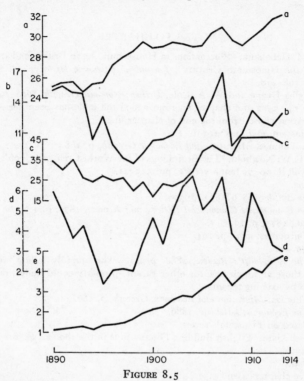

FIGURE 8.5

(a) Marriages, G.B. ('o,ooo). *B.H.S.*, p. 46.
(b) U.K. Emigration to U.S. ('o,ooo). Thomas (1), p. 296.
(c) Index of New Building in U.S. (Long.). Thomas (1), p. 299.
(d) Railway Miles Added in U.S. ('ooo). Thomas (1), p. 288.
(e) Bituminous Coal Output in U.S. ('o m. net tons of 2,000 lb.). Thomas (1), p. 287.

and so to set off an upward tendency, which was visible almost everywhere when the war came in 1914.

This is by no means a full account of the last building cycle of our uncontrolled economy. It has said nothing about internal migration, and there has been little in the way of regional analysis. It is, like most of its predecessors, a cycle that calls for a much longer and more rigorous study than we have been able to give it. Our aim has been simply to comment on one or two points that have been put forward by others, and to make a few observations of our own. In the next chapter we shall fall back onto some of these in attempting to outline a theory, and in assessing the implications of our rather tentative findings on theory, on future research and on policy.

NOTES TO CHAPTER 8

1. H. J. Habakkuk, 'Fluctuations in House-building in Britain and the United States in the Nineteenth Century', *Journal of Economic History*, vol. xxii, June 1962, pp. 198–230.
2. Phyllis Deane and W. A. Cole, *British Economic Growth, 1688–1959*, 1962, especially pp. 5–12 and chapter iii, from which the table has been derived. The long quotation comes from the end of chapter iii.
3. Feinstein, *ibid.*, pp. 219 ff.
4. Cf. Thomas, *Migration and Economic Growth*, p. 168.
5. J. T. W. Newbold, 'The Beginnings of the World Crisis, 1873–96', *Economic History*, vol. ii, no. 7, January 1932, pp. 425–41.
6. *Idem.*
7. *The Builder*, 28.6.1873, p. 509.
8. *The Economist's Commercial History and Review*, 1876, p. 1.
9. *Ibid.*, 1877, p. 19.
10. Cairncross, *ibid.*, p. 194.
11. *Op. cit.*
12. *The Economist's Review*, 1888, p. 26. The 'rapidly falling' rents were probably those at which new (or other vacant) property could be let, rather than rents paid by existing tenants.
13. Thomas, *Migration and Economic Growth*, p. 186.
14. *The Economist's Review*, 1889.
15. Based on Feinstein's series.
16. S. B. Saul, 'English Building Fluctuations in the 1890's', *Economic History Review*, 1962.
17. *Ibid.*
18. See chapters 4 and 5.
19. Thomas, *The Welsh Economy*, chapter 1.
20. *Ibid.*, p. 131.
21. Share prices have been examined with data taken from Brinley Thomas, *Migration and Economic Growth*, Table 99. This is based on P. Rousseaux, *Les Mouvements de fond de l'économie anglaise, 1800–1913*, Louvain, 1938, p. 272 and K. C. Smith and G. F. Horne, 'An Index Number of Securities, 1867–1914', *London and Cambridge Economic Service Special Memorandum, no. 37, June 1934.* Thomas took the average of the 1884 and 1896 values as 100.
22. Clapham, vol. iii, pp. 38–9.
23. Feinstein quotes on p. 279 of his thesis from *The Master Builders' Association Journal*, February 1900, p. 13.
24. Saul, *ibid.*, pp. 132–3.
25. Saul, *ibid.*, p. 121 and pp. 129–31.
26. On all of this see Musgrove, *op. cit.*

CHAPTER 9

SOME CONCLUSIONS AND THEIR
RELEVANCE TO THE INTER-WAR YEARS

A BOOK of this length cannot possibly deal adequately with a subject as vast as the interaction between building and the rest of the economy over a period exceeding two centuries. This is especially true because it is a subject which has become of interest to more than a small number of people only in recent years, so that it has not yet received enough examination and discussion from different points of view by people with different specialities at their command. It is too soon for us to feel that all the major points are settled, that all the relevant facts have been unearthed, and that all the relevant variables have been accorded their roles. Because of this, it is all the more important that we should test our theory. In the course of the last eight chapters we have asserted a number of causal relationships, without offering any proof. Historical fact has been put forward in support of our ideas, but even a professional historian with a very detailed knowledge of the period concerned can only sometimes be certain that his explanation is correct, for many important facts are never known, while others become lost either permanently or temporarily. Even when we seek to explain contemporary events we feel this ignorance, and while the past is sometimes easier to study because diaries and records unseal lips which never spoke during their lifetime, there is the grave disadvantage of a complete inability to ask questions. This is not to say that historical proof does not exist. It most certainly does. But it needs a far greater expert to recognise it than does a statistical proof; and on occasion the expert must declare that he sees no prospect of proof or disproof, unless some unsuspected data are revealed. So far in this book we have relied almost entirely on demonstrating the historical plausibility of our assertions. We have taken such facts as we have found, and attempted to produce a theory which is compatible with them. We cannot suppose that there is no other theory which is equally compatible, nor can we suppose that no facts contradicting the theory will ever come to light. On the other hand, the theory involves a number of well-defined causal relationships, and it may be possible to test the validity of at least some of these by statistical methods.

There is, however, one great difficulty. Many of our assertions have been put forward on a regional basis. We have not suggested that they should be verifiable or valid at a national level. Yet it is at that national level that many of the statistics exist, while usually there are none at the level at which we believe the relationships to be true. While they are testable in principle, they are not in practice. For this reason we have had to devise a totally different method of 'testing' our theory. Briefly it consists of building a simulation model, and examining the effects of varying certain assumptions and parameters. We shall have more to say about this in a moment, but it is clear, from the outset, that this method tests the correctness of a piece of reasoning, rather than a theory about the real world. It enables us to see the consequences in the model economy which we build of the assumptions we make, and the interactions we specify. It does not enable us to decide whether these interactions actually existed in the British economy. On the other hand, if we succeed in building a model which appears to behave in much the same way as the British economy did in those days, and which reacts to certain changes in parameter values in some 'realistic' way, then such a model may lend support to our ideas. If it does not behave in the way that the economy behaved, then it may be useful for us to enquire whether it is our assumptions that are inadequate or our reasoning from them, for one of the big points of a simulation model is that it enables us to use a computer to 'reason' out the consequences of far more simultaneous assumptions than any human mind can ever hope to manage.

This is a subject to which we shall return later in the chapter. It is more important now to summarise the theory, and to pay rather more attention to certain parts of it than we have done so far. The ingredients are derived from Jevons, Hawtrey, Cairncross and Thomas, with a sprinkling of Frisch. The last named writer has dwelt at length with the importance of shocks in generating cycles, and in preventing damping of fluctuations. Jevons took the harvest as one of the main shocks, and gave it an important role. Hawtrey has based a great deal of explanation on credit. Cairncross and Thomas have emphasised migration, both internal and international, and the terms of trade. But none of these writers has quite succeeded in explaining both the amplitude and the timing of the fluctuations, even though, in some cases, the explanation has possibly been implicit. Jevons's attempt to explain cycles sometimes broke down, as did Hawtrey's, and this seems to have been because neither paid adequate attention to the importance of the factor emphasised by the other, and because each looked upon cycles as being more or less of one kind. There was no adequate appreciation of the fact that the 'trade cycle' that embraces the peak of a building cycle is quite different from one half way up the slope. Cairncross and Thomas have brought in the building cycle, and births and marriages appear in their explanations. But not even Thomas has explicitly related the timing of the building cycle to the timing of a births cycle, even though he gets very close to doing so. Neither writer gives an important active role to the credit situation, although, once again, it seems to be implicit in a great deal of what they write. On the other hand, without the work of these writers the present theory would never have been formulated.

There is no need to repeat that part of the theory which appears in Chapter 3. Furthermore, since we do not suggest for one moment that every building cycle was the same as every other, there is no point in offering a theory of 'the building cycle'. Rather we must offer a theory of building cycles in the plural, in which alternative possibilities are allowed to operate.

The key to our theory lies in population, credit and shocks, and it is convenient to speak first of the last. Here there seems to be an example of an important, obvious but neglected principle: that shocks have to be taken in their context. It is customary in econometric work to allow for shocks by adding them at the ends of equations. The usual assumption is that a specified relationship does not exactly 'explain' a certain variable, but that the differences between the observed and the calculated values are normally distributed with zero mean. These differences may arise out of neglected variables, over-simplification or shocks. They represent everything about which we do not know enough to have a measure. But there are certain things which we do know about shocks, and which can be taken into account in a quite different way. Although the Principle of Shocks in Their Context has become apparent during the course of writing this book, it is clear, when one thinks about it, that it is not just an economic concept, and that in some fields it is already well established. It is well known in surgery that the shock of an operation can be stood by a fit person more than by an unfit one, as can the shock of bad or good news. For a person with a bad heart, either a good shock or a bad shock may have the same fatal result, while for a person suffering from severe depression a quite small piece of good news may at one time have tremendous effect while at another it has none, while bad news may have most serious consequences. In meteorology a small depression some distance

H

away may have no effect of any consequence if local conditions have been settled for some days; while if the weather is less settled this distant disturbance may make all the difference. In music, the effect of a mighty crash on the percussion is clearly very different if it occurs in a quiet peaceful passage than if it is in the middle of a loud crescendo. It is different, even when immediately prefaced by identical bars, if it occurs in the middle of a movement than if it occurs at the end. There is hardly need to present other examples of this principle which, although valid in so many fields, has so far found no general acceptance in economics. The reason for this is not far to seek. Economists are concerned about studying relationships and reasoning things out. If one is studying a whole chain of such relationships, then human reasoning breaks down if at every stage we have to consider not just what happens next, but what happens next if there is a shock of type A, type B or type C. It is easier, and in the past it has been more fruitful, to assume that there is no shock. In most cases one does not seem to go far wrong, because on the whole shocks have only minor effects on the economic system. But every now and again we go seriously wrong, sometimes because there is a big shock, or, more often, because we happen to have arrived at a context in which a little shock has a big result. My opinion is that the development of simulation models on computers can allow us to deal with this kind of problem. Furthermore, if what has just been said is correct, it seems to be important for us either to avoid reaching a situation in which small shocks can have large outcomes, or to be able to recognise these contexts when we approach them, so that remedial counter-shocks can be at hand if necessary.

In order to build a model in which shocks can be introduced in this way a number of simplifying assumptions have to be made. But the model must inevitably remain a complicated one. In an earlier draft of this book we presented a very long conceptual outline of a two-country multi-regional economy, in which each region had a building industry and a few others, and each country had a banking system. There was also a transport system, and migration of money and men. Harvests, bankruptcies and other features which we have stressed had their place. It was soon apparent that in its original form the model was too large for any existing computer. A smaller version of it, which retains the features just mentioned, but sacrifices many others is now being programmed; but this is a very long process, and it has been felt better to present the model and its results, after it has been run through the computer many times, in another work. For the time being we must content ourselves with obtaining some insight into its working, by drawing upon what we have already written.

Population is usually treated as an exogenous factor. Provided that there is no migration, this is a reasonable device if we are concerned with short runs. But economic factors clearly affect the volume of migration, and although it may be numerically small compared with the total population, or even compared with total population change, it may nevertheless be important because of its age and sex structure, or, indeed, because of its industrial composition. An emigration of fifty economists might have quite catastrophic consequences for one country or the other. Our model takes account of the industrial structure of migrants, and has room for varying assumptions about their age and sex structures. But to take account of migration is not enough if we are concerned with growth, for then natural population change also becomes important. Birth- and death-rates have to be considered, and since both the birth-rate and the demand for houses are affected by the marriage-rate we must also bring in this. If there is one lesson that history teaches us but which economists, on the whole, ignore, it is that whatever determines the long-run trend of these rates, quite severe fluctuations occur in them for reasons that are partly economic. This has been so in the past and it is not unreasonable to believe that it is so today, even in advanced economies. Economic conditions are more likely to exert sharp effects on the death-rate in subsistence economies, when hard times may, through sheer shortage of food, lead to increased deaths of people of all ages, but particularly the young and old. If there have been several years of prosperity, then the effects of a bad year may be less severe, simply because people will have a higher resistance. If the economy is a more advanced and prosperous one, then the effects on the death-rate are more likely to be on its long term trend than on year-to-year changes; and these effects may be favourable or otherwise according to the wisdom with which people spend their money and time. In our model, in its simpler version, we have assumed death-rates which have long-term trends, but have no other systematic changes. The more complicated version brings in the points we have just mentioned. The marriage-rate is probably more likely to be affected by economic conditions. Certainly our statistics seem to suggest this. We have made the principal variables in its determination the price of food, which depends on harvests, (and so on shocks as well as design) and the level of employment and incomes. The marriage-rate, like the death-rate, has to be thought of as a set of age-specific rates, and so it depends on the age-structure of the population.   If there is migration of a kind that upsets the sex-balance (which frequently happened in the nineteenth century, when country villages were depleted of males, who left to work in heavy industry), then the marriage-rate is further affected.   Similar factors affect the birth-rate.   Since birth-control has played an important role in our theory, our model will eventually have to have a birth-control trend — not necessarily a smooth one — built into it.   It will, for example, be interesting to bring in a sharp change in the birth-rate, such as that which occurred in the 1870's, and to see in what respects the course of the model economy differs from that of the same economy when this change is not introduced.

It is then, in their direct effects on population, including not only natural increase but also the decision to emigrate, that shocks have their first role in our model, operating through the harvest (or other factors that affect the supply of food), on the real incomes of the people.   These population changes have subsequent effects on demand, and on the supply of labour, either immediately or at some considerable time in the future.   They also affect the age composition of the population, and so have some effect on future population changes.

The other principal place where shocks come in is the monetary sector.   Here they operate in several ways.   One which we have emphasised is the impact of harvests on the balance of payments. Chaudhuri[1] has recently made a useful study of the role of the balance of payments between 1815 and 1875, and has suggested that during the first half of the century it imposed a ceiling on growth. At that time, our textile exports to areas other than North America, which were to some extent dependent on the amount of British currency available to these countries either through our purchases from them or through our loans, did not rise at the same speed as our own purchases from these countries.   One reason for this was that much of the profit made by the exporters in these countries remained in the pockets of the rich.   Another is that as our boom proceeded, the high income elasticity of imports of raw materials, and for stocks, tended to worsen our balance.   But essentially, according to Chaudhuri, the trouble was in the stickiness of our exports, which were so dependent upon a sort of self-financing, and an adequate marketing system.   These are clearly matters of great importance, which we have hitherto ignored.   They tie up with the observed inverse relationship between exports and home investment, on which Cairncross, Thomas and others have commented, and which we noted even early in the eighteenth century.   Our interest in this thesis is that it reaches conclusions similar to our own in some respects, for Chaudhuri emphasises the impact of the harvest on the balance of payments, and how, when this was already strained, such an impact could lead to a crisis. But it is important to see how this crisis comes about, and also to see whether a major crisis in our model necessarily arises through a balance of payments situation rather than in some other way.

The kind of crisis we emphasise is the credit crisis. Essentially this takes the form of certain people being unable to obtain renewals of short term loans, and so being unable to fulfil their contractual obligations. A credit stringency may mean a situation in which people are unable to obtain new loans; it becomes a crisis when it extends into the renewal of existing loans. In the former case, new activity has to be postponed, while in the latter case the obligations associated with recent and current activity cannot be met. How can either of these situations arise? They concern the excess of demand for short-term credit over its supply, and in order to answer the problem we have posed we must discuss the determinants of these. It is easiest for us to do so in terms of our model, which avoids complications which we believe to be comparatively unimportant.

We may consider first the merchants' need of credit. At the end of every month, or whatever other period is appropriate, merchants have to pay producers for the goods they have bought. It is possible that they will also have to pay some deposit on orders they are placing, but this need not now concern us. What matters is the payment that they have a legal obligation to make. At the same time they receive money from the public for goods they have sold. In general the merchant may expect the latter to exceed the former, but there are, in particular, two occasions when it may not. One is when prices are falling, or demand declining. Unless this is correctly anticipated by the merchant, he may find himself selling at less than the normal margin over his buying price, or his stocks rising at the expense of his sales. The other occasion is when, because of rising prices, or the expectation of a shortage, he buys more than he expects to sell, believing that by getting into debt this month he may make a large profit the month after next. There is also the possibility that he has placed an order without a firm price contract, and has to pay more than he expected. In any of these cases the merchant will try to meet his financial commitments either out of his own savings (if they are in a sufficiently liquid form) or by borrowing from a bank or a discount house, on the understanding that he will repay within a stated time. Before seeing what happens next, we must specify how a producer may land up in a similar position.

While it may be reasonable as a first approximation to make no mention of the merchants' wage bill, one cannot do this in the case of the producer, nor can one assume that the wages are paid out at intervals equal to the period of production. In some cases it may be possible to sell the product of a single day's work at the end of the same day, but in other cases it may take several months before any income can be received by the firm as a result of its expenditures, whether it be on labour or raw materials, while even longer will have to elapse before it recoups the cost of equipment. We may suppose that new equipment is financed through the issue of shares, or out of accumulated profits; but depreciation has to be debited against current income. This will depend on recent deliveries of finished output, at ruling prices, while current expenditure will depend on the current rate of purchase of inputs — which will be related possibly to expectations of sales in a fairly remote future, based partly on orders and partly on speculation. If the prices of the inputs are rising it may be possible to do something to prevent a deficit on current account by putting up the price of the output, but this may be made difficult or undesirable by contracts or sales resistance. In the latter case the firm is likely to cut down its output, in order to reduce its demands for inputs which it is no longer profitable to buy in such quantity. But if expenditure on inputs is rising because of increased activity, then the answer is not to put up prices, but to accept a current deficit and to try to finance it in some way so that future profits derived from an expanded output may more than pay for it. It may be financed out of accumulated savings or out of borrowing. Possibly the expansion of output will, acting through an increased demand for the inputs, drive up input prices. In this case the rising output may call for greater financial accommodation both because of the scale of the activity, and because of price effects.

One example of a producer who requires a great deal of credit because of the long gestation period is the builder, who is commonly paid in arrears in stages, yet has to use labour and bricks which must be paid for currently or obtained on credit. If he is a speculative builder then he is not paid until the building is completed, so that he needs credit for the whole of the construction period — or even longer — rather than for part of it. Building also impinges on the credit situation in other ways, which will become clear when we have looked at the factors determining the supply of credit.

Credit of the kind we have just described may be supplied either by a person or a firm directly, or by a bank. We must consider these three in turn. The individual can lend out of his savings from wages and dividends. These would otherwise be hoarded, saved in the bank, used for the purchase of industrial shares, or used for the purchase of government bonds. The amount of money that individuals are prepared to lend will therefore depend not only on the total amount of money at their disposal after making their purchases, but also on the relative attractions of the other uses to which it can be put. These will depend not only on their liquidity preferences but also on the returns to be obtained, or the expectations of returns to be obtained, from the various forms of investment.

Firms may be able to grant credit to customers, by agreeing to accept payments, for goods delivered, at a later date than the payment is due. If this is to be done then either the firm itself must have accumulated savings, which it can run down in order to meet its expenses, or it must be able to obtain credit from some other firm, from individuals, or from the bank. If it grants credit out of its current profit and/or past accumulations then it means that it is not using that amount of money for some other purpose, and the attractiveness of the other possible uses will therefore be a factor in determining whether the firm is willing to grant credit in this way. Another factor is that the firm, by granting credit to a customer, is doing something to increase its own business; and provided that the firm has faith in its customer then there is strong temptation to give him a limited amount of help.

Other credit will be granted by the bank. The amount that it is able and prepared to grant will depend on the ratios to which it is working, on the cash deposited with it, and on the gold reserves or other rules of the game. An adverse movement in the balance of payments will reduce its willingness to grant credit, while it will also reduce its loans if cash is withdrawn. In the more complicated model we must take into account the whole range of possible assets, and the variations in the banks' preferences for these, but to do so now would be simply to prolong what is deliberately a simplified account, without adding appreciably to either realism or understanding.

If one considers the mechanism that has just been outlined, it seems that there will possibly be forces at work which will lead to a weakening of the credit situation whenever there is a long period of rising activity. The reason for this is that as activity rises the amount of credit that is required also rises, but there comes a time when this rises more rapidly than activity. At the same time, although rising incomes may lead to increased savings in both monetary and real terms, there are other forces at work which tend to shift money out of bank deposits. We must look at this a little more closely.

The factors that tend to make the credit requirements eventually rise more rapidly than activity are physical or other shortages and speculation.   Once any input becomes in short supply — and in unplanned economies it is inevitable that this should occur at some time if activity keeps rising, while even with planning of a very high degree it is likely to happen by accident — then its price is likely to rise.   Either merchants or producers have to pay out more than they expected, and they are more likely to require credit as a result. Whether they are seriously or only slightly inconvenienced at first does not matter very much, for in the first case they are likely to make adjustments which simply postpone the evil day, unless the harm is so great that there is an immediate crisis.   Unless this last possibility occurs, the prospect of continuing price increases will lead to speculative buying of stocks, driving up prices even further. Larger than usual stocks are purchased at higher than usual prices, and much of this has to be done on credit.   The accompanying inflation raises incomes, and it is possible that savings increase; but the ability of a bank to grant credit depends on its total assets, rather than on current additions to these.   If rising incomes lead to an equal proportional rise in current savings then there is not anything like an equal proportional rise in the banks' reserves of cash.   If, at the same time, there is a building boom, with an increasing amount of speculative building, then this adds further to the demands for credit, to an extent that much exceeds the credit demands of some other form of activity that might be carried out on the same scale. Adding to the strain created in this way are two other factors.   One is that the boom is likely to be accompanied by rising profits, which make investment attractive.   People who would in more normal times put their money into deposit accounts, or lend it on short term loans, are more inclined to purchase industrial shares.   Instead of being saved and available for credit purposes, it is invested in new equipment or buildings, and although some of it gets back into the banks, much of it goes on consumption.   Finally there is the possibility of a gradual drain on our reserves, through the Chaudhuri mechanism.

Although this argument has not been worked out rigorously, and the validity of the result must depend on the values of a number of parameters, it appears to be a likely phenomenon.   The point to keep in mind, however, is that such a period of strained credit is likely to last only a comparatively short time in a free economy. In the absence of shocks, the high rates of interest, and the un-availability of new loans, will lead to a reduction in activity, just as high prices will eventually lead to a refusal of merchants to add further to their stocks, as they fear that the public will refuse to buy their product at high enough prices. It is intended to demonstrate this with the aid of the simulation model. If, however, some shock occurs then the period of strained credit may terminate with a credit crisis. The shock need not be an unfavourable one. Clearly a bad harvest, by causing abnormally high imports of food, may so upset the possibly already strained balance of payments that credit has to be curtailed. Merchants and others are unable to renew their credit, and fail to fulfil their commitments. Activity is curtailed, orders are reduced, employment falls, and the whole downward mechanism sets in: but the suddenness of the refusal to renew loans, as opposed to a refusal to make new ones, is almost certain to be accompanied by bankruptcies, and it is these that lead to a severe switch in confidence. People hold onto their money, and make the supply of credit even worse. Some activities, such as building, may be left half completed, as credit dries up. Others may carry on, as railway-building carried on, through calling up unpaid share-capital, which may add to the embarrassment, even though it may also have a counter-cyclical effect. All of this is fairly familiar. But the less familiar possibility is that in which some seemingly good news has a bad effect. If some industry suddenly seems to be highly profitable, either because of the publication of the accounts which reveal high profits, or because of some unexpected increase in demand, then there may be a shift of money into its shares. Whether this is through speculative buying and selling of existing shares, or the issue of new shares, there may still be a net withdrawal of money from a form in which it added to the supply of credit; and the consequence may be almost the same as that of an unexpected shift in the balance of payments. This kind of change is more likely to occur slowly — as, for instance, in recent years when the growing attractions of share purchases reduced the flow of money (at nominally short-term conditions) into building societies, and so reduced their ability to make long-term loans. But we have to keep in mind that it can occur quite suddenly. When credit is strained, a 'bad' shock is very likely to precipitate a crisis, while a 'good' one may, if it is of the right kind. So far we have emphasised only the former possibility; but it is not the only one.

The way in which population and credit are tied together in our theory of building cycles has already been explained. Basically it is that as children reach the age at which they begin to earn, so they liberate a demand for housing, which is more likely to be effective if there is some shock raising real incomes, at a time when credit is plentiful. New marriages add to demand, as may also the

H 2

growth of towns through internal migration.   The boom in building, accompanied by rising activity in other fields, continues until there is an inventory downturn, or some other form of recession.   But if this is in just one or two industries or localities, or of an essentially brief nature, then building is unlikely to decline to its former low level, partly because of the long period of gestation, which helps to carry it over, and partly because the basic demand from the population side is still present, and there has been no severe all-round fall in incomes of a kind that would cut out all hope of further profit from house-building. As conditions improve, building goes on apace. But once there is a severe credit crisis, brought on partly by the strain that building imposes on the credit situation, and partly by the generally high level of activity, then the impact of the crisis on the incomes of workers is so severe that there is no prospect of letting new houses.   Furthermore, in such bad times there is likely to be emigration, which makes the excess of houses over the effective demand more marked.   If there is no credit crisis, then an inventory downturn in building may eventually occur, as too many speculative builders seek to make their profit, and build too much.   The decline in building activity that follows has a downward multiplier effect on incomes.   In either case, there is less employment than there was, a falling demand, and, amidst other things, a tendency for the birth- and marriage-rates to fall.   Economic cycles impinge, once again, on population cycles, which in turn affect the economy.

A conventional two-country model, printed in the *Economic Journal*, March 1964, suggests that in the absence of shocks inverse cycles are likely to appear even when the balance of payments is preserved, if migration is allowed, and if there is a basic population cycle.[2]   The model is a simplified one, with a number of rather artificial assumptions, and it cannot be put forward as a proof of the universal correctness of the result we have just suggested.   On the other hand, it has a certain plausibility about it. This, too, is a matter that will have to be tested with the simulation model.   Another feature of this model is the place it gives to physical restrictions, and it is because it is so difficult to introduce these into conventional models that we have not devoted greater time to developing some of this theory in mathematical terms.   One restriction that is of immense importance is transport.   Without it, no trade can take place.   To provide it calls for heavy investment programmes with long gestation periods.   When it exists, a certain amount of trade is possible, but no more, until further investment occurs.   This is a matter which most trade theory ignores, and which introduces non-linearities and discontinuities of a kind that it is extremely difficult to take into account in any conventional way. We have suggested that the length of the building cycle is related to the length of a human generation, but if we seek to show this with the aid of a model that has no place for transport, for capacity limitations, and so forth, then our demonstration is not very useful. Nor is it very useful if we ignore shocks.

It is for this reason that we have chosen to rely on simulation studies. Despite their inevitable simplification, they can still be much more realistic than conventional analytical models. By varying the numerical values of certain parameters, and the precise nature of certain behavioural assumptions, it will be possible not only to examine the result, in the model, of different kinds of behaviour, but also to see these results in detail. We can, for example, introduce rent control, and see how this affects every single variable, at every moment of time. But there is an even more important reason why we should use the modern resources now placed at our disposal. Every economy is affected by shocks. Growth theory has devoted a great deal of attention to stability, but there has not been much attention to the problem of devising policies which will be most resilient to shocks. One may, for example, run the model for several periods, and chart behaviour of the major variables. One may then run it again, with everything exactly the same except the shocks. These can have their effects not only on the variables just mentioned but also on all others. When several runs have been made, one may introduce a new policy — a certain kind of tax, a different interest-rate structure, or something similar, and run through the revised model several times, with the same shocks as before. Comparison of the two sets of results may reveal not only different growth paths, but also different degrees of fluctuation. Although it will tell us nothing about anything but itself, the model may in this way suggest possibilities about the real world which would not otherwise be so apparent. The opportunity of learning in this way is very important.

It may, however, be argued that the model we have just outlined is based on a study of an era that has gone for ever; that economic control and regulation now play greater parts than they did in the nineteenth century, that institutions are different, and more resilient to shocks. This is undoubtedly true, and yet we must not forget that in a controlled economy the basic forces of the uncontrolled economy are still at work. They are not given free rein, and at times they may be a great deal less important than other forces arising out of the controls; but they still exist. To take just one example, we are particularly conscious today of the economic effects of the post-war bulge in births, and the way in which this is now causing a demand for additional university building, just as it also added to the embarrassment of the Government by providing an exceptionally large number of school-leavers to be found jobs just before a severe winter (foreseen by none of the manipulators of our primitive regulators) caused unemployment to rise so sharply. In a few years' time these school-leavers will themselves be creating demand for houses, and giving birth to yet another bulge. How important may this be, as a factor in demand, when compared with other factors, such as Government policy towards slum clearance? Before attempting to answer this question we may very briefly survey the course of house-building in the inter-war years, so that we shall better be able to see how policy and other factors interacted. The course of industrial building is summarised in Appendix 11.

Even without the First World War, house-building would certainly have presented very different economic problems in the twenties and thirties than it did around the turn of the century. This must be so for two reasons. On the one hand there was the problem of urban renewal. The houses that had shot up late in the eighteenth and early in the nineteenth century could not last much longer, while even those built in the forties and fifties were already being condemned by the standards of the times. Just as these earlier years had seen an unprecedented migration and boom in building, so now there was an unprecedented problem of slum clearance and replacement building. On the other hand was a revolution in transport which was to affect building in two quite different ways. As the motor-car and motor-bus, especially the latter in the earlier years, made it increasingly easier for more and more people to live further from their work and railway stations, the location of new building assumed new patterns. At the same time, convenience, and sometimes ostentation, led people to spend money on cars that they might otherwise have spent on housing. In the twenties this probably mattered very little, but even by then the trend had started, and today many people own cars costing at least half as much as their houses, and sometimes even more. Whereas a man in the nineties had but one way of adding to his comfort and importance by spending a large sum of money on a durable, in the twenties he began to have two. To a lesser extent a similar point may be made about the many accessories that began to creep into homes around the same time. Domestic appliances, apart from dethroning the domestic servant and so, in many cases, reducing the size of the household, made investment in gadgets compete with investment in bricks and mortar. Comfort and labour-saving became factors in consumer demand.

This impact of mechanical inventions upon the demand for houses has done much to improve standards not only for those who can afford whatever they fancy, but also for others, for desires always sooner or later become driving forces, either, through positive effort to increase one's income or through the determination of some manufacturer to be the first to convert a potential demand into a real source of profit by producing and selling sufficiently cheaply. War or no war, the development of motor engines and electricity, both well under the way before 1914, were bound to influence both the size and location of houses. So far as an added impetus was provided, war speeded the revolution in housing.

It was, however, the complete cessation of house-building during the war that really wrought the revolution. Nothing but this could have changed the percentage of houses provided by local authorities from an average of under 6 per cent in 1909–15 to over sixty per cent in 1919–22. So immense was the change that what had been negligible before the war became completely dominant; and even if we take the whole of the inter-war period, during which 4,400,000 houses were built in Great Britain, we find that over one third of them were built by local authorities and another half million with some Government assistance. The whole economics of the housing industry and market was completely changed, as politics and policy over-rode profit.

Even before the war housing had been at a generally low level for several years, although there were signs of some incipient up-swing, as empties began to dwindle and families to change their structure. The war itself brought a new migration of labour to the munition factories, and some cities, such as Glasgow, were unable to accommodate all of the new population that this and other changes brought them. The lack of new building added to the premium on accommodation and rents rose to fantastic levels. Although this was almost entirely in the field of working-class housing, there was some fear that in fact it would soon spread to other houses, whose rents would rise in sympathy. Even more important was the feeling that yet another group of people was making profit from the war, this time out of the worker. By 1915 the shortage had become acute and feelings were strong. In the same year the Increase of Rent and Mortgage Interest (War Restrictions) Act was passed. It stipulated that there should be no increase in the rents of working-class houses, which for this purpose were defined to be houses whose annual rateable value was not more than £35 in London, £30 in

Scotland, or £26 elsewhere. As a rough guide one can say that a house whose annual rateable value was £30 would have had a weekly rent in those days of about 15s. including rates. The tenants of these houses were given further protection by a clause that forbade their eviction. But it was appreciated that many of the landlords were in fact still paying for their property, and so the Act also forbade the increase of rates of interest on mortgages and the calling in of mortgages. Thus, at a time when the social changes arising out of the war were increasing rather than decreasing the demand for new houses, the Government, by stopping new building and controlling rents, threw a massive, if necessary, obstruction into the working of the ordinary price mechanism. It was intended that it should remain there until six months after the end of the war.

But peace brought no end to the control. Returning members of the forces, and a wave of post-war marriages, added to the accommodation problem that had already become acute. Builders were in short supply, and apprentices almost non-existent. The housing shortage was estimated at over six hundred thousand houses. The current political pledge was 'homes fit for heroes'. The removal of rent control would have been a political impossibility.

Yet some increase in rents had to be allowed, if only because of the increase in building costs, which had its origin partly in specific shortages of materials and suitable labour and partly in the general inflation, to which in turn it contributed. This increase made repairs more expensive, and in 1919 landlords were allowed to increase their rents by up to 10 per cent above the pre-war level, with a similar slight rise in the permissible mortgage rate. The annual rateable values above which control would not exist were doubled.

This interference with the price mechanism, along with the war-time cessation of building, was the first positive entry into housing economics by the Government. Previously legislation had been permissive, and much of it had had little effect. Now, having done something to create one problem, by easing another, and more inclined than formerly to embark on welfare programmes, the Government stepped in further with schemes for the provision of local authority houses. Dr. Addison introduced his Housing and Town Planning Act (1919) which, amidst other things, required, in very positive terms, that all local authorities should prepare schemes for working-class housing with rents fixed at pre-war levels. Any loss beyond the product of a penny rate would be borne by the Government, and thus both local authorities and builders were virtually guaranteed against loss by an Act which encouraged the authorities to plan without regard to costs. At the same time private building was attempting to get into its stride, aided by the Housing (Additional Powers) Act of the same year, which gave State subsidies to private builders in the form of lump sums. Industrial building was also going on. The combined effect of these sudden immense increases in activity was tremendous. Shortages appeared almost at once, prices rocketed further, and many more houses were begun than could possibly be finished. The rise in prices and repair costs was so great that in the very next year the Government was compelled to allow further increases in rent. First there was an increase of 30 per cent and then, in July 1921, of 40 per cent. The mortgage rates were allowed to increase further, up to a maximum of 6½ per cent, while the limits of rent control were put at rateable values of three times their original level. Thus rent control, which had begun in 1915 to protect the working-class tenant, spread to cover 98 per cent of the country's houses. Rents were not to exceed their pre-war levels by more than 40 per cent, and three-fifths of this sum was intended to cover the increased cost of repairs. It was far from adequate.

The shortage continued. New families arose more quickly than new houses, and by March 1923, despite the building of a quarter of a million houses since the war, the housing shortage had risen from 600,000 to over 800,000. To aggravate the position, older houses were becoming less and less habitable. Neville Chamberlain, who had had long experience of dealing with slums and other housing problems in Birmingham before becoming Minister of Health, wrote that beyond the trouble caused by the suspension of building during the war 'there stretches away behind a vista of range upon range of slums already unfit for habitation, and daily rotting into more complete decay under the operation of the Restriction of Rents Act'.[3] He began the process of decontrol, by shifting the control from the house to the tenancy. With certain exceptions, control of the rent of any house would last only during the existing tenancy. His second line of attack was to limit the Government contribution to local authority losses on working-class housing schemes to a maximum of £6 per annum per house for a period of twenty years, thereby dissuading the local authorities from the utter disregard of costs which some of them had shown. The local authorities were allowed to pass this grant on to private builders, and to increase it out of rates if they wished. This applied to the smaller houses, whether they were for sale or to let, but in practice they usually fell into the former category. From September 1927 the grant to private builders fell to £4 per annum (except in Scotland, where it was not reduced until two years later). In 1929 the scheme terminated in England and Wales, but it continued in Scotland until 1933.

But with local authority housing the tale was different. The Housing (Financial Provisions) Act, 1924 (the Wheatley Act), increased the subsidy up to £9 in urban areas, and up to £12 10s. in rural areas, for as long as forty years, provided that the houses were let under specified conditions. Preference was to be given to larger families, and there was to be no sub-letting. The rents were to be at pre-war levels except in so far as it might be necessary to limit the loss to be recovered out of the local rates — not the total loss — to a maximum of £4 10s. a year. These provisions were the subject of a great deal of disagreement. Chamberlain foretold that the competition between local authorities and private builders which the scheme engendered would drive up prices. Certainly something did. The subsidies were reduced in 1927, and the scheme of grants came to an end in 1932.

By then housing had become the victim of political as well as economic forces, and the former were undoubtedly dominant. Nobody was satisfied with the situation, and in 1930 the Marley Committee was set up to enquire into the working of the various Acts, of which we have mentioned only the principal ones. It was long overdue, for, quite apart from the catastrophe of the times, the slow decontrol of houses through the expiration of tenancy, and the building of more than a million and a half new houses since the war had led to numerous inconsistencies in rents. Often those who for some reason or the other had been compelled to move, or who had had the misfortune of being born a few years later than others, were paying rents far in excess of those paid for identical houses next door. At the same time there was still overcrowding, exaggerated by poverty, while one effect of the system of decontrol by change of tenancy was to discourage labour-mobility to the detriment of growth.

The Marley Committee was able to make use of material on rents that had been collected for the Cost of Living Index by the Ministry of Labour. I have been kindly allowed access to some of this material, and I hope eventually to produce a study of it, dealing with building, house prices and controlled rents in various towns. For the present it is adequate to report that while there were differences in activity between one town and another, and sometimes (especially in the early thirties) the rents charged fell below the controlled levels because the empty houses were so numerous, on the whole rents pressed against their permitted ceiling, rising with every increase in local rates. The official enquiry of 1930 was concerned with the national picture, and it found what one would expect to find after fifteen years of rent control and subsidised local authority building. Most of the houses built since the war had been either local authority houses, which were not subject to rent restriction, or houses built for owner-occupiers. Altogether some 1,500,000 houses had been built, but only a third of these were for rent. To the five or six million pre-war houses of working-class rent still available, the municipal housing schemes had added about another 600,000, thus increasing the stock by about 10 per cent. About one-eighth of the working-class houses controlled by 1919, if not earlier, had become decontrolled through a change of tenancy. The rents of these controlled houses stood at about 50 per cent above the pre-war level (40 per cent permitted increase plus allowance for increase in rates). The decontrolled houses of the same kind had rents around 85–90 per cent higher. In absolute terms, a pre-war working-class house with an inclusive rent of about 6s. would have had a controlled rent in 1930 of 9s. and a decontrolled rent of about 11s. 3d. A higher proportion of the more expensive, non-working class, houses had become decontrolled.

For the purpose of its recommendations the Marley Committee divided houses into three classes according to their rateable value on April 1st, 1931, or, in the case of Scotland, their value according to the 1931–2 Valuation Roll. Those in Class A had values exceeding £45 in London and Scotland, and £35 elsewhere. In class B were those with lower values but exceeding £20 in London, £26 5s. in Scotland and £13 elsewhere. Houses with values still lower than these fell into class C. It estimated that a third of the 900,000 houses of class A built before the war were already decontrolled, while another 350,000 new houses had been added to this range. On the other hand in the cheaper houses decontrol had gone less far, and still seemed to be less desirable. Accordingly the Committee recommended that houses in class A should be completely decontrolled, that those in class B should continue to be decontrolled at change of tenancy, and that those in class C should cease to be decontrolled at all. The recommendations were put into effect in 1933. Four years later the first Ridley Committee reported on the effects of these new regulations. It found that 56 per cent of the houses in class C and 35 per cent of those in class B, representing altogether about 44 per cent of rented houses, were still controlled. The average net rent of a class C house in England and Wales was about 6s. 9d. per week. There seemed to be little doubt that these should remain controlled, but class B proved to be too wide, and the

Committee recommended that the lower part of it should be kept under control. Accordingly the 1938 Act removed from control all those houses with a rateable value of £35 or more in London and Scotland and £20 elsewhere. The system of decontrol through change of tenancy, introduced in 1923 and partially abolished in 1933, was completely abolished. The result was that four million houses, being a quarter of the total stock, remained controlled twenty years after the end of the war. By the end of the following year another war had re-introduced control for all houses.

This broad outline of the course of housing policy between the wars has paid no attention to slum clearance, or to a number of other important features. Rather we have attempted to show how complex were even the major changes of policy as they impinged on the provision of housing. Marian Bowley[4] has provided a detailed and critical appraisal of policy during these years in her indispensable study of the period, and there is little point in going over ground that has been so well covered. H. W. Robinson[5] has provided a pioneering study of the economic forces at work, which seems to pay insufficient attention to policy and other non-economic forces, and also to suffer from being carried out at an over-aggregated level, but nevertheless contains a number of fruitful ideas. Neither of these works, however, pays much attention to the interaction of finance and the changing age-structure of the population, which is an important feature of the theory we have developed for the uncontrolled economy of the earlier years.

That the credit side was still important is underlined in a notable study carried out on behalf of the League of Nations by the Swedish economist Helger, who surveyed the course of urban and rural house-building in eight European countries, and of urban house-building in Canada and the United States, for the inter-war years. In his introductory chapter, which contains a valuable discussion of the theory of building fluctuations, he explains:

One of the chief reasons why supply is slow in adapting itself to demand after a slump in building is that financial institutions, anxious to preserve the value of their mortgage securities, and fearing that an over-production of dwellings may lower rents ánd property values, tend to restrict advances to builders. The credit institutions may further be influenced by the fact that a considerable part of their assets is in ageing buildings that are likely to be the first to be affected by a fall in rents, and to suffer heavy depreciation. So long as the erection of new house property proves to be profitable, contractors may of course find money elsewhere, by applying, for instance, to private individuals in a position to make them the advances they need. In most cases, however, the commissions and rates of interest they have to pay in such circumstances are much higher, so that some builders find it impossible to carry out their plans.[6]

This explanation of a certain slowness of response to demand relies upon the assertion that building contractors were dependent upon borrowed capital. Helger paid little attention to the building cycle, as we have described it,[7] and was not very concerned with the determinants of its downturn, but it is clear that if the industry was as dependent upon borrowed capital as he suggests in this quotation and elsewhere, then any forces which tended to reduce the supply of credit would operate in the way we have already described. There is, however, another aspect of this which Helger points out in his chapter on the United Kingdom:

Private construction is mainly carried on by speculative builders who buy land for development of new residential areas and sell houses to prospective home-owners or investors. As in other countries, there are a great number of small contractors without sufficient capital of their own who risk bankruptcy even in good times, and who must consequently pay a relatively high rate of interest for borrowed capital. But during recent years, a fairly large number of well-established big firms have specialised, not only in blocks of flats in the principal cities, but also in one-family houses. Such firms often construct up to 2,000 or 3,000 houses a year. They have been able to borrow part of their working capital at a relatively low rate of interest and have realised economies by improved technical methods, machinery, etc.[8]

The appearance of the large speculative house-builder, and the entry of building societies into the finance of tenement houses and blocks of flats, probably tended to make the industry a little less susceptible to changes in the credit situation, simply because the firms had greater resources on which to fall back, or were held in higher esteem by their creditors. But this is not to say that the supply of credit did not remain an important factor. Helger has argued that in the countries he studied the post-war bulge in marriages boosted demand, which was further stimulated by migration into the towns as peace-time production got under way. Yet building was

very little affected by this increase in demand. This may to some extent be attributed to measures restricting rents to a level that was far below the general level of prices and, in particular, below the level of building costs. It is conceivable, however, that the shortage of capital would in any case have impeded the resumption of building activity during the years immediately following the war. Since there was general anticipation of a fall in wages, in the prices of materials and in rates of interest, as a result of a return to more normal conditions, it is not certain that builders would have considered the moment favourable for starting work on new houses.[9]

As a final piece of evidence to support our contention that our analysis of the earlier building cycles is not irrelevant to the inter-war years, we may once again fall back on the same author:

During the economic depression which began in 1929, the course of building activity varied a great deal from one country to another. In those European countries which, by abandoning the gold standard, were able to check monetary deflation at an early stage and soon afterwards adopted a cheap money policy, building underwent only a temporary setback, followed by a resumption of greater activity than before. This was particularly the case in the United Kingdom and Sweden. Developments in the countries which remained on the gold standard and which, for that reason, had to adopt a policy of deflation, were entirely different. At first, lower building costs seem to have stimulated the erection of new dwellings. . . . But continued deflation, increased unemployment and the shrinkage of incomes ultimately led to a falling-off in the demand for new dwellings; rents fell, real-estate crises developed and building came to a stop.[10]

This is almost a description of mechanism of the classical downturn in building, and the distinction drawn between the experiences of those countries which remained on the gold standard and those that left it underlines that while we cannot expect our basic theory to present an adequate explanation of building in more controlled economies, it nevertheless describes the underlying forces against which the controls had to work. There is little doubt that the post-war births bulge worked in much the same way as did previous bulges, and probably it did more to accentuate the poverty of the early thirties than is generally realised, for it was then that the children were probably most burdensome. Shortages of raw materials provided constraints and contributed to inflation, and, as we have just seen, despite its international character, the Great Slump had something in common with the kind of crisis we have examined before, in which excessive demands on credit, and speculation, played their noticeable part. It is not insignificant that one of the early indicators of trouble adduced by Galbraith[11] was property speculation in America. It would be interesting to see whether, with appropriate (comparatively easy) modifications, our model may not be made to behave in a way that presents a fair simulation of this period; and then to see what happens in the model when migration is freed, when rents are decontrolled, or when the gold standard is restored. This is one of the simulation experiments on which I hope to report in a later work.

NOTES TO CHAPTER 9

1. P. K. Chaudhuri, 'Foreign Trade and Economic Growth: The Balance of Payments as a limiting factor in the British Economy, 1815–1875', M.Sc. Thesis in the Library of Cambridge University, 1963.

2. J. Parry Lewis, 'Growth and Inverse Cycles: A Two-Country Model', *loc. cit.*

3. K. Feiling, *The Life of Neville Chamberlain*, London, 1946, p. 86.

4. Marian Bowley, *Housing and the State, 1919–1944*, London, 1945, on which much of this chapter is based.

5. H. W. Robinson, *The Economics of Building*, London, 1939.

6. B. Helger, *Urban and Rural Housing*, League of Nations Economic Intelligence Service, 1939, p xi.

7. On page x of his book he refers to the fact that 'The building cycle sometimes tends to overbridge two consecutive waves of the general cycles. This seems to be the rule in the United States . . .'; but there is no attempt to explain this.

8. *Op. cit.*, p. 18.

9. *Ibid.*, p. xii. The demographic angle in the United Kingdom is discussed on pp. 13–17.

10. *Ibid.*, p. xx.

11. J. K. Galbraith, *The Great Crash, 1929*, London, 1954, p. 32.

CHAPTER 10

1950–2000

I

MEASURED at constant factor costs, the output of the construction industry stood some 50 per cent higher in 1963 than it did in 1948, while our gross domestic product had risen by almost exactly the same proportion. In 1948 building got off to something of a false start, as is shown in Figure 10.1, and its upward surge did not really begin until 1953. In 1956 it leapt upward quite dramatically, at a time when the domestic product rose

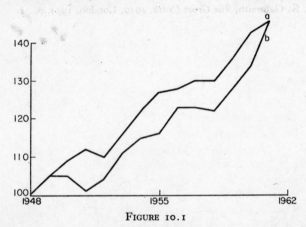

FIGURE 10.1

(a) Index of Gross Domestic Product at 1948 factor cost. *Annual Abstracts of Statistics*.
(b) Index of Output of Construction Industry at 1948 factor cost. *Ibid.*

but little, but in the next few years it failed to maintain its progress and the gap widened. During 1959 and 1960 both construction and the economy as a whole put on considerable spurts, and in 1961 construction maintained its rapid growth, and at last drew level with the rest of the economy which was progressing more slowly.

This great upward movement has now gone on for so long that any student of the building cycle must ask whether it is perhaps not time for a downturn ; but to ask this question without a number of qualifications is to forget that we now live in an economic climate far different from any that has existed before. An adequate study of post-war building would be a study of our whole economy in its international setting, for which clearly there is no room at this stage of our book. We can, however, make certain observations which may enable us to say something useful about the future, later in the chapter.

As the variety of building increases, so it becomes more difficult to measure. Appendix 11 discusses some of the problems involved in measuring the amount of industrial building between the wars, and the same kind of factors operate now. The number, value or area of works started in a year may have little relationship to the amount of work actually done; and the quantity of work finished may rise in a year when the amount of work actually done is falling. Indeed it is not unknown for the value of work done in a certain period to rise simply because new orders are not coming in. Everybody is put to work finishing projects in hand, which, being in the last stages of construction, often involve the most expensive parts of the contract such as electric wiring and finishing. It is for reasons of this kind that it is often extremely difficult to assess the importance of quarterly, or even annual, changes in various official and unofficial statistics.[1] It is, however, possible to make certain broad observations on what has happened since the war, by looking at a number of annual series, and commenting upon them in the light of current developments.

To understand the course of the economy since 1945 we have to take account of the facts that the war saw very little building, and that what did occur was almost completely directed towards the war effort; that the war also disturbed the course of marriages and births at a time when the people born in the bulge that followed the First World War would otherwise have been marrying and having children; that since the war there has been a very heavy re-armament drive, affecting the economy in many ways; and that there have been severe credit squeezes. Any list of this sort is bound to be criticised for what it omits, but if we concentrate on the factors just mentioned we shall be able to present a tolerable explanation of the course of building.

It is convenient to take the population factor first. In the late thirties United Kingdom marriages were averaging just over 400,000 a year, compared with about 350,000 in the early thirties when economic distress resulted in frequent postponement of the responsibility of a family. Perhaps, if the economic conditions had been more even in this decade the late thirties would have seen a slight decline, due to a dispersed echo of the lower birth-rate in the later years of the First World War, but whatever tendency there might have been in this direction was over-ridden by the opposing influence of economic improvement, and, no doubt, the improving housing situation. When the Second World War erupted the babies born in the bulge after the hostilities of a generation earlier were just reaching the age when they themselves would soon be contemplating marriage, and an immediate effect of the war was for many of them to marry at an earlier age than they would otherwise have done. This is made clear by the following table relating to the age of marriage of men in selected years.

ENGLAND AND WALES : MALES MARRIED, BY AGE
(ANNUAL AVERAGES OR CALENDAR YEARS)
(000's)

	1930–2	1938	1940	1941	1942	1943	1944	1945	1946	1948
Under 21	13·5	12·2	30·2	32·7	34·3	28·2	26·4	28·8	21·2	20·0
21–24	97·2	106·1	146·5	126·8	133·1	109·2	116·5	143·2	118·2	130·5
25–29	118·5	138·6	170·4	119·3	99·5	70·2	71·0	114·1	121·5	122·8
30–34	37·8	51·6	60·7	48·7	42·6	33·8	34·2	46·3	52·2	48·3
All ages	351·7	409·1	533·9	448·5	428·8	344·8	349·2	456·7	441·2	450·0

It can be seen from this table that, for example, in 1940, when the total number of marriages was at a peak just a third of them involved men aged under 25. In 1938 the proportion was 29 per cent while in 1942 it became 39 per cent. By this year, of course, another factor was that for most of the men marriage was geographically impossible.

The result of these changes was that except for 1943 and 1944, when it dipped to its level of the early thirties, the number of marriages in every single year of the forties exceeded the highest number of the thirties ; and even in the years 1940–4, the annual average of 421,000 was higher than at any time between the wars. It was not only the actual number of marriages that was high. The marriage-rate, expressed as a fraction of the total population, had also risen, and the Registrar-General commented on the 'very high' marriage-rates of the twelve-year period 1939–50 by saying that 'their maintenance over so long a period constitutes a record in the history of marriage-rates in this country during the past hundred years'.[2] The course of marriages during this period, and continued up to the latest available date, is charted in Figure 10.2.

Before commenting on some of the consequences of these movements we may look at births, which followed a somewhat different pattern, also shown in Figure 10.2. Whereas the number of marriages rose in the early years of the war, and then fell before rising again as peace came, the number of births first fell, emphasising that many of the marriages of 1940 were marriages of little more than a formal character followed almost at once by geographical separation. The boom in births set in with 1942, which saw the highest number of births since the twenties, and with the exception of a dip in 1945 it continued to reach its peak in 1947. The gradual decline to the trough of the mid-fifties, and the subsequent steady climb is shown in the same diagram.

The marriages of the war years are important not in their timing but in their total. They usually became real, and added to the number of households, only when the war ended. Within a few years it was apparent that the economic prosperity of the forties, compared with the thirties, and the presence of foreign troops and

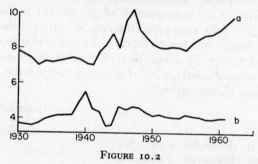

FIGURE 10.2

(a) U.K. Live Births ('00,000). *Annual Abstracts of Statistics.*
(b) U.K. Marriages ('00,000). *Ibid.*

refugees, had beaten the unfavourable effects of war. The total number of new families arising in the later forties, out of current marriages and the return of men married a few years earlier, was quite unprecedented. Between 1940 and 1947 the number of marriages registered in the United Kingdom was almost 3½ million.

The increase in the number of families was, of course, less than this, if only because of deaths ; but it was nevertheless substantially more than the gross addition to permanent and temporary houses during these years of less than half a million. Some crude estimate of a sufficient ratio of house-building to marriages may be derived from the fact that during the fifties there were·just under 3½ million weddings in England and Wales while the number of households increased between censuses by just over 1½ million. This suggests that it is roughly correct to think of the addition to households over a decade as being approximately equal to half of the number of marriages, and on this crude criterion we find that the formation of households during 1940–7 exceeded the gross addition to housing stock by about 1,300,000.

The problem facing the building industry was not simply the provision of houses to meet the demands of newly established households.   There was the replacement of houses which had been described as slums even before the war, and of many others which through bombing or inadequate repairs had fallen into that category meanwhile.   Other houses had to be repaired as speedily as possible to prevent them from the same fate, while there was also the vast problem of providing other buildings, such as factories, offices, schools and so on.   Housing and factory building were given top priority, and our scarce resources were allocated by a system of controls and licences.   In housing, the emphasis was placed on the provision of temporary accommodation in the first few years, but speedily shifted to the construction of permanent houses by local authorities.   The following table in terms of current value is illuminating, even though one has to be careful to note that housing work was also undertaken by employees of local authorities, and that there are all sorts of overlapping of activities beyond the boundaries of the statistical classifications :

	1946	Great Britain 1947 1948 (£ million)		1949
(1) By firms in the building and civil engineering industries employing one or more operatives :				
Permanent housing*	148	202	222	219
Temporary housing*	26	8	2	—
Housing repairs and adaptation, etc.†	173	168	197	‡
(2) By operatives of local authorities	65	88	97	103
(3) Prefabrication§	70	53	22	—
(4) By all agencies	885	1047	1181	1248

* Including site preparation.
† Including maintenance and conversion.
‡ In 1948 the total of this category and 'other work' came to £323 m. of which £197 m. was housing repairs, etc.   There is no split of the comparable total of £380 m. in 1949.
§ The costs of manufacture of components and fittings for prefabricated houses (both temporary and permanent) are included here 'in those cases where they are not included under other headings'.

Source : *Annual Abstract of Statistics*, No. 87, 1938–49, Table 186.

It shows, for example, that in 1947 at least 40 per cent of the total value of building and construction activity was concerned with housing, and that a similar proportion of housing activity was concerned with repairs and adaptations.   It is for this reason that a chart of the number of new houses completed, or commenced, gives only a partial picture of the progress that was being made.

It was, however, inevitable that the re-housing start should be slow, for the whole economy was out of gear, and industry was not immediately able to supply the materials and components. One may take the brick manufacturing industry as an example. In 1938 it had produced almost 8000 million bricks ; but in 1945 its output was less than one-sixth of this. In 1946 it rose to 3450 million and by 1949 output reached just over 5000 million bricks ; but stocks at the end of the year were a mere 179 million — perhaps a week's supply at the existing constrained rate of consumption. Cement output was substantially above the pre-war level, partly because the industry had been in greater comparative demand during the war ; but stocks were even lower than in the case of bricks.

The interim index of industrial production for the years immediately following the war showed building and contracting more or less keeping pace with the rest of the economy, but by 1950 a slowing down was clearly visible in the new index of building output. This was largely due to the deliberate cutting back of demands from private persons in order to make room for defence building and other activity which temporarily assumed greater immediate importance. Licences were used to impose delays on many projects. Official policy was to keep the number of houses completed at a steady level of 175,000 a year in England and Wales, and in both 1950 and 1951 the actual number completed lay between 170,000 and this target figure. It was a policy with was reaffirmed, as part of a balanced growth programme, subject to defence commitments, in February 1950.

This was just a year or so before the first post-war Census, which revealed that the number of households in England and Wales exceeded the number of houses by rather more than a million. Since marriages were proceeding at a trifle more than double the rate of new house-building, it is doubtful that anything was really being done to overcome this terrific backlog, and the continued dissatisfaction with the housing programme was one reason for the return of an alternative Government in 1951. The Conservatives were committed to a target of 300,000 houses a year, and proposed to reach it by giving greater freedom to the private builder, by stepping up the production of supplies, by the relaxation of various controls and the more widespread adoption of more economical designs and less traditional modes of construction. The new Government took office at a time of severe financial crisis, and immediately reacted by imposing a number of restrictions. Building licences were blocked,

credit was restricted, new labour controls appeared and only absolutely essential industrial expansion was permitted. The Bank rate
became, once again, an instrument of policy, rising by $\frac{1}{2}$ per cent late
in 1951, and within a few more months by a further point. Korea
was exacting its toll.

Even so, the building policy and particularly the house-building
policy, was kept well to the fore, and 1952 saw a slight increase over
1951 in both house and industrial building. As the defence programme eased and it became possible to devote more resources to
domestic expansion the first post-war boom got under way. It was
not without its difficulties. The control scheme for general steel
which had been removed in May 1950 had to be reintroduced early
in 1952, and the use of steel for multi-storey flats had to be restricted temporarily until output eased the situation in May 1953.
Later that year the licensing of timber consumption was abolished,
at some cost to our foreign currency, but local or national shortages
of bricks continued to hamper progress. In the very year that timber
became free, we had to import half a million tons of cement, despite
the restrictions on its use. In the delivery of cast iron pipes for
water and gas services there were delays of over a year, which
threatened to hold up the whole programme of house-building until
the increased production of 1953 came to the rescue. By now a
substantial boom was under way and the number of local authority
houses completed reached an all-time peak shown in Figure 10.3.
Its slight decline in the following year compares with the large
increase in the amount of private house-building, and 1954 saw the
target of 300,000 new houses in England and Wales being passed,
with well over a quarter of them provided by private builders.
Advances from building societies, which had been steady around
£265 million in the earlier fifties, rose to £375 million, of which, of
course, a substantial portion was for the purchase of existing houses.
The amount of new industrial building planned or commenced rose
rapidly, and the first signs of the commercial building boom appeared, in response to the announcement made late in 1953 that
licences could now be granted for large buildings other than those
connected with industrial purposes or nationalised industries. The
lower Bank rate and easier credit situation were helping to make
this expansion possible, and Mr. Butler's investment allowance
added encouragement. The urgent need to recover from the lost
years of the war had long been apparent, and once the frustrating
restrictions of the Korean period were lifted, and replaced by a
positively encouraging policy, a massive boom was bound to follow.
Yet it imposed considerable strains. Investment in houses and

factories was demanding resources of men and materials at the same time as consumer demands were rejoicing in their new freedom. Steel was needed not only for construction and for industrial plant but also for motor cars and refrigerators. Unemployment was down to a trough, the number of marriages was beginning to rise again, and the air was full of prosperity. Our demand for imports rose, and at the same time the terms of trade turned against us. Prices rose, and substantial wage-demands were made, at a time when there was a considerable speculative pressure on sterling. Official policy turned towards restraint. Bank rate rose sharply and a new credit squeeze was introduced. Its effect is seen clearly in Figure 10.3.

The modern credit squeeze affects industrial building in a different way from that in which it affects domestic building. Taken by itself, the rate of interest is more important if the period of borrowing is long than if it is short, for in the former case total interest payments form a larger fraction of the total amount ultimately repaid. If £1000 is borrowed for a period of five years at 3 per cent interest, with equal annual repayments of principal and interest, the interest being charged on the outstanding debt, then the annual repayment amounts to £219, while if the rate of interest is 6 per cent the annual repayment rises to £234. But if this same sum of money is borrowed for thirty years then the repayments at 3 per cent come to £57 and to £78 at 6 per cent. By no means all of our building is financed in this way, but when money is borrowed for industrial building or equipment the industrialist normally aims to repay his loan over a fairly short period, while the person who borrows for house-building has in mind a period that is often as long as twenty or more years. Local authorities borrow for even longer periods, and the fact that many individuals repay their mortgages long before the whole period has elapsed does not detract from the fact that at the time they negotiate the mortgage the levels of the current and expected interest rates loom large in their calculations. But this is only part of the story. Hire-purchase restrictions, special deposits, the reduction of investment allowances and a displayed reluctance to lend are all ingredients of the squeeze. Their combined influence on consumer spending is witnessed by many statistical series. A perfectly convincing one is that of unemployment, which is graphed in Figure 10.3, and may be compared with the course of the Bank rate, which comes in here not simply in its own right but as an indicator of the intensity of credit policy. Falling consumer spending, rising unemployment and a generally unfavourable official attitude cannot lead to optimism about the immediate future. Expectations of profits fall, and new industrial investment seems less worthwhile.

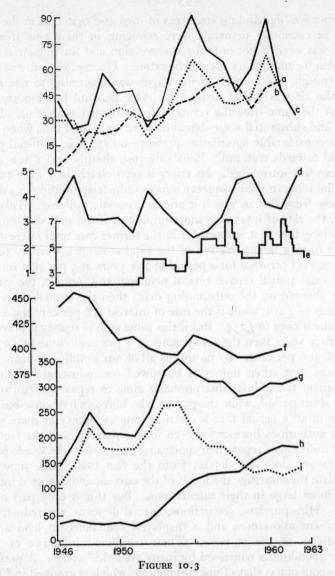

FIGURE 10.3

(a) Industrial Building Completed, G.B. (million sq. ft.). *Monthly Digests of Statistics.*
(b) Industrial Building Started, G.B. (million sq. ft.). *Ibid.*
(c) Industrial Building Approved, G.B. (million sq. ft.). *Ibid.*
(d) Registered Unemployed, G.B. ('00,000). Monthly Average. *Ibid.*
(e) Bank Rate (per cent.). *Financial Statistics.*
(f) Marriages, U.K. ('000). *Annual Abstracts of Statistics.*
(g) Permanent Houses Completed, U.K. ('000). *Ibid.*
(h) Permanent Houses Completed for Private Owners, U.K. ('000). *Ibid.*
(i) (g)–(h).

The area of development planned or commenced declines, not just because it has been made more costly, or because there is difficulty in getting finance — although these are of course factors to be taken into account — but because the barometer of confidence becomes unfavourable. How closely this pattern is followed is clear from Figure 10.3 where the new industrial building curves are almost perfectly inverse to unemployment and the Bank rate. The falling industrial investment adds directly and indirectly to the level of unemployment : but it is the expectation of unemployment as a result of expected falls in consumer spending that pulls the trigger.

All of this impinges on building in yet another way. Here there are four main points. First we must note the belief in the continuation of inflation, which results in a long-term tendency towards favouring investment in industrial securities, for these provide a better hedge, especially if they also have a certain solidity such as that engendered by the wide spread of unit trusts. With such attractions, the Post Office Savings Banks and building societies compete less and less favourably. This is most important. The man who lends £100 to a building society and so helps in the construction of a house, will receive only a small annual return that bears no relationship at all to the increasing capital value of the project he has helped to finance : but the investor of this sum in a new factory may eventually have a very large return. Of course, if he buys shares in a property company that builds houses as investments, then as the value of the houses increases so does the value of the shares. A company of this kind can offer terms quite as attractive as those of any industrial company, except for one thing. There is always the fear that renewed rent control, or other Government action, may reduce the profitability of the investment. This fear of political action is a deterrent to the flow of money into the private provision of rented houses. We shall return to this point later on. All we need note now is the long term tendency to put savings into industrial shares, rather than into building societies.

The second point is that when, perhaps due to a credit squeeze, employment falls and people have less to save, then all kinds of savings are likely to be reduced, including building society deposits.

The third point is that when times are temporarily bad, and share prices are low so that their yield is high, people who do have money to save may be more inclined to consider the high yield, and the prospect of capital gain, than the solidity of the building society. Thus to the long-term movement against investing in building societies, come at such times two short-term forces working in the same direction. It is no wonder that building society deposits show a pattern inverse to the Bank rate and (consequently) so similar to industrial starts. Whether the lag here is meaningful, and likely to persist so that changes in deposits may predict changes in industrial starts is a point that cannot now be followed. The movement is brought out clearly in Figure 10.4. Although deposits have risen in absolute terms, as a proportion of total assets they have fallen from about one-fifth in the late forties, to a mere fifteenth in the early sixties. Yet they remain very important, if only because of their liquidity. For example, in 1954 the net addition to share subscriptions was £194 million, and in 1956, when the credit squeeze had exerted its initial icy grip, the net addition was only £16 million lower than this. But instead of net deposits of £19 million, there were net withdrawals of £23 million. Deposits had fallen by £42 million, at a time when total assets had fallen by much less than half of this sum.

The fourth way in which building societies are hit by the credit squeeze arises from the fact that, at present, repayments of principal provide rather more than half of the sum advanced on new mortgages, while interest payments by borrowers account for about another third. In 1962, for example, advances totalled £613 million, repayments of principal £345 million, and payments of interest £199 million. These repayments are, of course, primarily a function of past activity, but current conditions affect them. In good times many people try to pay off their mortgages more quickly than the terms of their loan necessitates, while in bad times the repayments slip back to their contractual minimum, as is shown in Figure 10.4. Thus repayments tend to decline, or at least to rise less rapidly, at the same time as deposits are falling. If the rate of interest is raised then some of this loss may be averted : but in this case loans become more expensive. Whether the building society reacts to a credit squeeze by raising the rate of interest or not, the impact on the house-builder is much the same. Since funds are flowing into the society less rapidly, for the four reasons we have just elaborated, it will be difficult to get a loan. And if, in an attempt to attract more funds, the society raises its rate, then whatever loan there may be will be expensive.

The slackening in the rate of growth of private house-building that followed the credit squeeze of 1955 reflects the factors we have just discussed. Tighter building society policy, higher mortgage rates, and rising unemployment all acted in the same direction. At the same time the number of marriages resumed its decline, as less favourable times, including the greater difficulty of house-purchase, coincided with a period when the low birth-rate of the early thirties was most likely to have its main effect. Local authority housing declined sharply, partly because of the policy of encouraging private building at its expense, but also because the long-term loans made to local authorities for housing purposes became particularly expensive when the interest rates rose, and this made large rent increases

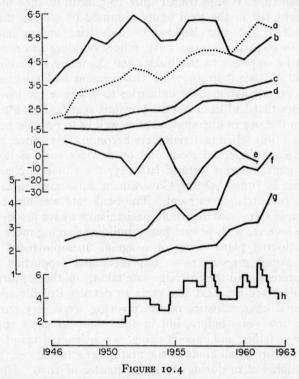

FIGURE 10.4

(a) Percentage Yield on 2½% Consols. *Annual Abstracts of Statistics.*
(b) Percentage Yield on Industrial Ordinaries. *Ibid.*
(c) Rate of Interest on Building Society Shares, 1946–7, *Ibid.*, 1958–62 ; *Financial Statistics.*
(d) Rate of Interest on Building Society Deposits. *Ibid.*
(e) Net Change in Building Society Deposits (£m.). *Ibid.*
(f) Building Society Advances on Mortgages (£'oo m.). *Ibid.*
(g) Building Society Repayments on Principal (£'oo m.). *Ibid.*
(h) Bank Rate.

so inevitable that many local authorities thought twice about their programmes. This became even more true after the withdrawal of the general housing subsidy in England and Wales at the end of 1956, and in the following year local authorities concentrated much more on the replacement of unfit houses.

Measured at constant (1958) prices, the total volume of building

I

and works continued to rise after 1955, despite the credit squeeze. The value of work on dwellings fell from its peak of £736 million in 1954, through £666 million in the following year, to a trough of £591 million in 1958. But other new buildings and works continued to grow even though there was a certain slackening in the pace of growth, as is seen from Figure 10.5, until in 1958 there was a very slight fall in the total figure obtained by adding these two components. The vast backlog of industrial orders had been sufficient to keep the industry busy, school building had necessarily expanded in response to the bulge, and commercial building had about held its own. In 1957 the Government had relented sufficiently to permit nationalised industries to continue the investment programmes that had been cut the previous year, and an attempt to slow down the rise in unemployment as well as to provide necessary services at a time when materials were becoming less scarce, resulted in higher expenditure on roads and on services such as hospitals. After the penal interest rates of late 1957 the situation changed so rapidly that in June 1958 the Government announced measures to encourage industrial investment. The bank rate was lowered in a series of rapid steps, and the whole mechanism we have just described went into reverse, with private house-building forging more steeply ahead, industrial plans rising once again, unemployment falling, personal savings growing to an unprecedented proportion of disposable incomes, and the marriage-rate taking another upturn. We need hardly trace the next few years in detail. Broadly speaking, the principal characteristics of the upswing were very similar to those of a few years before, but in 1960 ominous signs appeared. Exports were falling and imports rising, as was home demand. Total final expenditure of all kinds in the first quarter of the year was ten per cent higher than during the same quarter of 1959. Hire purchase controls were imposed at the end of April, and other credit restriction measures were announced. While some parts of the country had a certain amount of unemployment in the building industry, there were acute shortages of carpenters, bricklayers and other craftsmen almost everywhere. Cement shortages were reported, and local shortages of bricks and reinforcing rods were still giving trouble. 'But', said the *Treasury Bulletin for Industry* in July, 'the restraints on credit and the levelling out of public investment should help to bring demand and supply into better balance.'

If the intention of the measures taken in 1960 was partly to restore some balance to the economy as a whole with any speed, it is unfortunate that one of the sectors most out of balance was the building industry, for as we have already seen while the volume of work submitted for planning permission may fall quite rapidly, the amount of work actually being done may go on rising for some time, both because of the length of the period of production and because so often the value of the later stages exceeds that of the earlier stages. The quarterly figures for new orders for industrial building levelled off after the middle of 1960, but the amount of work done continued to rise. In the first quarter of 1961 the value of new private industrial building done by contractors was over a quarter above that of a year before, even after making allowance for price changes. Construction had, in fact, become the main contributor to the economy's growth, and the total real value of all new work done by contractors was 10 per cent higher than in the first quarter of 1960. Much of it was of a kind that would later be able to add to our production, but if the measures taken in 1960 were intended to ease home demand and to boost exports with any sense of urgency then the continued growth of building during this period was acting against them. Even if one were to forbid all new building activity, the total strain imposed on men, materials and money could continue to rise during several months as projects already under way entered their more expensive stages.

In May 1961 the building labour force was some 3 per cent higher than a year previously, having reached the total of rather more than 1,600,000, excluding, of course, workers employed in the manufacture of building materials. There was still a grave shortage of skilled labour, with six vacancies for every unemployed carpenter, and ten for every unemployed bricklayer. In some parts of the country, the position was a great deal worse than in others. Shortages of materials still existed, but it was significant that brick stocks were rising after allowance for the seasonal factor. In July, before the announcement of Mr. Lloyd's Pause, the *Treasury Bulletin for Industry* concluded with the warning that the building industry was expected to continue its expansion, but that 'a build-up of orders leading to too much work in hand may reduce efficiency'.

The impact of the Great Squeeze of 1961, following on the gentler pressure of the previous year, which had been quite enough to set some orders downwards, is clearly visible in the table overleaf, which shows the values of orders and work done in the various sectors.

Orders for new industrial building began to level off in the latter part of 1960, and to fall quite sharply in the last quarter of 1961 after the Great Squeeze. New orders obtained in 1962 totalled but three-quarters of the level of two years before. In private housing, the decline was much less severe. Here the orders totalled £476 million in 1960, compared with £465 million in 1962. Because of this, the value of work done in this sector continued to increase. Where there was no evidence at all of reduced orders was in the field of public authority work (in both housing and non-housing), and in the miscellaneous private development category, which consists largely of shops and offices.

New Housing		Great Britain (£ million)			
		1960	1961	1962	1963
(i) private	O	476	469	465	526
	D	389	437	445	461
(ii) public	O	257	273	343	454
	D	240	252	293	323
(iii) total	O	733	742	808	980
	D	629	689	738	784
Other New Work					
(i) private (*a*) industrial	O	341	312	260	279
	D	341	408	370	336
(*b*) miscellaneous	O	278	316	356	345
	D	251	286	338	346
(*c*) total	O	619	628	616	624
	D	592	694	708	682
(ii) public	O	489	556	646	747
	D	432	498	560	585
(iii) total	O	1108	1184	1262	1371
	D	1024	1192	1268	1267
Total New Work	O	1841	1926	2070	2351
	D	1653	1881	2006	2051

O = Value of new orders obtained by contractors.
D = Value of new work done by contractors.

The autumn of 1961 saw a slight lowering of the Bank rate, and the following March and April saw three further reductions, which brought it down to 4½ per cent. By then the pressure on the economy had eased considerably. Unemployment stood at 438,000, compared with 340,000 a year earlier. Throughout 1962 the seasonally adjusted level continued to rise, and notified unfilled vacancies to fall. At the end of the year, total instalments outstanding to hire-purchase companies and household goods shops was £40 million lower than at the end of 1961. The severe winter, which caused the unemployment figure for February 1963 to reach 878,000, and brought a great deal of building to a halt, compelled the government to stimulate the economy more quickly than it might otherwise have done, and a number of measures were taken to encourage industrial building, especially in development areas. Throughout 1963, approvals for industrial building moved on a slightly upward trend, as once again prospects became more favourable.

In all sectors building renewed its vigour. After seasonal adjustment, the volume of output of new work in the second quarter of 1964 was 48 per cent higher than the average quarterly level for 1958. Factory approvals accounted for 13·6 million square feet, compared with 8·1 million two years earlier. The number of houses in the United Kingdom whose construction began in that quarter was 117,000, while the number actually under construction at the end of the quarter was 432,000. Educational building was about level with its 1963 level, which was almost double that of 1959. Such was the pace of activity that, in July 1964, the stock of bricks amounted to only 77 million, representing the output of about three days. Stocks of cement came to less than a week's supply. To some extent these figures exaggerate the seriousness of the situation, for many builders had accumulated their own reserves of materials : but 'any builder placing an order now can expect to have to

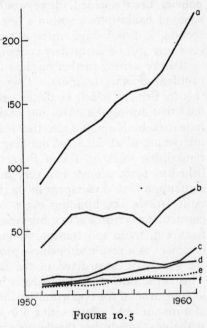

FIGURE 10.5

Value of Gross Fixed Capital Formation at 1958 prices in the following sectors (£'o million) (*National Income and Expenditure*, 1962, p. 61) :
(*a*) Total.
(*b*) Dwellings.
(*c*) Total Manufacturing.
(*d*) Wholesale and Retail Trade, and other Transport and Services.
(*e*) University and other Education.
(*f*) Gas, Electricity and Water.

wait a year before delivery of any engineering bricks, rather more than this for the standard varieties, and up to two years for yellow bricks'.[3] One consequence is that many of the smaller firms, less influential over suppliers, 'have recently had to put off work for six months or so'.[4] Bank advances to builders and contractors stood at £245 million in August 1964, representing 4·8 per cent of total advances. The average figure for 1963 was £202 million, being

4·5 per cent of the total, while in 1957 it was £64 million, representing under 3·2 per cent of all advances.

The situation in the summer of 1964 was thus almost that of the classic building cycle peak. Scarcity of skills and materials coincided with increasing demands for credit at a time when the balance of payments situation cried out for restraint. Had nineteenth-century policies been pursued, there would almost certainly have been a spate of bankruptcies within a few months. Even as we write this section, at proof stage, there is no certainty that the strain on the economy will be adequately contained.

Before writing further on the subject of policy, we must note the problem of office-building. There has been no adequate study of this in Britain, which is all the greater pity when one realises not only that during the fifties and sixties it behaved so differently from industrial building, but also that it is economically possibly the most interesting of all kinds of building. Warren and Pearson, in their remarkable work on *World Prices and the Building Industry*, published in 1937, present two very interesting charts illustrating their contention that skyscrapers in the large American cities are usually built late in the building cycle. They explain that 'Residential construction creates active business and results in profits in manufacturing, trade and transportation. The demand for office space increases as a result of business profits. Therefore, office buildings are generally constructed in the latter part of the building cycle. This is the time when individuals have the money or credit and are looking around for opportunities for investments or the construction of a monument.' After citing a long list of buildings which opened at the peak, or during the downswing, of a building cycle, they add

It frequently happens that monumental buildings are planned near the peak of a building cycle, opened at a time when they cannot be filled, refinanced in the depression, and occupied during the upturn of the next building cycle. The optimism necessary to finance such a building develops late in the building cycle, which is the wrong time to construct one. The best time for construction would be in the recovery part of the building cycle, but before costs have risen too much.

They also found that retail buildings tended to be constructed in the later stages of the cycle.

The control exercised over building until the middle fifties makes it difficult for us to decide whether the present high level of commercial building is due to the factors indicated by these authors, or to the desire to make up for the opportunities lost when demand was frustrated by licensing. When developers were given their freedom,

there began an upswing which still continues, as far as we can tell
from the available statistics. A powerful factor has been speculation,
which has relied upon prestige as a motive in demand. Reliable
data are scarce. A recent estimate is that in 1956 the amount of
office building constructed was about 10 million square feet, at a
cost of about £40 million. In 1962 the estimated area was double
this amount, and the cost stood at £100 million.

Costs of this magnitude represent only about 3 per cent of the
total value of building activity. The Labour Government's action
in November 1964, forbidding the further erection of offices in
London, stemmed not from a desire to ease the load on the industry,
but from a feeling that it was time to halt the growth of employment
in London. It came at an opportune time, for nobody can these days
walk the streets of London without being aware of the notices advertising vacant offices, in both old buildings and new. The same is
true in most of the major provincial centres. There is little doubt
that speculative building has exceeded current demands, and that
the artificial halt that has been called to office building in London
will save many speculators from embarrassment.

II

We saw above that in 1951 there were over a million more households than dwellings in England and Wales. The Census of ten
years later showed that the number of households had increased
over the decade by nearly 1,600,000, but the net addition to housing
stock was almost 2,600,000. In terms of national aggregates, the
housing shortage was all but over. In the three years that have
elapsed between the 1961 Census and the time of writing the net
addition to housing has probably exceeded the number of new
households by something approaching half a million, so that the
total number of houses is now well above the number of households.

National aggregates of this kind conceal a number of regional
and local shortages that are quite acute. In the London conurbation
for example, in 1961 there were 2,480,000 private dwellings to
accommodate 2,720,000 private households. The county borough
of Cardiff had a percentage deficiency almost as great, the number of
dwellings being 70,700 compared with 76,400 households. In other
areas there was fairly substantial surplus accommodation. An
analysis of the 509 local authorities which had at least 8000 dwellings
in 1961 shows that almost a third of the 86 districts in the London
area had fewer than nine dwellings for every ten households, and
in only two of these 86 districts was a surplus as high as 2·5 per cent.

In the rest of the country, however, almost a third of the 423 areas had surpluses higher than this, while another quarter had surpluses between 1·5 and 2·5 per cent. By now, in almost all of these areas the surplus will have grown. On the other hand a surplus of perhaps about 3 per cent is about the minimum that is necessary to allow for population movement within the area concerned, and where immigration from other areas is contemplated or natural growth of household formation is occurring, it is necessary to keep providing new houses even when voids reach a higher percentage of the total stock. The Housing White Paper [5] published in May 1963 estimated an overall deficiency, allowing for voids, of between half a million and a million houses.

Another factor that is masked by the statistics is the proportion of existing houses that are unfit for habitation, or are likely to become so before very long. According to the latest official estimates there are still 600,000 slums to be cleared, and there are many houses not officially so described which many people would put into the same category. These are concentrated largely in the northern conurbations, including Clydeside. Their existence is a legacy of the rapid unplanned housing developments of the early and mid-nineteenth century, when the seeds of our industrial greatness carried with them the more slowly growing weeds that choke. Had houses then been built more solidly, and better spaced-out, the slum problem of today would have been less acute, just as, also, the costs of some of our exports would have been increased ; for these were houses which were built to house the workers who flocked into urbanised industry, and the rent which had to be paid for them, whether subsidised by the industrialists or not, was a factor in the settlement of wage-rates, and of production costs. The position was worsened by fifty years of rent control, which often made repair unprofitable. It was a national policy which hit most badly those areas where, on the eve of the First World War, the housing standards were already showing the uneven incidence of regional contributions to the nation's growth in the previous century. Manchester's slums of today are part of the price paid for the country's growth a hundred years ago.

There are also many other old dwellings which cannot be described as slums. Of the houses now standing in Great Britain, about 2·8 million were built more than a century ago ; another 3·3 million arose before the end of the last century ; and about 1·5 million between 1900 and 1919. Taken together these houses constitute almost half of our present stock. Many of them are still structurally sound, and capable of modernisation or adaptation. Some of the larger ones can be converted into more than one home, and often it is possible to convert two adjacent smaller houses into one sizeable dwelling. Age alone is no ground for condemnation. The Government estimates that between 2 and 3 million of these houses are capable of being made into good homes, and it plans to expedite work on them. This still leaves something in the region of five million houses which, it seems, are considered as being unsuitable for conversion, adaptation, or long-continued use as they are. 'Some of them are too worn out to be worth improvement, or are too small and cramped. Many are badly laid out, crowded, airless, in drab and depressing streets. They cannot be described as technically "unfit", though some of them could soon become so. But they ought to be replaced and the opportunity taken to build a new environment as well as new houses.' The White Paper continues that 'the Government wants to see a vigorous drive launched for the redevelopment of the depressed residential areas just as soon as each town has cleared the worst of its slums and overtaken its present housing shortage'.

As the authors of the White Paper made clear, any programme of this kind is very long-term, and one has to take account also of population growth, and its additional demands. By the end of this century our population will be about 20 millions greater than now, and this calls for an increase in our housing stock of about 5 million houses. If, to take a simple example, we aimed at replacing by the end of the century all of the houses built before 1860 and half of those built between 1860 and 1900, then we would have to provide about 10 million houses during the next thirty-six years. This calls for an annual programme substantially below the current level of activity. If we wished to replace all of those built before this century then we would need to add about another 50,000 houses per annum. When we consider that this task would be tackled with a growing labour force, and a growing total population, it does not seem to be beyond our physical capabilities.

There are, however considerable dangers in this kind of approach. One arises out of the changes in housing standards. It is, for example, likely that more and more houses will be built with garages, or some other form of car protection. Broadly speaking one may expect houses to become more comfortable and laboursaving than those built today, even if they do not become bigger, and their construction will involve different problems. This is a point to which we shall return, and which is made here only to emphasise the danger of thinking of houses as a homogeneous static product.

The second danger comes from averaging out, over a long period, an activity which has a very definite tendency to a cycle in at least one of its components. Let us suppose for the moment that all houses last for ever, and are of good standard, so that there is no renewal or slum problem. The problem facing the industry then would be to provide the houses that are necessary to meet the present regional shortage, and to provide additional houses, in the right places, for new households. Except where housing shortages compel married couples to share houses with their parents, the main determinants in the number of actual households will be the number of marriages and the number of married couples who, through death or old age, cease to exist as independent households. The latter factor is less easy to compute than the former. A rough idea of fluctuations that can be expected in the marriage rate can be obtained by looking at the changes in the number of people aged 20–24, as in the table below. A very much rougher guide to the time-shape of the surrendering of houses through death and old age, but not, it must be emphasised, to the actual rate of surrender, may perhaps be obtained from the changes in the number of people aged 70–74.

EXPECTED POPULATION CHANGES — U.K.

(ooo's)

Quinquennium ending in	Additional Number Aged 20–24	Additional Number Aged 70–74
1967	645	135
1972	-38	192
1977	-44	223
1982	517	88
1987	499	-60
1992	106	53
1997	90	-15
2002	130	-69

Based on estimates of future population in the *Monthly Digest of Statistics*, April 1963, Table 11.

It is clear from this table that in the seventies we can expect a considerable fall in the demographic demand for houses, because of both a fall in marriages and a rise in the number of newly elderly people who are likely to begin to give up their homes. On the other hand, the eighties will see a reversal of both of these factors, the number of marriages rising very appreciably, and the number of newly aged rising much less quickly, and eventually falling. In the following decade marriages will continue to rise, even though less slowly, while the surrendering of houses through old age will probably show little change.

This is a very crude calculation, and of course it completely ignores economic considerations. But short of war, demographic

demand is not long thwarted, and there seems to be little doubt that
the eighties will see a substantial rise in the amount of building for
new households, and that the new high level will be carried forward
into the next decade.   The time when demographic demand is
likely to be slack is in the seventies, and it is during this decade that
the building industry will best be able to cope with the replacement
of slums, provided that other kinds of building do not absorb the
resources freed by the lowered demographic demand.   This argument also assumes that elderly people do, in fact, move into the
homes of their married children.   An alternative possibility is that
small bungalows or other special accommodation may be provided
for them, but even in this case they will be vacating other houses,
and liberating more space than they are about to occupy.   There is
clearly a strong argument for a more careful calculation of the
probably annual course of household formation, so that plans may
be made for an appropriate concentration of re-housing in the period
when demographic demand is slack.   In this way, the house-building
cycle can be ironed out.   If it is not done then we may find the
industry working below capacity for some years in the seventies and
then suddenly required to face increased demands to which it is not
geared.   In making these calculations one will have to keep in mind
that especially good times may bring forward the age of marriage,
just as less good times may shift it back a little.   We must also recol-
lect that the building boom of the 1870's means that shortly we shall
see an increase in the number of houses reaching ripe old age : but
age alone does not determine condition.   The recently expressed
views that we can shortly expect a sharp upswing in the number of
slums, because so many houses will become a hundred years old,
ignores the fact that, just as many of these dwellings have long been
slums, so many yet have years of useful life before them.

One must not, however, consider the house-building requirements of the country in isolation from its other building needs.
These are less easily predictable, but clearly they are related to
fluctuations in the level of demand.   In broad outline the demands
for some goods are clear functions of the number of people in certain
age-groups, even though changes of economic fortune may stimulate or thwart them, just as technical change and tastes may also
exert their longer-term influences.   A principal component in the
demand for furniture is the number of new households.   With
increasing standards of living the demand for motor-cars will depend
rather more than it does now on the number of people in their
later teens, who, with an income of their own and being old enough
to drive, will be important potential buyers of new and second-hand

vehicles. Most of our consumption function analysis is still inadequately geared to the age-structure of population. Adequate research into the spending patterns of people of different age-groups is still in its infancy in this country. It can be developed as an important tool for the prediction of potential demand, and an indicator of the capacity which will be needed in certain industries. As a rough guide to the likely course of net additional capacity requirements of industry one may take the shape of the net additions to housing stock, but this kind of approach is no substitute for the detailed estimates based on demand for the various industrial products.

Here, too, policy comes in. The growth of any country eventually comes up against barriers erected by physical shortages. Sometimes these act through the price mechanism to create financial difficulties, while at other times they result in controls, delays and possibly breakdowns. An example of the former is the restricted supply of coal in the early 1870's, while the shortage of pipes early last decade illustrates the latter. In times of boom, labour is needed both to provide capacity and to use it, and it is often the consequent labour shortage which drives up wages and prices, leading to excessive home-demand and adverse balances of payments. Even if the seventies see a high level of re-housing, the fact will remain that this period will not be accompanied by the same economic and demographic changes as those of the later sixties and the eighties, and detailed analyses of potential demand for industries' products may well suggest that during this time many industries will pause in their investment programmes. If this is so, then it will be the time not only to do more to increase our industrial efficiency by the provision of better transport, but also to use up some slack by deliberately anticipating demand, creating surplus capacity, especially in key industries, as a safeguard against future shortages of some products, and excessive demands on the building industry in a later period Although few private industrialists would of their own free-will follow this policy, investment allowances and other incentives could make it quite realistic. The cost to the nation of subsidising industrial investment may well be considerably less than the cost of the shortages that result from waiting for it to be done at a time when it is commercially profitable. It is a point calling for urgent consideration.

The table below shows the quinquennial increments in the male population aged 15–19 and 20–64. It shows quite clearly that whatever assumptions are made about either the compulsory or the voluntary age of leaving school there will be a considerable acceleration in the rate of growth of the labour force around 1980, and a further acceleration at the turn of the century. Around 1970, however, the rate of growth shows a tendency to slacken, and for the next few years the key to the situation will be the number of boys who opt to stay on in school. It is partly this pattern of growth in the male labour force which suggests the pattern of industrial building if it is left to itself. If re-housing and the provision of surplus industrial capacity are contemplated for the seventies, we will have to be careful not to be so enthusiastic that we assume too high a rate of growth of the labour force.

UNITED KINGDOM : CHANGES IN MALE POPULATION

(ooo's)

	Aged 15–19	Aged 20–65
1962–67	−2	528
1967–72	−68	301
1972–77	263	197
1977–82	257	540
1982–87	58	774
1987–92	43	854
1992–97	69	933
1997–2002	174	987

Educational building and other public projects have obvious relationships to age-structure which need not be described here. So has the remaining principal component of building — shops and offices.

It has been argued that house-building has now become so expensive that subsidies are essential. One of the most lucid sources of this argument is provided by Needleman,[6] in a paper published in 1961. He made careful calculations of the proportion of households able to afford the purchase or renting of houses of different sizes. Assuming that a household was able to spend up to a quarter of its income on housing, he found that in 1958–9 only 12 per cent could afford to buy a two-bedroomed house, costing £2250, with the aid of a twenty-year mortgage at 6 per cent, when allowance was made for legal and other fees and rates. The percentage able to rent such accommodation, with a rent worked out on the same basis but with the cost spread over sixty years, was 32. Further detail is shown in the table overleaf.

As it stands, the argument has a weakness. As Needleman has pointed out, over a third of our households now own, or are in the process of paying for, their own homes. This means that their current outgoings are based on the costs which existed at the time of purchase rather than those of today. A more important point is that there is a substantial market in second-hand houses. Even if the only course open to a new household were to buy or to rent a new house the relevant statistic would be the proportion of these new households (with a definition of 'new' that might be stretched to include those formed in the past three or four years), which would be able to afford the sums given in the table below. But the essential point is that this is not the only course open to them. Many people become occupiers of houses which were built several years ago.

Number of Bedrooms	Area in Square Feet	Cost	Annual Cost after allowing for Fees, Rates and Maintenance, if House is		Percentage of Families (1958–9) with Income at Least Equal to Four Times this Sum	
			Bought over a period of Twenty Years	Rented	If Bought	If Rented
2	770	£2250	£256	£192	12	32
3	1000	£2500	£284	£214	9	23
4	1240	£3000	£342	£258	6	12

Between March 1st and June 30th, 1962, the Co-operative Permanent Building Society recorded details of 6735 dwellings which were purchased for owner-occupation with the assistance of mortgage loans granted by the Society. Just over two-thirds of these mortgages were for existing dwellings. For both new and existing property, just over a fifth of the houses were priced at £3500 or over ; but whereas a negligible fraction of the new houses cost less than £1500, over a sixth of the existing houses sold for less than this. Although nine out of every ten new houses cost £2000 or over, over a quarter of all houses purchased cost less than this sum, while an eighth cost less than £1500.

Another survey, of 12,103 house purchasers who obtained mortgage loans from the Society in the first half of 1963 sheds further light on this matter. The easier lending policy is reflected in the rise in the number of purchases. This was so great that we must think in terms of absolute numbers as well as of percentages. For example, whereas the percentage of existing dwellings bought for under £2000 fell from 35 in the first half of 1962 to 28 a year later, the number of such houses rose from 1657 to 2106. Similarly while the proportion of new dwellings costing less than this sum fell from 11 to 6·5 per cent, the number rose from 235 to 304. In the former period new dwellings accounted for 32 per cent of the total number of transactions, while in the latter period the percentage rose to 38.

A fifth of the persons securing mortgages were aged under 25, and two-thirds were under 35. Over a quarter of those buying houses were earning under £16 a week, although this takes no account of other earnings in the family. Those with lower incomes tended to favour existing houses, even though this sometimes meant finding an appreciably larger proportion of the price as a deposit. Taking all properties together, the average loan amounted to £2250, requiring monthly repayments ranging from £16 8s. on a twenty-year mortgage to £12 19s. on a thirty-five year term.

Since 20 per cent of all dwellings cost less than £2000, and 17 per cent cost between £2000 and £2499, it seems likely that at least a quarter of all purchases cost less than the figure of £2250 on which Needleman based part of his argument, but it is not possible to argue from this about the fraction of all families that could afford such a house. The more telling point is the existence of an appreciable number of houses costing less than this, and the fact that if a man who already has a house which he can sell for £1500 wishes to buy a new house costing £3000, then what matters is not whether he can afford £3000 out of income, but whether he and somebody else can each manage £1500.

Part of Needleman's thesis, however, was that a large number of people at present living in rent-controlled or sub-standard houses would not be able to afford the economic rents of new accommodation. Here there is a real problem, for people already in houses whose rent is lower than they could afford to pay cannot be relied upon to move into the more expensive newer houses just to make room for the displaced tenants of the slums. To some extent a contribution to the solution of the problem can be a subsidy, and Needleman argues that this will clearly be necessary. But this is to take what seems to be an unwarrantedly pessimistic view of what can be done to reduce the costs of houses. Even though the person who is building a house for his own occupation, or buying one from somebody else for the same purpose, is not interested in one which has a short lifetime, there is no reason why the local authorities or even private persons or companies who wish to build houses for letting should take the same view. At the moment prefabrication is both expensive and unsatisfactory because it is not done on a large scale, but given the guarantee of large orders spread over several years from a consortium of local authorities, it seems reasonable to suggest that the costs of prefabricated components could be much reduced. The use of prefabrication techniques and factory-made components does not necessarily imply shorter life, but it can lead to considerable economies, especially if adequate attention is given to detail. In

South Africa, for example, it has been possible to effect very substantial economies, without impairing comfort, quality or efficiency, by asking such simple questions as what quantity of metal is needed in a window, and what strength it should be. Other economies arise from the reduction of variety, not necessarily in the completed house, but in the specification of the individual components out of which houses are made. When one considers that today we are making caravans, without any of the benefits that really large scale production could bring, and selling them at considerably less than the cost of a small new house, one cannot help but feel that a really concerted effort could produce houses with a life-time of (say) twenty years at a cost which would allow them to be let at an economic rent.

The consequences of shortening the life of a house need careful examination. There is a strong argument against overdoing it in the case of houses intended for owner-occupation, for the owner-occupier usually wishes to complete the payments during his working lifetime on a house that will last him through the years of his retirement. A man aged 40 who begins to buy a house would like to think that it is going to last him for at least forty years, even though he has only twenty-five years of working life before him. It is this factor which makes the owner-occupier a special case, for he is usually either unable or reluctant to spread repayment over the complete life of the house. In effect, he spends more than is necessary on housing in the earlier years in order to have smaller outgoings under this heading when he is on a pension. He is encouraged in this practice by the policy of building societies, who give preference to younger borrowers, and are usually reluctant to lend at a rate that requires a monthly repayment in excess of the weekly income of the head of the household, although there is a growing tendency to consider instead the income of the married couple, or some weighted sum of the two incomes.

In the case of houses built for letting the argument is quite different. We have to look at it from the viewpoint of the landlord, the tenant, and the community at large.

An adequate appreciation of the economic effect of shortening the life of a house, from the landlord's point of view, is obtained by considering a landlord who has some idle capital. He has to choose between investing it at compound interest, or building a house. If he does the latter he cannot devote the whole sum to construction, since he has to put aside some part of it to accumulate into a repair fund. Let us suppose that he does this, and invests his rent at compound interest. Over the life-time of the house he just uses up all of the repair fund, so that when the house falls down he is left only with the rent, accumulated at compound interest. If, instead, he had just saved his capital, then he would still have it, plus the interest. The question that arises is the rate at which he should fix the rent so that when the house falls down he is just as well off as he would have been if he had simply saved his money.

The answer is that if the sum of money involved is £C, and if interest is payable at r per cent, while the life of the house is n years, then the annual rent should be

$$R = \frac{rC}{100} \left[\frac{(1 + \frac{r}{100})^n}{(1 + \frac{r}{100})^n - 1} \right]$$

If n is large, then the square bracket tends to unity, especially if r is also fairly high, and so the rent R turns out to be little more than the interest payable on the total capital sum. For example, if the sum of money is £2000, which goes into building a house and setting up its repair fund, the rent payable when the rate of interest is 5 per cent and the house lasts for 100 years rather less than £101 per annum — compared with £100 interest that would have been paid on the capital sum. If, however, the life is shortened, then the rent rises away from the rate of interest. If it is shortened to twenty years it becomes £160.

There are two further points to consider. One is that the house with a shorter life may need a smaller repair fund than a house costing the same amount but intended to last longer. The other is that it should be possible to provide comparable comfort, but lower durability, at a lower cost. This means that if, for example, the sum of £1250 can provide a twenty-year house (and its repair fund) of a standard similar to that of a conventional house, designed to last a century, with an inclusive initial cost of £2000, then they can be let at identical rents. The possibility of achieving such a reduction in costs seems to be less remote when we keep in mind the repair fund. In the case of neither house should repairs be necessary in the first five years. For the 'temporary' house one has therefore to invest a sum which may be raided at intervals after five years, and has to last for another fifteen. In the 'permanent' case it has to last over six times as long. Without a more detailed knowledge of the time incidence of repairs it is difficult to say more than that it looks as if, from the landlord's point of view, temporary housing for letting need not be uneconomic.

It is, however, absurd to attempt a last word from the landlord's angle without looking at the tenant's ideas. On the one hand he is certain of a house that is not more than (say) twenty years old. But the chances are about one in five that the house is due for demolition within four years. Apart from any other consideration, moving is expensive. Because of such factors, tenants may be unwilling to move into the older temporary houses except at such low rents that it is uneconomic. User obsolescence has led to owner obsolescence,[7] and demolition and replacement may be advantageous to the owner before the physical limit of durability is reached. For this and other reasons there is something to be said for thinking in terms of houses whose expected physical life is a little longer than the lifetime on which the rent is calculated. Such a procedure would enable demolition to take place after the capital had been recovered, but before serious physical deterioration had set in, yet with a minimum waste. At the same time there would be a certain elasticity which could operate in favour of existing tenants.

The demolition of perhaps one-twentieth of the nation's stock of rented houses, and their replacement every year, would raise problems which bring us face to face with some of the more important economic considerations of housing policy. There would, in any case, have to be replacement at some rate. The question we have to consider is whether replacement at a rate of 5 per cent taken along with new additional building of temporary houses and whatever work is done on repairs would require greater resources than replacing at a rate of, say, 1 per cent, building houses of longer life, and performing repairs on these. The number of additional houses required would be the same in any case, and would probably amount to about 2 per cent of the housing stock, but not all of these would be for rent. A reasonable presentation of the picture might be as below.

	If Rented Houses last for	
	20 Years	100 Years
Replacement	5%	1%
Additions	$1\frac{1}{2}$%	$1\frac{1}{2}$%
Total	$6\frac{1}{2}$%	$2\frac{1}{2}$%
	+ repairs	+ repairs

We can expect repairs in the second column to be at least equal to the equivalent of an increase in the number of houses of $\frac{1}{2}$ per cent, and we shall suppose that in the first column they are equivalent to $\frac{1}{4}$ per cent. The implication is that in numerical terms we would require about double the annual level of building of rented houses if the life were shortened from 100 to 20 years. But the temporary houses we are considering would require lower inputs than the more substantial houses, and if the inputs can be reduced to the 5/8th ratio which we found to be economic from the landlord's angle, the increase in *total* building activity of all kinds would be quite low.

Nevertheless, there would probably be some increase. Would it be worth it ? What advantages would temporary housing have ? As we have considered it so far there has been no financial advantage to the tenant, for his rent has not been reduced. Indeed we have argued that a reduction of 37·5 per cent in the cost of building and repairs is necessary if the house is to be let at the rent of conventional accommodation. South African experience, our own school-building experience in recent years, and considerations of the untapped benefits of large-scale planning, ordering and production suggest that such reductions should be quite possible.

There is one important, and quite fundamental, objection to leaving the argument here, for, despite all that we have said, to build houses with an expected life of about twenty years would be sheer lunacy. It would mean that if any bulge in marriages gave rise to an increased amount of house-building, then in a generation's time there would be an increased amount of renewal required just at the time that the echo of the marriage bulge would also be leading to a high demand on the industry. This, however, gives us a clue about one way of evening out building fluctuations, for it suggests that houses with lifetimes of about thirty years may result in re-placement demand being high when demographic demand is low. The above calculations need reworking : but the effect is to make the necessary cost reduction rather smaller, and so to lend greater credence to the idea.

Before considering some of the other advantages of housing of this kind, we may look at the question of rent subsidies, for it is by no means certain that less durable housing or, indeed, other innovations will adequately lower costs.

At the moment the net rents of pre-war council houses are fre-quently above their economic level. The difference is used to help to subsidise the rents of post-war houses built at greater cost. The principle here is that rents should not vary just because of the date of building, or, in other words, that shelter should have a current price, common to all consumers, varying with the standard of shelter but not with the cost of providing it. Some local authorities accept this more wholeheartedly than do others. In Liverpool, for example, the average rent charged in 1962 for a three-bedroom Council house was 28s. 11d. a week in the case of a post-war house, and 25s. 6d. for a pre-war house. In Derby the average rent for a post-war house was 24s. 11d., while pre-war accommodation was let for 15s. In deciding upon these rents the local authority takes into account the size of its subsidy from the Government (totalling to £96 million in 1961) and the rate subsidies (which come to about a third of this sum, over the whole country).

While local authority housing is currently subsidised to the tune of £128 million per annum, private house-building is subsidised through Improvement Grants and through the reduction of income-tax when interest is paid on mortgages. As long as the Schedule A tax remained effective on owner-occupiers, it was possible to argue that the reduction of tax on mortgage interest was more or less negatived, but this is no longer the case. It has been argued by Miss Nevitt [8] that the rate of subsidy implicit in this arrangement is in some cases higher than that on local authority housing. Certainly it operates in favour of the higher income groups.

There is a social need for more houses. Anybody who builds a house for his own occupation is doing something to increase the ratio of houses to households. He is also using men, materials and money. If he is building a large house he is possibly using resources which could have provided less opulent accommodation for two households at present living in inadequate quarters. If he was previously living in a smaller house, which he sells, then he does not have to borrow the whole of the cost. His interest payments are low, and he gets little direct subsidy on his improvement in accommodation. The buyer of his old house is subsidised on his own interest payments, and so on down the line. In the end the subsidy distributed as a result of this single house being built may exceed the subsidy that would have been paid on the two smaller houses that could have been built in its stead.

This is but one example of many anomalies of the present system. The economic consequences of any income redistribution, especially one that is conditional, as in the case of a subsidy, are usually much more complex than any discussion in these terms is likely to reveal. How, for example, would the abolition of tax-relief on mortgage interest payments affect the demand for furniture and cars ? It is for this reason that one must put forward proposals for reform with some caution, as ideas to be examined rather than as recommendations. Keeping this in mind, one may suggest that a rational approach to the subsidy problem should begin with the premise that every household is entitled to a minimum standard of accommodation. If the economic rent of that accommodation exceeds a certain fraction of the household's income, or if the housing shortage compels a family to live in more expensive accommodation, then some form of subsidy is appropriate. But for any improvement in accommodation which arises out of desire rather than out of any scarcity of minimum standard housing the individual should pay the full cost. As a principle it seems to be worth keeping in mind. Every man has the right to food, shelter, clothing and medical care, and if his income does not allow him to receive these then it is appropriate for the community to bestow them upon him ; but if we feel that he also has a right to a television set then it is time that we said so, unequivocally, and set about supplying them to any family whose outlay on housing is so high that it prevents the acquisition of a set. Many of the people now living in condemned houses are eager to get out of them. When they move into local authority houses they will, presumably, be gaining some satisfaction, and it is not unreasonable that they should be asked to pay for it in so far as it is within their means. Whether the marginal worth of the improvement in housing exceeds the marginal loss of pleasure due to the surrender of a television set is doubtful. Usually they are not consulted about this. It may reasonably be argued that if the community compels them to move, without taking account of their preferences, then the community should pay some compensation in the form of a subsidy ; but if it is made clear that it will be reduced annually, and finally disappear, so that in time people pay for their accommodation at the proper economic rates, just as they pay for their clothing, then we shall be in a basically healthier state.

The impact of house-building on the supply of short-term credit and of loanable funds has also to be considered. A man who borrows £2000 for a long period, to build a house, and makes annual repayments of principal and interest of £200 is affecting the money market for as long as he is repaying the loan. He assumes command over £2000 worth of resources, and pays for them by curtailing his future expenditures over a period of perhaps twenty years. If, instead, 20 men can borrow £100 to buy refrigerators then although they command the same volume of resources they pay for them over a much shorter period. This means that other expenditure is reduced more severely, and that in three years' time the whole of the borrowed sum is once again available for some other purpose. Furthermore, the short-term credit required during building operations probably exceeds that required in the production and distribution of twenty refrigerators. Both short-term credit and longer term loans are at present in great demand. So are materials and skilled labour. There is, once again, something to be said for discouraging the expenditure of these items in ways that add to the comfort or status of a few, rather than to the number of people who can be provided with the minimum acceptable standards of accommodation. It cannot be overemphasised that when we grant a mortgage we compress into the present a demand for resources that is to be paid for over a very long period. The driving up of current demand inflates prices, and so effectively reduces the real worth of future repayments. This encourages further demands for mortgages, on the principle that the rate of inflation will reduce the real rate of interest. If resources are scarce, it seems to be both economic and social sense to encourage their allocation in a way that will bring maximum benefit. In present conditions it is doubtful whether the building of super-luxury houses and flats is the way to do this.

It is equally doubtful whether the provision of subsidised loans — in the form of loans at specially low interest rates — is a solution. In such a case it is quite possible that the initial stimulus to demand would be so high that shortages of one kind or another would quickly develop. In a free economy this could lead to an increase in prices so great that the financial benefits of a cheap loan would be lost. Alternatively the more important effect might be a shortage of loanable funds for some other purpose — which might ultimately hold back the development of the economy. There are many more possibilities.

We may now return to our examination of the advantages of building houses of a comparatively short life. One is that it is a move towards financing current accommodation out of current incomes. The capital cost of the house is less, and it is recovered more quickly. Command over resources is more nearly in keeping with the current ability to pay for them. The community is saddled with a smaller debt, even though its total outgoings on housing may be unchanged, and its stock of physical assets be of less value.

Two more arguments need mentioning. One is that the problem of providing for adaptability is reduced. In tackling our redevelopment and new building work we must be careful not to repeat the mistakes of a hundred years ago, and of much more recent times. We must build in a way that looks to the probable course of future development, rather than simply to present needs. This affects both the design of buildings and their location. Given the demand for buildings of a certain kind, and the supply of them, then the rent of newly let buildings is determined. There is, of course, usually a considerable degree of substitution, which means that rents of similar buildings or of buildings in different locations, will exert their effect on the demand schedule. Under any given set of circumstances, however, there is a maximum rent which a landlord can reasonably hope to obtain from his specified property.

As the building gets older it usually needs additional expenditure on maintenance. This is partly because the rate of depreciation tends to increase with age and partly because there is a tendency for building costs to rise, which makes any given amount of repair work more costly. These repairs have to be paid out of rent. If the rent has been properly fixed in the first case, then the main trouble will arise from the inflated building costs in later years, which may drive the maintenance expenditure to a very high level. This will be less true if its life is short. If the landlord can raise rents at the same rate then he still makes a profit ; but often he cannot do this. There is then no incentive to keep the property in repair. Deterioration accelerates. Demand for its occupation falls, and the possible rent probably falls as well, in real terms if not in monetary ones. Probably, too, adjacent property becomes less attractive because of this decay, and so the disease tends to spread until whole areas become blighted, as we have already described.

To prevent this we must devise means of ensuring that the property is not allowed to deteriorate in any way, either absolutely or relatively to other property. There must be no loss in accessibility (such as occurred when railway lines created huge physical barriers and reduced the ease of access). There must be no slow disintegration, or loss of tone in the surrounding area. And there must be continual bringing up to date. It is this last point which is the most important to us when we think of new building, for it means that what we build now should be modern by modern standards. Design must be forward-looking. This is not just a case of providing the latest, but rather of preparing for the probable course of future development. To build a house in which the only form of heating is the open fire, and a few electric points, is clearly to provide something which will need modernisation almost before it is up. To put in central heating is to be modern by modern British standards. But to provide a building in which floor heating of some kind can be introduced with least effort when that becomes more fashionable in this country is to take a positive step towards reducing the rate of ageing of our houses. As long as a house, or a shop, or a block of offices, can be modernised with little trouble and cost, so it will remain possible for the landlord to charge rather higher rents for improvements in order to cover his outlay. Even though the shell may be old, the inside of the building is in no way inferior to a modern building, and demand for its occupation keeps up. This means that we should also build in a way that anticipates changes in lay-out of rooms, and in their sizes ; and this means that as few internal walls as possible should be structural, while there should always be room to expand, either on to adjacent ground, or into next-door, horizontally or vertically. Sound Victorian houses have been converted into flats with little trouble, and have maintained their economic viability. Others, rather smaller, have been converted through extensions of one kind or another. It is noticeable that a great deal of slum property could be extended in this way only with very great difficulty. If a building has a short life, the problem of foreseeing the probable course of changes in demand is simplified.

The remaining, and perhaps most important, argument in favour of short-lived houses is that even if they are not actually transportable, they enable one to think in terms of greater mobility, since they need not be replaced in their old sites.

III

An adequate theory of urban land values has not yet been developed, and the work in this connection of such people as von Wieser, Hoyt, Roos and Pribram has not yet received adequate attention. For our present purpose we do not require a complete theory, but it is necessary to look at some of the forces at work.[9]

Urban land may be used for roads and railways, for recreational purposes, for car-parks or for the erection of buildings with, in some cases, their accompanying gardens, car-parks or yards. If we put roads, railways and public parks to one side, we are left essentially with land that is devoted to car-parks or covered (more or less) with buildings. From this land, the owner receives an income which depends on the location of the land, and the kind of buildings which is erected upon it. We now have to see how this income may change, and to discuss the consequences of such changes.

At any moment either the tenant or the landlord may decide that a given building is obsolete. There is a great deal of loose talk involving this term, and it is important to differentiate carefully between different types of obsolescence. This word is now used far too loosely. It always requires qualification with answers to the questions 'In what way?' and 'From whose point of view?' In an attempt to clarify this position we shall look at an imaginary town, in which all the land is held freehold, or on very long leases. The owner of a building also owns the land on which it is built. This is to simplify away what is in fact a very important complication : but it helps us to present the essential features of the story. We shall suppose that all buildings are rented, by their owners, to tenants. An owner may be his own tenant.

Let us now look at the building, and its location, from the tenant's point of view. For the privilege of occupying it, he pays rent. In it, he performs some function — which may be simply living, or may involve working, and even the employment of other people. Now usually this function could be performed somewhere else, and it is useful for us to ask why it is being carried on just where it is. We are not concerned with why a man is living, or a firm is employing resources, but with why this is being done in a particular building in a particular location, rather than somewhere else. Why is it that the tenant has chosen this particular place for his activity ? The answer must be that when he came along, he felt that out of all the alternative premises that he could have occupied, *at the time that he took up his tenancy*, no other was more suitable to his purpose, after making allowances for rent differences. Let us be more precise about this. The other property that he could have occupied fell into three groups — cheaper property, property charged at the same rent, and more expensive accommodation. We have suggested that the cheaper property was all, in some way or other, less suitable to a degree that outweighed the saving in rent ; that none of the more expensive property was so much more suitable that the additional rent would be justified ; while no property of the same rent was more suitable than the one occupied.

Over the course of time, all of this can change. The property may become more or less suitable, while the rent of the property itself, or of other properties, may change. Eventually the difference in suitability of the tenanted premises and some other available premises may, when weighed against the new differences in rent, make the tenant feel inclined to move. This can happen in several ways, of which we need here mention only a few. The suitability of the building may change because the function changes — the family grows or dwindles, the firm uses new techniques, and so on. Alternatively there may be legal changes, making the existing building not quite satisfactory as it stands. Changes in transport conditions, or in the sources of supply or the location of customers, will also exert their effect. In all of these cases the building becomes more, or less, desirable because of changes in other things. Another possibility is that the building itself may change. It may deteriorate in some way. A point we must not forget is the upgrading or downgrading of the surroundings, and its effect on the desirability of the building itself.

But our concern is with the suitability of one building compared with that of another. Consequently we have to take account of the above — and other — factors over quite a large area. In some cases we may even need to consider them over an area stretching beyond national boundaries ; but in other cases only a fairly small area will be relevant. A transport café designed to serve the crews of a municipal omnibus company does not have a great choice of where to go. But an office whose sole purpose is to correspond with bird-watchers has the whole of that part of the world that has postal services. The point to keep in mind is that the area of necessary comparison depends on the function for which the building is being currently used ; and a change of function may change this area.

We shall consider how rents may change in a moment. All we need say now is that in every case one has to consider not only the rent of the chosen building, but also the rents of all alternative accommodation, over the proper area of comparison.

Now we may think that whenever he is legally, or contractually, free to move on, the tenant makes himself aware of the market. He knows all about current rents and accommodation. Eventually he may decide that, after taking account of moving costs, and possible loss of local contacts, it will pay him to move to some other accommodation — which may have a lower, an identical, or a higher rent. In such a case, and only in such a case, we shall say that from the standpoint of the tenant the building (or, to be more precise, the occupation of the building) is obsolete. More briefly, we call this a state of *tenant obsolescence*. Whenever it is reached, it ceases to be, for the tenant moves, and the building remains empty until a new tenant moves in — and clearly he will move in only if the building is, for his purposes and pocket, the most suitable.

The landlord has a different approach. As the owner of both the building and the land — and that is where our basic simplification appears — he has to decide whether he is getting his highest return. Can he, by altering the rent of the existing building, make more money ? Can he make more by spending money on improvements ? Even more interesting is whether he can make more by knocking the building down, and replacing it with some other building, or even some other land-use altogether, such as a simple car-park. If the landlord believes that he can make more money by altering the rent of the building, we shall say that there is *rental obsolescence*. This may be divided into *upward* and *downward* categories according to whether the rent should be raised or lowered. Similarly, if, after taking account of the expenditure involved and of the income that could be obtained if that money were spent in some other way, the landlord could make more by improving the premises we shall say that there is *condition obsolescence*. We shall shortly modify this definition. If demolition and rebuilding is the most profitable, then there is *building obsolescence*. We may note that all of these are defined in subjective terms. They depend on the landlord's belief about what he can do. One may also define them in objective terms, in which the criterion is whether, in fact, it is most profitable to take a certain action. We must also note that rental, condition and building obsolescence are, in any case, defined from the landlord's point of view. From his point of view, too, we define another state. If the most profitable thing to do is to spend nothing on the building even after physical deterioration has set in, we shall say that the building is in a state of *decay*.

So far we have simply defined our terms and indicated how tenant obsolescence may arise. Before considering how to pull things together we may see very briefly how the other kinds of obsolescence — which may all be lumped under *landlord obsolescence* — can occur.

Clearly downward rental obsolescence occurs when the building is not always occupied at the current rent, but would be occupied if there were a reduction not so great that the total rental income would fall. Thus an empty building is a necessary, but not sufficient, condition for downward rental obsolescence.

Upward rental obsolescence occurs when the demand for the occupation of the building is high. It may even be profitable to raise the rent so much that sometimes the building is empty. An example is the kind of luxury flat into which newcomers to a town may move for a month or two while they look around. It is always going empty, but demand for some spring-board accommodation is so high that it never remains empty for long, despite the exorbitant rent. The fact that a building may be empty because of action designed to counter upward rental obsolescence emphasises the point just made that emptiness is not a sufficient condition for downward rental obsolescence.

Condition obsolescence may coincide with, but need not coincide with, rental obsolescence. This is convenient for our analysis, and since our definitions are tools of our analysis we might as well sharpen them until they suit us. We shall say that condition obsolescence arises when it would be more profitable to spend money on improvements and to receive a new rent as a consequence, than it would be simply to alter the rent so that there is no longer rental obsolescence. We may think of the owner of a rental-obsolescent building as first of all altering the rent, and then, on the next day, spending on improvements and charging an utterly new rent — which may in fact be the old rent, which now becomes realistic because the building has been improved.

Building obsolescence may similarly be thought of as arising only after rental and condition obsolescence have been removed, or carefully considered and rejected as being less profitable.

Clearly all of these states will depend on the demand for the use of the building and the site, and this demand will depend on what is available in other places, as well as on transport facilities and so on. There is no need to go into it in detail now. Let us instead see how these definitions help us in our theory.

A great deal of confusion has already been cleared away, for the definitions almost produce a theory as they stand. To see how it works we may consider a single building that is tenanted at the moment. When it became occupied it was the most suitable building for the tenant, and the landlord considered that the rent charged brought him greater profit than would any combination of improvement, demolition, or change in rent. This state of affairs may be upset from either direction. Either tenant obsolescence or some form of landlord obsolescence may set in. Let us consider them in turn, taking tenant obsolescence first.

This means that the tenant finds some other building more attractive, everything considered, and goes to it. Now since the initiative of the move has come from the tenant, it may follow that the building is immediately re-tenanted. If it lies empty for long, then the landlord may decide that it is profitable to take some action. One possibility is lowering the rent, which will mean that his expected future income will lie below that which he has previously hoped to have. For the landlord, downward rental obsolescence is never a happy thought. Perhaps, instead of it, the landlord will try to improve the building.

On the other hand, the departure of the tenant may provide an opportunity for the landlord to raise the rent. If this happens then it means that there was, or almost was, upward rental obsolescence. Even if the tenant had not moved for the reasons he did move, the landlord would possibly have hastened his departure by raising his rent.

Now usually whether rents change upwards or downwards — not necessarily in absolute terms, but certainly relatively to other rents — depends chiefly on the demand for the occupation of the premises. It is at this stage that we have to distinguish clearly between the building and the site. If the demand for the site is low, then it is unlikely that the landlord will profit from demolition of the building, especially if building costs are rising. Possibly it will pay him to forestall the state of condition obsolescence, but it is not unlikely that downward rental obsolescence will soon occur, as the landlord feels the impact of tenant obsolescence. There is, however, a limit to the extent of rent reduction, dictated largely by repair costs. If demand is so low that this limit is reached, then subsequently there is a state of decay, as it ceases to be profitable for the landlord either to demolish or to maintain the building.

The point to notice here is that this state of decay is reached through the initial onset of tenant obsolescence ; but it is also important to notice that this is only one of many possible sequences. Suppose, for example, that building costs rise, so that repairs become more expensive, while legal or contractual barriers prevent rents from rising in parallel. In this case the tenant sits happy until he suddenly becomes aware of decay : and it is not unlikely, if this happens, that many people are similarly placed, and that the tenant's only chance of improving his lot is to go elsewhere where rents are much higher. This may be less desirable than staying where he is. Decay not only occurs before tenant obsolescence, but may actually exist for a long time ; and when legal barriers are removed and it becomes possible for the landlord to raise the rent in order to finance improvements, the problem of tenant obsolescence rushes in — for at the new rents the tenants may feel more inclined either to seek other cheap accommodation, or to pay a lot more for superior accommodation. If controls cause decay to precede tenant obso-lescence, then the removal of controls may bring about an upward rental obsolescence, which causes such a wave of tenant obsolescence that decay returns.

Now take the case where building costs rise, and rents rise with them — or at least they are *allowed* to rise. Here the rising costs lead to upward rental obsolescence ; but if the incomes of tenants do not rise adequately, or if rents elsewhere are not rising as much, then tenant obsolescence soon sets in. This may prevent further increases in rent, and continued rising costs result in decay.

One can go on with this kind of analysis. The main conclusions are that decay can be brought on by a variety of economic causes ; that in the absence of controls it is usually preceded by tenant obsolescence ; and that this may arise out of rising costs, develop-ments elsewhere, or changes in the function of the tenant.

Before seeing what lessons can be learned from this, let us look at the reverse side of things : at development, which arises out of building obsolescence. This implies either an increased demand for the occupation of the site, or a demand for a different kind of building — a change in the desired land-use pattern. Initially the equilibrium is disturbed by upward rental obsolescence, leading perhaps to tenant obsolescence, but not to long periods of vacancy, for new tenants come in. This is especially true if there is no great change in land-use requirements. Eventually the landlord sees that he can get more by knocking down his three-storey offices and putting up a fifteen-storey block, and building obsolescence is reached. In such a case the demand for accommodation elsewhere rises, at any rate during the period of construction. The other kind of building obsolescence, involving a new land-use may occur not after upward rental obsolescence but (more probably) after either no change in rents or even after decay. The dying cinema becomes a dance-hall, or a garage. Sometimes it may be a good thing if the approach to decay is accelerated, so that new land-use arises sooner. There may be little disturbance of tenants — as when an empty cinema becomes something else — or there may be a great deal — as when slum houses are replaced by a university.

The position in some towns today is that while many buildings, especially houses, have reached the state of decay, partly through rent-controls and rising costs of repair, there is a great deal of building obsolescence, and redevelopment, coming after upward rental obsolescence. The buildings are demolished long before they have reached the state of decay. The question to ask is whether one can encourage re-development in areas of decay, rather than in areas which are thoroughly satisfying tenants as they are, and also enabling the landlord to make an income after payment of maintenance costs. A second question is whether it may not be possible in future to arrange that a building enters what we have called 'the state of decay' only when it is very near the end of its physical lifetime, so that it stands a greater chance of becoming so unprofitable that it may pay to knock it down. Another way of posing both of these questions is to ask under what conditions may building obsolescence shortly precede, or shortly follow, decay. The emphasis is on 'shortly'. To knock down a perfectly good and usable building just because such a large number of people want to occupy it that it becomes profitable to replace it with a bigger one is not a very sound use of our limited resources — especially if we can persuade some of these people either to occupy some other building (thereby postponing its entry into downward rental obsolescence) or to demand the erection of a new building on some site of decay. We want re-development to serve the purpose of destroying the more or less unwanted, rather than the over-wanted. How can this be done ?

To some extent one can do it by imposing controls, or financial penalties, on the demolition or other re-development of property under a certain age, or still in a certain condition. I think that this is worth trying because although people would soon become busy devising ways around it, there would be greater difficulties in the way of the demolition of usable property, and this would lead to redevelopment on the fringe of decaying areas, especially if perhaps there was some financial assistance given in this case.

But this is the kind of argument that is applicable to new commercial building; and it is doubtful whether all the new commercial building in the country requires a ground area equal to that covered by the slums of the north. We have to look elsewhere for adequate remedies, even though the scheme we have just suggested may be useful.

Basically it is a problem of increasing the demand for the site on which decay stands. Three broad ways of doing this exist. One is to make development anywhere else — even for housing — costly, difficult or impossible. This would be politically difficult, and is probably a last resort : but it must be kept in mind as a possibility. The alternative is to stimulate the demand in a more positive way, and this brings us to our second and third solutions. Without going out of one's way to discourage building elsewhere, one can adopt a policy of doing nothing positive to encourage it, while at the same time making the decaying areas as attractive as possible. The strategic siting of municipal buildings and parks, not all in a huddle but just far enough apart to make the intervening areas desirable, can do a lot to stimulate private demand, so that decay becomes overtaken by building obsolescence. Once a start is made, this sort of thing grows : but few private individuals have the resources needed for a sufficiently large start. The function of municipal development may well be not to clear and cultivate a corner of some weed-ridden field, but to scatter the seed of development more widely. This metaphor is chosen deliberately, for it immediately reminds us that weeds may kill ; and that if there are just a few isolated improvements here and there they may have no effect at all on the development of their surroundings. But if, instead of tending to develop a whole area, local and national authorities set about giving development a good push in several areas, by the careful siting of strategic schemes, then, in time, the areas surrounding these sites might show a greater total development than would have arisen if all the new buildings had been confined to one zone.

Whatever is decided about development of areas of decay, one has to be careful to remember that the erection of a new building may destroy amenities, and in particular it may block lines of communication, and especially of pedestrian communication, unless subways are provided, or the building put on stilts. Here we can conveniently bring in our third method, which is an essential partner of the second. Another basic variable in determining demand for a site is accessibility. The siting of new roads, and of road and rail improvements, and the routing of bus services can do a great deal to determine demand for a site, as can the provision of parking facilities. With municipal co-operation, a great deal can be done in this way to add to the demand for sites now condemned to decay. If, at the same time, schools are suitably located, and public buildings of a kind that attract ancillary development (such as law courts, or certain kinds of hospitals) wisely placed, then a few years may well show the beginning of a natural growth of new buildings. In such schemes, the importance of parks is paramount — and so is that of communities.

This excursion into town-planning may seem to be a strange exercise in a book of building cycles : but it emphasises some of the real forces at work in the determination of land values : and as such it has a prime place in any consideration of current economic problems. Today we are faced with a number of difficult decisions, full of economic significance, that stem from factors such as those we have just discussed. Sometimes those who cry loudest for slum clearance also are loudest in deploring profit from land sales. Yet if controls or physical planning can manipulate land values properly, these rising values can be a most effective instrument in urban re-development. This is just one of the many economic aspects of town and country planning to which we have paid far too little attention. That we are considering transport policy in terms of profits of undertaking, and congestion of main roads, rather than as part of an overall policy dovetailing into one of land values, population distribution and industrial efficiency is a sad condemnation of our piecemeal planning.[10]

The question of where we should build is being faced by our physical planners. It is, however, important for economic and physical planners to work together in these matters. The economics of an activity depend upon its location. Aggregative thinking, of a kind which specifies a rate of growth for exports, but does not ask from which ports they are to be sent, or where they should best be made, is as likely to lead us into errors as the kind of visionary physical planning which never looks at an aggregate. Just as economists too often ignore the map, so physical planners too often look upon their plans in isolation from the rest of activity. Whatever plans may be made for the distribution of new towns, or the implementation of new road schemes, in the end they may be vitiated by a shortage of bricks, credit, pipes or plumbers. Scarcities drive up prices, and the costs bear little relationship to those taken into account at the planning stage. If physical planning is not to run into economic difficulties, we must pay more attention to the timing of projects. We must do our best to forecast the demands that will be made for materials and skills, to forecast their supplies, and to make adjustments in programmes with the results of these forecasts in mind.

With such a rapidly changing building and construction industry, it is more important than ever that we should think in this way. Already the high level of demand has compelled the industry to search for new techniques. Some of those which have been adapted involve structural changes within the industry itself. Many of the new methods are economic only when large orders are available, and this has led to grouping of customers such as local authorities. Another consequence has been the tendency for some firms which have hitherto been engaged in building activity to turn towards the manufacture of components for their own use or for sale to other firms.

Changes such as these seem likely to have two victims. The small builder is likely to have to rely on repairs and maintenance for a larger proportion of his total work. The increasing use of new methods and materials will compel him to acquire new skills if he is to maintain his share of even this kind of work. Already some of the larger firms are operating successfully in this field. The other victim may be the merchant of building materials, who is a traditional source of credit for the industry. If we are to understand the full implications of the changing structure of the industry, we must make a much more detailed study of its financial structure than has hitherto been attempted. Indeed, without this we are still not properly able to assess the impact on the industry of such factors as a change in the Bank rate.

When one considers the importance of building as an economic activity, it is remarkable that we know so little about its economics. The improved training of managers is already showing effects on site efficiency and operational aspects : but we do not know enough about the economics of the industry as a whole to apply that large scale piece of operational research which is so necessary. Nor do we adequately appreciate the links between the industry and the rest of the economy. It is no accident that in the very week in which the Bank rate was raised to 7 per cent on a Monday, in November 1964, the Minister of Public Building and Works found it necessary to say that the industry was unable to cope with the demands being made of it. An overloaded building industry and a high Bank rate (or yield on Consols) have appeared together in our story before now.

K

Economists have long paid lip service to Walras. We all know about interdependencies. It is time now for us to plan in a way that takes account of them. Housing policy, transport policy, port policy and regional policy — all of which have been the subjects of separate reports in the last few years — must be all parts of one national policy. There can be local flexibility and freedom only if our national supplies of materials, money and men allow the scale of activity that these local plans require, when aggregated. The analysis contained in this book has possibly added to our understanding of the forces that operate. Possibly it will be of use, in this country and in others that are less developed, in helping us to build the right amount, in the right way, and in the right place at the right time. Before we can hope to do this we must know more about the industry itself. We must also think more about the economic and operational aspects of different kinds of physical plan. There is a great deal that can be done in this direction.

NOTES TO CHAPTER 10

1. Some of the more useful statistics relating to the industry are to be found in *The Builder*. These include a quarterly analysis by C. F. Carter, who has made this point.

2. *Registrar-General's Statistical Review of England and Wales, for 1946–1950. Text, Civil.*, 1954, p. 28. The table of male marital ages is based on information in this and earlier volumes.

3. *The Financial Times*, November 11th, 1964.

4. *Ibid.*

5. Cmnd. 2050.

6. L. Needleman, 'A Long Term View of Housing', *National Institute Economic Review*, November 1961. See also M. F. W. Hemming and H. Duffy, 'The Price of Accommodation', *loc. cit.*, August 1964.

7. These terms are alternatives to 'tenant' & 'landlord' obsolescence on pp. 270–1.

8. 'Tax Relief as Housing Subsidy', *The Guardian*, August 14th, 1963.

9. A slightly fuller treatment appears in G. C. F. Capper and J. Parry Lewis, 'Decay, Development and Land Values', *The Manchester School*, vol. xxxii, 1964, pp. 25–41. This forms part of an empirical and theoretical study sponsored by the Civic Trust for the North-West and the University of Manchester. The results of this research project will appear in a volume entitled *Urban Decay*, edited by the Director of the project, Franklin Medhurst. See Appendix 14.

10. Some further remarks on this subject appear in my paper, 'Economic and Physical Planning', due to appear in the 1964–5 volume of *The Transactions of the Barlett Society*. My views on it have been considerably influenced by Heinz Rau and Professor R. H. Kantorowich. Rau's views are summarised in his article 'National Prospect', *The Guardian*, April 23rd, 1963.

Appendix 1

AN ANALYSIS OF CYCLES IN ARTIFICIAL TIME-SERIES

BY DAVID BUGG

In order to observe the effects of superimposing random or exogenous shocks upon time-series with known characteristics, use was made of the facilities of the Manchester Computing Laboratory. The procedure adopted was to feed into the Mercury computer sets of artificial data representing 100 successive observations from series displaying simple systematic behaviour such as an exact linear trend, regular sine-waves about a zero trend, or other regular fluctuations. For each given set of data, 20 sets of 'shocks' were added, producing 20 series composed of different 'shock' elements superimposed upon the same 'systematic' data. In practice, each 'shock' was produced by means of the random-number generating facility in Mercury Autocode, a facility which can be used in exactly the same way as a page in tables of random normal numbers.

Programming the Mercury for this task was not difficult. However, even with a high-speed computer there remains the problem of economising on the quantity of output produced, both for the mechanical version and for the more mundane human limitations on handling whatever is produced. Consequently, only a limited objective was set. For *each* set of data, the computer generated *twenty* time-series of 100 observations. Consequently, much of this information which might possibly have been amenable to further very interesting examination and experiment was left irretrievably in the store of the computer. Even so, the analysis which was carried out resulted in a large amount of printed output, and consumed a good deal of machine time.

The point of interest was an examination of time-series for regular behaviour resulting in peaks and troughs (variously defined) which follow a consistent pattern of regular alternation. Let us consider a given set of artificial data, composed, say, of 100 successive observations from a sine curve with a 12-year periodicity. These are fed into the Mercury computer. One hundred 'shocks' are then added,[1] resulting in a new series of 100 observations which are now examined for peaks and troughs. First, a peak is defined as an observation X_t whose value is greater than

---

[1] The 'shock' for time period t was in general defined as $u_t = \rho u_{t-1} + \epsilon_t$ where parameter ρ varied from experiment to experiment, and ϵ_t was a random normal variate with zero mean, and variance equal to σ^2, this variance also changing from experiment to experiment.

those of the two previous and two succeeding observations. A trough is an observation smaller than the two previous and two succeeding observations. The Mercury searches for peaks and troughs so defined, and points out the number of such peaks and troughs in the series of 100 observations. In addition, since our interest is in *regular* behaviour, the dates of such peaks (i.e. the values of t for which observation $X_t > X_{t-2}, X_{t-1}, X_{t+1}, X_{t+2}$; $t = 0, 1, 2 \ldots 99$) and troughs (i.e. the values of t for which $X_t < X_{t-2}, X_{t-1}, X_{t+1}, X_{t+2}$; $t = 0, 1, 2 \ldots 99$) are printed if, and only if, peak alternates with trough over the *whole* of the series. Thus, if two successive peaks have no trough in between (using our definitions), then the required regularity is broken.   Only the *number* of peaks and troughs is then printed.

Next a peak X_t is defined such that $X_{t-3}, X_{t-2}, X_{t-1} < X_t > X_{t+1}, X_{t+2}, X_{t+3}$, and a trough such that $X_{t-3}, X_{t-2}, X_{t-1} > X_t < X_{t+1}, X_{t+2}, X_{t+3}$, i.e. the new definition is more restrictive, since it relates to *three* observations before and after X_t. Results of the inspection process are printed as before, and the analysis is repeated for peaks (troughs) defined as observations larger (smaller) than four, five, six, . . . twenty observations before and after X_t.

Thus, the results of our experiments will come from sets of artificial time-series, some exhibiting alternating peaks and troughs (variously defined) over the *whole* range of 100 observations, and some not. Our limited aim is merely to see whether it is likely that regular alternation will be produced by the random or exogenous shocks, in spite of a 'systematic' part of the series which does not itself alternate peaks and troughs over the whole range; or whether such regularity only occurs as a result of a dominant systematic part which itself shows the required alternation of peaks and troughs over the whole range.

THE RESULTS

Experiment I

Firstly, let us examine the case where the series to be examined consisted entirely of 'shock' elements — i.e. where the 'systematic' part consisted of zeros, and the 'shock' elements were generated according to the structure $u_t = \rho u_{t-1} + \epsilon_t$ ($t = 0, 1, 2, \ldots 99$). ϵ_t was a random normal variate with zero expectation. Four separate sets were examined, with $\rho = 0, \rho = 0\cdot25, \rho = 0\cdot75$, and $\rho = 1\cdot0$ respectively.   In each case, the variance σ_ϵ of ϵ_t was unity.

For the completely random series ($\rho = 0, \sigma = 1$), *six* out of the twenty generated series of observations displaced regularly alternating peaks and troughs over the whole range of 100 observations for some value of N less than 10 (where $N = $ No. of observations on either side of a given observation which are smaller than (greater than) that given observation, when that given observation is defined as a peak (trough) e.g., if $X_t > X_{t-3}, X_{t-2}, X_{t-1}, X_{t+1}, X_{t+2}, X_{t+3}$, but $X_t \not> $ either X_{t-4} or X_{t+4}, then $N = $

3.)   In detail, the values of t for each of these six series, with the appropriate values of N, were as in Table 1.

TABLE 1

Series 1
$N = 5$

Peaks	$t =$	5	22	29	36	44	57	69	81	92
Troughs	$t =$	16	24	30	39	54	68	75	82	

Series 2
$N = 7$

Peaks	$t =$	9	26	42	53	62	77	88
Troughs	$t =$	20	35	43	58	73	81	91

Series 3
$N = 7$

Peaks	$t =$	9	26	45	57	66	87
Troughs	$t =$	18	37	48	65	86	

Series 4*
$N = 7$

Peaks	$t =$	19	33	53	71	87
Troughs	$t =$	7	26	41	62	82

$N = 8 : N = 9$

Peaks	$t =$	33	53	71	87
Troughs	$t =$	26	41	62	82

Series 5
$N = 8$

Peaks	$t =$	9	21	34	47	69	86
Troughs	$t =$	13	26	42	63	81	90

$N = 9$

Peaks	$t =$	9	21	34	47	69	86
Troughs	$t =$	13	26	42	63	81	

Series 6
$N = 9$

Peaks	$t =$	26	43	61	74	
Troughs	$t =$	18	32	60	72	85

* *Note:*—Series 4 illustrates the fact that observations defined as peaks or troughs for $N = 9$, say, are automatically defined as peaks or troughs for all $N < 9$.

As many as 16 of the 20 series displayed 'regularity'[1] for some value of N between 10 and 15, though this is not surprising when one considers

[1] 'Regularity' will be used to denote regularity of alternating peaks and troughs over the whole range of $t = 0, 1 \ldots 99$ — i.e. unbroken alternations through the whole series.

that often only 2 peaks and 2 troughs were found for a value of N as high as, say, 14.

Several general comments arise from the detailed data of Table 1. To begin with, the table illustrates the general point that 'regularity' need not imply a pattern of cyclical fluctuations with constant periodicity (witness the irregular distances between successive peaks). In other words the fact that 3 out of 20 series of supposedly 'random' numbers produced 'regularity' of peaks and troughs for $N = 7$ does not imply oscillations of a kind which would throw doubt on the 'randomness' of those series.

Secondly, Table 1 does offer some kind of warning. While one cannot be foolish enough to claim that our relative frequency of 6/20 can be regarded as a *probability*, it suggests that there is some danger in merely examining time-series for the existence of alternating peaks and troughs. Our experiments provide some evidence that even random series may exhibit behaviour which a mere listing of peaks and troughs could confuse with cyclical or oscillatory behaviour. Behaviour in between peaks and troughs, regularity of oscillations apart from the actual peaks and troughs themselves, amplitudes of fluctuations, etc., are all crucial in describing a particular series fully. Table 1 illustrates quite clearly the limitations on the results of our experiments. We have confined our attention to the *location* of peaks and troughs within series, and have not examined the patterns of behaviour in series as a whole. That is, our interest in 'regularity', as we have defined it, should not be confused with an interest in 'cyclical behaviour' as it is more generally understood.

The set of 20 series generated by the same scheme of a zero systematic part, and a shock structure of $u_t = \rho u_{t-1} + \epsilon_t$, this time with $\rho = 0.25$, included 9 series displaying 'regularity' for some value or values of N less than 10 . . . see Table 2.

TABLE 2

Series No.	1	2	3	4	5	6	7	8	9
Values of N for which peaks and troughs alternate over whole range of $t = 0, 1 \ldots 99$	4 7 8 9	8 9	8 9	8 9	5	5 6 7	7	7	4

Thus, 7 out of 20 series produced alternating peaks and troughs with $N = 7$, 8 or 9 — i.e. peaks and troughs defined in relation to the 7, 8 or 9 elements in the series immediately before and after the 'peak' or 'trough' element. Again, of course, it should be noted that the behaviour of series *between* peaks and troughs may include all kinds of irregularities without affecting the results of Table 2.

Fifteen of the 20 series displayed 'regularity' for some value of N

between 10 and 15, although again, the 'regular alternation' of peaks and troughs defined for, say, $N = 12$ usually meant alternation of only 1 or 2 or 3 peaks with 1 or 2 or 3 troughs.

Tables 3 and 4 present the corresponding results for $\rho = 0.75$, and $\rho = 1.0$ respectively in the case of series consisting entirely of 'shock' components.

TABLE 3

Series No.	1	2	3	4	5	6	7	8	9	10	11	12	13	14	15
Values of N for which series displays 'regularity'															3
	4												4	4	
	5	5										5			
	6		6	6	6		6				6				
	7	7	7				7	7		7					
	8	8	8	8	8	8			8						
	9	9	9	9	9	9		9							

Thus 15 out of 20 series for $\rho = 0.75$, and 17 out of 20 series for $\rho = 1.0$ displayed 'regularity' for some values of N less than 10.

TABLE 4

Series No.	1	2	3	4	5	6	7	8	9	10	11	12	13	14	15	16	17
Values of N for which series displays 'regularity'	4	4	4		4												4
	5			5	5											5	
			6	6	6	6							6	6			
	7	7	7	7		7						7	7				
	8	8		8			8	8	8	8	8	8					
			9	9	9	9	9						9				

Taken together, therefore, for the case of time-series with a zero 'systematic part' we had 80 series of the form $u_t = \rho u_{t-1} + \epsilon_t$, 20 of which became truly random (with $\rho = 0$) and 60 of which were autocorrelated. Forty-seven of these 80 series displayed 'regularity' for some $N < 10$. (34 displaying 'regularity' for $N = 7, 8$ or 9): i.e. 47 of these series contained peaks and troughs which alternated regularly over a total series of 100 observations. The crucial feature of the evidence which makes this result rather less surprising, however, is the (cardinal) *number* of particular peaks and troughs which are found to alternate in each series.

Consider a series of 100 numbers X_t $(t = 0, 1 \ldots 99)$. Define a peak such that $X_t > X_{t+s}$ $(s = 1, 2 \ldots 7)$, and a trough such that $X_t < X_{t\pm s}$ $(s = 1, 2 \ldots 7)$, i.e. consider the case where $N = 7$. Then the maximum possible number of *alternating* peaks and troughs is 11 peaks, 11 troughs, which will be the case if peaks occur for values of t of, say,

$$7, 15, 23, 31, 39, 47, 55, 63, 71, 79, 87,$$

with troughs occurring for values of t of, say,

$$9, 17, 25, 33, 41, 49, 57, 65, 73, 81, 89.$$

Similarly, the maximum number of alternating peaks and troughs for $N = 8$, is 10, and the maximum number for $N = 9$, is 9. These maximum numbers will only be displayed if the series as a whole displays behaviour yielding peaks and troughs which are more or less evenly spaced, $N + 1$ items apart throughout the series. The smaller the number of peaks and troughs in a series (i.e. peaks and troughs for a particular value of N) the less restrictive are the conditions for alternation. For example if, for $N = 7$, there are 5 peaks and 5 troughs, we can have alternation for such differently spaced peaks and troughs as the following:

CASE A

Peaks	$t = 7$	15	30	75	83
Troughs	$t = 9$	28	40	79	91

CASE B

Peaks	$t = 7$	30	40	65	80
Troughs	$t = 9$	39	50	75	85

Thus, a series with *exact* cyclical behaviour of period $N + 1$ seems likely to produce a larger number of alternating peaks and troughs for given N than a series without such cyclical behaviour. However, whereas a large number of alternating peaks and troughs (up to the maximum) seems likely to indicate some sort of approximately cyclical oscillation, a small number of alternating peaks and troughs may reflect either the presence or complete absence of genuine cycles — it is impossible to tell. From our 34 series displaying 'regularity' for $N = 7$, 8 or 9, the numbers of peaks and troughs in each case are given in Table 5.

This table shows that the maximum number of peaks and troughs generated in such a way as to show regular alternation was 7 for $N = 7$, 6 for $N = 8$, and 6 peaks with 5 troughs for $N = 9$. In the majority of cases the number of peaks and troughs was even lower.

TABLE 5

	N = 7 — No. of Peaks						N = 8 — No. of Peaks					
Number of Troughs	2	3	4	5	6	7	2	3	4	5	6	7
2							2					
3		3	1				1	6	1			
4			4					1	4	1		
5			1	1	2				2	1	2	
6				1	2	3					2	
7						2						

$$N = 9$$

No. of Peaks

		2	3	4	5	6	7
	2	1	2				
	3	3	2	1			
Number	4		2	4			
of	5			3		2	
Troughs	6						
	7						

Experiment II

In contrast to the case of a zero 'systematic part', experiments were carried out with basic 'systematic' data consisting of a series of the following 100 values:

$$0, 3, 6, 9, 12, 15, 10, 5, 0, 3, 6, \ldots \text{etc.}$$

Here was a regular 'oscillation' with alternating peaks and troughs for values of N from 1 up to 7. For $N = 7$, the 10 peaks and 11 troughs were the values of X_t for t as follows:

Peaks	$t =$ 13	21	29	37	45	53	61	69	77	85	
Troughs	$t =$ 8	16	24	32	40	48	56	64	72	80	88

Once again a series of 'shock' elements generated according to the system

$$u_t = \rho u_{t-1} + \epsilon_t$$

was added to the original series, and the resulting elements analysed for peaks and troughs. Let us consider the results for various values of ρ and σ (the standard deviation of the ϵ_t).

1. $\sigma = 1; \rho = 0$. Here, the standard deviation of the systematic part of the series (4·8) dominated that of the random shocks. In 4 of the 20 series peaks and troughs were affected by the addition of random shocks to the extent that for $N = 7$ the observation of X_t for $t = 13$ no longer satisfied the definition of a peak. Thus the overall alternation was disturbed, and 'regularity' was destroyed by this relatively minor effect on the series as a whole. In addition, 4 of the series now showed peaks and troughs with regular alternation for N at some value or values between 8 and 10. Otherwise, the random shocks were too weak to disturb the system.

K 2

2. $\sigma = 3$; $\rho = 0$.   By increasing the standard deviation of the random element in the series to a fraction of $\frac{3}{8}$ of that of the systematic element, rather more changes were observed.   While all 20 series retained alternating peaks and troughs for values of $N = 3$, in not one series did the ordinal numbers of these peaks and troughs remain identical with those of the original 'systematic' series.   Further, only one series gave 'regularity' of alternating peaks and troughs for $N = 7$, and the cardinal number of such peaks and troughs was reduced from the original 10 and 11 to 9 and 8 respectively, as follows:

Peaks	$t = 13$	21	29	44	53	61	69	77	92
Troughs	$t = 16$	24	40	48	56	74	73	88	

This, together with the slight change in ordinal numbers of peaks and troughs, probably reflects a *slight* tendency for the cyclical nature of the original series to be affected and disturbed by the addition of random shocks.

The median cardinal numbers of peaks and troughs for $N = 7$ for all 20 series were 8 and 8 respectively.

3. $\sigma = 10$; $\rho = 0$.   When the standard deviation of the random shocks was increased so as to outweigh that of the original series, the resulting series lost almost all trace of its original 'regularity'.   In only 7 series did regular alternation of peaks and troughs occur for any value of $N \leq 7$, and in each case the ordinal and cardinal numbers of such peaks and troughs were changed.   In those two series displaying 'regularity' for $N = 7$, the values of X_t which constituted peaks and troughs occurred as follows:

Series 1 — 6 peaks, 7 troughs

Peaks	$t = 21$	29	44	60	68	84	
Troughs	$t = 7$	22	41	50	66	80	88

Series 2 — 5 peaks, 5 troughs

Peaks	$t = 28$	42	52	84	92
Troughs	$t = 17$	31	47	65	86

i.e. 'regularity' was maintained, but peaks and troughs no longer were consistently spaced.

As in the two previous cases, several series now yielded small numbers of alternating peaks and troughs for values of $N > 7$.

4. $\sigma = 1$; $\rho = 0.75$.   By introducing a non-zero value of ρ (i.e. an autocorrelated shock-series) we also introduced a problem of measuring the variance of that shock series.   The 'true' value of that variance would be $\dfrac{\sigma^2}{1 - \rho^2}$, but in our sample of 100 items we cannot expect this 'true' value to hold.   No precise statement can therefore be made about the relative weight of the shock elements in the final series examined in each case.   The results were very similar to the non-autocorrelated case with

$\sigma = 1$, with one exception. 'Regularity' was disturbed for $N = 7$ in 14 of the 20 series. The cardinal numbers of peaks and troughs in each of these cases was:

No. of Peaks: 10 10 10 10 10 10 10 10 10 10 10   9   9   8
No. of Troughs: 10 10 10 10 10   9   9   9   9   9   9 11 11   9

5. $\sigma = 3$ $\rho = 0.25$. Remarks similar to those made in the non-autocorrelated case with $\sigma = 3$ can be made here. Now, however, there was no series displaying 'regularity' for $N = 7$, and the median numbers of such peaks and troughs moved to 8 and 7 respectively.

6. $\sigma = 3; \rho = 0.75$. Increasing the degree of autocorrelation in the 'shock' series made *some* differences, though the broad picture was similar to the case discussed previously. One of the 20 series displayed 'regularity' for $N = 7$, appropriate values of t being as follows:

Peaks	$t = 12$	21	37	53	69	85
Troughs	$t = 16$	32	48	63	81	

The median numbers of peaks and troughs for $N = 7$ were now 6 and 6 respectively.

7. $\sigma = 3; \rho = 1.0$. Finally, in the perfectly autocorrelated case, 2 out of the 20 series showed no 'regularity' for *any* $N < 7$ (though both showed 'regularity' for $N = 8$). No series had alternating peaks and troughs for $N = 7$, and the median numbers of peaks and troughs for $N = 7$ fell to 5 and 5.

Experiment III

The 'systematic' series for this experiment comprised data corresponding to sine-curve oscillations, with regularly alternating peaks and troughs for all $N \leq 11$. The series consisted of the following 100 values:

0, 5, 8·66, 10, 8·66, 5, 0, −5, −8·66, −10, −8·66, −5, 0, 5, 8·66 . . . etc.

For $N = 2$, these data included 8 peaks alternating with 8 troughs, while for $N = 11$, values of t for which observations X_t comprised alternating peaks and troughs were:

Peaks	$t = 15$	27	39	51	63	75	87	(7 peaks)
Troughs	$t = 21$	33	45	57	69	81		(6 troughs)

For the case of completely random shocks ($\rho = 0$), the addition of a shock series with standard deviation $\sigma = 3$ caused *some* change in the pattern of peaks and troughs in all 20 cases. In all 20 series, the values of t for which observations X_t comprised alternating peaks and troughs changed for *some* t. And in no series were 'peaks' and 'troughs' now defined so as to satisfy the 'regularity' of alternation for *all N* up to $N = 11$. The median numbers of peaks and troughs for $N = 11$ for all 20 series were 4 and 3 respectively, compared with the original 7 and 6, and in only 4 cases did these alternate. (In each case with some values of t changed — e.g.

$$
\begin{array}{lccccc}
Peaks & t = 14 & 28 & 52 & 75 \\
Troughs & t = 20 & 33 & 56 & 81)
\end{array}
$$

For the autocorrelated cases ($\sigma = 3$, $\rho = 0 \cdot 25$; $\sigma = 3$, $\rho = 1 \cdot 0$) very similar results were observed, except for marginally more frequent changes in the values of t for which X_t comprised a peak or a trough, and except for a reduction in the cardinal number of peaks and troughs for most N. For example, the median numbers of peaks and troughs for $N = 11$ were, in the case of $\rho = 1 \cdot 0$, 3 and 2 respectively.

Thus, summarising the results of experiments II and III, the following points emerge. Consider a series comprising systematic oscillations, with regular alternating peaks and troughs which satisfy our definition of 'peak' and 'trough' for, say, $N = 7$ (and therefore all $N < 7$). Superimposition of a shock series of a random or autocorrelated nature will clearly affect the patterns of the series according to the magnitudes of the shock elements relative to the systematic elements in the series. While our original peaks and troughs will probably still satisfy our definitions of 'peak' and 'trough' for small N; it is unlikely that even relatively small shock elements will cause them to continue to satisfy the definitions for $N = 7$. That is, even small shock elements are likely to cause some reorganisation of 'peaks' and 'troughs', although the generally cyclical nature of the series may remain. (The series may, of course, still comprise 8-period cycles *almost* exactly, without yielding regularly alternating peaks and troughs for $N = 7$.) For larger and stronger shock series, the reorganisation and redefinition of 'peaks' and 'troughs' in the system seems much greater, and the basic underlying cyclical pattern is certainly much more difficult to pick out merely by examining and counting 'peaks' and 'troughs'.

Further Experiments

Similar experiments were carried out for other 'systematic' series, notably our two 'oscillating' series above with trend components incorporated in them, and data solely comprising a linear trend ($X_t = 0, 1 \ldots 99$). Little would be gained by presenting the results in detail, but one or two points can be made.

Firstly, as in the case of a zero systematic part, superimposition of a random or autocorrelated series onto a series displaying no oscillation and no peaks or troughs did generate (small numbers of) alternating 'peaks' and 'troughs' for *some* values of $N < 10$ in a fairly high proportion of cases. Thus, the dangers of interpreting a count of alternating peaks and troughs as evidence of 'cycles' *without* also examining the pattern of a series as a whole was illustrated.

Secondly, where genuine cycles *did* exist, small shocks did not greatly disturb the pattern of oscillation, as far as one could tell, though they did affect the *location* of 'peaks' and 'troughs' to some degree, even for small N. They did, however, cause observations which had previously satisfied definitions of 'peaks' and 'troughs' for some larger N to fail to satisfy such definitions.

Thirdly, the larger the shock elements' variation relative to that of the 'systematic' series, the more was the whole pattern of peaks and troughs changed.

Appendix 2

THE POSSIBLE REVERSAL OF LAGS ON AGGREGATING

WE stated in Chapter 2 that the aggregation of regional series into national series might lead to a sequence of peaks or troughs that is true for none of the individual regions. This phenomenon has been discussed by me more fully in a paper called 'Aggregation, Peaks and Troughs' in the *Review of Economic Studies* (volume xxix). Here it is sufficient to demonstrate with the aid of the table below. If the X series indicates rent and the Y series the level of building, then in both region A and region B the level of building falls after rents begin their decline: but on looking at the national data we find a reversal of this order. Clearly to rely on the sequence of peaks at a national level in order to explain a regional phenomenon may sometimes be to invite trouble.

Region A	X	35	40	45	50	49	48	X-peak precedes
	Y	30	35	40	45	50	49	Y-peak
Region B	X	45	50	49	48	47	46	X-peak precedes
	Y	48	49	50	40	30	20	Y-peak
Total	X	80	90	94	98	96	94	X-peak follows
	Y	78	84	90	85	80	69	Y-peak

Appendix 3

AN INVESTMENT MODEL WITH SHOCKS

THE purpose of this appendix is to provide an admittedly artificial model in which certain physical restraints are imposed on a multiplier-accelerator mechanism before we introduce shocks in a way that is rather unusual.

Despite the artificiality of the whole model, it points to some interesting possibilities. The precise specification has benefited from many discussions with Mr. David Bugg who undertook the whole of the programming and computing.

The model is developed in three stages, which may conveniently be denoted by *A, B* and *C*.

Model A

We shall think of all output as consisting of consumption goods and fixed investment. Denoting the total output of all goods in period t by Y_t, we shall assume that the level of consumption in that period is C_t, given by

$$C_t = cY_t \tag{1}$$

The actual output of consumption goods in period t will usually differ from the amount consumed in the same period. We shall denote it by O_t. If the volume of investment is B_t then

$$Y_t = O_t + B_t \tag{2}$$

Stocks are introduced by considering the difference between O and C. We suppose that producers plan to have stocks at the beginning of a period proportional to the level of sales they expect to have during that period. Furthermore, they expect sales in any period to be the same as actual sales in the previous period. Now at the end of period t, they know that in period $(t - 1)$ their sales were C_{t-1}. They therefore expect sales to be at this level in the coming period, and so they have to produce this much. But that is not all. They have some stocks of level K_{t-1}, so they only need produce $C_{t-1} - K_{t-1}$ if they want to manage, but only just. Instead of this they want to end period t with a level of stocks proportional to their expected sales in period $(t + 1)$, and this they put at kC_{t-1}. This means that, in order for stocks to be at the right level (if they have correctly forecast sales) they produce

$$O_t = C_{t-1} - K_{t-1} + kC_{t-1} \tag{3}$$

Now they begin the period t with stocks of level K_{t-1}, so that if actual consumption is C_t then the level of stocks K_t at the end of period t is

$$O_t + K_{t-1} - C_t = (1 + k)C_{t-1} - C_t$$

i.e.

$$K_t = (1 + k)C_{t-1} - C_t$$

and similarly for the previous period,

$$K_{t-1} = (1 + k)C_{t-2} - C_{t-1} \tag{4}$$

Substituting (4) in (3) gives us

$$O_t = (1 + k)(C_{t-1} - C_{t-2}) + C_{t-1}$$
$$= (2 + k)C_{t-1} - (1 + k)C_{t-2} \tag{5}$$

Thus we have related output of consumer goods to previous levels of consumption (in (5)) and levels of stocks to previous levels of consumption in (4). Consumption is related to income by (1), and income is defined to include the volume of investment, in (2).

We now have to determine how the volume of investment is decided. We shall let it have three components. There is an autonomous component A_t. There is also a component induced — in the accelerator fashion — by changes in income, defined by

$$I_t = v(Y_{t-1} - Y_{t-2}) \qquad (6)$$

and finally there is a replacement element defined by

$$R_t = zP_{t-1} \qquad (7)$$

Here P_{t-1} denotes the stock of capital existing at the end of period $(t - 1)$ and z a rate of depreciation, so that, if the stock is to stay the same an amount zP_{t-1} has to be built to allow for that which wears out. Thus, we may write

$$B_t = A_t + I_t + R_t \qquad (8)$$

where I and R are defined by (6) and (7), and P is defined by

$$P_t = (1 - z) P_{t-1} + B_t \qquad (9)$$

All this leads to

$$B_t = A_t + v(Y_{t-1} - Y_{t-2}) + zP_{1-1}$$

i.e. $\quad B_t = A_t + v(Y_{t-1} - Y_{t-2}) + z[(1 - z)P_{t-2} + B_{t-1}]$

and one can go on substituting back and back for P_{t-2} in terms of P_{t-3} and then P_{t-4} and so on. The initial stock of capital matters. If we are given this, and the initial level of output, then the whole thing is determined by the above set of equations. If there is no depreciation ($z = 0$) then $R = O$ and we have simply

$$B_t = A_t + v(Y_{t-1} - Y_{t-2}) \qquad (10)$$

which, with (1), (2) and (5), leads to

$$\begin{aligned} Y_t &= O_t + B_t \\ &= (2 + k)C_{t-1} - (1 + k)C_{t-2} + A_t + v(Y_{t-1} - Y_{t-2}) \\ &= (2 + k)cY_{t-1} - (1 + k)cY_{t-2} + A_t + v(Y_{t-1} - Y_{t-2}) \end{aligned}$$

and so yields the second order difference equation

$$Y_t - [(2 + k) c + v]Y_{t-1} + [(1 + k) c + v]Y_{t-2} = A_t$$

This may or may not oscillate, according to the numerical values of k, c and v. When we add in depreciation the result is more complicated. We have, however, worked it out in two cases, shown by the broken lines marked *Model A* in Figures A3.1 and A3.2, showing the values of Y, B and K for 150 periods, with $Y_1 = Y_0 = 1000$, $P_1 = 5000$, and $A_t = A = 200$. In Figure A3.1 the incomes Y_t have a slightly damped oscillation about a slightly rising trend, with a period of about 20 time units. This is for $k = 0.05$, $c = 0.9$, $v = 0.05$ and $z = 0.02$. In Figure A3.2, we have a bigger accelerator, $v = 0.25$, which leads to a more violent set of cycles. Y quickly becomes negative, and we are no longer interested. We may note that while negative income is not allowed, negative stocks are — for we can always borrow from another country. In *Model A* with $v = 0.05$, the rising income trend is echoed in the stocks, which soon pass out of negativity completely. They exhibit a cycle of the same periodicity as the income cycle, but with the peaks in stocks half-way down a downswing in income. The investment cycles are much less pronounced and precede the income cycles.

Model B

We now make the model a little less artificial. First we introduce a small random element into consumption, so that

$$C_t = (1 + u)cY_t$$

where u is a random number of zero mean, normally distributed with a standard deviation of 0.025. This means that we can expect it to lie almost exclusively between -0.075 and $+0.075$, so that consumption pretty well never deviates from what one would expect from equation (1) by as much as 8 per cent. If, however, we have a value of u in one period of, say $+0.05$, and in another it is -0.05, then these values may considerably influence the changes in stocks, as may be seen from equation (4).

The second alteration to the model has a greater influence. As we have framed it so far we have assumed that there is no need to ask whether productive capacity is able to produce the goods. We should try to ensure that the total output in a period is a possible one, bearing in mind the amount of investment we have at our disposal. We can do this by specifying a capacity restraint, that

$$pY_t \leq P_t$$

where p is some constant — taken by us to be 3. This means that in order to produce a total output of 1000 in a given period, the total accumulated net value of investment must be at least 3000.

When this is done the whole thing changes, as may be seen by looking at the dotted *Model B* curves in Figues A3.1 and A3.2. In both cases the initial upswing given by the broken line is too steep. Although the model begins with a building stock P_0 of 5000, and an initial income Y_0 of 1000, so that there is plenty of excess capacity, the parameter values we have chosen soon lead to a Y exceeding capacity. This cannot be, so we reduce both O and B in the same proportion, until their total is just equal to capacity output. When this is done then total output Y creeps along the capacity level for about 30 periods. Around this time *Model A* would have shown a downswing, and so, as it happens does *Model B*. The slow steady

growth of this strained economy begins to give way to cycles. The steady
income growth has robbed the stock-changes of their cyclical character,
and investment has had less smooth fluctuations than before, but has still

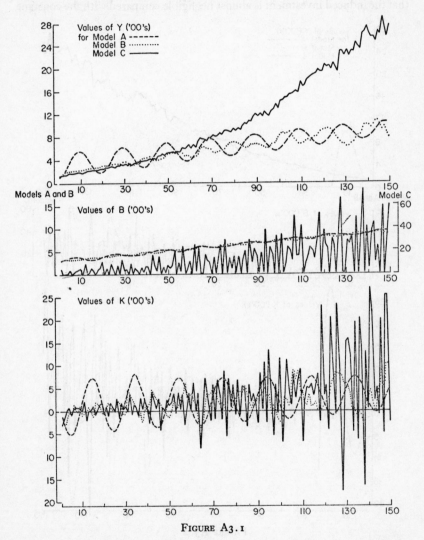

FIGURE A3.1

been pretty steady. In fact, in both the low accelerator ($v = 0 \cdot 05$) and the
high accelerator ($v = 0 \cdot 25$) versions, investment in *Model B* has behaved
pretty well as in the low accelerator *Model A* case. This is because the
accelerator comes in through the investment term, which it increases by a
certain fraction of the recent increase in income. When income hits the

ceiling imposed by capacity, it can subsequently grow only at a rate allowed by the expansion of capacity; in the models we are considering this rate is quite slow, and the successive changes in income are so small that the induced investment is almost negligible compared with the constant

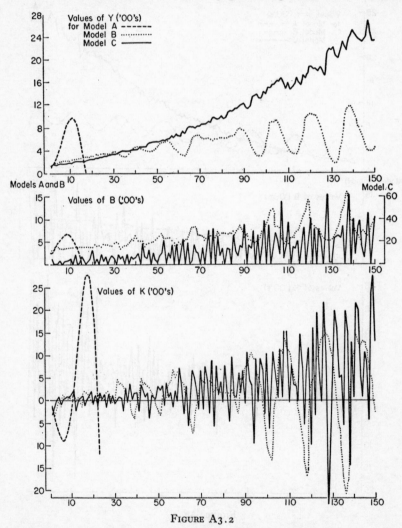

FIGURE A3.2

autonomous part, and the small addition due to replacement. The high accelerator has no chance of being effective, initially because it calls for the impossible, and then because the income changes are so small that it operates on a negligible quantity. For all it can do, it might as well be small itself.

But as investment creeps along at its low-accelerator *Model A* values (more or less), and so adds to capacity, income has crept along at an average far below that of the *Model A* cycles. Eventually capacity reaches — in this model — an accumulated level that begins to be more than enough to produce the level of income that the model requires. It may be asked why, since the straight-line path has existed for so many periods, there should now be a break away from it. Why should the model require less output than the slowly growing capacity can now provide? There are two answers to this. One is that there may be a purely chance effect. arising from the random element in consumption, which causes income in one period to fall below that of a preceding period. This means that investment will tend to fall, through the accelerator, and the difference equation describing the path of income may enter into a cumulative downswing. If this sort of thing happens when the values dictated by the equation exceed the possibilities of capacity output, then it does not much matter, since the lowered values may still be above capacity, and the fall will be cloaked by the ceiling. But if capacity has been built up then the ceiling may be too high to cloak a fall. The second answer does not depend on the random element. If, for the moment, we ignore the problem of replacement investment we can write our difference equation for the successive values of income in the high-accelerator model as

$$Y_t - 2 \cdot 095 \, Y_{t-1} + 1 \cdot 195 \, Y_{t-2} = 200$$

provided that these values are not greater than a third of the existing capacity. This equation can be used to find the condition under which Y_t may be less than Y_{t-1} even though Y_{t-1} has been greater than Y_{t-2}. We have that

$$Y_t - Y_{t-1} = 200 + 1 \cdot 095 \, Y_{t-1} - 1 \cdot 195 \, Y_{t-2}$$

and so the left hand side is negative if

$$1 \cdot 195 \, Y_{t-2} - 1 \cdot 095 \, Y_{t-1} > 200$$

i.e., if $\qquad 0 \cdot 1 \, Y_{t-2} > 200 + 1 \cdot 095 \, (Y_{t-1} - Y_{t-2})$

Now if we begin with fairly low values of Y this is unlikely to be the case, even if the values increase only slowly. If, for example, Y_{t-1} exceeds Y_{t-2} by 50, then the above inequality will not hold unless Y_{t-2} is well over 2500. This means that if, in fact, income grows steadily at the rate of an additional 50 every period, because the model is not free to operate in its unrestrained way since there is not enough capacity, then provided we start at a fairly low level there will be no departure from the steady growth for several periods. But eventually a critical value will be reached, when the above inequality will hold, and instead of growing income will fall. If this happens to be a time when capacity is not so low that even the diminished Y exceeds it, then the fall will be revealed. Thus, although the random element may bring about a departure from the steady trend, this may also occur for other reasons, once income has become high enough compared with its rate of increase, and capacity has become more or less adequate for the demands upon it.

Once the departure from the steady trend has begun then, short of a favourable random influence, it is likely to continue to decline for a while, as the model operates in its complete freedom. It may eventually lead to rising incomes that hit the ceiling once again, but this need not be so. The ensuing fluctuations in these models are less regular than formerly, partly because of the random element in consumption, and partly because of occasional collisions with the ceiling. In the low-accelerator case they are around what seems to be the same trend as that followed in *Model A*, while in the high accelerator case they are rather more violent and appear to be around a slightly lower trend than that of the low-accelerator version. We may notice that in the high accelerator case investment fluctuates more markedly than in Figure A3.1. It may be noticed that high stocks tend to coincide with low fixed investment and vice versa. This is true for both values of the accelerator, but with the higher value, the fluctuations become more violent, and this means that sometimes the stocks are very negative.

Summing up we may say that in the low-accelerator case, the effect of the ceiling and the random element in consumption has been to delay the appearance of fluctuations, and then to make them less regular and of different timing, but not to alter the trend. In the high-accelerator case the same broad effect has held, but now the delay in fluctuations has actually staved off the day of negative incomes, although the increasing amplitude of the cycles makes it look as if it will occur within about 250 periods. The low accelerator seems to have led to the higher trend, for although the maxima of the high-accelerator incomes slightly exceed those of the other variation, the minima are very much lower.

Model C

Finally we attempt to work in the idea that the impact on investment of an exogenous event depends on the level of credit. We hope to do this in a much more realistic fashion elsewhere, but in order to derive a rather interesting result, which was unsuspected until this model was worked out (even though it is obvious enough now) we shall proceed with a very artificial attack on the problem here.

The basic model is exactly the same as *Model B*, but instead of writing

$$B_t = A_t + I_t + R_t$$

we write

$$B_t = \beta(A_t + I_t + R_t)$$

where β is a function of the level of credit and a random component. In this model the only thing that can possibly be credit is the level of stocks. If one goes back to the idea that goods are always bought with goods, then a high stock of goods can be taken as meaning that there is an abundant supply of goods (or money) with which to finance operations of a long gestation period. Now in this model the gestation period has not been mentioned, but is implied to be a unit period, and the whole thing is extremely artificial from beginning to end, but in order to see what happens let us invent a function of the level of stocks and a stochastic impulse which will have the property of increasing the level of investment if the shock is favourable and stocks are high, of leaving it only slightly increased if the shock is favourable and stocks are low, of much reducing it if an unfavourable shock coincides with low stocks, and slightly reducing it if an unfavourable shock occurs when stocks are high.

We define a random variable v of zero mean and standard deviation of 2 with extreme limits of ± 6. We also define

$$L_t = \frac{\gamma K_{t-1}}{A_t + I_t + R_t}$$

where γ is an arbitrary constant. This ratio, apart from the γ, expresses the level of stocks at the beginning of a period as a fraction of the level of investment that the *Model A* would require to take place. A high value for L means that from a credit point of view, investment is easy. We shall assign a lower limit of zero to the value of

$$B_t = A_t + I_t + R_t$$

so that there is no net negative investment, and also a lower limit of zero to L, so that negative stocks mean a zero value for this quantity. We impose an upper limit on L of 5.

Now let us define β to have the values shown in the body of the following table:

	$0 \leq L < 1$	$L \geq 1$
$v < 0$	$L\sqrt{1 + \dfrac{v}{6}}$	$\sqrt{L\left(1 + \dfrac{v}{6}\right)}$
$v \geq 0$	$L\sqrt{1 + v}$	$\sqrt{L(1 + v)}$

Examination of this table shows that β is zero only when there are zero stocks, or when there is a highly adverse v (giving, in view of our extreme limits, a zero under the root sign). An adverse v will result in a value of β greater than unity if L is high enough, or, to be more precise, if

$$L > \frac{1}{1 + \dfrac{v}{6}}$$

Since we have imposed an upper limit of 5 on L, this means that if v is less than -4.8 then β is bound to be less than unity. No level of credit can completely nullify the cramping effect of a very bad shock. On the other hand, a positive v will result in an increased volume of investment provided that stocks are not too low. To take the extreme case of $v = +6$, we find that investment will be higher than in the simpler model provided that the value of L — stock ratio — is not below 0·378. Such a favourable value of v is, by definition, rare. Taking a more likely one of $v = 3$, then in order for investment to benefit the stock-ratio will have to be at least 0·5.

For each period the combination of v and L modifies the amount of investment, and it is this that takes place provided that, once again, the total income is not beyond capacity. If it is then both the output of consumer goods and investment are reduced proportionately. The model is thus the same as the B model except that investment has become the victim of a very artificial function relating a random shock to the level of stocks. The time-path of Y and of B under these circumstances is plotted, for the two levels of the accelerator, in Figures A3.1 and A3.2. We see that initially it seems to be the old story, as far as total income goes. The values are a bit lower than in the case of *Model B*, but they have a pretty steady path hugging the *Model B* path quite closely. After the first forty or fifty periods the whole trend of the economy, for both values of the accelerator, turns upwards, with a growth rate far exceeding that in either of the other models, and it is this which gives the exercise its unexpected twist. Before looking at the fluctuations themselves, we must attempt to explain this change in trend.

We look first at investment, noting that in the diagrams it has been drawn on a different scale from that in *Models A* and *B*. Its behaviour is clearly very different from that in the other models, and in rather more than a quarter of the periods it is zero. On the other hand, in other periods it far exceeds the levels reached in the other models (remembering the scale difference). Generally its behaviour is a great deal more erratic, and this is bound to rid income, of which it is a component, of its smooth fluctuations. Because of this, stocks also change more erratically. That they fluctuate over a wider range is not surprising when one considers that the level of income is so much higher than in the other models.

The whole of this arises simply because of the way in which we have related investment to the level of stocks and the random component. If we had kept the same basic formulation but had allowed some investment to proceed when stocks were negative then we would have had zero investment less often; and probably some semblance of a wave would have appeared. This is one of the points we are still examining. As it stands, negative or zero stocks in one period lead to a zero L in the next period, to a zero β and to zero investment. If stocks are positive but below some level that is considered to be desirable for a certain level of investment, so that L is less than unity, then the actual volume of investment will be related simply to the level of stocks and the shock. The planned volume will just not enter into it, once it has been decided that under ordinary circumstances (i.e. a neutral shock) the level of credit will not support the amount of investment that is planned. But if L exceeds unity then the volume of investment going on is related to the amount planned, and when the shock is favourable it exceeds the planned amount.

The result of all this is that we have allowed shocks to reduce investment from its planned level down to zero, if the shock is very bad or the level of stocks non-positive; while we have also allowed them to boost it very considerably — to three times its planned level if the shock is extremely favourable and credit is most abundant. Now in fact this is not quite as biased as it sounds, since if investment is very low, boosting it will not result in a colossal activity, while if planned investment is high the stocks will have to be enormous if L is to be high enough to allow ρ to magnify it very much. Nevertheless, there does seem to be a built-in upward bias arising here, and it is this that allows investment to become so large, and pushes up the whole economy, both through the multiplier effect of the extra investment and through ensuring that there is less likely, eventually, to be any capacity restraint.

This is a most artificial model, but possibly there is something of real importance here. If the impact of a shock does in fact work through the credit system, then it seems to be true that, *if the impact is restricted to the period in which the shock takes place*, then the worst that it can do is to stop investment altogether, while the best that it can do is dictated only by capacity considerations. And so, if investment is rather on the low side, a favourable shock in one period will possibly multiply it several times, while an unfavourable shock will simply stop it. In fact, of course, the impact of shock may last over several periods, and perhaps one should introduce some sort of moving average into the picture, weighting the various shocks according to their dates, and then assessing the influence. This may result in low investment for several periods because of a single bad shock: but it can also result in high investment for several provided that the level of stocks permit it. There is no need to go into it more fully here, because this is in any case simply a very preliminary model, and the more realistic one on which we are now working deals with it further: but it certainly seems that perhaps we are assuming too much when we argue that shocks balance out in the long run. It may well be that if, instead of being just added as an afterthought, *they are worked into the system in the way in which they actually affect it*, then they give the trend a definite bias in one direction or the other.

We may conclude by drawing attention to a few other features of this model. If one places Figure A3.1 on top of Figure A3.2 one will notice first that the two values of the accelerator do not seem to exert very different influences on the trends in *Model C*. For the first thirty or so periods the income paths are much the same, then the high-accelerator model grows just a trifle more quickly than the low-accelerator version, until a pronounced fall, after just over a hundred periods, pulls down the high-accelerator incomes, and they then continue to grow around a trend that — as far as our results go — remains beneath the low-accelerator trend. We may also notice that towards the end of the 150 periods we are considering the two curves move very similarly, and it may be worth looking into this a bit further.

We may start by looking at periods 107 onwards, when the fall in the high-accelerator incomes sets in. If we look at the course of investment we find that in both curves it falls sharply from 107 to 108. In the high-accelerator case it then rises a little in 109, but in the other case it remains low. Both cases see a rise in 110 to about the same levels, and then it falls to zero in 111. It is clear that the fall in income that occurs in only one case is not to be explained through differences in investment activity. In fact it arises in only one case because the low-accelerator model has a considerable consumer output boom in 108–111, followed by a high plateau lasting for several periods, while the other model has a sharp decline, which happens to coincide with the fall in investment. In that the high-accelerator model makes induced investment a larger proportion of the total, it is not surprising that here both investment and income have tended to move together, but with our peculiar distortion of the volume of investment we must not expect this to happen very often.

From period 120 onwards the similarity between the two cases becomes most noticeable. Once this sort of thing begins there is bound to be a tendency for it to go on, for both variations have been fed with the same random numbers and this means that, except for the different influences of the accelerators, one must expect stock changes in the one case to behave very similarly to stock changes in the other case. The income changes are in the same direction, and so the planned investment changes tend to be. If things have once become approximately equal then the similar stock changes and the identical shocks will tend to make the similar planned investment levels result in similar levels of actual investment and so the two systems move on together. But this cannot last indefinitely, for at some time quite a small difference, due to the different accelerators, may have a great significance, and set the two models onto their separate paths once again. Yet, an extreme shock, good or bad, may soon pull them into line again, given the right levels of stocks.

Since we have let investment be dominated not by the conventional accelerator, but by shocks in a credit context, it is not surprising that the major fluctuations in income seem to be chiefly shock determined. But the time lags and actual economic relationships have ensured that there is some continuity in the system, and that income does not just fluctuate at random.

We have not succeeded in producing long cycles in this model. Perhaps, by allowing investment when there are negative stocks, we will. But this is unimportant. The main purpose of the model has been to illustrate the effects of restraints and shocks, and to show how, when they are related to a simple form of credit, they result in behaviour absolutely different from that dictated by the simple model. In that reality does bring in restraints and shocks, and even the credit problem, it seems useful for us to try to work them into the classical multiplier-accelerator model.   It must be admitted that there are many ways of working them in, and that especially in *Model C*, we have chosen a rather peculiar way: but that does not detract from the point that without these features the classical model may be utterly misleading, both about the cycles and about the trend.   On the other hand, it may not.   We take up this problem in a more realistic way in the simulation model on which we are now working.

Appendix 4

INDICES OF HOUSE-BUILDING, 1851–1913

The Main Sources

THE main source of information is the register of plans kept by the local Surveyor.   Weber obtained data for thirty-three towns, either directly from these registers or through correspondence with the local authorities. For Liverpool there were supplementary data covering 1838–66 in *The Builder*, May 18th, 1867.   He also used the data for London mentioned below.   For twenty-five of his thirty-three towns his information related to houses erected.   For the remaining towns it consisted of the number of houses on approved building plans.[1]   The towns covered were spread over the country from Exeter to Glasgow, and their industrial composition was weighted rather heavily in the direction of export industries, as is evident from a glance at his list.   On the other hand, most of our growing towns were biased in the same direction.

Richards tackled the South Wales coalfield and its ports, obtaining data for five towns from 1856 or earlier, and gradually accumulating more until he reached the total of thirty-eight towns by 1902.   These data included a series for Cardiff obtained from local records by Lewis, who was able to extend Weber's series for this town over a longer period, and made use of the Weber series for Newport (Mon.).   All his other material was obtained directly from the Registers of Plans, from Council Minutes or the Reports of the local Medical Officers of Health.[2]

The next collection was for thirty-nine towns in the Manchester conurbation.[3]   Almost all of this information came from plan registers. The data for Manchester itself are described separately below.

[1] B. Weber, 'A New Index of Residential Construction, 1838–1950', *Scottish Journal of Political Economy*, 1955.
[2] J. Hamish Richards and J. Parry Lewis, 'House Building in the South Wales Coalfield, 1851–1911', *The Manchester School*, vol. xxiv, 1956, pp. 289–300. I am very grateful to Mr. Richards for placing a copy of his papers at my disposal.
[3] J. Parry Lewis, 'Indices of House-building in the Manchester Conurbation, South Wales and Great Britain, 1851–1913', *Scottish Journal of Political Economy*, vol. viii, 1961, pp. 148–56.

Regional data for fifty-one local authorities in North Eastern England, beginning at various dates from 1853 onwards, were collected from plan registers and similar sources by Kenwood.[1]

Saul obtained data from over one hundred local authorities — including some covered by the other workers in this field — for various periods beginning in 1909 or later.[2]

Plans, Erections and Boundary Changes

The main problems in analysing these statistics stem from boundary changes and from the fact that for some towns we have information about houses erected while for others our only data relate to approved plans. In some towns both series exist, and in others there is abundant evidence of entries having been deleted if the plans did not materialise. But often this was clearly not done, and on the whole it looks as if the series of 'plans' is likely to overstate the amount of activity. A further point is that planning approval was in any case bound to precede the actual construction. Where the registers record all the relevant detail, including the date of completion, it is possible to make some estimate of the time-lag here. Few houses seem to have been erected in less than six months after receipt of planning approval, and in the case of large building schemes the activity sometimes went on for two years or even longer. The favourite months for obtaining approval were those between April and July,[3] which means that the houses would be completed from October onwards, but that a substantial proportion of them would not be ready until the following year. If we take the position in Rhondda in 1908 as an example we have the following situations, which must not be taken as typical in every respect,

	J.	F.	M.	A.	M.	J.	J.	A.	S.	O.	N.	D.
Approved	15	12	46	67	141	237	116	96	163	61	30	235

although it was not uncommon to see a winter month with a high number of approvals. The total number of houses involved was 1239, and if we assume completion within six months at the earliest, then we see that 701 of these could not possibly have been erected in that year. If, on the other hand, we look at 1895, when 629 houses obtained planning approval, we find that more than two-thirds of them could have been completed in the same year. Clearly any attempt to convert approvals into erections is

---

[1] A. G. Kenwood, 'Residential Building Activity in North Eastern England, 1853–1913', *The Manchester School*, vol. xxxi, 1963.

[2] Some of these data appear in S. B. Saul, 'English Building Fluctuations in the 1890's', *Economic History Review*, 1962. Professor Saul gave me access to all of his data.

[3] This statement is made on the strength of the experience of both Richards and myself in examining the registers of about 80 towns. August was usually a poor month. In some towns the committee never met at this time, and applications were concentrated into July and September.

complicated both by the problem of determining how many plans never went further and by the difficulty of deciding the correct time-lag.

Yet it is necessary to have some idea of the time-shape of aggregate house-building activity, and so it is equally necessary for us to overcome the difficulties we have just mentioned. Using our examination of about fifty registers, and the views of Weber and Richards as guides, we converted the 'plans approved' data into 'erections' by multiplying by 0.85 and then lagging them by six months. This means that if n_1 house plans were approved in year 1, and n_2 in year 2, then the estimated number of houses built in year 2 is given by $0.85 (n_1 + n_2)/2$. There are obvious criticisms to be levelled at this device: our only defence is that it seemed to be a more appropriate device than any other.

The next problem is that of boundary changes. These were located from Census information, and local records. As a basic guide we assumed that if a boundary change caused the population to increase from P_1 to P_2, then the number of houses that would have been erected (or planned) in the enlarged area before the change occurred would approximate to the number in the smaller area multiplied by P_2/P_1. Clearly this tends to be an over-estimate in some years and an under-estimate in others. Long before the change there might have been little building in the surrounding country, while just before it there would possibly be more building in these suburbs than in the old town itself. In an attempt to allow for this we examined old maps, where possible, and also looked at any existing population data about the absorbed area. Then we modified our multiplication by P_2/P_1 by introducing a time factor t, whose value altered from year to year, usually increasing by constant amounts from P_1/P_2 to unity. However the actual values used depended on our detailed analysis of the area concerned.

In the end we thus produced for each town a series purporting to show the course of actual house-building within the area covered by the most recent boundaries from as far back as the earliest available statistic. The graphs presented in the text show these converted series, rather than the raw data. However, our tables in this appendix just give the raw data, so that readers who object to our manipulations may perform their own.

London and Manchester

For London and Manchester special devices were necessary. In the case of London the basic source is J. Calvert Spensley's series of the number of new houses in the Metropolitan Police District,[1] 1871–1916. We also have a series from 1856 due to Cooney,[2] showing the fees obtained by District Surveyors in the Metropolitan Board of Works District of

[1] J. C. Spensley, 'Urban Housing Problems', *Journal of the Royal Statistical Society*, vol. lxxxi, Part II, 1918, p. 210.
[2] E. W. Cooney, 'Capital Exports, and Investment in Building in Britain and the U.S.A., 1856–1914', *Economica*, 1949.

London (London County Council from 1889). In their overlapping period these two series have a very similar time-shape, and after introducing a slight lag it is possible to splice them, with considerable conviction, by the usual methods.

Manchester is more difficult. Basically the problem arises from the fact that while there is a useful series from 1851 to 1868, and another from 1891, there is a gap of over twenty years when we have no directly relevant data. Added to this difficulty are boundary changes.

There were three guiding lights. The Medical Officer of Health reported in 1880 that between 1869 and 1879 there had been 7628 new dwellings erected, and 3031 old ones pulled down. This meant that the basic problem for the seventies was the determination of the distribution in time of a known total for the decade. As indications of this time shape we could fall back on the course of building in neighbouring towns, especially Salford, and the increase in annual rateable value of property in Manchester, which, of course, would tend to lag after building activity but to show some broad conformity to its general pattern. It would have been possible to use these data to compute 'best' estimates of the course of building in Manchester, but this would not have taken account of contemporary newspaper evidence of a qualitative kind. Eventually we plotted the series just mentioned, and used them and our qualitative evidence to obtain estimates for the missing years. Our aim was to produce a series having a good compromise fit to the course of building in neighbouring towns, and to changes in rateable values, subject to the qualitative check afforded by newspapers. Clearly the accuracy of this series cannot be defended. But I doubt very much whether the timing of the principal peaks and troughs or the comparative levels of these would be much modified if the truth were known to us. Some check on this point is provided by the rent-index described in Appendix 6.

The Indices

The information for the separate towns was combined into a series of area or regional indices. For the South Wales coalfield a single regional index was produced, although Richards's thesis contains indices for various groups of towns according to their location or main industrial characteristic. Another index was compiled for the Manchester conurbation, but here we also computed indices for each of several smaller groups of towns in the conurbation. These centred upon Salford, Oldham, Bolton and the other principal centres of industry. Obviously there was some arbitrariness in the allocation of some of the smaller towns to one group or the other, but as it happened this never caused the main characteristics of any of the indices to alter.

These area indices are useful as an illustration of some of the points made in Chapter 4. They also provide abundant evidence, during the course of their construction, to support the reasonableness of our procedures for

allowing for boundary changes. This important point arises from the
fact that clearly the effects of such changes largely cancelled out, as one
town gained at the expense of its neighbour. Construction of indices, by
allowing for boundary changes in the way we have described, showed very
little difference from those obtained by cancelling out any boundary
effects wherever possible.

The method used for constructing these indices may be conveniently
illustrated by referring to the Ashton-under-Lyne district. Here we
had data for Ashton itself from 1851, for Hyde from 1864, Stalybridge
from 1868 and other towns from later dates. This means that we can have
a one-town index from 1851, a two-town index from 1864, a three-town
index from 1868, and so on. All of these indices are based on the average
of 1901–10 as 100. Over part of their span they go as the unbracketed
figures in the following table.

		Index for	
	1 Town	2 Towns	3 Towns
1861	134·8	(121·2)	
1862	71·7	(64·5)	
1863	45·9	(41·3)	
1864	22·9	20·6	
1865	22·0	27·1	
1866	34·4	29·2	
1867	79·3	59·6	
1868	52·6	80·1	67·2
1869	41·1	49·3	44·1

The bracketed figures in the two-town index are simply those of its left-
hand neighbour shifted downwards a little in the ratio 20·6/22·9 dictated
by the 1864 values. The extended 'two-town' series for 1861–7 may
now be converted into a backward extension of the three-town series, by
multiplying it by 67·2/80·1, and so on.

There are obvious criticisms of this method, but it does have certain
merits. In the above table the peak of the one-town index in 1867 comes
a year before the peak of the two-town index, but the addition of third
and subsequent towns hardly ever shifted the peaks or troughs, and usually
even the addition of the second town left these unchanged. Usually,
too, the addition of a town and the conversion of part of an n-town index
into an $(n + 1)$-town index resulted in a lowering of the former series.
As the number of towns grows so the adjustment tends to become less
important, but it is still usually in the downward direction. This seems
to be as it should be, if we are seeking an index for an area that consists of
a central town and its suburbs. Clearly if the level of building in, say,
1860 in the central town is equal to the average level in the first decade of
the next century, the one-town index will stand at 100 for that year.
But it is highly unlikely that building over the whole area, including the

suburbs, amounted to as much in 1860 as it did forty years later. The downward shifting of the one-town index thus seems to be a move in the right direction: but whether it is also of the right magnitude we cannot say. In the later years the locations of the peaks and troughs are very reliable guides to the changes in activity over the whole area, but, as we have seen, they are a little less reliable in the early years of the index. For all that the index must be thought of as providing a better guide to cycles than it does to trend. When one considers both the deficiencies of the data and the method of construction of the index, one should not need to be warned against attaching significance to small changes between consecutive years, or even to larger differences in level between two widely separated years. If it is ever used in econometric work then one should certainly use methods that take account of errors in the data: but there is also a trend in the errors.

This description of the construction of the area-indices around Manchester also applies to the construction of the Regional Indices for South Wales and the Manchester Conurbation. Kenwood constructed his index for North East England in a similar way.

The 'national' index presented more difficult problems. These arose from the unrepresentative selection of towns. Eventually two indices were computed. One just absorbs all the towns as they come along, without paying any attention to bias. One big deficiency in this index is that it is dominated in its earlier years by London. It is true, of course, that London saw a great deal of building, but the proportion of national activity that was located in the capital was not as high as that accorded to it in the early years of the index. As data for more towns become available so the weight put on the fluctuations in London or any other single town declines to something nearer its proper level.

This dominance of the index by London is apparent even in the seventies and eighties, and as the course of building in the Metropolis differed considerably from that elsewhere it is important to try to give it its proper weight if we are not to be misled. As a step in this direction we constructed a second 'weighted' index. This has four strands — the Manchester conurbation index, the South Wales index, the London index, and another index built out of all the available data for the rest of the country. These indices were added together with weights proportional to the contribution of net house-building in these areas to the net national increase in 1901–11. It has been assumed that the 'Other Towns' index can be taken as representative of the rest of the country, and the appropriate weight has been given to this. This seems to be a fairly reasonable assumption from about 1865 onwards, but it may well be wrong in the earlier years. The weights used were London 16·3, South Wales coalfield 5·5, Manchester Conurbation 8·6, Other Towns 69·6. The series for the North East did not arrive in time to be included in this index. If it were included it would probably slightly pull up the values for the mid-sixties, definitely leave the peak of 1876 unchanged, slightly steepen the

ensuing decline, show a very minor peak in 1884, and make the peak of
1898 more distinct from the value of next year.   The peak of 1903 would
be preserved, but the next few years would be a little less determined in
their downward path.   In other words, there would be very little difference.
The object of collecting more data must now be that of facilitating regional
analysis rather than of improving the national series — which is still
remarkably close to the one produced by Cairncross's crude computations
and enviable intuition.

The data appended show:
(a) The crude data, unadjusted, for various towns.
(b) The relevant data for Manchester.
(c) The indices for areas around Manchester.
(d) The regional and national indices.

1. *Raw data for selected towns*

The following table contains the basic data for most of the towns
included in the index of building activity.   The exceptions are the towns
in the Manchester Conurbation, London, and the other towns for which
more detailed information is given elsewhere in the book.

Most of these data are for calendar years.   The exceptions are Cardiff
(year ending August 31st), Glasgow (year ending August 31st after 1872),
Ealing (year ending March 31st from 1900), Leyton (March 31st) and
Wimbledon (March 31st).

All data relate to the numbers of houses for which planning permission
was obtained, except in the following case when they refer to houses
erected:

Birkenhead before 1875 and after 1892	Bath
Birmingham after 1900	Middlesbrough
Burton-upon-Trent	Macclesfield
Gateshead after 1899	Smethwick
Newcastle after 1880	Dudley
Swindon	Wimbledon
Nottingham after 1880	West Hartlepool
Crewe after 1899	Leeds
Burnley	Gloucester
Bromley	Wakefield
Ealing after 1900	Barnsley
Barrow-in-Furness	Colchester
Preston	Sunderland
Halifax after 1898	Derby
Leyton	

From 1871 the figures for Cardiff include shops.

Italicised figures appear for years in which boundary changes are
known to have taken place.

	Birkenhead	Swansea	Cardiff	Newport	Aberdare	Merthyr Tydfil	St. Helens	Birmingham	Glasgow	Llanelly M.B.	Burton-on-Trent	Exeter	Mountain Ash
1850	32												
51	52	272	380										
52	28	252	328										
53	10	199	190										
54	18	100	123										
55	67	82	192	93	453								
56	201	51	356	114	392	198	233						
57	169	187	284	103	234	293	156						
58	210	704	240	139	97	163	254	605					
59	184	255	160	76	164	183	240	674					
1860	281	272	83	20	183	131	99	778					
61	567	159	40	35	66	69	142	811					
62	874	92	40	11	58	12	83	1160					
63	452	87	16	10	36	12	78	1489					
64	263	155	60	16	68	7	60	1273	448				
65	133	193	107	47	128	25		1056	778	89			
66	66	243	59	54	200	40		1289	772	54	301		
67	38	268	152	89	73	59		1221	1195	62	175	102	30
68	28	215	152	91	67	45		1363	2204	53	107	41	44
69	31	184	130	76	37	60	80	1536	3184	67	69	100	4
1870	21	199		69	37	19	193	1597	3325	86	29	79	6
71	51	214	277	38	41	58	139	1537	3841	61	42	46	2
72	47	213	251	72	43	144	104	1064	2735	31	37	42	0
73	116	337	273	56	164	162	48	845	4463	100	45	51	64
74	115	380	539	87	187	90	158	1611	4392	99	87	50	31
75	175	820	648	163	156	26	217	3395	5582	239	189	25	29
76	149	365	552	172	134	176	445	2903	5746	143	221	65	80
77	205	330	611	191	10	17	490	2700	3963	75	279	153	21
78	340	189	564	151	5	40	534	1205	1033	58	402	85	1
79	425	113	618	67	5	10	473	1197	501	63	430	92	16
1880	321	129	771	118	5	137	316	1301	492	77	372	198	68
81	1093	179	904	84	2	56	179	1236	419	52	361	83	25
82	1336	192	686	87	2	41	175	666	512	61	321	47	19
83	1405	123	980	203	1	147	169	876	391	61	174	72	76
84	916	190	1445	243	3	51	260	922	587	66	133	175	149
85	174	218	1345	189	29	180	194	1049	764	69	111	151	141
86	169	273	1201	349	12	231	235	1000	1262	76	123	216	76
87	155	390	1226	139	39	87	282	989	1021	76	187	137	131
88	138	382	1062	275	6	34	438	2034	1202	135	182	210	29
89	145	414	603	110	10	107	453	938	1545	184	163	207	44
1890	121	422	745	183	15	163	267	1061	1253	140	149	48	35
91	137	288	730	114	36	158	245	1884	1561	114	305	34	300
92	132	420	990	433	77	193	395	1491	2051	84	180	100	91
93	108	479	1456	594	79	247	551	1658	2573	234	142	102	226
94	139	459	1206	544	200	297	378	1790	3466	162	159	90	350
95	175	473	1507	515	158	162	254	1806	3497	86	141	127	220
96	255	319	1196	760	180	222	302	1852	3370	121	156	145	466
97	349	134	1247	522	125	255	342	1836	4870	120	160	126	211
98	438	62	1258	390	91	446	375	2308	5618	82	148	82	292
99	434	63	624	300	140	824	288	2145	3730	74	148	69	112
1900	408	47	267	307	149	419	317	1630	2536	22	144	211	116
01	420	89	230	567	109	923	382	3249	2446	33	242	182	169
02	646	244	185	410	161	720	672	3440	5349	52	240	270	418
03	897	182	398	365	253	283	584	3562	4837	42	203	288	289
04	643	145	228	426	64	251	428	2497	2894	213	164	211	430
05	848	393	389	298	149	181	502	2372	2085	144	156	560	495
06	472	305	291	446	329	147	281	2950	2863	145	118	449	389
07	685	226	222	481	259	451	213	3093	1442	174	62	421	41
08	550	379	307	427	233	267	111	2841	1028	196	50	219	94
09	293	432	377	319	120	564	135	2442	1167	173	26	95	53
1910	255	439	307	261	88	424	142	1785	1283	97	23	36	39
11	232	390	208	244	94	530	224	1166	284	217	17	66	53
12	273	311	325	171	98	161	286	1107	200	309	10	46	31
13	339	249	325	199	87	147	243	1531	461	203	6	44	17

	Gateshead	Newcastle	Swindon	Nottingham	Crewe	Blaenavon	Ebbw-Vale	Wolverhampton	Leeds	Penarth	Gloucester	Wakefield	Neath M.B.
1850													
51													
52													
53													
54													
55													
56													
57													
58													
59													
1860													
61													
62													
63													
64													
65													
66													
67													
68	397	349											
69	526	399											
1870	273	384											
71	246	337	161										
72	163	366	153										
73	323	370	84										
74	575	611	171	644		40							
75	626	1102	116	883	163	72	25						
76	542	832	187	1338	83	33	4	1152	1738				
77	234	428	352	1084	145	17	2	369	2147	28			
78	357	242	326	1270	110	5	6	369	1848	112	119	34	
79	86	249	93	1043	183	2	0	269	1419	75	252	40	
1880	89	417	50	1296	217	0	0	391	1088	195	203	49	19
81	162	489	126	1859	203	0	1	272	1053	197	169	52	13
82	217	483	196	2289	37	5	4	418	1022	175	80	20	14
83	169	728	211	2603	65	8	59	50	1024	136	213	19	17
84	159	757	275	1645	95	9	28	116	1179	50	77	12	21
85	253	1031	142	1125	150	32	23		1135	82	50	51	1
86	341	1158	224	874	116	13	4	300	1182	106	58	26	5
87	325	1114	171	633	127	24	5	132	1594	174	110	37	4
88	284	1334	379	425	91	4	16	427	1609	124	167	14	20
89	312	963	361	290	136	22	7	167	1689	59	157	53	3
1890	198	953	625	201	93	46	15	168	1041	52	107	36	10
91	329	862	674	135	139	11	25	230	1610	43	242	19	28
92	314	875	414	120	145	17	55	285	1905	85	196	18	60
93	259	736	159	135	150	25	64	162	1941	33	200	34	61
94	280	617	234	245	207	17	26	1461	1768	82	268	29	59
95	334	688	159	470	245	20	21	417	1688	67	311	65	123
96	753	895	367	683	265	30	33	731	1869	70	199	89	140
97	512	1173	475	892	342	35	139	727	2282	44	207	83	114
98	599	1256	813	888	282	32	42	1121	2777	77	201	81	71
99	436	863	575	877	275	37	122	856	3020	113	124	97	94
1900	556	741	212	857	230	23	123	173	3037	44	301	45	62
01	472	655	201	1156	226	1	136	394	2408	45	201	19	84
02	736	976	269	1537	257	6	140	271	2479	53	133	30	74
03	409	1000	286	1322	304	3	213	260	2835	18	172	49	184
04	212	633	353	1050	181	17	101	168	2562	27	91	18	28
05	322	615	473	1088	135	11	224	135	1921	13	94	13	68
06	120	890	442	1192	106	28	177	212	1288	37	177	18	100
07	247	892	540	1061	64	31	98	207	973	38	106	13	37
08	168	618	161	1020	58	62	247	106	856	32	136	21	23
09	215	473	53	1096	45	30	323	224	647	36	73	64	60
1910	117	365	22	1056	35	60	248	250	525	65	37	93	74
11	122	313	33	724	28	26	111	101	389	51	55	174	82
12	37	145	58	495	16	36	179	106	252	38	56	122	98
13	37	111	63	384	13	n.a.	256	106	270	32	60	97	21

L

	Tredegar	Rhondda	Barnsley	Rhymney	Neath R.D.	Abertillery	Glyncorrwg	Colchester	Chatham	Sunderland	Derby	Llwchwr	Nantyglo & Blaina
1850													
51													
52													
53													
54													
55													
56													
57													
58													
59													
1860													
61													
62													
63													
64													
65													
66													
67													
68													
69													
1870													
71													
72													
73													
74													
75													
76													
77													
78													
79													
1880	13	399	166										
81	12	275	63	6	5	7							
82	2	295	54	7	29	5							
83	69	482	52	8	21	10	11						
84	3	599	49	2	34	46	24						
85	31	180	75	0	20	59	67	91	265	216			
86	18	271	59	0	39	44	23	116	226	332	395	248	31
87	0	202	69	0	30	19	45	153	51	188	554	164	12
88	1	280	103	2	21	18	8	70	53	300	381	186	5
89	2	371	70	1	39	51	89	142	87	102	305	294	2
1890	8	888	103	4	57	179	80	225	111	116	322	140	14
91	91	1008	166	0	85	134	8	124	126	118	309	85	3
92	4	918	118	1	52	63	13	146	187	188	252	84	18
93	16	702	186	0	93	183	15	120	262	199	368	140	12
94	21	1239	181	1	97	184	92	180	290	240	390	111	8
95	36	629	197	2	127	180	94	102	150	509	463	120	9
96	30	441	294	0	71	343	53	188	141	410	420	93	27
97	8	496	206	0	99	175	44	142	107	331	508	63	32
98	31	151	123	13	116	306	72	127	198	506	721	62	18
99	30	103	133	3	200	181	27	118	334	373	649	55	10
1900	5	291	90	27	152	191	25	326	165	448	542	115	13
01	16	433	119	104	249	268	67	286	216	306	624	104	98
02	2	687	148	128	328	316	54	245	460	529	728	156	60
03	146	347	285	187	395	324	29	320	727	310	363	252	56
04	56	393	257	31	268	274	105	300	194	385	280	165	47
05	70	382	287	44	175	311	140	200	203	338	293	262	26
06	91	463	158	33	224	105	21	120	102	306	249	367	15
07	125	957	178	23	557	159	90	125	20	282	226	453	26
08	154	1239	185	57	387	313	96	69	26	183	283	401	87
09	208	1397	264	7	347	615	77	96	70	105	307	475	22
1910	195	1079	230	26	316	172	343	110	57	95	220	555	56
11	176	692	201	40	348	182	12	67	87	77	180	404	11
12	75	401	163	6	182	100	18	50	78	24	123	621	1
13	52	325	144	63	278	172	15	50	106	17	114	426	11

	Pontypridd	Burnley	Ogmore & Garw	Ealing	Barrow-in-Furness	Bromley	Bedwellty	Preston	Reading	Caerphilly	Llantrisant	Maesteg	Oxford
1850													
51													
52													
53													
54													
55													
56													
57													
58													
59													
1860													
61													
62													
63													
64													
65													
66													
67													
68													
69													
1870													
71													
72													
73													
74													
75													
76													
77													
78													
79													
1880													
81													
82													
83													
84													
85													
86													
87	259												
88	81	452	16	106	2								
89	154	*569*	20	110	23	125	74	*309*	*385*				
1890	389	584	161	108	7	123	2	261	162	41	24	9	129
91	260	444	128	50	30	89	*157*	200	215	60	90	28	122
92	219	434	138	102	80	142	55	119	421	48	69	97	188
93	*274*	358	93	131	71	174	40	135	262	56	16	181	166
94	*212*	376	224	133	93	76	9	176	239	115	64	42	*239*
95	147	588	167	144	50	98	108	174	348	277	64	64	170
96	246	584	95	240	7	*169*	102	172	273	183	92	217	227
97	89	589	123	396	133	*85*	141	277	307	151	60	128	158
98	37	381	89	495	96	278	27	242	631	203	19	135	233
99	43	197	88	526	109	295	90	237	329	245	37	64	144
1900	44	192	56		223	265	19	413	551	219	26	154	228
01	100	280	86	285	252	238	32	248	866	109	48	116	159
02	114	177	80	*511*	*384*	259	259	259	563	410	90	259	101
03	361	162	132	729	594	329	529	170	514	366	83	246	175
04	214	142	196	1045	539	280	371	242	426	249	37	251	182
05	343	188	101	805	178	272	253	266	*288*	311	49	214	205
06	193	289	121	809	241	270	268	336	296	416	85	117	195
07	291	327	120	764	283	246	78	259	122	206	347	176	225
08	428	339	142	685	208	121	99	205	185	170	154	266	146
09	436	267	169	484	190	143	186	209	128	239	178	366	187
1910	365	255	77	571	148	105	362	169	108	188	177	175	128
11	219	*290*	371	509	152	43	177	193	*114*	318	290	71	128
12	88	378	100	455	180	38	214	143	83	210	329	63	129
13	56	425	102	358		99	616	142	n.a.	123	88	50	34

	Lincoln	Halifax	Leyton	Bath	Runcorn	Middlesbrough	Macclesfield	Smethwick	Dudley	Wimbledon	W. Hartlepool
1850											
51											
52											
53											
54											
55											
56											
57											
58											
59											
1860											
61											
62											
63											
64											
65											
66											
67											
68											
69											
1870											
71											
72											
73											
74											
75											
76											
77											
78											
79											
1880											
81											
82											
83											
84											
85											
86											
87											
88											
89											
1890	74	285	501	41	83	276	40	413	20	155	227
91	151	201	417	66	78	278	27	140	45	100	197
92	233	304	567	45	103	307	2	302	31	212	171
93	178	181	645	35	92	397	14	155	78	210	305
94	383	285	507	87	8	392	14	202	120	298	439
95	175	114	708	76	47	363	14	239	84	295	396
96	258	408	919	80	27	437	40	337	71	321	655
97	289	305	831	108	0	326	31	436	110	292	645
98	303	605	874	136	4	781	41	620	115	372	634
99	225	448	829	109	5	600	37	750	170	457	596
1900	542	428	1011	111	7	607	46	596	195	465	610
01	323	240	904	108	2	570	63	356	109	447	557
02	320	281	985	148	4	550	15	350	201	290	636
03	153	279	934	149	0	447	28	397	321	321	586
04	218	180	984	175	14	469	18	296	316	310	257
05	416	170	708	161	29	608	25	445	140	357	154
06	398	170	481	156	56	458	30	289	116	268	148
07	241	176	323	121	46	342	11	420	150	470	130
08	163	114	335	94	71	439	14	422	107	429	122
09	122	73	258	66	58	390	11	438	120	383	57
1910	385	90	258	54	58	423	22	248	68	266	64
11	330	63	218	n.a.	33	253	36	35	82	227	30
12	194	87	111	n.a.	12	274	83	51	32	126	21
3	269	54	131	n.a.	23	221	68	22	51	n.a.	32

2. *House-building Statistics for the Manchester Region*

The minutes of Manchester Borough Corporation include statistics of 'new properties inspected and reported upon' by the officers of the Building and Sanitary Regulations Committee, 'whilst in the course of building'. These data relate to years ending on April 30th of the year stated. From the 1854 figure onwards, one column relates to 'shops and houses', but for the earlier years a few miscellaneous buildings were included. No figure has been found for the year ending in April 1858. For the other years the figures are:

1851	1134	1856	410	1861	352	1866	868
1852	2040	1857	325	1862	662	1867	735
1853	2673	1858	—	1863	652	1868	659
1854	2513	1859	304	1864	861		
1855	815	1860	229	1865	714		

Reliable data for the seventies and eighties do not seem to exist, but the Medical Officer of Health reported in 1880 that between 1869 and 1879 some 7628 new dwellings were erected in the city and 3031 old ones were demolished.

The City Architect supplied Weber with the following statistics of houses erected between 1891 and 1913

1891	722	1897	2210	1903	1598	1909	1706
1892	909	1898	2772	1904	1678	1910	1595
1893	687	1899	2939	1905	1928	1911	1056
1894	1129	1900	2305	1906	1945	1912	606
1895	1087	1901	1680	1907	2020	1913	646
1896	1968	1902	1662	1908	1712		

Estimates for the years 1869–90, based on the total for 1869–79, on movements in rateable values, and on behaviour of building in the surrounding areas, were used in the compilation of the conurbation and national indices.

The district indices in the following table are based on an increasing geographical coverage, as described in the text. The dates when new areas were added are given below:

Principal District	*Districts incorporated in index, with dates of entry*
Ashton-under-Lyne (1851–1913)	Hyde (1864), Stalybridge (1868), Dukinfield (1880), Denton (1888), Droylsden (1896), Audenshaw (1897), Mossley (1899)
Bolton (1855–1913)	Farnworth (1864), Little Lever (1875)

Principal District	Districts incorporated in index, with dates of entry
Altrincham (1863–1913)	Sale (1868), Stretford (1869), Urmston (1878), Hale (1879), Ashton-on-Mersey (1895), Boundary extensions to Altrincham (1901)
Salford (1865–1913)	Eccles (1873), Swinton and Pendlebury (1877), Worsley (1878), Irlam (1879)
Oldham (1866–1913)	Royton (1870), Crompton (1878), Failsworth (1879)
Stockport (1866–1913)	Bredbury and Romiley (1876), Hazel Grove and Bramhall (1901)
Bury (1868–1913)	Heywood (1879), Prestwich (1885)
Rochdale (1868–1913)	Whitworth (1875), Middleton (1885), Littleborough (1889)

DISTRICT INDICES IN THE MANCHESTER REGION
1901–10 = 100

	Ashton under Lyne	Bolton	Altrincham	Salford	Oldham	Stockport	Bury	Rochdale	Manchester Conurbation
1850									
1	228·3								134·8
2	224·8								190·9
3	159·6								196·6
4	50·1								105·9
5	26·5	31·3							41·6
6	36·5	29·7							27·3
7	25·1	52·7							24·3
8	12·2	85·2							29·3
9	80·9	86·1							31·5
60	36·5	115·6							37·9
1	100·9	127·9							56·5
2	53·7	94·9							60·7
3	34·3	59·0	54·5						61·4
4	17·2	54·2	45·5						55·6
5	22·7	23·7	69·6	18·4					55·6
6	24·5	48·4	30·4	88·5	88·1	12·4			53·2
7	50·5	72·3	97·0	29·1	88·1	17·4			58·6
8	67·2	204·0	32·6	40·6	80·6	15·3	84·2	20·7	65·1
9	44·0	220·5	68·5	75·3	245·8	27·4	100·7	58·8	83·8
70	50·3	168·9	47·1	73·3	150·6	23·3	85·5	101·8	88·7
1	120·7	153·2	21·5	86·3	173·8	40·2	132·8	114·1	87·3
2	76·6	153·8	23·6	53·7	234·3	69·2	135·0	115·7	89·9
3	36·0	132·2	30·8	156·9	199·1	49·0	80·8	133·8	96·0
4	114·4	91·6	72·7	205·0	262·9	55·0	137·5	152·8	110·5
5	166·1	131·0	105·5	271·5	383·1	88·9	77·4	176·6	141·6
6	193·3	201·3	106·5	224·2	533·5	86·0	231·8	163·7	169·7
7	261·8	135·5	100·6	223·2	618·1	70·0	256·0	167·0	168·2

	Ashton under Lyne	Bolton	Altrincham	Salford	Oldham	Stockport	Bury	Rochdale	Manchester Conurbation
1878	207·9	68·2	98·8	183·7	217·7	107·7	107·1	156·7	136·7
9	103·4	59·3	50·9	86·0	180·0	65·7	69·8	136·4	94·7
80	147·4	38·8	41·6	58·2	213·9	59·9	96·4	69·0	69·9
1	85·0	17·0	42·8	62·0	160·0	44·0	61·9	32·2	58·4
2	65·7	50·1	23·3	62·5	150·3	99·4	46·4	33·7	51·7
3	96·7	36·8	13·7	54·1	177·1	53·4	60·1	27·3	53·0
4	86·6	54·2	19·8	37·5	251·7	44·2	54·5	34·3	53·3
5	106·2	87·1	19·3	36·1	237·5	31·6	78·5	40·5	61·1
6	153·9	80·5	34·6	45·9	247·6	64·3	50·0	48·4	65·1
7	121·0	78·2	25·1	45·6	154·2	69·4	48·6	88·3	63·7
8	102·3	104·2	32·2	80·8	107·8	81·1	19·3	104·2	61·7
9	103·4	89·0	28·9	70·2	73·9	93·7	42·0	104·0	64·0
90	97·9	134·1	50·3	80·0	60·6	85·4	41·8	98·6	67·2
1	70·6	81·6	28·5	50·1	70·5	85·6	32·9	93·5	62·8
2	78·6	91·8	50·6	79·7	96·6	91·5	36·0	100·0	65·3
3	78·4	87·2	54·5	92·3	97·1	93·7	54·3	84·6	69·8
4	90·4	120·8	153·6	78·8	107·6	67·3	49·3	79·0	77·9
5	104·2	113·2	110·9	138·6	144·9	75·9	74·4	85·2	88·4
6	130·9	151·1	106·5	137·1	164·5	79·3	71·0	167·0	118·8
7	133·9	130·6	123·2	180·0	198·7	150·3	83·8	173·6	137·4
8	164·1	130·3	99·3	134·8	202·2	88·4	81·9	163·8	146·6
9	171·7	111·9	141·5	143·5	162·8	95·4	82·9	161·9	142·3
1900	100·9	114·3	109·3	126·1	119·1	69·6	69·6	160·6	126·8
1	77·9	80·1	101·8	117·2	107·0	82·4	59·4	117·2	101·4
2	82·9	91·5	108·4	72·1	92·4	77·2	90·8	107·6	92·9
3	210·1	76·5	121·8	128·2	121·2	85·0	62·1	93·3	98·5
4	119·6	130·3	132·5	88·4	54·5	95·4	53·6	79·7	102·3
5	92·5	90·0	107·3	114·2	41·2	119·9	74·6	73·9	99·7
6	97·0	85·3	102·7	106·0	76·3	110·2	102·2	81·8	99·0
7	86·7	81·3	107·3	70·1	81·9	104·2	164·3	103·1	100·8
8	79·8	140·3	88·9	160·1	146·8	106·6	108·7	124·4	102·9
9	65·2	113·0	63·8	78·0	143·8	114·7	149·0	123·8	106·5
10	88·2	111·6	65·5	65·7	135·0	104·4	135·3	95·2	95·9
11	73·4	75·4	60·8	67·8	107·3	95·4	105·3	89·7	80·8
12	39·5	70·2	44·3	50·7	93·2	72·7	64·0	78·2	60·6
13	46·8	66·1	16·6	32·3	73·3	69·6	40·8	65·4	51·0

3. *Regional and National Indices*

The table below presents the South Wales Coalfield index, and the Manchester Conurbation index. In the next column these are combined in an attempt to approximate to an index of areas engaged essentially in exporting their produce. Simply to see how it behaves, the next index is for all the towns for which we had data at the time of computing it, other than London and towns covered by the Manchester or South Wales indices.

Column (5) relates to all of the towns for which data were available, other than London, while the next column includes the London figures.

None of these series covers all the towns for which data exists. It has not, however, seemed to be worth while to amend the index every time new data is unearthed. Such amending as we have done from time to time suggests that only the discovery of a great deal of data exhibiting fluctuations quite different from those we have noted will cause any appreciable effect on the index. The one town that does have an unusual series, and which is big enough to affect the index, is London. This can be seen from the table, which also shows that the index that excludes only London differs little from that which also excludes the Manchester and South Wales conurbations.

The last column, showing a weighted index, combines the London, South Wales and Manchester Conurbation indices with weights proportional to the contribution that net house-building in these areas made to the net national increase in 1901–11. A weight proportional to the contribution of the rest of the country has been given to the index for the remaining towns. The weights given were, London 16·3, South Wales 5·5, Manchester Conurbation 8·6, and Other Towns 69·6.

This is admittedly not a very satisfactory procedure. It is to be hoped that the production of other regional indices, along the lines of Kenwood's recent work, will enable us eventually to produce a more refined index: but I doubt that it will differ much from that which we now have.

The towns included in the index are listed below.

INDICES OF HOUSE-BUILDING ACTIVITY

	(1)	(2)	(3)	(4)	(5)	(6)	(7)
	South Wales coalfield	Manchester conurbation	South Wales and Manchester conurbation	'All' towns excluding London, Manchester conurbation and South Wales	'All' towns excluding London	'All' towns	Weighted index
1850				19·7	29·0	23·8	
1		134·8	134·3	38·9	57·2	46·9	
2	72·6	190·9	190·2	50·9	79·4	65·2	
3	55·3	196·6	189 7	40·9	76·0	62·4	
4	37·7	105·9	104·7	33·5	49·4	40·5	
5	35·2	41·6	47·6	35·7	36·3	29·8	
6	43·4	27·3	37·6	41·7	37·9	31·2	37·2
7	42·3	24·3	35·3	35·5	33·4	27·5	33·7
8	48·9	29·3	41·4	39·0	37·7	34·4	37·1
9	43·7	31·5	40·1	40·5	38·1	35·2	38·8
60	29·7	37·9	36·9	38·8	36·0	37·7	37·9
1	21·0	56·5	43·3	39·9	38·8	41·2	39·3
2	11·7	60·7	41·2	49·3	43·9	41·3	47·6
3	7·9	61·4	39·7	54·0	46·4	50·1	52·1
4	10·3	55·6	37·5	58·9	48·7	57·0	54·9
5	16·6	55·6	40·7	48·1	43·0	53·1	48·7
6	22·5	53·2	42·0	50·3	44·9	58·4	51·4
7	25·9	58·6	46·8	58·0	51·3	65·8	57·7
8	24·8	65·1	50·6	64·7	56·6	69·3	64·1
9	22·0	83·8	61·4	75·0	66·5	78·9	70·1
70	22·7	88·7	64·8	83·3	72·7	72·0	75·2

INDICES OF HOUSE-BUILDING ACTIVITY—*contd.*

	(1) South Wales coalfield	(2) Manchester conurbation	(3) South Wales and Manchester conurbation	(4) 'All' towns excluding London, Manchester conurbation and South Wales	(5) 'All' towns excluding London	(6) 'All' towns	(7) Weighted index
1871	23·6	87·3	64·3	87·6	74·9	65·2	77·1
2	26·6	89·9	66·9	91·3	78·1	70·1	82·0
3	36·3	96·0	74·3	83·6	80·4	60·1	75·0
4	48·3	110·5	87·8	97·1	93·9	67·2	86·5
5	61·0	141·6	112·2	120·5	117·8	85·0	108·0
6	62·4	169·7	130·7	135·0	133·9	100·4	123·0
7	47·6	168·2	124·6	124·7	125·1	99·4	115·9
8	37·2	136·7	100·8	103·0	102·6	94·1	99·4
9	31·4	94·7	71·7	76·6	75·2	90·5	80·2
80	36·9	69·9	57·6	69·5	65·5	93·0	75·9
1	42·8	58·4	52·3	70·3	64·0	95·1	76·8
2	39·8	51·7	47·1	69·2	61·2	87·0	73·1
3	49·2	53·0	51·5	72·7	65·0	84·3	74·5
4	62·5	53·3	56·7	74·1	67·9	79·8	74·2
5	62·2	61·1	61·4	67·6	65·7	72·6	68·3
6	60·5	65·1	63·3	67·0	66·0	64·8	65·4
7	59·9	63·7	62·2	71·4	68·4	66·6	68·6
8	54·6	61·7	59·0	70·3	66·5	65·4	67·3
9	50·5	64·0	58·7	70·5	66·5	64·2	66·9
90	58·3	67·2	63·7	64·7	64·3	61·1	62·9
1	70·6	62·8	66·3	64·0	64·6	63·5	63·6
2	76·7	65·3	70·4	70·5	70·4	65·7	68·0
3	86·6	69·8	77·2	79·5	78·8	73·9	76·5
4	96·9	77·9	86·2	79·4	81·2	75·6	77·8
5	98·5	88·4	92·6	80·7	83·9	77·9	79·9
6	102·1	118·8	111·0	93·5	98·2	93·5	94·6
7	106·1	137·4	122·8	107·9	111·9	105·4	107·8
8	89·6	146·6	120·1	132·6	129·8	127·3	129·8
9	73·1	142·3	110·2	131·4	126·4	128·7	129·6
1900	60·4	126·8	95·9	121·2	115·4	117·6	118·7
1	64·2	101·4	84·1	117·6	109·7	116·5	115·7
2	88·8	92·9	91·0	126·8	118·4	120·4	121·5
3	101·8	98·5	100·0	127·9	121·4	123·8	124·2
4	96·9	102·3	99·8	114·4	111·0	112·0	112·0
5	93·4	99·7	96·7	102·4	101·0	103·0	112·5
6	94·2	99·0	96·8	98·4	98·1	100·1	99·3
7	99·4	100·8	100·2	90·0	92·4	93·0	92·2
8	111·3	102·9	106·9	79·3	85·7	80·0	81·0
9	124·8	106·5	115·0	76·3	85·5	79·8	80·0
10	125·0	95·9	109·5	67·0	77·0	71·5	71·3
11	109·6	80·8	94·2	55·8	64·8	60·4	60·0
12	91·3	60·6	74·9	45·5	52·4	48·7	48·4
13	79·6	51·0	64·3	39·4	45·2	44·4	43·1

Towns included in indices by first year of inclusion

E = statistics of houses erected

P = statistics of houses planned

W = included in South Wales Coalfield index

M = included in Manchester Conurbation index

1850 Liverpool (E); Birkenhead (E 1850–74, P 1875–93, E 1894–1913).
1851 Manchester (M) (E 1851–69, 1890–1913. Estimates for 1870–89. See text).
1852 Swansea (W) (P); Cardiff (W) (P); Ashton-under-Lyne (M) (P).
1853 Bradford (P 1853–89, E 1890–1913); Hull (P).
1855 Newport (W) (P); Aberdare (W) (P); Bolton (M) (P 1855–96; 1897–1913).
1857 London (basically erections. See text); Merthyr Tydfil (W) (P); St. Helens (P. 1857–89, E 1890–1913).
1859 Birmingham (P 1858–1900; E 1901–13).
1865 Glasgow (P); Altrincham (M) (P); Farnworth (M) (P); Hyde (M) (P).
1866 Burton-on-Trent (E).
1867 Stockport (M) (P 1866–99, E 1900–13); Salford (M) (P 1867–91, E 1892–1913); Oldham (M) (P); Llanelly R. D. (W) (P).
1868 Rochdale (M) (E).
1869 Gateshead (P 1868–99, E 1900–13); Newcastle (P 1868–80, E 1881–1913); Exeter (P); Mountain Ash (W) (P); Stalybridge (M) (P); Sale (M) (P); Bury (M) (P).
1871 Swindon (E).
1872 Stretford (M) (P 1872–90, E 1891–1913); Royton (M) (P).
1875 Nottingham (P 1874–81, E 1882–1913).
1876 Crewe (P 1875–99, E 1900–13); Leeds (E); Blaenavon (W) (P); Ebbw Vale (W) (P); Eccles (M) (P); Little Lever (M) (P); Whitworth (M) (P).
1879 Wolverhampton (P); Gloucester (P 1879–89, E 1890–1913); Penarth (W) (P); Bredbury and Romiley (M) (P); Swinton and Pendlebury (M) (P); Worsley (M) (P); Urmston (M) (P 1879–90, E 1891–1913); Crompton (Shaw) (M) (P).
1881 Neath M.B. (W) (P); Tredegar (W) (P); Rhondda (W) (P 1881–97, E 1898–1913); Irlam (M) (P); Heywood (M) (P); Hale (M) (P); Failsworth (M) (P); Dukinfield (M) (P).
1882 Oldham (M) (E); Barnsley (E).
1886 Colchester (E); Sunderland (E); Derby (E); Chatham (P); Rhymney (W) (P); Neath R.D. (W) (P); Abertillery (W) (P); Glyncorrwg (W) (P); Prestwich (M) (P); Middleton (M) (P).
1888 Sheffield (E); Burnley (E); Barrow-in-Furness (E).
1889 Preston (E); Bromley (E).

1890   Leyton (E); Dudley (E); Wimbledon (E); Bath (E); Smethwick
        (E); Middlesbrough (E); Macclesfield (E); Denton (M) (P);
        Littleborough (M) (P); Pontypridd (W) (P); Bedwellty (W) (P).
1891   Doncaster (E); Hornsey (E); Nuneaton (E); Warrington (E);
        Carlisle (E); Reading (E); Oxford (E); Lincoln (E); Accrington (E);
        Ogmore and Garw (W) (P); Maesteg (W) (P); Caerphilly (W) (P);
        Llantrisant (W) (P).
1892   Leicester (E); Coventry (E); Willesden (E); Enfield (E).
1894   York (E); Ilford (E); Brighton (E).
1895   W. Bromwich (P); Gillingham (P); Gelligaer (W) (P); Llanelly
        R.D. (W) (P).
1896   Shrewsbury (E); Gourock (E); Tottenham (E); Keighley (E);
        Ashton-on-Mersey (M) (P); Crickhowell (W) (P); Penybont (W)
        (P); Bridgend (W) (P).
1897   Eastbourne (E); East Ham (E); Sutton Coldfield (E); Norwich
        (E).
1898   Cowbridge (W) (P); Llwchwr (W) (P); Nantyglo and Blaina (W)
        (P); Droylsden (M) (P); Audenshaw (M) (P).
1899   Halifax (E); Nelson (Lancs.) (E); Edmonton (E); Hereford (E);
        Bristol (E); Bournemouth (E).
1900   Croydon (E); Huddersfield (E); Darlington (E).
1901   Mossley (M) (P); Hazel Grove and Bramhall (M) (P); Risca (W)
        (P); Pontardawe (W) (P).

Appendix 5

BUILDING IN BRADFORD, 1852–1951

In 1952 the Town Clerk of Bradford supplied Weber with detailed
statistics of building over a period of a hundred years, and the following
extracts from reports of the Building and Improvements Committee:

1854

The Committee, in presenting their annual report, have to con-
gratulate the Council on the elasticity of the commercial spirit in the
Borough, evidenced by the number and extent of the building plans
which have been presented to them for their approval, in a time when
the staple trade of the district has laboured under considerable depression.

The Committee have reason to believe that the number of new
houses would have fully equalled that of the preceding year, had not

the depressed state of trade combined with the high price of building materials, which has prevailed during the year, somewhat checked the demand for and supply of new dwellings. And it must also not be forgotten, that Mr. Salt has lately erected at Saltaire, 140 houses, accommodating 700 people, the greater proportion of whom previously resided within the Borough; thus diminishing the demand to that extent.

1855

In laying before the Council a Report of the proceedings of the past year, your Committee would observe that the depressing effect of the continuance of the war, and other disturbing causes of the Trade of the Town, has operated considerably (though perhaps not more than might have been expected) in limiting the extension of Buildings in the Borough. The increase is still more than sufficient to meet the natural and ordinary increase of Population arising from excess of births over deaths, but is by no means so large as in former years.

1856

Last year your Committee had to note a decrease in the number of new buildings, etc., coming under their cognizance, and the war with Russia was then referred to as one of the causes for this falling off in building enterprise. The return of peace has been too recent for its effects to be visible in the increase of building operations, and accordingly the statistics for this year show again a decrease, as compared even with the preceding one.

1857

In the Statistics which your Committee has this year to submit, in their Annual Report to the Council, it will be seen, that there is a marked decrease in the number of Plans of new Buildings deposited, as compared with some previous years, with reference to which fact, your Committee deems it proper to remark, that it does not see any reason to conclude, that the increase in the population of the Borough, has been in the same proportion, less than during former years, as your Committee does not altogether concur in the opinion expressed in some former reports, that the number of new Buildings erected, is a measure of the increase and prosperity of the Borough, seeing that the class of Buildings by far the most numerous, is that, which is almost exclusively in the hands of speculating builders, and your Committee believes that the excessive activity of such speculators, during the four years previous to 1856, was greater than was required to meet the permanent increase in the population of the Borough. One great reason for the demand for new Houses during that period, especially of the lower classes, will be found in the superior character of, and convenience afforded in the new Buildings, owing to the operation of the Improvement Act, and the natural tendency of the population to abandon the Old Houses for new and more salubrious localities.

This demand for new Buildings, could of course be only temporary, as the owners of the older property, on realising the position, would find themselves compelled to take one of two courses, either to improve their dwelling, or to reduce the rents, as an inducement to tenants to remain.   This has been done to a very considerable extent during the last two years, and in the opinion of your Committee is the greatest cause of the large deficiency in the number of new Buildings erected, as shewn in the present year's statistics.

Your Committee is, however, glad to be able to report, that the Plans generally have been for Buildings of a somewhat improved character, as respects the extent of open space for yards, etc., and with few exceptions, they have found the proprietors more willing to adopt its suggestions, and observe the regulations of the Council.

1862

It will be seen from the foregoing statements, that building operations have been active during the past year, as more than double the number of houses and other premises have been erected than in the year previous. The greatest number of houses have been built in the Townships of Manningham and Horton, and the smallest number in the Township of Bowling.

The new Bye-Laws have now been in operation two years, and your Committee are glad to be able to state that the influence which they have exerted has now been shewn to be most beneficial.   Owners and others concerned in the erection of new houses have gradually become accustomed to their operation, and with very few exceptions, the requirements of the Bye-Laws are complied with; and the increased accommodation and improved arrangements, which are necessary to secure clean, well ventilated, and convenient dwellings, are generally provided for on the Plans, when first submitted to the Committee.

If the houses which have been built under the operation of these Bye-Laws, be compared with others, erected previously, it will be found that there are most important points of difference between them, some of which may be briefly stated — instead of long rows of houses built back to back, one half having no prospect but over a narrow yard, crowded with privies and ashpits, no access but through a covered passage three and a half feet wide, and having no means of ventilation beyond what can be obtained at one side of the house, from the atmosphere of the yard, tainted with emanations from a cluster of privies and ashpits immediately before the door, will be found houses having in every instance a frontage to a street, and at the side or rear, an open space appropriated as a separate yard for the use of the house, in which every occupier can have the conveniences, and outbuildings, kept exclusively to themselves; and every house having also, at least two sides, from which complete ventilation can be secured. It was stated previously to the adoption of the Bye-Laws, and some fears were entertained, that the effect of their operation would be to retard the increase of the Town, by preventing the erection of houses in so free and unrestricted a manner as heretofore; that this has not been the case is clearly shewn by the statistical information contained in the first portion of this Report, from which it appears that the number of houses erected during the past year, has been equal to that of any other of the three years prior to the time when the Bye-Laws came into force.

Your Committee have reason to believe, that the effect of these improved arrangements will be most beneficial on the general sanitary and social condition of the inhabitants, of the town, and that occupiers of houses will gradually appreciate and seek to avail themselves, to the full extent, of the great conveniences and advantages offered by the improved arrangements of the new buildings.

The statistics of building, which follow, are for years ending on August 31st in the year stated. They relate to buildings for which plans were approved, and to certificates of habitation granted in respect of completed houses. In later years a seeming discrepancy between these data arises because houses built by the Corporation were not subject to approval by the plans committee, and consequently do not appear in the statistics of plans approved. A point of some importance, especially after 1946, is that plans approved for the building of new houses were valid for three years after the date of approval. The annual figures printed here include plans that were re-submitted in order to keep them 'alive'. In the years after 1946 this device was necessary because of the difficulty of obtaining a licence to build, even though planning approval had been obtained. There were substantial boundary changes in 1873, 1882, 1899, 1930 and 1937. Dashes indicate that there is no record of the statistics. In some cases they were probably zero.

Year	Dwelling-houses	Mills and Warehouses	Public Buildings	Mis-cellaneous	Certificates of Habitation
1852	1358	27		216	
1853	1552	67		352	
1854	1401	34		232	
1855	637	18		214	
1856	598	26		214	
1857	410	21		98	
1858	202	3		82	
1859	234	15		86	
1860	234	24		98	
1861	111	17		67	
1862	233	28		79	
1863	153	34		102	
1864	273	72	3	70	
1865	429	69	4	110	
1866	690	53	2	130	
1867	1758	38	1	226	
1868	1428	31	3	189	
1869	1708	33	4	149	
1870	1808	75	5	198	
1871	1769	125	4	134	
1872	1926	91	1	143	
1873	1654	67	1	151	
1874	1860	67	4	253	
1875	1869	49	2	299	
1876	1750	31	3	258	
1877	1213	36	2	246	
1878	1701	28	—	275	
1879	720	20	1	409	
1880	714	30	1	248	
1881	577	19	2	238	
1882	319	30	2	383	
1883	219	22	1	271	
1884	210	33	—	474	
1885	402	15	10	363	
1886	690	28	1	324	
1887	1019	27	5	435	
1888	915	21	1	433	725
1889	1054	64	2	474	938
1890	1265	20	2	511	1070
1891	869	22		378	826
1892	583	25		455	675
1893	1036	20		437	782
1894	535	28		445	641
1895	532	15		346	498

	Building Plans							Certificates of Habitation		
Year	Dwelling houses	Houses and shops	Warehouses	Mills	Workshops	Lock-up Shops	Misc.	Corporation houses	Privately built	Total
1896	712	—	36	—	—	—	392	—	—	490
1897	796	—	26	—	—	—	442	—	—	578
1898	1146	63	32	2	14	39	521	—	—	851
1899	1216	52	9	2	17	63	441	—	—	731
1900	1007	45	13	5	20	48	540	—	—	1240
1901	1145	21	12	4	16	25	409	—	—	967
1902	1167	42	19	—	26	23	370	—	—	1023
1903	1538	41	14	6	23	36	418	—	—	1238
1904	1425	44	4	2	17	50	429	—	—	1458
1905	897	34	10	1	12	29	454	—	—	1057
1906	689	16	18	3	19	15	617	—	—	655
1907	737	32	22	—	9	10	430	—	—	637
1908	542	14	15	6	16	19	578	—	—	486
1909	769	25	9	1	15	20	570	—	—	476
1910	564	19	15	6	24	15	563	—	—	626
1911	430	23	35	6	19	18	414	—	—	396
1912	525	18	16	8	27	22	487	—	—	393
1913	395	7	24	9	30	13	487	—	—	349
1914	457	11	12	1	13	11	540	—	—	394
1915	312	16	15	1	28	10	389	—	—	306
1916	110	0	17	1	51	1	345	—	—	128
1917	34	1	7	—	32	12	269	—	—	32
1918	41	—	2	—	16	4	218	—	—	38
1919	77	2	11	2	31	1	408	—	—	6
1920	95	4	30	3	49	15	706	12	26	38
1921	691	3	8	3	37	13	515	—	—	446
1922	99	10	5	1	16	23	1068	228	38	266
1923	392	9	15	2	18	34	1231	140	105	245
1924	529	5	9	3	34	18	987	375	323	698
1925	875	1	6	4	18	19	948	947	562	1509
1926	966	30	3	1	3	13	959	1241	1005	2246
1927	755	62	2	—	1	31	912	1115	954	2069
1928	668	64	4	1	3	18	771	1273	654	1927
1929	655	21	4	—	6	24	855	258	700	958
1930	404	2	2	—	6	18	803	210	298	508
1931	488	3	—	—	2	20	629	120	484	604
1932	552	19	—	1	1	6	532	684	445	1129
1933	1635	13	—	—	2	5	689	18	1123	1141
1934	1309	14	5	2	3	11	738	8	1447	1455
1935	1735	12	5	3	11	4	941	164	1360	1524
1936	1580	7	1	—	8	6	986	108	1360	1468
1937	1091	—	4	—	1	3	1051	330	1320	1650
1938	1183	33	1	—	3	—	1215	640	1161	1801
1939	733	4	5	—	3	11	906	458	893	1351
1940	36	—	—	1	—	—	337	150	188	338

Year	Building Plans							Certificates of Habitation		
	Dwelling houses	Houses and shops	Warehouses	Mills	Workshops	Lock-up Shops	Misc.	Corporation houses	Privately built	Total
1941	—	—	3	—	6	—	167	—	19	19
1942	—	—	1	—	7	—	274	—	4	4
1943	4	—	5	—	6	1	272	—	4	4
1944	5	—	2	—	3	—	346	—	3	3
1945	7	4	1	—	3	—	455	9	6	15
1946	189	—	2	—	6	1	861	269	45	314
1947	34	1	4	—	24	2	851	207	49	256
1948	521	1	6	—	9	4	1688	304	31	335
1949	277	1	16	—	30	3	575	386	9	395
1950	4	—	14	—	14	—	1285	494	—	494
1951	—	—	—	—	—	—	—	638	12	650

Appendix 6

HOUSE-RENTS IN MANCHESTER, 1868–1890

IN an attempt to obtain some idea of the behaviour of house-rents in the Manchester area, we examined the advertisement columns of the *Manchester Guardian*. These proved to contain large lists of houses for rent, and as an experiment an index of rents of houses advertised to let was constructed. It excludes houses outside the Manchester conurbation, as now defined, and consists chiefly of houses in Manchester, Salford and the immediate neighbourhood.

The rents of houses advertised on the Tuesday nearest to the seventeenth day of each odd-numbered month were noted. For each year there were thus six sets of data, providing between them anything up to about six hundred individual rents. The index was compiled by taking the median and quartile values for each year, and thus consists of three parts. Because the rents tended to be concentrated around certain round figures, the quartiles and median were not calculated in the usual fashion. For example in 1880 the annual rents had a frequency distribution from which the following is an extract. In all 585 houses were advertised. The first

RENT ($£$)	24	25	26	27	28	29	30	31	32	33	34	35
FREQUENCY	23	34	21	4	31	0	49	2	10	3	6	29

quartile is therefore the rent corresponding to the 147th house. There were 141 houses with rents under £24, and another 23 houses with rents of £24. The quartile rent was put at exactly £24 rather than at £24$\frac{6}{23}$ which would be dictated by the usual method. A glance at the distribution shows the reason for this step.

The index obtained is shown below:

	Lower Quartile (£)	Median (£)	Upper Quartile (£)
1868	17	25	40
1869	22	30	40
1870	20	30	40
1871	19	28	40
1872	19	30	40
1873	20	30	40
1874	18	27	40
1875	20	32	50
1876	17	24	37
1877	18	27	40
1878	19	28	36
1879	20	29	40
1880	24	30	46
1881	23	30	46
1882	23	30	46
1883	24	33	48
1884	25	34	45
1885	25	32	40
1886	25	32	40
1887	25	31	40
1888	25	30	40
1889	26	32	44
1890	22	28	45

There are obvious problems in the interpreting of this index. Clearly even the lower quartile around £20 per annum was a higher rent than that charged for most industrial cottages, and the index is hardly representative of all houses currently being let. Furthermore, although large numbers of houses became vacant after 1876, the index moves upwards after this year. This seems to be because there were so many vacant houses of the cheaper kind that there was little point in advertising. The upward movement reflects not a rise in average rents, but a failure to advertise houses which, though cheap, could not be let.

Despite its uselessness as an index of rents, it nevertheless is useful as a guide to changes in the housing market. Clearly something happened to this market around 1875. Clearly, too, something happened around 1884. But the index cannot tell us what.

Appendix 7

WEBER ON INTERNAL MIGRATION

WEBER was particularly skilful in his use of decennial changes, and in extracting from them conclusions which at first they seem to conceal. The following edited account of his look at rural-urban migration is useful both for its content and as an example of his work.

He compared natural increase in urban areas with changes due to migration, and concluded that the latter was quantitatively of minor importance; but it considerably affected the time-shape of growth:

'Net migration to towns was quantitatively a smaller factor in town growth. Its highest contribution to total urban population increase in the period 1861–1911 occurred in 1861–71 and amounted to 30 per cent but the average for the whole period was considerably lower. Its impact on town-growth did not, however, depend merely on the number of migrants but even more so on the fluctuating progress of migration and this was extensive enough largely to determine the time pattern of urban population growth.'

He estimated net migration to the towns by setting actual population change against natural increase, relying on the Registrar-General's annual data for 1841 onwards. For the earlier years he looked simply at the relative overall growth of towns and rural areas. His analysis is worth quoting fairly fully:

'The enumeration areas used for the calculations are the Registrar-General's Registration Districts and in some cases Sub-Districts and prior to 1841 the Poor Law Union Areas which areas were generally adopted as Registration Districts when the latter were established. These areas do not correspond to the administrative areas but they can be grouped so as to approximate to the population in towns. The population in rural districts is then obtained by simple subtraction of the former from the total. A difficulty — familiar to any student of population changes — is that the boundaries of Registration Districts were changed from time to time. Fortunately there were relatively few large changes. Some of these do not affect our calculations since it is with population in the total of rural and urban areas respectively that we are concerned, and changes in boundaries between urban (or rural) districts alone do not affect the totals. In the few cases when this does not arise — such as for instance the creation of Middlesbrough — the necessary adjustment to ensure comparability could be carried out. Smaller changes in boundaries are more plentiful but their effect is hardly important enough to upset the conclusions drawn from the figures.

'All towns with a population exceeding 20,000 in 1891 as well as a number of smaller townships are included in the urban areas, and the Registration Districts covering them were so selected as to approximate to the areas getting to be fully built up in the period before the First World War. In this way the problem of overspill into suburbs and the failure of administrative boundaries to keep pace with urban growth was overcome. The disadvantage of this procedure is that some Registration Districts are larger than the actual towns and that consequently some rural population is included in urban districts. The proportion of the latter increases, moreover, as the figures are carried back into the earlier nineteenth century, when the strictly urban parts contain a smaller population. Our main concern, is however, to adjudge variations in urban population movements rather than obtain numerically accurate estimates of town-growth, and these variations are little affected by changes in the rural fringe of towns. It will be evident also that our rural areas contain a proportion of the townships not exceeding 20,000 in 1871.

'Returns of births and deaths have ceased to be made for the old Registration Districts in 1911 and the areas were not made use of by the Population Census after 1921. Comparison of pre-1914 and post-war experience cannot therefore be made on the same basis.

'Total urban population, its first and second differences, the natural increase and the net gain by immigration, are set out in Table 1.

TABLE 1

GREAT BRITAIN: URBAN POPULATION CHANGES, THE NATIONAL INCREASE
AND IMMIGRATION, 1801–1911
(000's)

	(1)	(2)	(3)	(4)	(5)	(6)	(7)
	Population in Urban Reg. Dis.	Increases in Col. (1)	Second Differences of Col. (1)	Natural Increase	Increase (+) or Decrease (−) in Urban Population due to Net Immigration	Increase in Col. (4)	Increase in Col. (5)
1801	4305						
1811	5112	807					
1821	6264	1152	+ 345				
1831	7690	1426	+ 274				
1841	9244	1554	+ 128				
1851	11028	1784	+ 230				
1861	13102	2079*	+ 295				
1871	15599	2526*	+ 447	+ 1761	+ 765		
1881	18827	3222*	+ 696	+ 2433	+ 789	+ 672	+ 24
1891	21825	2985*	− 237	+ 2715	+ 269	+ 282	− 520
1901	25119	3298*	+ 313	+ 2776	+ 522	+ 60	+ 253
1911	27780	2608*	− 690	+ 3199	− 591	+ 423	− 1114

* The figures diverge slightly from the increase in col. (1). Col. (1) relates to entries in the actual Census year whereas the figures from 1861 in col. (2) were obtained by taking increases in comparable areas between one Census and the next.

'After a high start in the 1810's the additions to the urban population increase show a steady fall in the 1820's and 1830's and they provide therefore no evidence of extra pressure for houses, on this count, in the 1830's. If a major house-building boom did occur at that time — and some evidence to that effect is on hand — then either it was not due to the growth of overall population, or it did not occur in the towns. The next thirty years show a steady rise in the additions to urban population increases. Excepting the 1840's — which period is subject to some doubt — there appears however to have been no corresponding rise in the level of house-building activity until the 1860's. In the 1870's and the 1890's towns grew faster than in any other comparable period and the 1880's and 1900's were the only times in the period 1811–1911 in which population increases actually declined. In these decades the correspondence between house-building and town growth is striking.

'A breakdown of the total urban population increases into components of natural increase and net migration is possible from the 1860's, and of the changes in these items from the 1870's. It serves to indicate the dominating influence of migration on the pattern of town growth. In the 1880's, the 1890's and 1900's changes in the course of net migration were quantitatively the greater and in the 1880's and 1900's they were of opposite sign. The fluctuations in town growth may be said therefore to be largely determined by migration. Only in the 1870's was the natural increase the greater. In that decade migration was also on the increase and between them the two factors accounted for the highest-but-one increase in urban growth in the century.

'Emigration, in the later nineteenth century, came to dominate the pattern of growth in the total population. At the same time it deflected large and varying parts of population from the rural-urban flow and directed them abroad. Hence a high level of emigration meant a reduced rate of growth of the home population and a smaller rural surplus for the towns. And a lower level of emigration increased the rate of population growth and made possible a greater volume of immigration to urban areas.

'This is what happened in the 1860's and 1870's. In the 1880's the rural exodus turned outwards. The net outward flow of population more than trebled while internal migration to towns amounted to no more than a third of the level reached in the 1870's. As a consequence towns grew more slowly (there was also a smaller natural increase) and the total population increases exhibited their only decline in the century. In the 1890's the pattern was again reversed. Net migration abroad declined, the population increase became greater, migration from the countryside to the towns increased and towns grew faster. And finally the same relationships persisted in 1901–11 though this time with a variation in the theme. Net migration abroad rose sharply and decline in population increase was still accompanied by a slower growth of towns. But for the first time, towns actually lost population by migration thus indicating that in this decade most of the emigrants came from the towns.

'These relationships are in marked contrast to those manifest in the earlier part of the century when emigration played a more insignificant role. Total population was dominated very largely by the natural increase rather than migration abroad and the rural-urban movement was — with emigration being lower — less affected by its alternating rhythm.

'In the early nineteenth century, urban population grew ever faster. At the same time total population grew in a fluctuating manner, with its second difference sometimes rising and sometimes falling, although the variations never reached the amplitude of the later decades. Each followed in these early years a movement largely independent of (and unaffected by) the course of emigration, although there is evidence that despite its quantitative insignificance, emigration did tend to rise at a time when home-construction fell, even in the twenties and thirties.

'It remains to examine the developments in rural areas. What was the pattern of population growth in the countryside? And was it accompanied by similar movements in house-building? Were the residential building fluctuations, in fact, a national or merely an urban phenomenon?

'In spite of the heavy loss of population by migration, rural population more than doubled between 1801 and 1911 and rose by 30 per cent in between 1861 and 1911. There was an increase in population in each decade but only twice before 1901 were the second differences positive, implying that for most of the period the rate of increase was becoming smaller. The reversal of this tendency in 1891–1911 is equally striking. It is due to the decline in migration from the rural areas. Only some 165,000 migrated from the countryside in 1901–11 as compared with 1,088,000 in 1881–91. Aside from 1891–1911 two other periods can be distinguished in which rural areas grew faster than at other times: in 1811–21 when occurred an increase second only to that of 1901–11. This is largely attributable to the return from abroad of the armies fighting the Napoleonic Wars; and in 1861–71 when the increase was probably affected by agrarian prosperity in the period of "High Farming". In addition the 1830's witnessed if not actual rise in population increase — at least an arrest of the prevailing tendency towards a rapid decline (the population increase in 1811–21 was 970,000, by 1851–61 it was down to 234,000). In the 1860's came the increase we have mentioned. It was followed by a decade of no change and finally a further fall in the 1880's.

'Annual statistics of rural house-building are unfortunately not available but some idea about the progress of house-building can be obtained from the net increase in housing stock in Census decades. They were obtained by subtraction of the corresponding urban figures from the totals for the country as a whole; and the urban housing stocks were in turn estimated by extracting the number of houses in all urban Registration Districts from the Population Censuses. The resulting figures correspond therefore in coverage to our estimates of urban and rural population and are subject to the same qualifications as the latter. They lcoud not be carried further back than 1851 and they refer to England and

Wales only.   The reason for the exclusion of the Scottish figures being
the break in the definition of a house in 1881 which makes comparability
with previous years impossible.

'Changes in the increase in rural housing stock are shown in Table 2,
and changes in rural population in Table 3.   It can be seen that the
periods of higher population growth are generally also periods in which
the housing stock increased faster.   This was the case in the 1860's and
even more so in the 1890's and 1900's, but it did not apparently apply
in the 1850's when the rural housing stock increased in spite of a fall in the
increase of population.   In the 1870's the increase in rural population
remained the same as in the previous decade and the net increase in rural
houses fell but later declined in the 1880's.

'Thus we see that urban fluctuations are supplemented by variation
in rural house-building and both show a clear relation to changes in
population increase and immigration.   The movements diverge in
direction in the 1850's and again in the two important periods of the
1870's and 1900's.   But since rural variations in building activity are of
much lesser quantitative importance and do not in any of the decades in
which their movement is opposite to that of urban building, determine the
pattern of total national building activity — we may conclude that the
major residential building fluctuations under discussion are essentially
an urban phenomenon.   Their urban character is accounted for by
internal migration.   The function of rural-urban migration has in fact
primarily been to transfer part of the increase of rural population, and
therefore part of the new housing demand, into the towns.   This is self-
evident from the fact that the overall rural loss by migration has never
exceeded the natural increase and that building has in each decade
occurred for new population; even though the magnitudes involved were
small in relation to the towns.

'But in the process of concentrating housing demand into the towns,
intense immigration has also had the effect of increasing housing demand
over and above that of new population and replacement.   One reason
for this can be statistically demonstrated.

'An increase in national housing demand directly attributable to
internal migration may arise if there are some absolute decreases in
population leading to a surplus of habitations in some areas and to a need
to rehouse the population decreases elsewhere.   In a closed economy
this population factor (minus the number which could be housed in the
houses normally falling to be replaced in the declining areas) is a measure
of the extra housing demand generated.   But if the economy is "open",
and there is emigration, part of the whole of this population factor may
find its way abroad and the increase in national building activity will
correspondingly be reduced.

'In Table 4, the Census Registration Districts have been grouped
so as to distinguish between Districts which suffered absolute decreases in
population (areas B) in 1871-81.   The totals for England and Wales,

TABLE 2

CHANGES IN URBAN AND RURAL HOUSING STOCK IN ENGLAND AND WALES, 1841–1911

(000's)

	(1) Total Housing Stock	(2) Housing Stock in Urban Reg. Dis.	(3) Housing Stock in Rural Reg. Dis.	(4) Increases in Col. (1)	(5) Increases in Col. (2)*	(6) Increases in Col. (3)*
1841	3117	1549	1568			
1851	3432	1784	1648	315	234	81
1861	3924	2175	1749	492	394	98
1871	4520	2658	1862	596	483	113
1881	5218	3264	1954	698	605	93
1891	5824	3788	2036	606	521	85
1901	6710	4517	2193	886	729	157
1911	7550	5116	2434	840	599	241

* The figures diverge slightly from the increase in cols. (2) and (3) respectively. Cols. (2) and (3) relate to entries in the actual Census years whereas cols. (5) and (6) were obtained by taking increases in comparable areas between one Census and another.

TABLE 3

GREAT BRITAIN: RURAL POPULATION CHANGES, THE NATIONAL INCREASE AND MIGRATION, 1801–1911

(000's)

	(1) Population in Rural Reg. Dis.	(2) Increases in Col. (1)	(3) Second Differences of Col. (1)	(4) Natural Increase	(5) Decreases (−) in Rural Population due to Net Immigration	(6) Increases in Col. (4)	(7) Increases in Col. (5)
1801	6196						
1811	6858	662					
1821	7828	970	+308				
1831	8571	743	−227				
1841	9290	719	−24				
1851	9788	498	−221				
1861	10027	234*	−264				
1871	10473	417*	+183	1508	−1091		
1881	10883	416*	+1	1462	−1046	−46	+45
1891	11203	333*	−83	1421	−1088	−41	−42
1901	11881	674*	+341	1318	−644	−103	+444
1911	13051	1223*	+549	1388	−165	+70	+479

* The figures diverge slightly from the increases in col. (1). Col. (1) relates to entries in actual Census years whereas the figures from 1861 in col. (2) were obtained by taking increases in comparable areas between one Census and the next.

and the natural increase and net gain or loss by migration for each group are also given.

TABLE 4

CHANGES IN POPULATION, THE NATURAL INCREASE, IMMIGRATION AND HOUSING STOCK IN ENGLAND AND WALES, AND REGISTRATION DISTRICTS GROUPED INTO AREAS DECLINING IN POPULATION AND AREAS GAINING POPULATION, 1871–81

(000's)

	(1) Population Increase (+) or Decrease (−)	(2) Natural Increase	(3) Net gain (+) or loss (−) by Immigration	(4) Net increase (+) or decrease (−) in housing stock
England and Wales	+ 3262	+ 3426	− 164	+ 698
Areas A (suffering absolute population decline)	− 345	620	− 965	− 20
Areas B (gaining population)	+ 3607	2806	+ 801	+ 718

'Net migration from areas A amounted to 965,000 in 1871–81. They lost the whole of the natural increase (620,000) and a further 345,000 of the population stock as constituted in 1871. The country's loss by net migration abroad was 164,000 so that 801,000 of the migrants were left to be swallowed up by the areas making up group B. 620,000 of this total formed the natural increase of areas A and this component of the migration total had no effect on building demand other than transferring it from areas A to B. But the remainder, e.g. 181,000, is an indication of housing demand which in the absence of internal migration would have been non-existent. Assuming a ratio of five persons to a house the displacement of 181,000 persons corresponds to a demand for 36,000 houses. To obtain the net national increase in demand we must, however, deduct the number of houses not replaced in areas A, e.g. 19,500. We are left with a total of approximately 16,500 houses to be added to the normal housing demand for replacement and the increasing population, which is directly attributable to internal migration.'

Appendix 8

BUILDING IN LIVERPOOL, 1838–1913

THIS appendix summarises data of house and other building obtained from a variety of sources.

1. *House-building by Rental, 1838–66*

This series was extracted by Weber from *The Builder*, May 18th, 1867, p. 354.

	(1) Total No. Houses Erected	(2) Houses Erected, Rentals under £12 p.a.	(3) Houses Erected, Rentals £12–£25	(4) Houses Erected, Rentals £25–£35	(5) Houses Erected, Rentals from £35
1838	1052	451	452	93	56
1839	997	390	471	86	50
1840	1576	623	760	131	62
1841	1761	628	873	188	72
1842	2027	724	914	305	84
1843	1390	440	794	114	42
1844	2450	1040	950	333	127
1845	3728	1212	2007	332	177
1846	3460	710	2328	236	186
1847	1220	59	925	167	89
1848	656	74	506	48	28
1849	446	90	258	63	35
1850	420	41	297	41	41
1851	837	101	578	88	70
1852	1136	223	727	76	110
1853	924	52	754	79	39
1854	829	16	655	102	56
1855	1355	63	1144	99	49
1856	1703	17	1455	125	106
1857	1520	124	1055	181	160
1858	1717	114	1299	182	122
1859	1758	85	1315	277	81
1860	1549	161	1129	163	96
1861	1250	45	1040	102	62
1862	1516	22	1145	208	141
1863	2015	110	1714	117	74
1864	2400	123	1962	217	98
1865	1496	—	1185	170	141
1866	1098	—	907	131	60

2. *House-building and Demolition, 1872–1913*

Provided to Weber by the Town Clerk of Liverpool:

NUMBER OF HOUSES ERECTED AND TAKEN DOWN

Year	No. Erected by Private Enterprise	No. Erected by Local Authority	Buildings Taken Down
1872	1559		530
1873	1071		536
1874	1266		371
1875	1495		94
1876	2343		197
1877	2134		228
1878	2657		159
1879	2338		212
1880	2095		334
1881	1696		222
1882	1232		395
1883	1136		916
1884	1460		800
1885	1180	282	766
1886	580		467
1887	866		464
1888	586		180
1889	601		284
1890	543		449
1891	371	102	437
1892	441		660
1893	333		525
1894	377		463
1895*	247		529
1896	1199		747
1897	1656	129	738
1898	1977		810
1899	2358		781
1900	1573		899
1901	1963	182	464
1902†	2061	237	548
1903	2453	209	528
1904	2174	380	293
1905‡	2186	139	980
1906	2453	194	818
1907	2342	155	386
1908	1850		447

* The City was considerably extended November 1895 and the estimated number of dwelling-houses in the additional area was 23,263, rising from 106,962 to 130,225.
† Garston was incorporated November 1902 and the estimated number of dwelling-houses in this district was 3300.
‡ Fazakerley was incorporated November 1905 and the estimated number of dwelling-houses in that district was 730.

NUMBER OF HOUSES ERECTED AND TAKEN DOWN—*contd.*

Year	No. Erected by Private Enterprise	No. Erected by Local Authority	Buildings Taken Down
1909	2149	49	280
1910	1710	114	595
1911	1234	108	473
1912	878	224	482
1913	767	68	498

3. House-building, 1867–72

Weber also obtained the information that between 1845 and 1872 'plans were passed for a total of 9131 houses'. He used this as a guide in estimating data for the missing years, 1867–71.

4. Houses Erected, 1896–1913, by Rental

Obtained by Weber from Reports of the City Building Surveyor for Liverpool:

	Total No. Houses Erected	Houses Erected, Rentals under £12	Houses Erected, Rentals £12–£18	Houses Erected, Rentals £18–£25	Houses Erected, Rentals £25–£35	Houses Erected, Rentals £35 upwards
1896	1199	7		944	204	44
1897	1656	95		1138	389	34
1898	1977	63		1276	539	99
1899	2358	4	821	769	607	157
1900	1573	—	436	602	402	133
1901	1963	222	558	633	441	109
1902	2061	85	590	962	323	101
1903	2453	201	363	1058	706	125
1904	2174	258	284	1067	449	116
1905	2186	78	394	872	638	204
1906	2453	243	547	1039	422	202
1907	2342	115	609	1022	444	152
1908	1850	—	418	1102	195	135
1909	2149	149	283	1369	191	157
1910	1710	—	119	1279	168	144
1911	1234	132	151	768	109	74
1912	878	—	41	717	64	56
1913	767	68	92	537	43	27

5. *House-building by District, 1883–1913*

(a) Professor Saul has supplied me with the following data:

	Liverpool 1835 Boundary	Walton W. Derby (rural) Wavertree Toxteth (rural)	Garston	Fazakerley	Tipton	Wednesbury
1890	543				22	29
1891	371				44	48
1892	441				18	55
1893	333				30	21
1894	377				41	46
1895	265				32	70
1896	358	841			30	53
1897	696	960			50	60
1898	475	1502			128	85
1899	335	2023			183	151
1900	107	1466			185	70
1901	316	1647			245	101
1902	227	1834			401	62
1903	405	1749	299		48	91
1904	417	1607	150		117	49
1905	111	1739	236		39	88
1906	584	1692	163	14	30	119
1907	521	1522	251	48	41	75
1908	255	1326	246	23	60	90
1909	223	1671	192	63	65	50
1910	48	1550	81	31	12	45
1911	355	819	53	—	17	42
1912	35	860	52	8	4	26
1913	90	621	56	—	10	54

The 1835 boundary lasted till Walton, Wavertree and rural West Derby and Toxteth were taken up in 1895. In 1902 Garston was added and Fazakerley in 1905. The statistics show houses for the old areas only in the years when the boundary was extended. In 1913 Woolton was taken in and in 1914 sixteen houses were built there. These have been subtracted from the Liverpool old area. The Tipton and Wednesbury figures are 'plans'. They go back a little further than shown in the table:

	Tipton	Wednesbury
1883	30	—
1884	14	—
1885	38	24
1886	19	47
1887	31	26
1888	18	24
1889	13	32

(b) Weber extracted the following data from Reports of the City Building Surveyor:

	(1) Total No. of Houses Erected	(2) No. Erected in Wavertree	(3) Erected in West Derby	(4) Erected in Walton	(5) Erected in Old City	(6) Erected in Toxteth Park	(7) Erected in Garston (Not incorporated before November, 1902)	(8) Erected in Fazakerley (Not incorporated before November, 1905)
1896	1199	185	41	313	358	302		
1897	1656	330	149	270	696	211		
1898	1977	538	216	445	475	303		
1899	2358	777	532	474	335	240		
1900	1573	481	373	300	107	312		
1901	1963	475	584	391	316	197		
1902	2061	509	776	482	227	67		
1903	2453	641	471	432	405	205	299	
1904	2174	329	624	525	417	129	150	
1905	2186	265	577	452	211	445	236	
1906	2453	318	594	494	582	286	165	14
1907	2342	582	536	394	521	10	251	48

6. *Other Building, 1877–1913*

The following data were supplied to Weber by the Town Clerk for the periods 1877–95 and 1907–13:

BUILDING WORK — CITY OF LIVERPOOL
1877–95

	(1)	(2)	(3)	(4)
Year	New Workshops, Stables and Minor Buildings	New Public Buildings and Manufactories	New Warehouses	Alterations and Additions
1877	61	22	11	302
1878	114	45	28	366
1879	110	30	22	358
1880		228*	25	377
1881	152	54	24	325
1882	132	22	26	433
1883	173	55	26	462
1884		136*	45	359
1885	146	36	23	406
1886	—	—	—	399
1887	—	—	—	478
1888	—	—	—	—
1889	—	—	—	—
1890		105*	3	492
1891	72	9	2	527
1892	59	22	9	465
1893	81	14	9	453
1894		104*	27	499
1895		82*	9	398
1907	87	37	1	492
1908	87	30	2	496
1909		128*	—	551
1910	100	39	1	586
1911	18	6	—	668
1912	107	25	2	594
1913	99	34	1	522

* No detailed figures.   — No record kept.

He also obtained the data for 1896–1907 which appears overleaf from Reports of the City Building Surveyor:

	New Workshops, Stables and Minor Buildings	New Public Buildings and Manufactories	New Warehouses	Additions and Alterations	Dwelling-houses	Buildings taken down: Workshops, Stables and Minor Buildings	Public Buildings, Offices, Manufactories	Warehouses
1896	82	55	4	663	747	9	3	6
1897	138	44	3	759	738	14	4	1
1898	149	34	2	753	810	12	9	—
1899	123	56	4	634	781	7	6	—
1900	116	47	3	628	899	37	11	5
1901	118	36	3	575	464	11	6	—
1902	123	29	—	537	548	17	6	—
1903	127	49	4	756	528	19	4	13
1904	110	41	1	997	293	12	10	—
1905	117	42	3	758	980	16	10	—
1906	140	32	1	704	818	17	7	1
1907	87	37	1	672	386	28	5	3

Appendix 9

DATA RELATING TO BUILDING IN
KINGSTON UPON HULL SINCE 1852

THE following remarkable set of data was provided to Weber by the City
Architect.

KINGSTON UPON HULL CORPORATION

MISCELLANEOUS BUILDINGS

PLANS DEPOSITED, REJECTED AND APPROVED

TYPES OF BUILDINGS ON APPROVED PLANS

BUILDINGS ERECTED

TOTAL PLANS AND BUILDINGS ADDED AREAS

1859–1939

SUMMARY

Building Bye-laws	Total No. of Plans Deposited	Total No. of Plans Rejected	Total No. of Plans Approved	Approved Plans						Buildings Erected					
				Warehouses	Factories	Offices	Alterations and Extensions	Miscellaneous	Total	Warehouses	Factories	Offices	Alterations and Extensions	Miscellaneous	Total
Pre-1894	9312	1664	7648	614	771	241	3415	2962	8003	331	413	147	1614	1665	4170
1894	7874	1177	6697	259	478	257	2203	3751	6948	3	5	4	7	24	43
1916	4709	293	4416	58	294	182	1492	2624	4650	—	—	—	—	—	—
1929	10136	38	10098	59	184	151	1588	9107	11089	32	117	93	1118	7688	9048
1939	141	1	140	2	4	3	38	112	159	2	4	1	32	92	131
Added Areas Taken Over in 1930	490	7	483	—	8	5	95	419	527	—	8	5	95	419	527
	32662	3180	29482	992	1739	839	8831	18975	31376	368	547	250	2866	9888	13919

PRE-1894 BUILDING BYE-LAWS

Year	No. of Plans Deposited	No. of Plans Rejected	No. of Plans Approved	Approved Plans						Buildings Erected					
				Warehouses	Factories	Offices	Alterations and Extensions	Miscellaneous	Total	Warehouses	Factories	Offices	Alterations and Extensions	Miscellaneous	Total
1859	66	3	63	8	8	1	26	22	65	8	8	1	23	22	62
1860	143	4	139	13	7	2	42	75	139	13	7	2	38	72	132
1861	101	5	96	15	4	3	33	47	102	15	4	3	27	33	82
1862	125	10	115	12	10	7	43	49	121	10	9	7	24	36	86
1863	155	14	141	6	18	6	62	60	152	5	13	6	34	46	104
1864	131	14	117	8	18	4	38	56	124	8	15	4	33	50	110
1865	162	27	135	17	17	6	44	67	151	15	17	6	44	66	148
1866	235	33	202	22	31	9	68	78	208	22	29	8	66	70	195
1867	298	44	254	15	21	4	93	128	261	13	20	4	88	120	245
1868	346	79	267	10	20	6	99	132	267	8	20	6	95	127	256
1869	355	87	268	26	19	1	144	100	290	25	18	1	124	94	262
1870	330	101	229	13	22	3	111	89	238	9	17	3	92	76	197
1871	339	80	259	10	15	5	158	71	259	—	—	—	—	—	—
1872	267	54	213	11	20	7	129	52	219	—	—	—	—	—	—
1873	336	66	270	8	17	2	185	58	270	—	—	—	—	—	—
1874	282	56	226	19	22	10	111	79	241	—	—	—	—	—	—
1875	342	44	298	26	48	10	147	82	313	—	—	—	—	—	—
1876	386	69	317	23	51	19	161	108	362	—	—	—	—	—	—
1877	353	57	296	23	27	11	179	74	314	20	22	11	155	63	271
1878	343	70	273	17	42	5	145	76	285	14	36	5	122	59	236
1879	210	42	168	14	19	6	70	66	175	10	14	6	55	51	135
1880	199	36	163	16	16	13	79	52	176	14	13	11	60	42	140
1881	244	42	202	18	21	13	105	56	213	11	16	11	82	38	158
c/f	5748	1037	4711	350	493	153	2272	1677	4945	220	278	94	1162	1065	2819

— Records incomplete.

PRE-1894 BUILDING BYE-LAWS

Year	No. of Plans Deposited	No. of Plans Rejected	No. of Plans Approved	Approved Plans						Buildings Erected					
				Warehouses	Factories	Offices	Alterations and Extensions	Miscellaneous	Total	Warehouses	Factories	Offices	Alterations and Extensions	Miscellaneous	Total
b/f	5748	1037	4711	350	493	153	2272	1677	4945	220	278	94	1162	1056	2819
1882	192	39	153	8	20	13	67	60	168	8	17	10	50	43	128
1883	277	63	214	23	31	11	82	86	233	23	28	11	58	68	188
1884	295	66	229	26	31	6	89	85	237	—	—	—	—	—	—
1885	260	45	215	30	25	5	87	73	220	—	—	—	—	—	—
1886	258	35	223	16	29	1	101	79	226	—	—	—	—	—	—
1887	271	36	235	16	26	4	104	96	246	—	—	—	—	—	—
1888	322	36	286	14	13	2	115	150	294	—	—	—	—	—	—
1889	335	47	288	28	11	8	129	119	295	—	—	—	—	—	—
1890	338	60	278	30	17	11	95	130	283	20	16	8	84	109	237
1891	359	58	301	29	23	9	95	163	319	27	23	9	90	151	300
1892	401	93	308	31	37	10	90	156	324	27	36	9	86	151	309
1893*	256	49	207	13	15	8	89	88	213	6	15	6	84	78	189
To Summary	9312	1664	7648	614	771	241	3415	2962	8003	331	413	147	1614	1665	4170

* January–September.　— Records incomplete.

1894 Building Bye-Laws

Year	No. of Plans Deposited	No. of Plans Rejected	No. of Plans Approved	Approved Plans					
				Warehouses	Factories	Offices	Alterations and Extensions	Miscellaneous	Total
1893*	77	16	61	4	6	5	10	39	64
1894	381	80	301	22	12	11	98	176	319
1895	376	92	284	23	14	9	109	134	289
1896	377	71	306	16	15	16	123	173	343
1897	414	47	367	9	30	17	126	191	373
1898	374	28	346	14	37	14	128	169	362
1899	321	24	297	16	36	14	98	134	298
1900	360	57	303	11	43	20	52	179	305
1901	385	60	325	14	25	16	102	173	330
1902	397	72	325	11	23	11	115	166	326
1903	348	41	307	12	25	11	82	179	309
1904	322	58	264	9	13	13	44	196	275
1905	319	63	256	10	18	12	79	146	265
1906	328	71	257	6	25	15	66	170	282
1907	331	39	292	10	10	9	119	183	331
1908	330	33	297	17	19	10	94	165	305
1909	350	57	293	8	20	14	126	126	294
1910	295	30	265	10	25	9	75	160	279
1911	337	49	288	11	12	4	105	165	297
1912	350	54	296	8	33	10	103	144	298
1913	397	53	344	9	14	6	117	202	348
1914	340	55	285	3	9	6	101	179	298
1915	231	19	212	5	9	1	85	130	230
1916	134	8	126	1	5	4	46	72	128
To Summary	7874	1177	6697	259	478	257	2203	3751	6948

* In this year the statistics run from September to December. 3 warehouses, 5 factories, 4 offices, 7 alterations etc., and 24 miscellaneous items were listed as actually erected.

1916 BUILDING BYE-LAWS

Year	No. of Plans Deposited	No. of Plans Rejected	No. of Plans Approved	Approved Plans					
				Warehouses	Factories	Offices	Alterations and Extensions	Miscellaneous	Total
1916*	75	7	68	1	3	—	30	34	68
1917	208	11	197	5	16	5	74	101	201
1918	164	8	156	2	13	4	61	76	156
1919	501	53	448	14	44	29	173	213	473
1920	539	37	502	7	59	26	155	272	519
1921	300	18	282	2	20	12	101	158	293
1922	343	26	317	5	19	16	92	197	329
1923	406	37	369	3	19	21	109	256	408
1924	372	34	338	2	16	17	119	210	364
1925	323	26	297	3	20	10	105	172	310
1926	317	15	302	1	10	6	112	182	311
1927	375	8	367	2	13	14	118	240	387
1928	389	6	383	3	17	11	116	272	419
1929	368	5	363	8	23	10	124	220	385
1930†	29	2	27	—	2	1	3	21	27
To Summary	4709	293	4416	58	294	182	1492	2624	4650

* August–September.   † January 1st–2nd only. See next table.

1929 BUILDING BYE-LAWS

				Approved Plans						Buildings Erected					
Year	No. of Plans Deposited	No. of Plans Rejected	No. of Plans Approved	Ware-houses	Fac-tories	Offices	Alterations and Extensions	Miscellaneous	Total	Ware-houses	Fac-tories	Offices	Alterations and Extensions	Miscellaneous	Total
1930	296	3	293	5	12	13	121	185	336	—	—	—	—	—	—
1931	310	2	308	4	17	15	99	249	384	—	—	—	—	—	—
1932	555	2	553	10	16	13	138	632	809	—	—	—	—	—	—
1933	893	8	885	2	15	13	106	852	988	1	11	11	90	800	913
1934	1195	5	1190	6	15	13	163	1055	1252	5	14	13	158	1013	1203
1935	1412	8	1404	5	20	14	215	1228	1482	4	19	13	203	1172	1411
1936	1567	5	1562	12	30	16	222	1429	1709	10	26	11	210	1370	1627
1937	1479	3	1476	5	13	20	206	1314	1558	5	11	17	182	1263	1478
1938	1550	1	1549	7	31	22	194	1392	1646	5	26	19	175	1348	1573
1939*	879	1	878	3	15	12	124	771	925	2	10	9	100	722	843
To Summary	10136	38	10098	59	184	151	1588	9107	11089	32	117	93	1118	7688	9048

* January–August.

— Records incomplete.

1939 BUILDING BYE-LAWS

Year	No. of Plans Deposited	No. of Plans Rejected	No. of Plans Approved	Approved Plans						Buildings Erected					
				Warehouses	Factories	Offices	Alterations and Extensions	Miscellaneous	Total	Warehouses	Factories	Offices	Alterations and Extensions	Miscellaneous	Total
1939*	141	1	140	2	4	3	38	112	159	2	4	1	32	92	131

* August–December.

ADDED AREAS: TAKEN OVER 1930

No. of Plans Taken Over	No. of Plans Rejected	No. of Plans Approved	Buildings Erected				
			Factories	Offices	Alterations and Extensions	Miscellaneous	Total
490	7	483	8	5	95	419	527

KINGSTON UPON HULL CORPORATION
HOUSES AND FLATS

PLANS DEPOSITED, REJECTED, APPROVED
TOTAL HOUSES ON PLANS APPROVED
HOUSES ERECTED BY PRIVATE ENTERPRISE
HOUSES AND FLATS ERECTED BY HULL CORPORATION
AVERAGE NO. OF ROOMS
HOUSES NOT TO BE ERECTED
TOTAL HOUSES IN ADDED AREAS
1852–1939

SUMMARY

Building Bye Laws	Total Plans Deposited	Total Plans Rejected	Total Plans Approved	Total Houses on Approved Plans	Total No. of Houses Erected	Average No. of Rooms in Erected Dwellings		Hull Corporation Houses and Flats Erected	Total Houses not to be Built
						Private	Corp.		
Pre-1894	7835	1135	6700	46797	—	—	—	—	4710
1894	3373	328	3045	25297	—	—	—	—	132
1916	1016	34	982	5055	3716	4–6	—	4804	—
1929	1695	2	1693	16249	12640	4–5	—	6023	—
1939	5	—	5	50	—	—	—	—	—
	13924	1499	12425	93448	16356	4–5–6	5	10827	4842

	Total Plans Taken Over From Added Areas	Total Houses Erected Added Areas	
	713	1925	

PRIVATE   16356

CORPORATION   .   .   10827

TOTAL HOUSES ERECTED (PRIVATE AND CORPORATION)   .   27183

M 2

Year	No. of Plans Deposited	No. of Plans Rejected	No. of Plans Approved	No. of Houses on Approved Plans	No. of Houses not to be Built
			Pre-1894 Building Bye-Laws		
1852	109	12	97	195	
1853	89	18	71	155	
1854	64	14	50	94	
1855	61	2	59	78	
1856	108	5	103	174	
1857	111	10	101	166	
1858	203	8	195	367	
1859	199	8	191	480	
1860	184	4	180	540	
1861	192	10	182	770	
1862	213	13	200	726	
1863	204	17	187	731	
1864	204	25	179	816	
1865	224	26	198	1084	
1866	178	19	159	792	
1867	248	37	211	1348	
1868	201	35	166	750	
1869	196	35	161	975	
1870	209	41	168	1232	
1871	235	51	184	1613	
1872	216	68	148	1103	
1873	166	42	124	863	
1874	272	52	220	1886	
1875	226	52	174	1231	
1876	275	52	223	1358	
1877	240	30	210	1306	
1878	236	50	186	1296	
1879	160	35	125	920	
1880	108	24	84	1121	
1881	132	26	106	795	
1882	122	24	98	464	
1883	208	53	155	1702	
1884	222	42	180	1355	
1885	155	21	134	786	
1886	151	17	134	1542	
1887	148	9	139	991	
1888	167	23	144	1044	72
1889	163	29	134	1609	387
1890	158	25	133	1138	161
1891	189	19	170	1763	216
1892	200	24	176	2107	360
1893	489	28	461	7331	3514*
To Summary	7835	1135	6700	46797	4710

* 99 per cent Lapsed Plans.

Year	No. of Plans Deposited	No. of Plans Rejected	No. of Plans Approved	No. of Houses on Approved Plans	No. of Houses not to be Built
		1894 Building Bye-Laws			
1893	23	5	18	3	3
1894	110	20	90	374	45
1895	101	17	84	386	14
1896	162	15	147	483	69
1897	209	21	188	1355	
1898	200	12	188	1597	
1899	284	22	262	2352	
1900	233	24	209	2071	1
1901	248	30	218	1687	
1902	202	15	187	1562	
1903	212	25	187	1661	
1904	213	30	183	1626	
1905	179	14	165	1236	
1906	126	13	113	1325	
1907	123	7	116	925	
1908	136	4	132	1187	
1909	160	10	150	1506	
1910	121	8	113	1206	
1911	73	10	63	487	
1912	88	9	79	821	
1913	88	9	79	738	
1914	62	7	55	504	
1915	20	1	19	205	
To Summary	3373	328	3045	25297	132

Year	No. of Plans Deposited	No. of Plans Rejected	No. of Plans Approved	No. of Houses on Approved Plans	No. of Houses Erected (Private)	Average No. of Rooms in Erected Dwellings		Hull Corporation Houses and Flats Erected
						Private	Corp.	
1916 Building Bye-Laws								
1916	7	1	6	22				
1917	3	2	1	3				
1918	Nil	Nil	Nil	Nil				
1919	8	—	8	10				
1920	52	8	44	186	8			—
1921	14	—	14	25	82			217
1922	54	2	52	88	41	5–7		334
1923	124	6	118	796	109	5–7		12
1924	130	5	125	658	213	5–6		162
1925	167	3	164	1029	692	5		342
1926	132	4	128	738	885	5		1006
1927	114	2	112	548	755	4–6		1269
1928	111	—	111	504	470	4–5		1008
1929	100	1	99	448	461	4–5		454
To Summary	1016	34	982	5055	3716	4–6	5	4804
1929 Building Bye-Laws								
1930	188	—	188	1417	379	4–6		714
1931	200	1	199	1518	985	5–6		428
1932	227	—	227	1535	1246	4–6		1679
1933	203	1 withdrawn	202	1558	1443	4–5		184
1934	219	—	219	2044	1367	4–5		538
1935	191	—	191	2030	1411	4–5		268
1936	187	—	187	2598	1178	4–5		680
1937	140	—	140	1800	2085	4–5		525
1938	108	—	108	1124	1320	4–5		609
1939	32	—	32	625	1226	4–5		398
To Summary	1695	2	1693	16249	12640	4–5	5	6023
1939 Building Bye-Laws								
1939	5	—	5	50				
To Summary	5	—	5	50	—	—	—	—
Added Areas				713	1925			

Estimated Cost of Dwelling Houses, 1929–51

Summary

Year	PRIVATE ENTERPRISE			KINGSTON UPON HULL CORPORATION		
	No. of Houses	Estimated Cost	Cost Per Unit	No. of Houses	Estimated Cost	Cost Per Unit
		£	£		£	£
1929	450	206,060	457·9	908	338,646	372·9
1930	1379	571,435	414·3	553	207,206	374·6
1931	1417	696,220	491·3	2305	760,813	330·0
1932	2041	573,521	281·0	134	40,618	303·1
1933	1654	561,961	339·7	448	132,198	295·0
1934	1598	521,780	326·5	196	72,490	369·8
1935	1689	555,109	328·6	660	192,676	291·9
1936	2573	661,351	257·0	497	157,229	316·3
1937	1681	468,544	278·7	444	144,011	324·3
1938	976	306,201	313·7	284	97,708	344·0
1939	639	199,280	311·8	—	—	
Total Pre-war	16097	£5,321,462		6429	£2,143,595	
1945	38	43,740	1151·0	—	—	—
1946	305	361,042	1183·7	410	473,270	1154·3
1947	19	29,968	1577·2	240	328,857	1370·2
1948	17	25,587	1505·1	484	619,149	1279·2
1949	88	124,187	1411·2	528	627,270	1188·0
1950	54	66,654	1234·3	837	887,936	1060·8
1951	63	82,384	1307·7	938	1,119,367	1193·3
Total Post-war	584	£733,562		3437	£4,055,849	
	16681	£6,055,024		9866	£6,199,444	
Add: Conversion to Flats	214	£77,036				
	16895	£6,132,060		9866	£6,199,444	
Add: Rebuilding War Destroyed Houses	529	£676,837	£1279·4			
Total	17424	£6,808,897		9866	£6,199,444	

Total No. of Private Enterprise and Kingston upon Hull Corporation: 27,290 Units
Total value of Private Enterprise and Kingston upon Hull Corporation: £13,008,341

ESTIMATED COST OF DWELLING HOUSES, 1929–51

Year	1929				1930			
	Private Enterprise		Kingston upon Hull Corporation		Private Enterprise		Kingston upon Hull Corporation	
Month	No. of Houses	Estimated Cost	No. of Houses	Estimated Cost	No. of Houses	Estimated Cost	No. of Houses	Estimated Cost
		£		£		£		£
January	28	13,100	34	11,901	15	6,895	110	37,782
February	40	19,500	—	—	24	14,625	8	6,923
March	63	26,950	480	178,868	29	19,850	8	5,900
April	71	32,525	244	92,138	136	46,475	—	—
May	51	26,900	—	—	117	48,225	—	—
June	32	14,650	—	—	17	9,570	31	13,410
July	27	11,850	—	—	405	155,180	—	—
August	5	3,190	—	—	121	53,275	—	—
September	25	13,670	150	55,739	121	57,890	42	13,960
October	65	24,200	—	—	130	46,360	—	—
November	16	8,000	—	—	176	73,215	354	129,231
December	27	11,525	—	—	88	39,875	—	—
To Summary	450	£206,060	908	£338,646	1379	£571,435	553	£207,206

Year	1931				1932			
		£		£		£		£
January	84	34,060	—	—	153	61,940	—	—
February	79	32,500	—	—	104	42,550	—	—
March	121	90,875	—	—	82	32,570	—	—
April	34	17,850	1032	336,492	121	44,615	112	33,265
May	216	127,810	—	—	82	41,275	22	7,353
June	260	103,615	12	5,520	52	21,320	—	—
July	91	33,525	—	—	86	33,095	—	—
August September }	420	208,660	58	17,294	430	153,889	—	—
October	31	15,065	—	—	145	47,760	—	—
November	19	8,325	1203	401,507	565	18,992	—	—
December	62	23,935	—	—	221	75,515	—	—
To Summary	1417	£696,220	2305	£760,813	2041	£573,521	134	£40,618

Year	1933				1934			
		£		£		£		£
January	431	135,585	—	—	80	25,892	32	8,918
February	143	46,160	—	—	151	48,560	—	—
March	152	56,135	—	—	134	45,855	—	—
April	68	22,860	—	—	100	33,365	—	—
May	81	27,605	144	41,952	144	54,785	—	—
June	168	56,125	—	—	78	28,885	—	—
July	140	50,775	—	—	321	96,425	—	—
August September }	204	79,366	—	—	215	68,940	164	63,572
October	61	21,945	—	—	48	17,305	—	—
November	81	27,130	304	90,246	243	78,770	—	—
December	125	38,275	—	—	84	22,998	—	—
To Summary	1654	£561,961	448	£132,198	1598	£521,780	196	£72,490

ESTIMATED COST OF DWELLING HOUSES, 1929–51—contd.

| Year | 1935 | | | | 1936 | | | |
| Month | Private Enterprise | | Kingston upon Hull Corporation | | Private Enterprise | | Kingston upon Hull Corporation | |
	No. of Houses	Estimated Cost	No. of Houses	Estimated Cost	No. of Houses	Estimated Cost	No. of Houses	Estimated Cost
		£		£		£		£
January	119	44,295	—	—	38	13,190	—	—
February	54	24,075	—	—	64	21,905	—	—
March	99	37,045	20	—	175	44,830	—	—
April	166	59,611	20	5,570	188	60,070	306	91,606
May	82	26,565	640	187,106	355	90,045	—	—
June	107	45,710	—	—	239	60,795	—	—
July	87	41,060	—	—	261	76,085	—	—
August }	193	64,913	—	—	384	90,301	15	10,657
September }					26	7,930		
October	544	146,490	—	—	41	12,150	176	54,966
November	145	42,015	—	—	376	84,815	—	—
December	93	33,330	—	—	426	99,235	—	—
To Summary	1689	£555,109	660	£192,676	2573	£661,351	497	£157,229

Year	1937				1938			
		£		£		£		£
January	33	11,990	—	—	99	23,942	88	37,200
February	206	51,810	—	—	81	25,964	92	26,060
March	88	34,915	48	10,134	80	28,155	104	34,448
April	184	48,870	166	56,600	115	37,325	—	—
May	309	75,335	—	—	55	22,810	—	—
June	83	27,365	—	—	229	69,500	—	—
July	106	34,120	—	—	78	25,730	—	—
August	42	14,829	—	—	28	8,800	—	—
September	38	10,235	—	—	41	13,260	—	—
October	37	15,130	—	—	11	3,925	—	—
November	410	105,215	230	77,277	111	31,070	—	—
December	145	38,730	—	—	48	15,720	—	—
To Summary	1681	£468,544	444	£144,011	976	£306,201	224	£97,708

Year	1939				1945			
		£		£		£		£
January	67	18,295	—	—	—	—	—	—
February	23	13,720	—	—	—	—	—	—
March	479	144,660	—	—	—	—	—	—
April	15	4,050	—	—	—	—	—	—
May	18	4,640	—	—	—	—	—	—
June	19	7,535	—	—	—	—	—	—
July	4	1,480	—	—	—	—	—	—
August	14	4,900	—	—	—	—	—	—
September	—	—	—	—	—	—	—	—
October	—	—	—	—	30	34,620	—	—
November	—	—	—	—	—	—	—	—
December	—	—	—	—	8	9,120	—	—
To Summary	639	£199,280	—	—	38	£43,740	—	—

ESTIMATED COST OF DWELLING HOUSES, 1929–51—contd.

Year	1946				1947			
	Private Enterprise		Kingston upon Hull Corporation		Private Enterprise		Kingston upon Hull Corporation	
Month	No. of Houses	Estimated Cost	No. of Houses	Estimated Cost	No. of Houses	Estimated Cost	No. of Houses	Estimated Cost
		£		£		£		£
January	2	1,900	260	272,720	1	900	—	—
February	45	51,900	—	—	—	—	—	—
March	—	—	—	—	—	—	—	—
April	37	43,125	—	—	—	—	—	—
May	152	185,148	—	—	14	21,624	—	—
June	40	46,608	22	29,414	3	6,157	—	—
July	—	—	42	56,154	—	—	84	109,901
August	28	31,876	—	—	1	1,287	86	136,465
September	—	—	—	—	—	—	50	59,912
October	—	—	—	—	—	—	20	22,579
November	—	—	—	—	—	—	—	—
December	1 (flat)	485	86	114,982	—	—	—	—
To Summary	305	£361,042	410	£473,270	19	£29,968	240	£328,857

Year	1948				1949			
		£		£		£		£
January	8	11,352	—	—	—	—	34	42,241
February	—	—	—	—	—	—	30	38,467
March	—	—	116	172,385	15	22,307	105	128,149
April	1	1,596	20	14,793	50	69,680	2	2,461
May	—	—	40	53,260	1	1,625	159	188,103
June	—	—	12	16,401	—	—	—	—
July	—	—	40	49,757	—	—	110	129,515
August	1	1,378	—	—	10	14,259	64	72,361
September	6	6,987	62	76,101	4	5,100	—	—
October	—	—	132	161,301	5	6,958	24	25,973
November	—	—	62	75,151	3	4,258	—	—
December	1	4,274	—	—	—	—	—	—
To Summary	17	£25,587	484	£619,149	88	£124,187	528	£627,270

Year	1950				1951			
		£		£		£		£
January	—	—	54	58,833	—	—	—	—
February	11	13,793	322	344,685	—	—	114	127,358
March	1	2,588	100	96,148	—	—	20	23,278
April	8	9,198	82	81,567	13	18,073	116	139,398
May	10	12,236	40	41,237	2	2,794	142	167,074
June	20	23,784	40	42,299	4	6,090	—	—
July	2	2,495	26	31,749	19	28,857	158	198,250
August	—	—	153	187,797	1	1,370	—	—
September	—	—	20	23,621	—	—	24	30,670
October	—	—	—	—	—	—	242	290,060
November	—	—	—	—	24	25,200	—	—
December	2	2,560	—	—	—	—	122	143,279
To Summary	54	£66,654	837	£887,936	63	£82,384	938	£1,119,367

ESTIMATED COST OF REBUILDING WAR-DESTROYED HOUSES
AND CONVERSION OF HOUSES INTO FLATS

	No. of Dwellings	Estimated Cost
Total number and cost of rebuilds as at 31.12.51	529	£676,837

	No. of Units	Estimated Cost
Total conversions to flats as at 31.12.51	214	£77,036

Note.—The above figures are taken from the records of licences issued.

Appendix 10

HOUSE-BUILDING AND THE TRADE CYCLE

WE have already seen that regional industrial activity, influencing local prosperity, had an impact on house-building in the region concerned, but that other factors, including the supply of credit and raw materials, which were all tending to be functions of national conditions, and the age-structure of the family, also exerted their influence. There is no point in repeating the detail of this argument, but it is useful to look at the story at a different level of aggregation. If, for example, house-building in the country as a whole tends to be high when other building is low, or when general activity is low, then the consequences are quite different than they would be if aggregate house-building tended to conform with aggregated other activity. There has already been a substantial difference of opinion about this. Barnes thought that 'in the normal way building will be quiet in a period of great commercial and industrial activity . . . and brisk in the time immediately succeeding. . . .'[1] H. W. Robinson, writing sixteen years later, held that housing had a cyclical pattern inverse to that of the trade cycle,[2] while Grebler has held that in the United States this was true for the period 1900–13 but not for the inter-war period, chiefly because much inter-war housing was relying on public funds which were more lavishly expended in good years.[3]

These studies were all made at a national level of aggregation. Cairncross, looking at Glasgow, found that the annual increments in occupied and empty houses followed a marked cyclical pattern in accord with the

[1] H. Barnes, *Housing*, London, 1923, p. 43.
[2] H. W. Robinson, *Economics of Building*, London, 1939, p. 156.
[3] L. Grebler, 'House-Building, the Business Cycle and State Intervention', *International Labor Review*, 1936, vol. xxxiii, pp. 337–55 and 468–78.

trade cycle, but that these cyclical fluctuations in demand found 'no or little echo in supply'. Fluctuations in demand were taken up predominantly by opposite fluctuations in the stock of empty houses, and residential building was comparatively insensitive to the trade cycle, even though building plans for houses of one room showed a distinct cyclical pattern.[1] Beveridge asserted that there was little connection between house-building activity and the trade cycle before 1913,[2] while Marian Bowley[3] reached the same conclusion for inter-war house-building. On the other hand, Bowen, working with regional employment statistics, found a very high positive correlation in the period 1927–36, and concluded that 'in all regions building activity was closely connected with the trade cycle'.[4]

In America, C. D. Long, J. R. Riggleman, J. M. Clark and W. H. Newman have all asserted that before 1914 building and general business activity tended to go together, with building tending to lead activity.[5]

After studying these contributions to the subject Weber felt that it was desirable to examine the long waves and short waves separately, since they 'appear to be caused largely by different factors'. He therefore expressed his building index (or, to be more precise, a slightly earlier version of his index, which differed little from the one that he finally published) as a series of percentage deviations from a nine-year moving average, thereby 'abstracting from the trend and isolating the minor fluctuations in building'. He then distinguished 'some fifteen building cycles with an average duration of 5–6 years ... over the period 1842–1913. Some of these appear to be more or less independent random movements but the pattern of fluctuation as a whole indicates without doubt that they should be regarded as an integral part of the trade cycle.' For the period up to 1859 he excluded London from his index, which means that it creeps into the moving average over a period of four years, when the splicing comes. The index for the earlier years was based on very few towns but he saw 'no reason ... to query the general outline of (the) cyclical fluctuations'.

Weber then took Beveridge's index of industrial activity, being a weighted arithmetic mean of the deviations of some twenty-three series from long-term trends. He was aware of many criticisms of this index, but checked it, for the period after 1870, against Prest's estimates of real national income. He asserted that apart from the amplitudes, 'agreement

---

[1] Cairncross, op. cit., pp. 22 and 28–9.

[2] W. Beveridge, Unemployment, London, 1930, pp. 335–9.

[3] M. Bowley, 'Fluctuations in House-Building and the Trade Cycle', Review of Economic Studies, 1937, vol. iv, no. 3, p. 167.

[4] I. Bowen, 'Building Output and the Trade Cycle (U.K. 1924–38)', Oxford Economic Papers, 1940, no. 3, p. 126.

[5] C. D. Long, Jr., 'Long Cycles in the Building Industry', Quarterly Journal of Economics, 1939, vol. liii, p. 380. J. Riggleman, 'Building Cycles in the U.S., 1875–1932', Journal of the American Statistical Association, 1933, vol. xxviii, no. 182, p. 182. J. M. Clark, Strategic Factors in Business Cycles, 1949, N.B.E.R., p. 28, W. H. Newman, 'The Building Industry and Business Cycles', Journal of Business, University of Chicago, 1935, vol. viii, no. 3, part 2.

in the broad pattern of fluctuation was found to be very close'. The comparison of the deviations from the Weber index of building, and Beveridge's index is shown in Figure A10.1. He concluded as follows:

'The conclusions to be drawn from the comparison of fluctuations in house-building and economic activity in general defy simple and

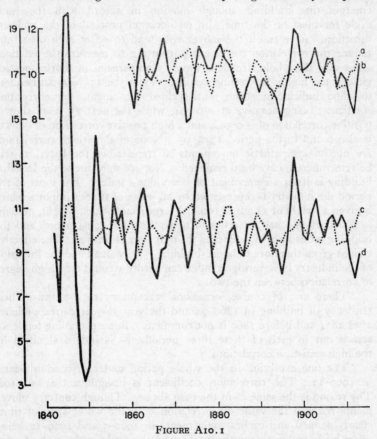

FIGURE A10.1

(a) and (c) Beveridge's Index of Industrial Activity. Percentage deviations from 9-year moving average.

(b) Weber's 26-Town House-building Index. Percentage deviations from 9-year moving average.

(d) Weber's 25-Town House-building Index (being (b) with the exclusion of London). Percentage deviations from 9-year moving average.

unqualified generalisation. Taking the period from 1842 to 1913 as a whole, neither an emphatic anti-cyclical movement in building nor the reverse can be established unequivocally. The correlation co-efficient measuring the closeness of relationship in fluctuation between building and Beveridge's index in the period 1842–1913 yields the result of 0·418 which appears to be statistically significant, and the conclusion seems warranted that house-building has tended, on the whole, to move in line with the trade cycle. Closer study of the fluctuation, however, suggests that the relationships involved are not adequately summarised by the numerical value of this coefficient. It emerges that building, though moving in accord with the trade cycle for most of the time, did on occasion proceed in the opposite direction. As a result the movements tend to offset each other and reduce the correlation coefficient purporting to measure the relationships over the whole stretch of time. Comparisons of shorter periods yield some highly interesting results. Thus the 15 years subsequent to 1860 indicate a strong anti-cyclical movement, the correlation coefficient being negative at −0·704, while the next 25 years show a positive correlation of +0·594, and a high positive correlation of −0·720 is also found in the period 1842–59. None of these high correlations are due to sympathetic movements in trend since the latter, as will be remembered, have been removed. Nor are they due to the fact that building is itself a component of Beveridge's index. For most of the period the industry is represented by an index of timber imports which is given a weight of 14 out of 100. A large share of that weight, perhaps as much as one half, attaches to non-residential construction and the building industry is by no means the only user of timber. The effective weight given therefore to house-building is very small and the inclusion of the industry in Beveridge's index can hardly account for a high degree of correlation between the two.

'There are, of course, occasional exceptions to the anti-cyclical tendency of building in 1860–74 and the year-to-year correspondence after 1874 and before 1860 is not complete. But a prevailing tendency stands out in each of these three periods, as is indeed signified by the high statistical correlations.

'The one exception in the whole period under discussion relates to 1900–13. The correlation coefficient is insignificant at +0·102. The reason is the same as in the case above. Though contrary movements reduced the value of correlation over the whole span of time, clearly defined anti-cyclical movements in 1900–5 and 1909–12 being offset by homologous movement around the trade cycle peak of 1907 and after 1912.

'It appears that two conflicting forces affect the pattern of house-building behaviour during the course of the trade cycle: variations in rates of interest and building costs in relation to rents, and variations in real income. The ratio of rates of interest and costs to rents rises in the upswing of the trade cycle and falls in the downswing and tends, therefore, *ceteris paribus*, to exert an anti-cyclical influence. Fluctuations in real income, on the other hand have the opposite effect. Both operate simultaneously but one or the other may exercise a stronger pull and predominate, thus determining the relation between building and general business activity. Prima facie, there appears no reason why one or the other should persistently be the more important and why their relative force should not change from trade cycle to trade cycle, remain stable over the duration of a number of cycles, change within given cycles or vary from region to region — thus accounting for the differences and complexities in the pattern of building behaviour.

'Yet building has broadly moved in line with economic activity for approximately two-thirds of the period under dicussion and it appears to have continued in this vein in the inter-war period. Only in the 1860's and part of the 1870's, and in some years in 1900–14 did a clear anti-cyclical tendency prevail. The reason for this divergent behaviour in these two periods is perhaps to be found in the rising *trend* of building costs and interest rates, itself a reflection of the general environment of rising prices. The trend of building costs moved firmly upwards in both periods and the long-term rate of interest, as indicated by the yield on Consols, followed a similar course in 1900–14 though it apparently did not rise in the 1860's and early 1870's. It is to be expected that in an environment characterised by a rising trend of prices and costs, the latter would exercise greater force also in the ordinary cyclical fluctuations and that building activity would, *ceteris paribus*, be affected relatively more by movements in cost and interest than by movements in real income. In the upswing, costs and interest charges are likely to rise more sharply and to a higher level, thus accentuating anti-cyclical tendencies. In the downswing, the fall in costs and interests is likely to be less severe, but the low level of building activity in the preceding years of boom, as well as the fact that the movement of costs *has been reversed* and is downwards, may be sufficient stimulus to revive house-building.

'Similar effects may arise from trend movements in real income. The long fluctuations here do not manifest themselves in absolute falls and rises but appear as accelerations and retardations in the rates of growth, which are of no lesser significance for the economy. It is likely that the income-demand for houses in the course of the trade cycle will, *ceteris paribus*, be of greater influence on house-building when the rate of growth of real income is rising and of less importance when it is falling. This appears to be confirmed by Prest's figures of real national income. They indicate a rate of growth rising steadily from 1880 to approximately 1898 and falling in the remaining years before the First World War. Their movement after 1898 would therefore further accentuate the relative importance of interest and cost conditions in shaping the direction of building fluctuation within the trade cycle.

'At other times, the trend in real income was in the reverse direction to costs and interest rates and it can be shown that chronologically this tended to occur in periods in which building moved in accord with the trade cycle. The evidence is least satisfactory for the 1840's and 1850's when costs and the yield on Consols, if anything, did fall but not sufficiently to be of importance. It is clear enough in 1875–99 when costs and the yield on Consols were falling steadily while the rate of growth of real income rose from 1880 onwards. The same explanation applies in the inter-war period when similar trend movements in interest, building costs and real income prevailed.

'A general chronological agreement, though not without exceptions, between rising trends in interest and costs (and in 1900–14 a declining rate of growth of real income) and stronger anti-cyclical tendencies in house-building, and conversely, seems established. We conclude that the anti-cyclical tendencies of residential construction assert themselves more or less effectively according as the prevailing long-run cost and income environment is favourable or not.

'It is important, however, not to exaggerate the anti-cyclical tendencies of house-building. The broad pattern of behaviour was sympathetic rather than opposite to the trade cycle, as is indeed shown by the positive correlation coefficients calculated. Anti-cyclical pressures though operative all along have only occasionally, when the trend of interest and costs was upwards, been strong enough to dominate the direction of building activity. At other times, notably in 1905–9 even that was not sufficient.'

Apart from the imperfections of the data, there is not much wrong with the above analysis. It is at what purports to be a national level of aggregation, but it carefully speaks of broad tendencies rather than of detailed mechanisms. My own view, expressed in the main text, is that on the whole house-building in any region tended to fluctuate with the prosperity of the region, as reflected in demand for increased labour, wage-rates and so on, but was also influenced by other factors, such as food prices (which would eventually also affect other demands, and so, perhaps, activity) and the level of empties or potential demand. Broadly speaking, I think, one can sum it up by saying that there was a tendency for the direction of changes in house-building to conform with those in local activity, but for the magnitudes of the changes to differ, for reasons we have already examined. The aggregation of regional activities, complicated by weighting problems and differences in timing, and resulting in a series based on a moving average technique, which is then compared with the Beveridge series in which all of these factors again may cause trouble, cannot be expected to lead to any kind of firm statement, or to an explanation of sequences. But it does give some indication of how the fluctuations in total activity have tended to move, and Weber's analysis is useful in that it summarises these tendencies.

· Weber's next step was to look at turning points to see whether there was any consistent lag between residential building and the trade cycle. He found that in twenty-two of the twenty-six peaks and troughs recorded in the period 1842–1914, house-building preceded or coincided with the

turning points in business activity.   He attempted to explain this in terms
of the accelerator, but his argument, which probably was by no means in its
intended final form, has several weaknesses as it stands and there is little
point in reproducing it.   As must be clear from the text, I am not very
happy about this kind of analysis.   To complete the story one could
produce a single explanation for a lag of this kind at a national level, in
terms of accelerators, multipliers and differing speeds of adjustment: but I
am not certain that it would have any value, not simply because it might be
at the wrong level of aggregation, but also because it is perfectly clear
that downturns in building activity were of at least two different kinds.
There were the downturns which coincided with major downturns, and
usually had part of their origin in a credit crisis; and there were the other
purely minor downturns, which were usually associated with an inventory
downturn in some industry, or some region.   Even if, in both cases, the
building downturn precedes that in general activity, there is little point
in attempting to find a single explanation when the actual phenomena were
so different — for in the one case a major component is the drying up of
credit for builders, while in the other case it is not.   This is not, however,
to say that there is no point in observing the extent to which leads and
lags seem to have occurred, which is what Weber did.

Appendix II

NEW INDUSTRIAL BUILDING IN GREAT BRITAIN 1923–38: A PROBLEM IN MEASUREMENT[1]

INDUSTRIAL building is easily recorded but measured only with difficulty.
From various dates in the nineteenth century local authorities kept
registers of plans submitted and approved for buildings of all kinds.
Houses, schools, chapels, mills, factories and almost every other kind of
structure were all recorded, sometimes with precise descriptions, sometimes very inadequately.   These registers have already been used as a
source of historical statistics on house-building,[2] but it is less easy to obtain
satisfactory series for industrial building.   Usually the registers simply
record entries such as 'new mill', 'tool factory', 'extension' or 'shed',

[1] Reprinted from the *Scottish Journal of Political Economy*, vol. viii, pp. 57–63.
[2] See B. Weber, 'A New Index of Residential Construction, 1838–1950',
Scottish Journal of Political Economy, 1955, pp. 104–32, and J. Hamish Richards
and J. Parry Lewis, 'House Building in the South Wales Coalfield, 1851–1913',
The Manchester School, 1956, pp. 289–300.

and give little guidance about the size of the project. Sometimes, when the actual plans still exist, it turns out that an extension would more than double the original size, while a shed might be anything from a weaving shed capable of employing scores of people to a shelter for a bicycle or a gate-keeper. For this reason, while the number of industrial plans passed in any year is certainly some measure of the number of industrial concerns who are planning expansion, it is a very inadequate measure of either the volume or the value of building. A single plan passed in one year may represent a greater investment than twenty passed in the following year, and it may mean several years of building activity. Alternatively it may just not materialise. The number of industrial plans passed is a measure of optimism, rather than of anything else, lagged by the time taken to prepare a plan and to get it passed. Useful series of this kind have been obtained for Glasgow, Hull, Coventry, Bradford, Birkenhead, Oldham, Bolton, Salford and a number of smaller towns around Manchester. Some of these series go back to 1850, but as yet they are too few to warrant a detailed analysis of industrial building in the nineteenth century, even within the limitations just indicated.

From 1911 an important change took place. The Board of Trade began to publish the estimated cost of the buildings for which plans had been approved in a large number of towns. The data were broken down into various sub-groups of which one was headed 'factories and workshops'. Originally 78 towns were covered. In 1922 building costs fluctuated so much, and so many approved plans were abandoned, that no data were published for that year, but in the following year the series re-appeared for 146 towns,[1] broken down on a regional basis. Publication of the statistics was discontinued at the outbreak of war in 1939.

Valuable as this series is, it suffers from certain defects. The 146 towns, with a 1931 population of about 17,500,000, excluded the whole of the London County Council. The Local Authorities were given no precise definitions, but were simply asked for the total number of buildings and the total estimated cost under each group. There was no ruling, for example, on whether a power-station should be counted under ' Factories and Workshops' or put into the group headed 'Other Buildings; and Additions and Alterations to Existing Buildings'. Certain statutory authorities were exempted from the necessity of submitting their plans to the local authorities, and buildings erected by them were therefore not covered. Another defect arises out of the changing costs in the building industry. This is not simply the problem of expressing building values in terms of constant prices, but also of assessing the reliability of the original estimates of cost. Even in times of stable prices the estimates

---

[1] The number of towns covered by the returns published in the Ministry of Labour Gazette fluctuated slightly, due chiefly to delayed replies from a few towns. The *Abstracts of Labour Statistics of the United Kingdom* provide adjusted figures for most of the years. In the other years the necessary small adjustment has been made by considering population figures.

might frequently be wrong. When prices change, the margin of possible error seems to be greater, unless (and there is no way of checking) the estimates attempted to allow for price changes. All one can be sure about is that the estimated cost almost certainly differed from the actual cost. Table 1 shows the course of the value of new factory and workshop

TABLE 1

ESTIMATED COST OF NEW FACTORIES AND
WORKSHOPS FOR WHICH PLANS WERE APPROVED
IN 146 TOWNS IN GREAT BRITAIN, 1923–38 (£m.)

Year	Original Data	At Constant (1930) Costs	Year	Original Data	At Constant (1930) Costs
1923	3·62	3·22	1931	2·73	2·77
1924	3·78	3·46	1932	3·07	3·26
1925	4·35	4·09	1933	3·70	4·08
1926	3·75	3·52	1934	6·07	6·70
1927	4·98	4·74	1935	7·67	7·91
1928	5·43	5·27	1936	10·06	10·01
1929	6·24	6·24	1937	9·28	8·68
1930	4·58	4·58	1938	7·47	6·99

Source: See text.

plans passed during 1922–38 and an attempted deflation of this series in terms of 1930 building costs, but not too much reliance should be placed on the deflated series because of the inevitable approximations involved in compiling and applying an index of costs.

Another source of information is the Censuses of Production for 1924, 1930 and 1935. A detailed inspection of these allows one to estimate the total value of new construction of factories and workshops (including electric power stations, gas-works, etc.). These estimates are presented in Table 2, which also expresses them as percentages of the 1930 value for purposes of comparison with the estimated values of plans approved in 146 towns.[1]

TABLE 2

INDUSTRIAL BUILDING IN GREAT BRITAIN IN 1924, 1930 AND 1935

	1924	1930	1935
1. Total value of new factory and workshop construction. Census of Production. £m.	14·0	16·6	21·2
2. Row 1 in index form, 1930 = 100	84·3	100·0	127·7
3. Index of estimated value of factory and workshop plans approved in 146 towns, 1930 = 100	66·5	100·0	119·7

[1] In his article 'Building Output and the Trade Cycle (1924–38)', *Oxford Economic Papers*, no. 3, February 1940, pp. 110–30, Professor Ian Bowen obtains rather lower estimates, namely £m. 11·8, 14·0 and 16·0. The main reason for the difference is that Professor Bowen does not seem to have taken account

Between the two indices shown in Table 2 there is a considerable divergence. According to the Census data, industrial building was about a fifth higher in 1930 than in 1924; on the other hand there was an increase of nearly half in the value of plans passed. This discrepancy cannot be explained in terms of any uniform lag, as is apparent from the figures for plans passed in (for example) 1923 and 1929 given in Table 1. It is a discrepancy that is to be expected and it underlines the danger of relying too heavily on plans passed as a measure of buildings erected.

Almost certainly many of the plans passed in 1930 were never translated into structures, and others were doomed to gather dust for a few years until industrial demand became brighter. There is also the point, of course, that the 146 towns were not a very representative sample, as is shown by the complete exclusion of the whole of the L.C.C.

Yet there were deficiencies in the Censuses themselves, and it is useful that there is another indirect means of checking the reliability of the plans-passed series as an index of activity. Between 1932 and 1938 the Board of Trade published a series of annual *Surveys of Industrial Development*, based on reports received from Factory Inspectors and on information collected from the Ministry of Labour. They contained particulars of new factories, extensions, employment generated and factories closed. The information was given by regions and industries and covered factories employing at least 25 persons at the end of the year. Establishments not engaged in manufacturing or processing goods (such as laundries) and certain Government establishments were excluded.

Table 3 summarises the principal data from this source. The first series, showing the number of new factories opened, represents, of course, the termination of building. A peak year in this series could easily be a year later than the peak in some series showing the number of factories actually under construction. In times of depression the tendency to suspend or to slow down building already commenced could so delay the opening of the factories as to exaggerate the lowness of activity in some years and yet to understate it in others; the longer the building period, the less reliable is a series of factories opened as an indicator of factories being built. For these reasons one must be careful not to read too much into the differences between consecutive years, especially in times of rapid economic change. Statistics of factories opened are useful indicators of new productive capacity available for immediate use; but they are very imperfect indicators of building. Quite apart from these considerations there is the fact that the first series in this Table, showing the number of factories opened, says nothing about their size. There are two possible ways of overcoming this deficiency. One is to consider the second

---

of building carried out by Government Departments, utilities and other trades not classified under Building and Contracting. The 1935 figure is especially low because the Final Report of the Building and Contracting Trades for the 1935 Census was not published until four years after the publication of Professor Bowen's paper.

series in the Table which indicates the numbers of jobs provided by the new factories, but this can be considered as only a rather crude measure of the volume of building. It is, however, interesting to notice the contrary movements of these two series between 1937 and 1938, which emphasises the inadequacy of the former series. Finally these series suffer from the exclusion of smaller factories and certain other establishments.

TABLE 3

INDUSTRIAL BUILDING IN GREAT BRITAIN, 1932–38

	1932	1933	1934	1935	1936	1937	1938
1. Number of new factories opened	676	467	520	514	542	522	414
2. Employment provided by (1) (000)	44·1	29·8	40·5	50·0	49·5	45·3	53·2
3. (1) as an index (1932–8 = 100)	129·5	89·4	99·6	98·4	103·8	100·0	79·3
4. (2) as an index (1932–8 = 100)	98·8	66·8	90·7	112·0	110·9	101·5	119·2
5. Estimated cost of factories and workshops for which plans were approved in 146 towns (1932–8 = 100)	45·4	54·7	89·8	113·5	148·8	137·2	110·5
6. (5) expressed in terms of constant costs (1932–8 = 100)	48·1	60·1	98·7	116·5	147·3	127·7	102·5

Source: See text.

Table 3 is completed by the conversion of the absolute figures in the first two rows into index numbers taking the averages for 1932–8 as bases, and the inclusion of two more indices, derived from Table 1, showing respectively the estimated value of approved plans for new factories and workshops in 146 towns, and the same data adjusted for changes in costs, both expressed as index numbers on the base 1932–8 = 100. It will be noticed that the adjustment for cost makes no difference to the direction of change between one year and the next. Of course, since planning precedes building while the opening of a factory follows it, there is bound to be some lag between these series.

The most obvious feature of the table is the amplitude of the oscillation in plans passed. During 1933–5 the new employment index rose from 66·8 to 112·0 — an increase of 68 per cent: but the value of plans passed more than doubled (and almost doubled even if allowance is made for changes in costs). If a lag of one year is introduced, so that we consider the plans of 1932–4, the result is virtually the same. One reason for this wide discrepancy could be that much of the building of

1933 arose out of plans passed before 1932.   Another could be the failure of plans to materialise, as excessive optimism gave way to more realistic appraisals of the future, and to some slight extent this is substantiated by the fall in new employment between 1935–6.   Probably both of these factors were operating, along with others.   The fall in the value of plans passed in 1937 and 1938 suggests that very probably many of the 1936 plans were either abandoned or held up, and perhaps some of the rise in employment in 1938, associated with a fall in the number of new factories, is due to plans passed in 1936 or earlier for large factories which took a long time to complete, partly because of their size and partly because of slower building due to a less optimistic outlook.   Some of the difference between the series must also be due to the large part played by small industrial concerns whose factories would appear in the plans series but not in the others.

To sum up it seems that we know very little about the actual amount of industrial building going on in any year.   The best documented years are 1924, 1930 and 1935, in which, for all their shortcomings, the Censuses or Production provide useful estimates of building actually taking place. For the other years we have on the one hand a somewhat hazardous estimate of costs of intended new building in a non-representative sample of towns, and on the other hand two series relating to new factories opened of which neither is an adequate measure of actual investment.   We can be tolerably certain that during 1924–9 building boomed, and that it then fell until some time in 1931–3.   The years 1934 and 1935 saw increasing activity: but except that no dramatic fall is likely to have occurred it is difficult to say much about 1936–8.

Appendix 12
ANNUAL PRODUCTION OF SANDSTONE IN SCOTLAND, 1900–1948

Year	Thousands of tons Total Sandstone Production	Year	Thousands of tons Total Sandstone Production
1900	1239	1924	277
1901	1315	1925	303
1902	1616	1926	286
1903	1452	1927	251
1904	1143	1928	246
1905	1094	1929	192
1906	1019	1930	188
1907	780	1931	202
1908	760	1932	215
1909	680	1933	180
1910	743	1934	188
1911	607	1935	178
1912	457	1936	233
1913	571	1937	288
1914	390	1938	289
1915	227	1939	286
1916	248	1940	505
1917	81	1941	593
1918	81	1942	210
1919	95	1943	220
1920	162	1944	227
1921	186	1945	79
1922	209	1946	126
1923	256	1947	113
		1948	102

Supplied privately to B. Weber by the Scottish Council (Development and Industry).

Appendix 13

WEBER'S INDEX OF HOUSE-RENTS COMPARED WITH THOSE OF CAIRNCROSS AND SINGER

Year	Weber*	Cairncross†	Singer‡	Year	Weber*	Cairncross†	Singer‡
1845			55·6	1888	92·9	93·0	92·0
48			57·7	9	92·7	93·9	
51			57·9	90	92·7	93·9	
53			60·3	1	92·7	94·8	
57			63·0	2	92·9	94·8	
61			67·5	3	94·5	95·7	93·9
64			71·1	4	95·4	95·7	
67			75·7	5	95·6	96·5	
70		87·0	79·2	6	95·8	96·5	
1		87·0		7	96·1	92·4	
2		87·8		8	98·4	98·3	97·7
3		88·7		9	99·3	99·1	
4	82·6	89·6		1900	100·0	100·0	
5	83·5	90·4		1	101·8	100·9	
6	86·3	91·3	85·6	2	102·3	101·7	
7	87·8	92·2		3	102·7	102·6	102·6
8	88.5	92·2		4	102·8	102·6	
9	89·7	91·3		5	102·5	102·6	
80	90·5	91·3		6	102·5	102·6	
1	90·8	91·3		7	102·7	102·6	
2	91·6	92·2	90·5	8	102·3	101·7	
3	92·0	92·2		9	105·6	101·7	
4	91·9	93·0		10	103·5	100·9	103·1
5	92·5	93·0		1	102·2	100·9	
6	92·7	93·0		2	102·2	100·9	
7	92·7	93·0		3	102·4	100·9	

* Index of average house rentals in Great Britain (1900 = 100) calculated as described in text.
† Index of rents in England and Wales (1900 = 100) calculated by A. K. Cairncross.
‡ Index of rent on buildings in England and Wales (1898–1903 = 100) calculated by H. W. Singer.

Appendix 14

POSTSCRIPT: JULY 1965

EXCEPT for a few brief insertions at the galley stage in November 1964, this book is as it stood in January of that year. There is not now space to do justice to the events of the eighteen months that have since passed : but a few points may be made very briefly.

The credit squeeze that was introduced by Mr. Callaghan differed from its immediate predecessors in several respects. Perhaps it will turn out that one of the most important of these is the way in which the pressure points have varied. Initially the high Bank Rate penalised borrowers, and reduced the flow of funds into building societies. There can be little doubt that the consequent inability of so many societies to balance their income flows was one reason for the subsequent reduction of the Rate. At the same time, hire purchase controls were invoked. Despite the continued reluctance of banks to provide finance for bridging the gap between the mortgage and the buying price, the lot of the house-purchaser eased a trifle, while the car-purchaser found it more difficult. It is still too early to speak of the full consequences of these changes. We may however, note that the mortgage shortage has probably affected the building industry more severely than statistics of starts or completions are likely to show. Builders have been further hit by the more general aspects of the squeeze. Some are currently offering as much as 20 per cent interest for short-term privately negotiated loans. By spreading the area of pressure through the use of hire-purchase controls, the Chancellor has done something to help the industry. Any squeeze must hurt, and since it is the house-purchaser who adds so much to the strain of the economy, by commanding resources so much in excess of his annual outgoings (*vide* pages 265–6), it may well be that the most effective squeeze is the one which is concentrated on this single point : but a spate of building bankruptcies can lead to even more embarrassing long-term problems.

The return of money to the building societies, when the Bank Rate was lowered, was dramatic. It would probably have been less dramatic if equities had been more in favour. Partly because of political uncertainties, and partly because of the imperfectly understood — but unfavourable — consequences of the Capital Gains Tax, they failed to rally when the Rate was lowered, and for once they did not compete with the building societies. The impact of the Capital Gains Tax on the direction in which loanable funds flow must be both permanent and considerable, but it is hardly likely that in normal times it will work quite as much to the advantage of the building societies as it seems to be at the moment. Fathered by the building clubs of the eighteenth century, the societies are a nineteenth-century invention which is just beginning to become a little out of date. As we have argued on page 243, the absence of any prospect of capital gain for the lender works against them. We may yet see societies adopting schemes which enable the lender to share in the fruits of inflation. One way of doing this would be to offer the borrower the choice of paying either a high rate of interest on the sum borrowed, or a lower rate of interest on the current value of the property. One may, for example, borrow £4000 at 8 per cent. If, after ten years, half of it has been repaid, the current interest payment is £160. Alternatively one may pay at the rate of 5 per cent on a current value basis. If, in such a case, the house has doubled its value over ten years, but half of the sum borrowed has been paid back, then the current value of the sum outstanding is £4000, and the interest payment is £200. For a person who expects his income to increase, a scheme of this kind may be quite attractive, while the societies could offer lenders either high rates of interest or, in the case of longer term loans, substantial bonuses every fifth year. Some local authorities, by charging rents for pre-war houses that are related to current building costs, have already gone some way towards spreading the burden of rising costs over occupiers irrespective of their vintage. Essentially they are facing a very similar problem.

Whether the building industry could have coped with the additional demands that would have fallen upon it if mortgages had been available is doubtful. Shortages of cement and plaster-board have arisen in any case. Probably others would also have occurred, prices would have risen — despite Mr. Brown — or some form of rationing would have been necessary. All of this simply illustrates the importance of ensuring that housing policy is always part of economic policy. No devices for bringing mortgages within the reach of more people, or for increasing the supply of land for local authorities,[1] merit a moment's consideration unless there are also devices for increasing the supply of materials and the supply and efficiency of skills.[2] The National Economic Development Office has recently initiated a study of means of measuring the capacity of the industry, and the Department of Building at Manchester College of Science and

[1] Since writing this book, the importance of a thorough study of urban land economics has become more apparent to me. It is a subject which is peculiarly neglected in England. Amongst American works I have found R. V. Ratcleff, *Urban Land Economics*, New York, 1949, particularly useful. A very different book is W. Isard, *Location and Space Economy*, Cambridge, Massachusetts, 1956. (Isard wrote two pioneering papers 'Transport Development and Business Cycles', *Quarterly Journal of Economics*, vol. lvii, November 1942, pp. 90–112, and 'A Neglected Cycle : the Transport-Building Cycle', *Review of Economic Statistics*, vol. xxiv, November 1942, pp. 149–58, which should be read by any student of the building cycle.) The need in this field seems to be an integration of the vast effort now going into urban model building and measurement. A way of bringing this about is suggested in my forthcoming paper 'Towards a Generalised Urban Model'.
[2] It is chiefly the failure of the authors to consider how their housing policy, by increasing the effective demand for houses, may impinge on the economy and so, perhaps, end up by reducing demand, that spoils an ingenious and valuable book, *Housing Finance and Development* recently written by A. J. Merrett and Allen Sykes. (London, 1965).

Technology is hoping to evolve forecasting techniques.[1] The Ministry of Public Building and Works has sponsored a more limited regional forecasting study at Liverpool, and has financed a study of factors affecting growth and efficiency in the building industry now beginning at Exeter University. At the Building Research Station, further forecasting work is in progress. All of these studies will add to our knowledge of the building sector, and help us to understand its links with the rest of the economy: but there is still a great deal to be done.

[1] The proposed techniques are an outcome of a study sponsored at the College by the D.S.I.R. on the Structure and Economy of the Building Industry, which is now nearing completion. They are elaborated in *The Builder*, May 14, 1965, by Gordon Bayley.

N

INDEX TO SUBJECTS

Note : (1) Where a further reference is given in italics it refers to an entry under that word or subject as a main heading. Where it is not in italics it refers to a sub-heading under the original main heading.
(2) Only the more important references to building and housing come under these headings. Other references appear elsewhere without specific mention of building or housing.
(3) Some minor references are omitted.
(4) Appendices are indicated thus : A1, A2, etc.

Board of Health 64–7
Board of Trade 134, A11
Boer War 147, 205–6
Boilermakers and Iron Shipbuilders 145
Bolton 35, 65, 69, 81, 106–7, 120–2, A4, A11
bonds 37, 92, 218–19
borrowing 13, 22, 87, 192, 217, 218, 241 (*Advances, Credit*, etc.)
boundary changes 65, A4, A8
Bournemouth A4
Bowling A5
Bradford 65–7, 91, 106–7, A5, A11
Bramhall A4
Brazil 100
bread, *Harvests*
Bredbury and Romley A4
brewing 103–4 (*Beer*)
bricklayers
 shortage 246–7
 strikes 73–4, 85
 wages and hours 26–7, 135
bricks
 beer and 79–81
 delivery 249
 duty on 22, 40, 61, 64
 East Wales 62
 Glasgow 148
 Government expenditure 12, 23, 26, 150–1, 193
 'home construction' indicator 182–183
 house building and output 36–7, 62–4, 81
 Leeds 62
 Liverpool 62, 64
 London 20, 40, 62, 64, 148
 Manchester 62
 new towns 276
 Norwich 61
 output of 12, 22, 26, 36–7, 61–4, 81, 194, 239–46, 249, 276
 prices of 148
 quality of 20
 railways and 36–7, 61–3, 78, 81–5, 182–3
 rate of interest and 12, 23, 26, 77, 150–1
 regional variations 61–2, 240
 Rochester 62
 Savings 79–80
 shortage 239–40, 246–9, 276
 statistical ambiguities 194
 Surrey 62
 timber imports 12, 15, 22, 39–40
 Uxbridge 61

bricks—*contd.*
 other variables 12, 23–6, 30, 61–4, 77, 82, 150, 193, 249
Bridgend A4
bridges 19, 21, 100, 196
Brighton 35, A4
Bristol 27, A4
brokers 94
Bromley A4
Bubble, South Sea 16
builders
 credit for 13, 56–7, 194, 230–2, A14 (*Credit, Working Capital*)
 exaggerate shortages of materials 249
 labour relations 26–7, 73 ff., 85, 135
 Parliament 73
 private, *Private*
 reaction to temporary recession 55–65
 speculative, *Speculative*
 supply 85, 226, 246–7 (*see skill concerned*)
Builder, The 85, 99, 100, 135–6, 198–9, A4, A8
building
 bye laws 64–7, A5
 controls 250–1 (*Controls*)
 costs, *costs*
 cycles
  American, *America, Inverse*
  births and 19, 43–60, 187–8, 191, 194, 212–13, 222–3, 263
  common features 42
  credit and 59, 191, 213, 221–2 (*Credit*)
  evidence for 4–5, 11–18, 186–7, A1
  Glasgow 2, 130, 180–1
  inverse 17, 34, 59, 106, 130–2, 197, 199, 222
  land values and 158–61, 276
  London 16–17, 130–2, 139, 191
  Manchester, *Manchester*
  migration 34, 52, 180–1, 188, 191, 201, 222
  removal of 255, 263
  shops and 250
  slums, clearance and 7
  South Wales, *South Wales*
  theories of 38, 42–60, 106, 133, 148, 155–60, 212–13, 222
  timing of 18–21, 139, 144–5, 212–213, 222–3
  trade cycle and 187, 213, 222, 233
  transport and 131, 135, 139
  trend 18–19, 144–5, 191
  unique nature 4, 28, 42

INDEX TO PERSONS

PRINTED BY R. & R. CLARK, LTD., EDINBURGH